Currents of Ar

CURRENTS OF ARCHIVAL THINKING

SECOND EDITION

Heather MacNeil and Terry Eastwood, Editors

An Imprint of ABC-CLIO, LLC
Santa Barbara, California • Denver, Colorado

Dedicated to Sigrid McCausland
friend, valued colleague and inspiration

Library of Congress Cataloging-in-Publication Data

Names: MacNeil, Heather, editor. | Eastwood, Terry, 1943- editor.
Title: Currents of archival thinking / Heather MacNeil and Terry Eastwood, editors.
Description: Second edition. | Santa Barbara, California : Libraries Unlimited, 2016. | Includes bibliographical references and index.
Identifiers: LCCN 2016038364 (print) | LCCN 2016050735 (ebook) | ISBN 9781440839085 (paperback) | ISBN 9781440839092 (ebook)
Subjects: LCSH: Archives. | Archives—Philosophy. | Archivists.
Classification: LCC CD972 .C87 2016 (print) | LCC CD972 (ebook) | DDC 027—dc23
LC record available at https://lccn.loc.gov/2016038364

ISBN: 978–1–4408–3908–5
EISBN: 978–1–4408–3909–2

21 20 19 18 17 1 2 3 4 5

This book is also available as an eBook.

Libraries Unlimited
An Imprint of ABC-CLIO, LLC

ABC-CLIO, LLC
130 Cremona Drive, P.O. Box 1911
Santa Barbara, California 93116-1911
www.abc-clio.com

This book is printed on acid-free paper ∞

Manufactured in the United States of America

Contents

Introduction: Shifting Currents

Terry Eastwood and Heather MacNeil

The second edition of *Currents of Archival Thinking* (*Currents2*) continues the exploration, begun in the first edition, of the shifting, converging, and cross-currents of archival thinking about the nature and purpose of archives and the role of archivists and archival institutions in the creation, use, and preservation of society's documentary record. As was the case with the first edition, contributors to *Currents2* were invited to reflect and speculate on a wide range of topics, but the questions they addressed in their respective essays were very similar: How has this area of archival concern been understood historically? How is it understood today? Where are the points of continuity and contestation in discussions of this topic? How have technological changes affected the way we think about it? How have currents of thinking in other disciplines about this topic influenced our own understanding of it?

Some of the essays included in this second edition are updated versions of ones that appeared in the first edition; others are new contributions that explore topics not covered in the first edition. The essays have been organized under three broad headings. *Foundations* focuses on the roots and subsequent development of archival theory and the history of archival institutions. *Functions* reflects on what it means to manage current records; identify, preserve, and make available for use records of enduring value; and communicate to the general public the role of archives and archival institutions. *Frameworks* examines a few of the broad social and political movements that are reshaping the archival endeavor in the twenty-first century.

SHIFTING FOUNDATIONS

The archival body of knowledge that took shape in the nineteenth and early part of the twentieth centuries was rooted in jurisprudence, positivist history, and a centuries-old body of written reflection and experience about the nature of records and recordkeeping practices of administrative entities from previous centuries. As Terry Eastwood explains in his essay, the traditional organic concept of archives as the natural, interrelated, and unique outcome of a record creator's activities and their consequent value as authentic and impartial sources for history grew from these roots.

In contemporary archival discourse, this traditional view has been contested on the grounds that it is incompatible with current understandings about the nature of records and recordkeeping environments and fails to account for the manifold ways in which human, social, and ideological forces impinge on the use, production, and transmission of archives through time and space. Out of that contestation, Eastwood suggests, a broader and more nuanced view of the nature of archives has come forth, one that takes into account their mutability, the fluidity of contemporary recordkeeping environments, and the social contexts that determine the archives' formation both before and after they are transferred to archival custody. Such view, he maintains, does not displace the traditional one so much as it reinterprets it in light of the changing environment.

A related shift in thinking is discernible in the way archivists interpret the principle of provenance. When it was first articulated in the nineteenth century, the principle was understood primarily as an organizing device for the physical arrangement of closed fonds. In the contemporary archival literature, it is more commonly understood as an umbrella term for the multiplicity of contexts in which a body of records is created, used, transmitted, and preserved. The relationships between and among records, their creators, and custodians as well as the sociohistorical circumstances that have shaped the records over time are all considered under this umbrella.

In her essay, Jennifer Douglas traces the evolution of provenance from organizing principle to physical and conceptual construct and to sociohistorical context, considering, along the way, the influence of new technologies, fluid recordkeeping environments, the writings of postmodernist theorists, and the call for social justice on that evolution. Douglas views the expansion of the boundaries of provenance that has occurred in the wake of its most recent repositioning as sociohistorical construct as a positive development inasmuch as it acknowledges "the complexity of archival origins." She wonders, however, whether collapsing all the various contexts of records creation into the amorphous conceptual category of *provenance* may have the inadvertent result of leveling some of that complexity and proposes means by which to mitigate that possibility.

Adrian Cunningham's essay shifts our attention from the origins and evolution of archival theory and method to the diverse histories of archives as physical and conceptual spaces. Over the centuries, archival repositories have been positioned variously as arsenals of administration, bastions of citizen and state rights, laboratories of history, physical and virtual sites of collective memory, and metaphoric sites of knowledge and power. Cunningham traces the myriad ways in which "the archiving impulse and imperative" has manifested itself in different times and places and considers how archival understandings of archives as place are changing yet again in response to contemporary shifts in the technological, social, political, and philosophical landscape in which archives are situated. His historical and comparative analysis demonstrates that the concept of archives as place is a mutable, dynamic, and contingent one.

SHIFTING FUNCTIONS

Changing circumstances and intellectual ferment have influenced consideration of archival functions. Gillian Oliver surveys the field of records management, which she sees as a "contested and confusing area." After a brief survey of the history of the management of current records, she assesses the effects of shifts from paper to digital records, from the life cycle model of phases of records management to a more holistic view of all the actions performed on records characterized in the continuum model, and from records management as a paraprofessional to a professional practice grounded in theory and standardized methods adequate to the digital age. She ends with reflections on the growing recognition of the role of effective records management in enabling people "to establish and reconstruct their lives" in instances when institutional behavior or community trauma has affected them.

Fiorella Foscarini approaches the discourse about the function of archival appraisal using Terry Cook's idea about the four shifting concepts that have animated archival discourse over time in what he calls the evidence paradigm, the memory paradigm, the identity paradigm, and the community paradigm. Foscarini walks us through the considerable appraisal literature assessing the tenor and strengths and weaknesses of the ideas expressed in each of these paradigms. Her exemplar in the evidence paradigm is Hilary Jenkinson, whose prime aim was to protect the evidentiary value of archival documents. She concludes that although "evidence has become a more complex and contested notion, the relationship between recordkeeping and accountability is still a guiding idea for archivists, especially those embedded in some organizational context, where protecting the authenticity and integrity of the records remains a fundamental aspiration." In the memory paradigm, the use of archives in the writing of history was the guiding frame of reference for appraisal. Here memory is primarily "conceived of as institutional memory" and evidence conceived of as "human and organizational activity." The aim of appraisal was the extraction and preservation of usable resources for cultural memory. Writers in the identity or perhaps society paradigm began to search for "a justifiable rationale" for appraisal, which was conceived as being deeply implicated in very political processes of fashioning collective and individual identities and in which postmodern ideas played a strong role. In the community paradigm, appraisal broadens its outlook and draws on many of the ideas of advocates of social justice and inclusiveness. "Putting community and people at the center," writes Foscarini, "is the hallmark of the paradigm in which we are [now] immersed."

Glenn Dingwall examines the shifting perspective on digital preservation, from its inception in the machine readable age of flat file databases to the current age of cloud computing. In a section entitled "What Is Digital Preservation?" he explains the principal risks met in preserving digital records and then reviews some of the means of overcoming those risks. As both he and Oliver observe, digital records must ideally come with sufficient metadata to indicate their context of creation, use, maintenance, and transmission so that they can be preserved as authentic and reliable records that are meaningful to future users. The archival community developed a conceptual understanding of what was involved in digital preservation even before much actual preservation had been achieved. Dingwall explains how the past decade or so has changed with the development of standards and technological tools that have become widely accessible and usable for archival institutions and programs, such that we are in a time of transition from the earlier speculative era to one that can build on actual experience of digital preservation. He also examines the phenomenon of digital curation and how it squares with the archival perspective on digital preservation, the pros and cons of cloud computing from the same perspective, and the skills and funding needed for digital preservation. Despite all the changes in the digital environment that we have gone through (and will undoubtedly go through in the future), he sees the task as reaching to achieve the long-standing archival goal to preserve meaningful records for use into the future.

Geoffrey Yeo comprehensively assesses the growing writing about description, the purposes it serves, the strengths and weaknesses of standards guiding it, its role in contextualizing and facilitating access to archival material, and the challenges and opportunities it faces in the digital age. Reading his essays leaves one with a strong sense of the complexity of descriptive issues and the variety of perspectives on addressing them. Echoing Oliver and Dingwall, he says that there are strong arguments for "integrating the previously separate control regimes for records management and archives' ... and for archivists reusing metadata rather than re-creating them." As Foscarini does in her examination of appraisal, he detects growing recognition of the mediating role of archivists and sees the need for a "self-critical perspective on the archivist as author of descriptions." As Oliver and Foscarini do in their essays, he detects a growing realization in the literature of the need to take the concerns and interests of those documented in records when conducting description and sees engaging users in the process as one way of doing that. Having exposed the considerable contestation about descriptive matters, he concludes that the profession needs "to acknowledge that description can never be reduced to simple certainties and to continue its exploration in different modes of thought."

Wendy Duff and Elizabeth Yakel reconceptualize archival reference services as interaction. They assess the literature on all aspects of the process: the reference interaction between users and archivist, between users and records, and between users and archival systems characterizing records and their context. Obviously users are at the center of the interactive process, but Duff and Yakel walk us through how recent studies have begun to show us how complex these interactions are, how we are only beginning to understand them, and where and how greater understanding would improve each aspect of the process. As is the case with other functions, this interactive process is being revolutionized in the age of the Internet, with all its promise, and some pitfalls, to bring users, archivists, and archival systems together remotely in the process of facilitating access to archival holdings. Despite the growth and sophistication of the literature on archival interaction, most of it issued in this century, Duff and Yakel conclude that "we still lack a strong theoretical foundation to explain the individual behaviors and social conventions surrounding reference service and interactions," which they see as vital to the effort to overcome "the notion of the passive user and embrace the researchers as active, participatory partners."

In her chapter, Sigrid McCausland traces the evolution of the concept of public programming and its distinction from related activities such as outreach, public/reference service, and advocacy. She finds that public programming has slowly become an accepted core function in which "archives present themselves, their collections, and their services to their audiences." She reviews ideas about the aims and orientation of public programming, assesses some notable examples of public programs, and concludes that public programming has already helped increase public appreciation of archives and stands to capitalize on the promise of digital technology to reach even wider audiences.

SHIFTING FRAMEWORKS

For much of the twentieth century, discussions about the purposes of archives and the societal role played by archivists and archival institutions were framed largely in terms of the needs and interests of history, administration, and law. Contemporary discussions about those purposes are framed in relation to more broadly defined societal needs and interests and revolve around issues of accountability, social justice, participation, convergence, and community. Such issues, which have already been identified as thematic threads in many of the essays included in the first two sections of *Currents2*, constitute the primary focal point of the essays in the third and final section.

Issues of democratic accountability underpin Elizabeth Shepherd's essay tracing the evolution of the legal and policy frameworks within which citizens have exercised their right of access to government information, including archival legislation, freedom of information laws, and open data initiatives. Drawing on examples from a variety of jurisdictions, Shepherd explores similarities and differences in the interpretation of the right to information and some of the impediments to its realization. Throughout the essay, she underlines the critical role that the keepers of current and historical records can and should play in supporting and reinforcing that right as well as the complexities that present themselves in connection to that role.

David Wallace draws on a range of disciplinary perspectives, including philosophy, history, and political economy, to construct a framework for understanding the meaning of the term *social justice*, recognizing the historical complicity of archives in the politics of memory and forgetting and promoting social justice consciousness within the archival profession and discipline. For Wallace, a significant barrier to promoting an archival social justice agenda has been the valorization of archival neutrality, the insistence that archivists should not "take sides." Breaking down that barrier, he argues, requires that the archival community acknowledge and defend the inherently political character of such an agenda and commit itself to critically assessing the impact of historical injustices on the documentary record and, where possible, working toward the alleviation of that impact.

In "Participatory Archives," Alexandra Eveleigh penetrates below the surface rhetoric surrounding the transformative possibilities of technology-mediated forms of user participation to expose the complex web of motivations, perspectives, and interests that are driving it and the questions it raises about the role of archivists and archival institutions in an increasingly participatory culture. Many of the debates about participatory archives, Eveleigh observes, focus on "the implications of a participatory paradigm for archival theory and practice, including issues of professional function, power and identity." She points to the need for more critical investigation of the kinds of knowledge generated from user participation and the means by which competing community interests can, or should, be negotiated in participatory archival spaces; only through such investigation will the archival community arrive at a deeper understanding of the logical limits as well as the transformative possibilities of the participatory paradigm.

In Jeannette Bastian's essay, we turn from participatory culture to convergence culture. Bastian outlines some of the institutional, technological, and social forces driving contemporary calls for convergence between and among libraries, archives, and museums (LAMs), reviews the arguments for and against convergence, and considers what archives stand to gain and lose in the so-called urge to converge. As with debates about participatory archives, debates about LAM convergence are fueled, in large part, by uncertainty about its impact on core values and concepts. As Bastian puts it, "Archives, libraries and museums each have strong and specific theoretical frameworks that have been carefully honed and shaped . . . [and] that are difficult to reconcile in ways that are equitable, both to the materials themselves as well as to the stewards and users of the materials." Without disputing the value of increased collaboration among LAMs, Bastian emphasizes that such collaboration must be built on a foundation of respect for the distinctiveness and integrity of the professions involved.

Rebecka Sheffield's essay, "Community Archives," concludes the *Frameworks* section, and in it we return to the theme of the mutability of the concept of archives as place explored by Cunningham in *Foundations*. Sheffield demonstrates the ways in which community archives and community archiving practices are simultaneously enriching our understanding of shared cultural heritage and challenging traditional understandings of what it means to create and preserve archives. She traces the history of the community archives movement, examines a number of frameworks that help to elucidate how and why communities come together to build collections, and, drawing on the life cycle of social movements, charts the trajectory of activist-oriented community archives from emergence to decline. Her analysis underscores the critical importance of community archives as "democratizing projects" and the consequent need for the mainstream archival community to "engage with community archives and to support those organizations in a manner that is respectful, constructive and meaningful."

It is evident in reading these essays that the historical and contemporary currents of archival thinking they trace are the result of a complex interplay of human, social, and technological forces. Also evident is the breadth and depth of reading and reflection—drawing on insights from a range of humanities and social science disciplines—that have informed thinking about the archival endeavor and the multiplicity of opinions and perspectives that have been brought to bear on particular issues and topics. And, as was the case with the first edition of *Currents*, each contributor has put his or her own distinctive stamp on each essay, offering diverse and nuanced interpretations of the evolution of thinking on a given topic. Taken altogether, the essays also attest to the thriving state of archival literature. Many of the contemporary issues and debates investigated in *Currents2* were in their infancy when the first edition was published in 2010. The welcome growth in the diversity and depth of the archival discourse in just six years is, we believe, an encouraging sign of the vitality and increasing maturity of the archival profession and discipline more generally.

PART I

Foundations

1

A Contested Realm: The Nature of Archives and the Orientation of Archival Science*

Terry Eastwood†

Archivists have long engaged in characterizing the nature of archives. Ideas they have and assumptions they make color the way they carry out every aspect of their work and fuel the discourse on any number of matters of concern to the profession. Characterizing the nature of a thing is complicated both culturally and philosophically. Eric Ketelaar argues that until we understand how archival concepts are construed from culture to culture, we cannot begin to arrive at "universally guiding or controlling principles" (Ketelaar 1997, 147). "With the decline of positivism and essentialism,"

*This is a revised version of the chapter of the same title in the first edition of the book of this title.

†I wish to acknowledge Stefano Vitali's contribution to this essay. The original idea for it, the structure it eventually took, and its perspective on several issues were shaped by several exchanges he and I had about the development of archival science over the past two centuries.

Geoffrey Yeo observes, "many scholars question whether language has the capacity to provide a reliable means of capturing the identity or the meanings of things we encounter in the world" (Yeo 2007, 315). Despite these difficulties, this essay seeks to frame the ideas applied by archivists over time in characterizing the nature of archives to demonstrate how thinking about the nature of archives has been at the heart of the orientation of the archival body of knowledge.

SOME PARAMETERS

It is useful to begin with a little brush clearing in order to allow a view of the field of our interest. When we speak of the nature of a thing, we are speaking about the particular combination of qualities belonging to it by its origin and constitution. We are trying to characterize or describe the properties or attributes it has. To make one of those assumptions, archives are social creations in the sense that they are a product of human society. So, many of the ideas about their nature inevitably conjure the circumstances in which they come into being, are formed, and are transmitted through time and space and the qualities they take on as a result of the processes they undergo. This central assumption of archival science makes it a social science in the sense that it builds knowledge of the human production and care of archives. When archivists try to characterize the nature of archives, they usually try to characterize the qualities or properties and attributes with which all archives, no matter the situation of their creation, are endowed. At least, that is the end they have in mind.

Archivists' discourse about the nature of archives, as opposed to others' exploration of the subject, also assumes that we are speaking about a determined body of material, as in the archives (or, as it is often now stated, the archive) of X or Y. Yet, as we shall see, it is not clear that archivists are always talking about the same thing when they speak of the nature of archives. Sometimes, they use the word in the sense of it used in this essay to refer to the whole of the archival documents or records[1] of some organization, agency, office, officer, individual, or family, but at other times, they characterize archives as the sum of the holdings of an archival institution or repository or even all of the holdings of all repositories in some sphere and thereby try to illuminate the collective qualities of all archival material. In this essay, both individual bodies of archives and the collective holdings in the custody of archival institutions will be referred to as historical archives.

In the English language discourse, discussion of the characteristics of archives has recently been overshadowed by consideration of the properties common to all records. The advent of electronic records has heightened the interest in exploring these properties. In fact, the two discussions on the nature of archives and the nature of records are interdependent, because archives are made up of records and records make up archives. For that reason, it will be necessary to examine what archival thinkers have said about both archives and records, but the aim is still mainly to speak about the nature of archives.

In this essay, the term *archival science* refers to the body of knowledge concerned with understanding and treating archives. It will be taken that, at its core, archival knowledge encompasses: theory, seen as elucidation of fundamental concepts applied to archival material and its treatment; methods, seen as ideas on how to treat the material; and practice, seen as the results of treatment of particular material. Other aspects of archival knowledge surround this core, such as writings about particular bodies of archival material, the history of recordkeeping and of archival institutions, and so on. Although this essay is mainly about the theory of the nature of archives, it will from time to time point out the significance of particular ideas for methods and practice.[2]

THE TRADITIONAL VIEWPOINT

A revolution in thinking about archival material occurred in the nineteenth century with the rise of historical archival institutions. Efforts to classify and organize historical archives according to their pertinence gave way in European institutions to respect for the origins of archives and the structure given to them by entities creating them. By the end of the century, archivists with extensive education in history, ancient languages, palaeography, and diplomatics needed to read and understand early records came to dominate the major European public archival institutions. Writing in 1860, Sir John Romilly, master of the rolls in Great Britain and titular head of the Public Record Office, observed that the archivist:

> must understand ancient French and medieval Latin. He must be able to decipher every form of handwriting from the earliest to the latest period .... He must make himself perfectly acquainted with the Law in terms and with the usages existing in the management of public business. He must understand the ancient method of dating documents ... and a variety of technical details not to be mastered without much labour. (Quoted in Levine 1986, 23)

Archivists were then dealing in the main with written, textual documents produced by civil administrative bodies of bygone centuries. The whole of the surviving documents, passed down from these bodies, presented archivists with entities whose characteristics they began to describe. The most common metaphor employed to describe archives was drawn from the natural world. As the famous Dutch manual, which was published in 1898 and translated into German (1905), Italian (1908), and French (1910), on the arrangement and description of archives put it, "an archival collection is an organic whole, a living organism, which grows, takes shape, and undergoes changes in accordance with fixed rules."[3] In a footnote, the authors of the manual concede that they are speaking about "an organism which has lived, for the archivist generally receives the archival collection into his custody when it is dead, or at any rate only the parts of it which must be considered as closed." In the main, then, archivists at this time were confronted with bodies of archives to which documents were no longer being added, subtracted, or reordered, which had reached a fixed state, the structure and order of which it was the archivist's duty to discover and preserve when treating them (Muller, Feith, and Fruin 1968, 19). It is true that some archives came down to archivists not in the ideal fixed state that they had reached at some point in time at the hands of the body or person that generated them but were instead reordered in some measure by others before they reached the archivist's hands, hence the long debate about the very notion of a primitive or original order and whether, if it had been disturbed, to restore it.

The organic metaphor was meant to emphasize that archives come into being, as the manual says, "as a result of the activities" of the entity producing it and always reflect the producer's functions (Muller et al. 1968, 19). Most traditional definitions of archives, however their wording varies, stress that archival documents come into being naturally, as it were, in the course of the conduct of the activities of the body that produces them and according to its needs. Of course, archives are not of the natural world but rather are social creations. Nonetheless, in describing them as being produced naturally as a result of the activities of their creator, archivists were attempting to describe the crucial characteristic that they believed all archives share: that they are an outcome of human beings taking actions, conducting affairs, or accomplishing tasks in the world and therefore speak in some, obviously circumscribed, measure of those actions, affairs, or tasks and the larger events or experience of which they were a part. It is this utility of archival documents to speak of past actions, affairs, tasks, and events that motivated the rise of modern institutions to preserve archives, which in the nineteenth century assumed the status of the principal primary sources for historical studies.[4] As the founder of the State Archives of Florence, Francesco Bonaini, put it in the 1860s, where once archives were preserved to attest to rights and privileges, they should now, he believed, be preserved in "real scientific institutions ... mainly devoted to benefit historical disciplines" (Bonaini 1866, vii, ix). In Germany, theorizing along organic lines "corresponded to the 'historical thinking' of a generation that had come to the archives from the classes of Ranke, Droysen, Sybel, and other luminaries of a great period of German historiography," who took it that their purpose was to reveal past reality (Posner 1967, 41).

Archival writers often contrast the naturalness of archives with the artificiality of collections of archival documents or copies of them brought together from various sources as a result of the interest of the collector, according to some determined theme or for some overt historical purpose.

The authors of the Dutch manual cite the case of an artificial collection of copies of documents of diverse origin brought together from various records depositories and placed in the Archives of the General Staff at The Hague for the sake of convenient reference to past actions and events of interest in the conduct of military affairs (Muller et al. 1968, 19, fn. 7). The contrast between the "naturalness" of archives and the "artificiality" of collections does not mean that the latter are unworthy of preservation or do not speak in some measure of the activity of their creator, as is obvious in this Dutch case. It is rather that the two are formed in different manner, and the character and outcome of their formation must be identified and respected. Archivists are bequeathed all kinds of so-called artificial collections. Such collections are often made up of documents once individually produced in the course of activity of one creator or another, what Yeo usefully (although I shade his meaning) calls "elementary records," (Yeo 2008, 133), but such collections do not have the same qualities as archives, and archivists do not treat them by the precepts they developed to treat so-called naturally generated archives. "The archival document," says Michel Duchein, "contrary to the object for collection or the file for documentation made up of heterogeneous pieces of diverse origins, has therefore *a raison d'être* only to the extent that it belongs to a whole" (Duchein 1983, 67). Artificial collections have their own coherence dictated by the purposes for which or the circumstances in which they were formed, which determine the cast they have.

Something needs to be said about the entities that produce archives. There is no doubt that traditional European thinking privileged archives generated by organizations. A distinction was commonly made between public archives, those generated by agents of the sovereign authority, and private archives, those generated by organizations not part of the state's apparatus. As the authors of the Dutch manual put it, "It is unquestionable that private civil bodies also form archival collections." By private civil bodies, they were referring to what we would call corporate bodies of all kinds, such as businesses, nonprofit organizations, and private societies, clubs, and so on that abound in the contemporary world. It is not so clear where personal archives fit into this traditional view of archives. In much of Europe, personal archives were often consigned to libraries in this period, and many works, such as the Dutch manual, addressed archives generated in an organizational context. At one point, the authors of the Dutch manual say that "the rules for ordinary archival collections ... cannot be applied to family archives," because "very often they have been gathered together in the strangest manner and lack the organic bond of an archival collection." At another point, they say that "private manuscripts ... are, however, not archival documents," even if, at yet another juncture, they do say that "private individuals may have archives" (Muller et al. 1968, 20, 22). Whether organizational archives and personal archives share the same nature or differ and therefore need different treatment, has been a matter of continuing discussion in archival circles, some of which will be reviewed later in this chapter.

The second cardinal characteristic of archives is obliquely suggested in the phrases "an organic whole" and "the organic bond." The idea that the whole body of documents are bound together by a process governed by "fixed rules" posits that archives are characterized by the relationships of their constituent documents with their producer and among themselves. The documents of so-called organic archives were said to have "a structure, an articulation and a natural relationship between parts, which are essential to their significance .... Archive quality only survives unimpaired so long as this natural form and relationship are maintained" (Jenkinson 2003, 238–39). In this view, understanding the meaning of any individual document depends, among other things, such as its context, on knowing its relationship with the entity that produced it, the purposes the entity pursues, the entity's manner of pursuing its purposes, the purpose the document serves, and its place in the scheme the entity devises for its documents. The analysis performed by archivists in their work of arrangement and description then came in the nineteenth century to turn on study of the body that produced the archives in question, its reason for being, structure, functions, procedures, activities, and recordkeeping practices. In this traditional view, there was rarely the sense that archivists would select only some of the documents of such an organic whole as was presented to them. The Dutch manual speaks of archives as comprising the whole of the documents "in so far as these documents were intended to remain in the custody" of the entity that produced them. The task was to carry that whole forward in time. To eliminate documents from a body of archives reduces its capacity to bring to mind facets of past activity and events not only by the fact of eliminating documents and their contents but also by limiting the possibility of understanding the significance of what remains. In this view, a signal objective of archival arrangement is to detect the various relationships evident in a body of archives, which determine its structure in identifiable groupings or aggregations of documents, while archival description aims at elucidating those relationships and aggregations.

The uniqueness of archival documents is a quality closely associated with the quality of interrelatedness. The notion is that each document has its place in the whole dictated by its relationships. A passage from an article by Duchein captures how naturalness, interrelatedness, and uniqueness are closely related:

> The archival document is present at the heart of a functional process, of which it constitutes an element, however small it may be. It is never conceived, in the beginning, as an isolated element. It always has a utilitarian character, which may only appear clearly if it has kept its place in the whole of the other documents which accompany it. Theodore R. Schellenberg cites an excellent case of

> a geographic map existing in the archives of an exploring expedition. The fact that the map is there constitutes, in itself, an important historical particular about the expedition; the same map, taken from these archives and placed in a collection of maps would lose a great deal of its interest. (Duchein 1983, 67)

The qualities of naturalness, interrelatedness, and uniqueness together constitute the core of the traditional organic concept of archives. It was these qualities that were impaired when archival documents were classified and reorganized on the basis of their pertinence for the purpose of facilitating, as it was erroneously supposed, their use as historical sources.

The English theorist Hilary Jenkinson discusses two other qualities often associated with this traditional view: authenticity and impartiality. The concept of authenticity was often enough mentioned by Europeans writing in the nineteenth century, but its meaning was rarely spelled out in any detail in texts about archives. The Italian theorist Giorgio Cencetti observes that a body of archives, "because of its provenance, should be considered authentic with regards to the entity that produced it." The authenticity of a body of archives, as opposed to the authenticity of any constituent document within it, refers to its determined relationship with its creator (Cencetti 1965, 49, 51). Diplomatists, who were interested in establishing whether or not an archival document was a forgery and therefore whether or not it testified reliably to the facts of some matter, had established that authentic documents were those that followed the practice of the time and were duly attested by those competent to make them. The most common archival sense of authenticity has been that archives have not been tampered with in the interest of some deception. Authenticity is about establishing that the thing in question is what it says it is. Jenkinson connected the authenticity of archives with their continuous, responsible custodianship. Because the entities producing archives have an interest in protecting them from corruption in order to be able to rely on their archives as effective artificial memory, continuous custody by the creating entity and, as Jenkinson adds, "their legitimate successors" lend archives a quality of *prima facie* authenticity, the case of any given document being open to specific tests of authenticity.

Impartiality is a quality familiar to both archivists and historians but rarely by that name. Jenkinson used the term *impartiality* to denote a "feature" of archives connected with the character of the intention behind their production. In his most succinct formulation of the idea of impartiality, Jenkinson said that archives are "by their origin free from the suspicion of prejudice in regard to the interests in which we now use them." Because Jenkinson also said that "provided, then, that the student understands [archives'] administrative significance they cannot tell him anything but the truth," many of his readers have supposed that he meant simply that archives tell the truth in some direct and unmediated way about the past (Jenkinson 1922, 12). The French historian Marc Bloch put it more clearly when he wrote that "it is not that this sort of document [an archival one] is any less subject to errors or falsehood than the others ... neither all ambassadorial accounts nor all business letters tell the truth. But this kind of deception, if it exists, at least, has not been especially designed to deceive posterity" (quoted in MacNeil 2000, 58). In our own historically conscious time, when some authors of records, perhaps those holding high office in government, may be tempted to make records for contemporaries with an eye on the opinion of posterity, we may see that impartiality is a relative quality of archives associated with the use of archives as historical sources and therefore most fully explored in the realm of historical methods of evaluating evidence. After all, Jenkinson discussed both impartiality and authenticity under the heading "Archive Quality and the Historical Criticism of Archives." Not everyone accepts that impartiality is a quality of archives deserving the attention of archivists. For instance, Schellenberg was loath to entertain its consideration in his writings.[5] Nevertheless, as we shall see, recent writers have criticized the notion of the truth bearing quality of archives in stringent terms, so it is a concept for continuing archival exploration.

This traditional thinking about the nature of archives slowly permeated archival methods and practice. By the early twentieth century, these European-born ideas were widely accepted in the principles of respect for the origins and primitive or original order of archival material, a notable exception being the treatment of private archives in the United States (and no doubt elsewhere), particularly personal archives, in what Richard Berner calls the historical manuscripts tradition (Berner 1983). It is true that theoretical justification followed rather than led to these principles of method, which were at first justified on practical grounds (Horsman, Ketelaar, and Thomassen 2003, 254). It is also true that the complications of jurisdictional and administrative change and custody and transmission of archives bedevilled efforts to realize the abstract concept of an organic whole, the value of which even the writers of the Dutch manual came to doubt (Horsman et al. 2003, 261). This was true in particular when it came to determining the precise body of archives to treat for the purposes of arrangement and description. Still, as reception of the Dutch manual across Europe and later in North America revealed, the organic theory of archives and the qualities of naturalness, interrelatedness, and uniqueness were accepted, whether explicitly or implicitly, as the theoretical underpinnings of methods of arrangement and description. Questions about the authenticity and impartiality of archives were considered to be primarily the concern of interpreters of archival material. One thing was clear: by the middle of the twentieth century, archival science was rooted squarely in this traditional conceptualizing of the nature of historical archives, with emphasis on developing the methods of their treatment, then called the historical method, which Ernst Posner nicely describes as "application of respect for historical growth to the sources of historical research" (Posner 1967, 41).

THE IMPETUS FOR NEW THINKING ON THE NATURE OF ARCHIVES

In the second half of the twentieth and into this century, deep and complex developments in scholarship, administration, information and communication technology, and society in general made a remarkable impact on archival institutions, the role they play in contemporary societies, and the expectations placed on them, on the one hand, and promoted rethinking many traditional archival concepts, methods, and practices, on the other. As Terry Cook and Joan Schwartz contend, classic archival texts "have shaped archival practice, but the evolution of communication technology and its impact on records and record-keeping, changing concepts of the nature and uses of memory, and shifting notions of authority, evidence, and truth severely undermine the ongoing relevance of these manuals" (Cook and Schwartz 2002, 184).

First of all, historical study has evolved. Its methods, the sources it uses, and the way in which it looks at and interprets those sources have undergone a deep transformation. Where once historical writing was mainly oriented to investigate the origins, development, and relationships of the national states and made use almost exclusively of political and diplomatic sources, in the last half of the twentieth century, historians widened the scope of their study to cover innumerable aspects of human endeavor, which led historians to exploit a much wider range of archival sources than they had in the past. At the same time, the view of archival institutions as laboratories of history was undergoing change: that archival material is an important component part of the national and local cultural heritage and that its preservation and availability can contribute to the sense of identity of nations, communities, organizations, and individuals changed the way in which individuals and societies look at and appreciate archival material. In the past, archivists and historians shared common interests, a common cultural background, and the same approach to archival sources. Today, archivists find themselves performing a complex role as mediators between archives and different categories of users with different backgrounds and needs. Moreover, cultural artifacts of all kinds, from literary texts to works of art, and the built heritage have come to be viewed through the lens of various forms of constructivist and relativist thinking "conveniently labeled as 'postmodernist' " (Yeo 2007, 316).

The second transformation concerns the relationship between active or current records and historical records. As Luciana Duranti observes, with the rise of historical archival institutions, there arose a "material and theoretical distinction between administrative and historical archives," that is, between records still in the care of the entity that generated them and records preserved as historical archives (Duranti 1989, 9). The relationships between active administrations and archival institutions were often weak and problematic, particularly in the process of disposition of records. All over the world, archivists wrestled with the problem of articulating systematic means of the disposition and acquisition of records that would identify those of enduring value and serve the manifold needs of society for access to the record of its past. This need for systematic disposition, or, as seen from the perspective of archival institutions, systematic acquisition, turned archivists' attention to the way in which contemporary organizations and individuals formed and cared for their archives.

The third change occurred in the context of recordkeeping. The advent of the welfare state (in some societies at least) and the active intervention of all levels of government to regulate an ever-widening range of economic, social, and cultural affairs expanded public bureaucracies into new realms. Both for-profit and nonprofit private corporations also spread into new realms and grew in the complexity of their operations. The hierarchical organization of old gave way to administrative arrangements privileging innovation in production or service delivery. The pace of administrative change became almost bewildering as new, and in some cases, freer administrative units were created, regularly transformed, or abolished in the search for more effective and efficient work processes. As a consequence of these transformations, the rate of records production grew dramatically, and managing records and appraising and selecting those deemed worthy of enduring preservation became increasingly complex tasks. Recordkeeping became so fragmented and unregulated in some settings that it became difficult to sustain a regime of reliable records, with obvious implications for the quality of archives.

As an aspect of these changes in bureaucracy and administration, communication and information technology transformed recordkeeping and complicated thinking about the nature of archives and caring for them. Even before the digital age, new technologies for creating and storing images and sound, and the two combined, complicated thinking about the nature of archives and the tasks of caring for archives. For example, Schwartz has observed that "because the advent of the photograph had profound implications for modes of communication, frameworks of knowledge, and uses of memory, archives are implicated in such upheavals" (Schwartz 1995, 41). Soon after the invention of photography, photographic images began to appear as records on their own accord or were imbedded in textual records. "In Canada, for example, photography was quickly adopted as a means of recording, ordering and disseminating information, and research indicates that by the late 1850's government records and personal papers had begun to include cased images, bound albums, illustrated reports, loose prints, and collections of negatives" (Schwartz 1995, 41). The same can be said of the various technologies used over time to produce and store audio and audiovisual documents. However, the bodies generating such records often treated them so poorly as to obscure their connections with other records.

Even in historical archival settings, for preservation purposes, they were removed from physical connection with the textual records of which they were a part and often organized separately to facilitate access to them. How much traditional precepts had to be altered in the face of these technologies fuelled archival discussions. The advent of computer technology and the information management practices that go with it only increased archivists' unease. "In many areas of work," Yeo observes, "entry of data into data bases has replaced the creation of documents as the preferred means of creating records" (Yeo 2007, 332). In this environment, questions arise about whether such data stores can be treated by archival precepts.

Over the course of the twentieth century, the character of archival acquisitions changed in tune with these changes in society. As access to archives was liberalized and regimes of disposition perfected, records were transferred to archives sooner than they had been in the past. Archivists dealing with relatively recent records, most of which were created within their lifetimes, did not have the same need of deep knowledge of unfamiliar times, languages, forms of records, and scripts as did their nineteenth-century European professional ancestors. They needed knowledge of entities of their own time and their production of archives. Unlike their forebears, they rarely received the whole of the surviving records of some entity distant from them in time, but rather the discrete parts of the whole articulated in the modern processes of selection and acquisition. Even where personal archives were concerned, the mobility of people and their changing recordkeeping practices made it imperative to intervene at a propitious time to select records for enduring preservation. All these changing circumstances have challenged archivists to rebuild a more robust theory of the nature of archives suited to the contemporary world.

CONTESTING TRADITIONAL IDEAS

Archival thinkers of the last half century or so have continued to wrestle with the question of the nature of archives and the implications of theoretical constructs for methods and practices. It is possible in this essay to touch on only some of the highlights of this thinking in order to extract from it some sense of its continuity with the past and departure from traditional ideas. One feature of recent thinking is its reliance on concepts from disciplines other than historical science that so dominated in the era when traditional theory emerged.

The Mutability of Archives

Writing in 1959 in *The American Archivist* about Australian experience in records and archives management, Ian Maclean argued that archival theory:

> ... in whatever form it may ultimately take, is also the essential ground-work of archival training. I say in whatever form because I am well aware that, even if its main principles continue to stand up to professional criticism, it needs much clarification and adjustment, not only in terms of logical argument but also in light of the practical experience of [current day] archivists and records managers.(Maclean 1959, 399)

Later, Chris Hurley would characterize the nub of the problem Maclean and his associates faced in the 1950s and 1960s in their efforts to arrange and describe records of the twentieth century of the Australian national government:

> For obvious practical reasons ... it was necessary to classify and describe records in a manner which allowed for continuing and sometimes frequent changes in status (whether of location, arrangement and recordkeeping system, or provenance and control). There were simply no archives in the old-fashioned sense (a stable, finite, physical body of records held outside the continuum [of the records' existence]) to be described. What [was needed] was a system which could be applied to any records, regardless of custody or location, from the moment of creation and throughout the continuum, which would also reflect *both past and future* [my italics] changes in status (provenance and control) and recordkeeping system. (Hurley 1994, 151)

Maclean firmly believed that "archivists have ceased to be concerned primarily with collecting the records of the past for use by the present generation and are now concerned with organising the records of the present for use in the immediate future" (quoted in Upward 1994, 113).

Maclean's colleague, Peter Scott, made the case for abandoning the record group concept as the method of observing provenance and original order in an article in *The American Archivist* in 1966. The record group concept was the American version of the European concept of the fonds—in theory the whole of the records of an entity, in practice the whole of the records of an entity in archival custody. Scott detected an important issue about the nature of archives:

> In essence, the central problem of the creating agency record group for the physical arrangement of archive series arises from the fact that the lifespan of the series and that of its creating agency are not necessarily coextensive. Series are begun and ended, agencies are established and abolished, but such events do not necessarily coincide. To attempt to fit the series into the record group is to deny the real nature of the series and to attempt the impossible, whatever ingenious compromises one may resort to. (Scott 1966, 495–96)

With colleagues, Scott elaborated his ideas in five articles in the late 1970s and early 1980s, in which he drew insight from the distinction in linguistics between synchronic analysis (of a thing at a point in time) and diachronic analysis (of a thing over time) to explain the processes influencing the formation of archives (Scott et al. 1978, 1979, 1980a, 1980b, 1981). They wrestled with long-standing problems of identifying and describing archives in the increasingly fluid conditions of contemporary administration. They argued essentially that provenance is mutable and multifaceted, not to be fixed in time and space. Their solution was to document all the actors contributing to the formation of records series (i.e., a distinct, organized body of records) through time in order to identify all the relationships of provenance, custody, and control as well as the makeup of series, thereby to piece together a picture of whole of the records of large organizations like governments, wherever those records might be. Following Maclean's insight that the management of modern archives required a holistic approach to the entire spectrum of records, not just those in the historical repository, successors in this tradition would theorize about the continuum of all the processes of records creation, maintenance, use, and transmission and enduring preservation, all of which, it was argued, were within the purview of archival science.

In many ways, this archival thinking further articulated the traditional organic concept but without its metaphorical overlay. From the moment records are created through all the processes visited upon them, things are constantly happening that influence the formation of archives. Thinking about these actions on records and how they are to be understood and documented in the manifold interests of records creators and users changed the orientation of archival science and, eventually, raised questions about the stance of the archivist. It was not that archives grew, as it were, at the hands of their creators to a point in time when, in a fixed state, they reached the archivist's hands. They were continually subject to change. Archivists themselves unavoidably became involved in these processes, particularly, of course, in their own processes of carrying records determined to be of enduring value forward in time and space. It was not just that you could not and should not see a fixed body of records outside the continuum of their existence; you could not and should not see the archivist existing outside it either. As Scott said, it is impossible to fix in time and space a thing that is mutable by nature. Archives are indeed like language in this respect; they are ever forming. Rich veins in recent archival literature play on this theme. This insight has profoundly changed archival science, even if we may detect in its new guise an important reflection of the notion of historical growth that was at the heart of the traditional organic concept. Indeed, it may be doubted that our forebears were as unaware of the contradictions inherent in their efforts to fix the state of records as recent writers sometimes suppose. Nevertheless, conceptually speaking, archivists have gone a long way toward characterizing "the way in which a web of records and their relationships is formed and reformed over time" (MacNeil 2008, 9).

Naturalness and Intentionality

Frank Upward contends that Maclean's ideas can be "read as suggesting that records creation is not a natural process, but involves a conscious decision to capture a record . . . . The intention of keeping the record at the time of creation matters, [and] in a sense denies the naturalness of the process" (Upward 1994, 113–14). It may be assumed that Upward does not mean to quarrel with the idea that records are inextricably connected with activity. It is true that not all actions are memorialized in records. It is true that all the processes of records creation, maintenance, use, and transmission (and therefore of archives formation) are undeniably subject to purposeful human intention. Those who create and control archives are guided by their own needs and circumstances in organizing and husbanding archives, and they often utilize them for ideological purpose. "Studies now reveal that archives were collected—and later weeded, reconstructed, even destroyed—not always to keep the best juridical evidence of legal or business transactions, but to serve historical, sacral, and symbolic purposes—and only for those figures and events judged worthy of celebrating, or memorializing, within the context of their time and place" (Cook 2001, 26).[6] Yet, a fine and important distinction must be made between the intentional context of archives and their naturalness. Yeo's extensive analysis of efforts to define records draws out this distinction very well. His analysis leads him to characterize records as "persistent representations of activities, created by participants or observers or their authorized proxies" (Yeo 2007, 337). He makes a strong case that it is not necessary when defining records either to specify the reasons for creating or keeping them or to make mention of their capacity to provide evidence, information, or memory. In effect, he argues that it pays dividends not to think about what he calls the affordances of records when trying to characterize the fundamental and universal characteristic of their nature that distinguishes them from other documentary materials, that is, their connection with and representation of activity.

Another current of thinking looks at the formation of archives from the traditional functionalist perspective but in terms of the management of information in organizations. David Bearman and Richard Lytle "advocate a much more aggressive leadership role for archivists in the wider management of information resources." To achieve this position they believe that "a *practical* understanding must be gained of organizations as living cultures or organisms which create and use information; upon this sound foundation, sound information management can be developed." They argue that archivists' acceptance of "the nineteenth-century view of organizations" structured hierarchically in superior-subordinate relationships misses "significant formal and informal relationships in an organization which together explain its mission, structure and activities." Recognizing the same problem with which Scott wrestled, they contend that "the problem is that the current archival model does not fit such living organisms." They argue that refining provenance-based information in general is the key to the inferential process of effective location and use of records (Bearman and Lytle 1985–1986). The essential difficulty here is that records creators often understandably organize their records to facilitate use of them, and in so doing, to lesser or greater degree as the case may be, often obscure the records-activity connection. Records may be natural (in the sense of the word developed in this essay), but the processes visited upon them are social in nature. It is not enough to understand the nature of archives to understand their character. Such understanding must be complemented by careful analysis of the social context of the formation of archives. In an article in 1984 on "information ecology," the always prescient Hugh Taylor characterized this thrust of thinking:

> ... we must be prepared to abandon the concept of archives as bodies of "historical" records over against so-called active records which are put to sleep during their dormant years prior to salvation or extinction. Records are active in direct proportion to the relevant information that can be retrieved from them, and dormancy is closely related to the inability to retrieve information .... We should then, by the nature of our training, be thoroughly equipped not so much with knowledge of academic history as with knowledge of automation, communication theory, records management, diplomatic, and use of records in administration—a vast and little-explored intellectual field with historical dimensions of great importance. (Taylor 1984, 30–31)

As might be expected, the play of naturalness and utility occurs prominently, indeed bedevils thinking about archival appraisal for selection and acquisition. Assuming that records are kept and destroyed for some reason in which human decision plays a part, the processes of appraisal (all along the continuum, if you like) constitute a vital element of the context in which historical archives are formed. Much recent thinking therefore asserts that the appraisal decisions archivists make crucially influence the formation of historical archives, and, by implication, undermine their naturalness. "As they make determinations about archival or historical value," Brien Brothman says, "archivists in effect create, initiate or perpetuate an axiological commitment which is manifested in the order that emerges" (Brothman 1991, 81). Guided by values of their society, archivists are implicated in forming the archives our time bequeaths to the future, which are anything but "the objective unadulterated record of the past" at which it is alleged traditional archival science aimed its practice (Brothman 1991, 83).

Although it is not always acknowledged, criticism of traditional archival science along these lines assumes that all the reasons why decisions are made to keep or destroy records amount to statements, articulated or otherwise, about their utility (see Eastwood 1993). Often such statements are complicated by reference to the outcome serving some generally conceived purpose, such as revealing decision making (Menne-Haritz 1994) or leaving trace of the image of society (Cook 1992). Other thinkers try to limit the play of subjective utilitarian reasoning in the processes of appraisal by elaborating the proper method of analysis employed in appraisal, such as by evaluating the creating entity's structures or functions or both, not records and their content. Behind such thinking there is the assumption that records follow activity and reflect it and its context and the further assumption that the total fund of archives a society preserves reflects its ways of being and doing. Despite all the objections to the positivism and essentialism of traditional writers, there is a measure of continuity between historically oriented archivists of the past and their postmodern critics. When archival science is conceived as an adjunct to historical science, writes Martine Cardin, "archival documents are traces of the past bearing witness to their creators and to the society they inhabited, the preservation and appreciation of these representations of the past constitute the goals of archival science, and the archivist is a participant in the construction of an historical discourse" (Cardin 2001, 115).

Even though Cardin places herself in the camp that sees archival science as a historical science, rather than a branch of information science, as some scholars of archives do, she has developed "a context-based approach . . . for characterizing archives." She argues that archival documents can be seen as objects that have a concrete reality, as tools that serve purposes, or as appearances, for lack of a better word, seen philosophically in terms of values and ideologies. "However," she says, "the sum of all the dimensions of an object can never produce a global reading of it. Rather than [being] the sum of the various dimensions, an object is an emergent whole created by their intersection" (Cardin 2001, 118–19). Such global reading is a worthy aim of archival science. Cardin's work, which draws heavily on the ideas of sociologist Edgar Morin, illustrates an important aspect of recent investigation into the nature of archives. Archival thinkers have viewed their own thinking through the prism of other disciplines to draw out the complexities of the nature and context of archives, the latter no doubt being part of the former, if we accept, as all this work powerfully suggests, that their many contexts influence how archives are formed and so become a part of their nature.

Not all contexts in which archives are generated are the same. It is easy enough to see that records generated in corporate settings have the utilitarian nature ascribed to them by Duchein. The same cannot be said of personal archives. Even though it is possible to see that the documentary output of individuals can be connected with the activities they engage in, those activities may not be strictly speaking utilitarian in nature. Rather personal archives are made up of the documentary output of the life lived by the individual producing them. As the recent and growing literature on personal archives reveals, individuals create documents, use them, and husband them in idiosyncratic ways that often defy straightforward application of certain traditional archival concepts and principles. These documents are most often not connected with the kinds of transactions of both public and private corporate businesses that generate records. Rather they accumulate as the person goes about his or her own private work and life's activities and are ordered (or not) to suit the individual's proclivities and needs. In some cases, they may be intermixed with records generated in the course of the person holding some position in an organization. These characteristics of personal archives have been the cause of considerable debate among archivists about both how to regard personal archives and how to treat them. It is not possible here to review the growing, recent literature on personal archives, much of which was reviewed by Catherine Hobbs in the first edition of this volume (Hobbs 2010), except to say that all sides in the debate recognize that individuals do produce archives that, for all their differences from those generated in corporate settings, deserve to be understood for what they are and to be treated as much as possible by the precepts of archival science.

In engaging other disciplinary perspectives, archivists have augmented their theory, methods, and practice with insights not of their own making but by no means foreign to their way of thinking. In some cases, these insights are surprising. Archivists have long recognized that records are a principal means of rendering account of actions, but the growing recognition that they themselves need to render more adequate account of their own actions on archives only came home to them through the literature on constructivist thinking about social memory. Similar insight has led them to probe their own traditional concepts: "Archival principles, such as *respect des fonds*, are likewise revealed as historically contingent, not universal or absolute" (Cook 2001, 27).

Questioning Impartiality and Authenticity

Traditional notions of impartiality and authenticity have become the lightening rod of criticism of traditional ideas. Jenkinson's notion of impartiality is at bottom a version of the concept of reliability of records. His notions of impartiality and authenticity posit that archival documents can be trusted as reliable sources of the past. "When archivists express their commitment to the protection of records and reliable and authentic evidence of action they are expressing a commitment to a philosophical ideal of truth" (MacNeil 2001, 37). Jenkinson, who inherited the rationalist tradition of legal evidence scholarship and the positivist tradition of historical scholarship, believed fervently in the archivist's commitment to the integrity of archives. In a lecture in 1947, he characterized the archivist's credo: "His Creed, the Sanctity of Evidence; his Task, the Conservation of every scrap of Evidence attaching to the Documents committed to his charge; his Aim, to provide, without prejudice or afterthought, for all who wish to know the Means of Knowledge" (Jenkinson 2003, 258).

Critics of these rationalist and positivist traditions argue that there is no certain knowledge or truth, which is always contingent upon its seeker. They question simplistic equation of records and evidence. To compress a few phrases of Brothman, archives are not sources of truth but rather traces of thought, expression, and activity that have to be interpreted to serve specific interests and purposes. Records do not reflect past reality; they are part of our conceiving of it; and we can only achieve purposeful conception of the past, not recapture its reality (Brothman 2002, 337–38). Although he definitely believes that thinking along these lines has implications (yet to be worked out) for archival science, he also urges the archival community

> to articulate more carefully ... its social and political philosophy of public affairs and public interest; a consideration of the sometimes conflicting claims upon archivists of politics, law, ethical principles, moral values, reason, scientific method, technological power, and epistemological issues in government, public administration, and society. Discussion of philosophical choices must move from the periphery to the centre of archival discourse. (Brothman 2002, 341)

Indeed, one could argue that in great measure, archival discourse has been dominated of late by consideration of these very choices.

Critics of the traditional orientation of archival science believe that the simplistic archival view of the connection between records and evidence distorts its theory and methods and blinds it to the ways archives are wielded to ideological purpose. Perhaps the most penetrating critic of traditional archival concepts, Verne Harris, contends that "the words and concepts which are archivists' basic tools are anything but simple, stable, and uncontested. The ground is shifting" (Harris 1997, 135). He stringently critiques the notion that archives/records reflect reality, and argues that archivists should make fewer claims about the power of archives to speak of the past and deliver more by providing "a richer contextualization of what is preserved" (Harris 1997, 136). He also believes that the traditional custodial orientation of archivists ill-fits the fluid organizational world and electronic recordkeeping of our time. He wants the work of archivists to be oriented not narrowly in terms of the "shaping of the record as a carrier of memory" but, rather, more broadly in terms of its "participation in the processes of memory formation." His native South African experience leads him to call for preservation of a wider range of archives to contribute to a more just and inclusive process of memory formation (Harris 1997, 133). Echoing Harris, Cook, and Schwartz enjoin archivists to "celebrate their historicity," and, recognizing it, to perform their tasks openly and accountably to allow others, who participate in shared historical discourse, to pierce the ways in which archives are connected with and support the exercise of power (Cook and Schwartz 2002, 185).

This critique calls for reorientation of the archival enterprise rather than wholesale abandonment of the traditional view of the nature of archives. It is more about the role archivists and archival institutions should play in society than it is about elaborating the theory and methods that guide practice. It reflects currents in recent intellectual history that have definitely alerted us that our view of archives is contingent upon a host of factors of their production, use, and transmission. It is indeed true that little about archives is simple, stable, and uncontested. It may be advanced that all sides in the debates about the orientation of archival science and archival work can agree that humanity does indeed rely on archives in many ways. They oil the wheels of governance and commerce; they help render account of the discharge of responsibilities; they provide essential and unique access to what was done in the past; however, much our view of the past is mediated by the purposes of the viewer and limited by the circumstances in which archives are formed and communicated through time.

ENDNOTES

1. The terms *archival document* and *record* carry the same meaning in this essay and should be taken to include not just familiar textual documents but also graphic documents and audio, visual, audiovisual, and digital documents. Neither the form nor the medium of a document determines its archival nature.
2. This necessarily brief description of archival knowledge owes a debt to the far more extensive explanation in Chapter 2 in Livelton (1996, 25–58).
3. Although the translator chose the term *archival collection* for the Dutch word *archief*, it is quite clear that the authors are speaking of archives, not an artificial collection of archival documents, as explained below.
4. For a cogent discussion of the status of archives as historical source, see Chapter 3, "Trusting Records as Historical Evidence: Modern Historical Methods," in MacNeil (2000, 57–85).
5. For instance, although he did discuss authenticity, he did not discuss impartiality in the chapter on "The Nature of Archives" in his *Modern Archives: Principles and Practices* (1956, 11–16).
6. Cook cites a number of studies that reveal cases of archives turned to ideological purpose.

REFERENCES

Bearman, David A., and Richard H. Lytle. 1985–1986. "The Power of the Principle of Provenance." *Archivaria* 21: 14–27.

Berner, Richard C. 1983. *Archival Theory and Practice in the United States: A Historical Analysis*. Seattle: University of Washington Press.

Bonaini, Francesco. 1866. *Rapporto sugli Archivi Toscani Fatto a Sua Eccellenza Il Barone Giuseppe Natoli*. Firenze, Italy: Cellini.

Brothman, Brien. 1991. "Orders of Value: Probing the Theoretical Terms of Archival Practice." *Archivaria* 32 (Summer 1991): 78–100.

Brothman, Brien. 2002. "Afterglow: Conceptions of Record and Evidence in Archival Discourse." *Archival Science* 2: 311–42.

Cardin, Martine. 2001. "Archives in 3D." *Archivaria* 51: 112–36.

Cencetti, Giorgio. 1965. *Scritti Archivistici*. Roma: Il Centro di Ricerca Editore.

Cook, Terry. 1992. "Mind over Matter: Towards a New Theory of Archival Appraisal." In *The Archival Imagination: Essays in Honour of Hugh A. Taylor*, edited by Barbara Craig, 38–70. Ottawa: Association of Canadian Archivists.

Cook, Terry. 2001. "Fashionable Nonsense or Professional Rebirth: Postmodernism and the Practice of Archives." *Archivaria* 51: 14–35.

Cook, Terry, and Joan M. Schwartz. 2002. "Archives, Records, and Power: From (Postmodern) Theory to (Archival) Performance." *Archival Science* 2: 171–85.

Duchein, Michel. 1983. "Theoretical Principles and Practical Problems of *Respect des fonds* in Archival Science." *Archivaria* 16: 64–82.

Duranti, Luciana. 1989. "The Odyssey of Records Managers." *Records Management Quarterly* 23: 3–11.

Eastwood, Terry. 1993. "How Goes It with Appraisal?" *Archivaria* 36: 111–21.

Harris, Verne. 1997. "Claiming Less, Delivering More: A Critique of Positivist Formulations on Archives in South Africa." *Archivaria* 44: 132–41.

Hobbs, Catherine. 2010. "Reenvisioning the Personal: Reframing the Traces of Personal Life." In *Currents of Archival Thinking*, edited by Terry Eastwood and Heather MacNeil, 223–24. Santa Barbara, CA: Libraries Unlimited.

Horsman, Peter, Eric Ketelaar, and Theo Thomassen. 2003. "New Respect for the Old Order: The Context of the Dutch Manual." *The American Archivist* 66: 249–70.

Hurley, C. 1994. "The Australian ('Series') System: An Exposition." In *Ian Maclean and Australian Archives First Fifty Years*, edited by Sue McKemmish and Michael Piggott, 150–72. Clayton, Victoria: Ancora Press in association with Australian Archives.

Jenkinson, Hilary. 1922. *A Manual of Archive Administration Including the Problems of War Archives and Archive Making*. Oxford, England: The Clarendon Press.

Jenkinson, Hilary. 2003. "The English Archivist: A New Profession." In *Selected Writings of Sir Hilary Jenkinson*, edited by Roger H. Ellis and Peter Walne, 236–59. With a new introduction by Terrence [Terence] M. Eastwood. Chicago, IL: Society of American Archivists.

Ketelaar, Eric. 1997. "The Difference Best Postponed? Cultures and Comparative Archival Science." *Archivaria* 44: 142–48.

Levine, Philippa. 1986. "History in the Archives: The Public Record Office and Its Staff, 1838–1886." *The English Historical Review* 101: 20–35.

Livelton, Trevor. 1996. *Archival Theory, Records and the Public*. Lanham, MD: Society of American Archivists and the Scarecrow Press.

Maclean, Ian. 1959. "Australian Experience in Records and Archives Management." *The American Archivist* 22: 383–418.

MacNeil, Heather. 2000. *Trusting Records: Legal, Historical, and Diplomatic Perspectives*. Dordrecht, Netherlands: Kluwer Academic Publishers.

MacNeil, Heather. 2001. "Trusting Records in a Postmodern World." *Archivaria* 51: 36–47.

MacNeil, Heather. 2008. "Archivalterity: Rethinking Original Order." *Archivaria* 66: 1–24.

Menne-Haritz, Angelika. 1994. "Appraisal or Documentation: Can We Appraise Archives by Selecting Content." *The American* Archivist 57: 528–42.

Muller, S., J. A. Feith, and R. Fruin. 1968. *Manual for the Arrangement and Description of Archives: Drawn up by Direction of the Netherlands Association of Archivists*. Translation of the Second Edition by Arthur H. Leavitt. New York: H.W. Wilson Company.

Posner, Ernst. 1967. "Max Lehmann and the Genesis of the Principle of Provenance." In *Archives and the Public Interest: Selected Essays by Ernst Posner*, edited by Ken Munden. Washington, D.C.: Public Affairs Press.

Schellenberg, T. R. 1956. *Modern Archives: Principles and Techniques*. Chicago, IL: Chicago University Press.

Schwartz, Joan M. 1995. " 'We Make Our Tools and Our Tools Make Us': Lessons from Photographs for the Practice, Politics, and Poetics of Diplomatics." *Archivaria* 40: 40–74.

Scott, Peter J. 1966. "The Record Group Concept: A Case for Abandonment." *The American Archivist* 29: 493–504.

Scott, P. J., et al., 1978, 1979, 1980a, 1980b, 1981. "Archives and Administrative Change: Some Methods and Approaches." In five parts in *Archives and Manuscripts* 7 (August 1978): 115–27; 7 (April 1979): 151–65; 8 (June 1980): 41–53; 8 (December 1980): 51–69; and 9 (September 1981): 3–18.

Taylor, Hugh. 1984. "Information Ecology in the 1980s." *Archivaria* 18: 25–37.

Upward, Frank. 1994. "In Search of the Continuum: Ian Maclean's 'Australian Experience Essays on Recordkeeping." In *Ian Maclean and Australian Archives First Fifty Years*, edited by Sue McKemmish and Michael Piggott, 110–30. Clayton, Victoria: Ancora Press in association with Australian Archives.

Yeo, Geoffrey. 2007. "Concepts of Record (1): Evidence, Information, and Persistent Representations." *The American Archivist* 70: 315–43.

Yeo, Geoffrey. 2008. "Concepts of Record (2): Prototypes and Boundary Objects." *The American Archivist* 71: 118–43.

2

Origins and Beyond: The Ongoing Evolution of Archival Ideas about Provenance

Jennifer Douglas

The principle of provenance[1] has guided archivists' work since its development in the early- to mid-nineteenth century and has throughout that time remained a central topic in archival debate and discourse. In this chapter, I trace various meanings associated with the principle, from its origins in the new or evolving repositories of nineteenth-century Europe, through its "rediscovery" (Nesmith 1993) by North American archivists, to the various ways in which archivists have proposed we rethink it in recent years. This chapter is an updated version of the chapter titled "Origins: Evolving Ideas about the Principle of Provenance," which appeared in the first edition of this book, and it includes discussion about some of the ways thinking about the principle of provenance has continued to evolve since the book was published in 2010.

As was the case with the first "Origins" chapter, this chapter, while it explores the evolution of the principle of provenance in archival discourse, does not purport to trace *all* the ways in which the principle has been discussed in the archival literature but rather attempts to draw out different meanings that have been associated with the principle over time and, in so doing, to call attention to the changing nature of archivists' interpretations of it. The chapter first focuses on three distinct yet related ways in which provenance has been understood since its origins in nineteenth-century Europe, that is, as organizing principle, as physical and conceptual construct, and as sociohistorical context; it next identifies some of the issues associated with expanding definitions of provenance and considers these in light of recent research on the notion of creatorship in personal archives. In the chapter's final sections, I look at two particular recordmaking and recordkeeping environments where discussion about the principle has been particularly robust and/or provocative in the six years since I wrote the earlier version of this chapter that appeared in the first edition of *Currents of Archival Thinking*. The article concludes—as did that first version—by affirming the continually evolving nature of archival principles.

PROVENANCE AS ORGANIZING PRINCIPLE

Although the principle of *respect des fonds* and the principle of respect for original order are considered component parts of the overarching principle of provenance, the principle of *respect des fonds* developed prior to the principle of respect for original order. Peter Horsman insists that the principle of *respect des fonds* "is not an invention of the French," having been "anticipated" in "practical application" in a number of European countries in the early nineteenth century (Horsman 2002, 6), but English-language archival literature has tended to focus on the primacy of French archivists' role in its development. Prior to the articulation of the concept of *respect des fonds*, archivists at France's *Archives Nationales* employed an "arbitrarily devised 'methodical' " classification scheme derived from library practice in their arrangement of historical records. T. R. Schellenberg explains that the first heads of the *Archives Nationales*, Armand-Gaston Camus and Pierre-Claude-François Daunou, established broad record groups to which they assigned letter symbols and which were further divided into subgroups. Over time, the record groups and subgroups "changed in character" as new records were added and contents were rearranged (Schellenberg 1956, 169). This arrangement practice was consistent with prevailing attitudes about the importance and function of archival documents. As Ernst Posner explains, following the French Revolution, records began to "acquir[e] the dignity of national monuments," and their care was entrusted to learned scholars who had trained in libraries and for whom "the needs of scholarly investigation and research were held so preponderantly important that it seemed obvious that records should be arranged and cataloged in a manner that would facilitate every kind of scholarly use." Records were therefore organized according to classification schemes meant to facilitate scholarly research, and their "original connection[s]" were frequently obscured or expunged (Posner 2006a, 30–31).

The first "major theoretical departure" in the manner of organizing archival material at the *Archives Nationales* occurred in 1839 when François Guizot issued regulations for the arrangement of archives in the *départements* that operated under the direction of the central archives. These regulations were later elaborated and explained in a circular issued by the Minister of Interior, Count Duchatel. The circular, entitled *Instructions pour la mise en ordre et le classement des archives départementales et communales*, and issued on April 24, 1841, outlined three general rules for arrangement. First, the circular commanded that records be grouped in fonds: "all records which originated with a particular institution, such as an administrative authority, a corporation, or a family, were to be grouped together and were to be considered the *fonds* of that particular institution." The second rule outlined in the circular stipulated that within the established fonds, records should be "arranged by subject-matter groups, and each group was to be assigned a definite place in relation to other groups." Finally, the circular allowed departmental archivists to arrange items within these subject-matter groups as "circumstances might dictate, either chronologically, geographically, or alphabetically" (Schellenberg 1956, 170).

At a meeting of the Archives Commission held on June 8 of the same year, Natalis de Wailly provided a "more definite statement" of the rationale for the rules laid out in the circular. He argued as follows:

> A general classification of records by *fonds* and (within *fonds*) by subject matter is the only way properly to assure the immediate realization of a regular and uniform order. Such a classification offers several advantages: in the first place, it is more easily put into practice than any other system, for primarily it consists of nothing more than bringing together items, only the origin of which it is necessary to determine. In a large number of cases this classification is made easier, since it involves simply the reproduction of the order of the former custodians: this order might perhaps be effected by means of existing inventories, in which case it is sufficient to collate the documents inventoried to arrange them in their original order. If, instead of following this method, a theoretical order is proposed, based on the nature of things, all these advantages are lost. (Quoted in Schellenberg 1956, 172)

Some archival scholars have highlighted the practical undertones evident in de Wailly's statement, arguing that the development of the concept of *respect des fonds* was more pragmatic in nature than theoretical. Nancy Bartlett, for example, argues that rather than attempting to articulate a principled and theoretical argument concerning the proper arrangement of archival materials, the circular and de Wailly's statement instead simply prescribe a practical methodology as a "means of insuring that beginning archivists [in the departmental archives] without the benefit of direct supervision might not cause too much intellectual damage to vulnerable records in their care." Bartlett contends that "the language of the original decree, the method of its enforcement, and the lack of any evidence of an intended role in professional discourse or practice in Paris" together indicate that the principle was primarily devised in the hopes of supervising and standardizing practice in the departmental repositories. For these reasons, she concludes that the principle of *respect des fonds* is not due the level of "intellectual mystique" it has since acquired (Bartlett 1992, 108, 111).

Other archival scholars, however, recognize a distinct theoretical advancement in the French articulation of *respect des fonds*. For example, although Schellenberg acknowledges that the new principle was "not consistently followed in France after its formulation in 1841," he concludes that "an important step forward" had been initiated:

> The old system of arranging records according to some arbitrary scheme of subject matter had been abandoned, at least theoretically, and had been replaced by a system based on a generally applicable principle. This principle is that public records should be grouped according to the nature of the public institutions which accumulate them. (Schellenberg 1956, 173)

Posner likewise asserts that the enunciation of the principle of *respect des fonds* reflected a new conviction about the nature of archives, that is, "archives bodies correspond to a former or existing administrative unit and should be preserved accordingly" (Posner 2006b, 31).

Both Schellenberg and Posner credit Prussian archivists with extending the principle of *respect des fonds* as outlined by Duchatel and de Wailly. In July 1881, Heinrich von Sybel, director of the Prussian Privy State Archives, issued the *Regulative für die Ordnungsarbeiten im Geheimen Staatsarchiv*. These regulations, drafted by Max Lehmann, were based on two principles: the *Provenienzprinzip*, which stipulated that the records of one administrative unit should be kept separate from those of any other, and the *Registraturprinzip*, which further stipulated that records be maintained in the order in which they had been kept by the administrative unit that created them and with their original designations (Posner 2006b, 31). Thus, with the articulation of the *Registraturprinzip*, the Prussian regulations extended respect for creators by respecting also the manner in which creators conducted their affairs and maintained the records of such conduct.

Although many of the arguments for adopting the *Registarturprinzip* were based on practical concerns (e.g., in a country with well-developed registry systems, maintaining original order was easier and less time-consuming than reorganizing records according to subject or chronology), Posner points out that the new principle was more than just a "technical knack." The development of the *Registraturprinzip* was also a response to contemporary trends in historical study that demanded respect for the origins of historical sources; records kept in their original order began to be considered more likely to reveal the nature of the agencies that created them and the unfolding of the activities in which they participated (Posner 2006a, 41). Posner quotes Friedrich Meinecke who maintained that with this new understanding of the nature of provenance, "the registry of every single agency . . . now became a living organism of its own with its peculiar principle of life"; the application of the *Registraturprinzip* "injected all of a sudden an incredible amount of vitality and individuality into the entire Archives" (quoted in Posner 2006a, 41–42).

The idea of the archive as a living organism was central also to the thinking of Dutch archivists Samuel Muller, J. A. Feith, and R. Fruin, who together compiled the *Manual for the Arrangement and Description of Archives*, published in the Netherlands in 1898. Muller, Feith, and Fruin described the fonds, or *archief*, in their words, as an "organic" outgrowth and reflection of the body that creates it. Rather than resulting from the collection activities of historians or archivists gathering disparate records into groups, the archival "whole" "comes into being as the [direct] result of the activities of an administrative body or official"; the *archief* is "an organic whole, a living organism, which grows, takes shape and undergoes change" in accordance with the growth, development, and change that take place within the administration that creates it. Thus, each *archief* is "always the reflection of the functions" of the body that creates it and possesses, therefore, "its own personality, its individuality" (Muller, Feith, and Fruin 2003, 19).

Muller, Feith, and Fruin are adamant that the organic nature and individual personality of the archival whole must be respected. Each whole must be kept separate from each other whole, and like Lehmann and von Sybel, the Dutch trio insist that rather than "forcing" the *archief* into an "alien mold," the arrangement of records within an *archief* must be based on its "original organization." They explain that not only is this system the only one that can be "consistently applied," but it is also the only one that allows archives "to accomplish the usefulness for which they were intended." In Section 16 of the *Manual*, Muller, Feith, and Fruin argue that the original arrangement of an *archief* will "naturally correspond in its main lines to the old organization of the administrative body, of whose function the [*archief*] is the product." In other words, the structure of the *archief* is assumed to reflect the structure of the organization, its internal divisions, and the processes by which it achieved its ends (Muller et al. 2003, 54–56).

The Dutch manual is widely recognized as having gathered together and elaborated on ideas about the arrangement and description of archives that had been circulating in various European countries over the previous century. As Schellenberg puts it, the authors supplied "theoretical justification" for ideas that were already gaining currency in archival institutional practice

(Schellenberg 1956, 175). Speaking on behalf of the three archivists, Muller acknowledged that they had not "invented the *Provenienz Prinzip*; it was just in the air ..." (quoted in Horsman 1994, 53). In Italy, for example, archivists had arrived at a similar conclusion about the archive as a reflection of the body that created it. In the mid-1850s, Francesco Bonaini undertook to create a "truly historical institution" by arranging the Tuscan State Archives to reflect the history of the forms of government in Florence and Tuscany; on the shelves, the archives would be "ordered according to a pattern that was to convey immediately the idea of a systematic development of the history which had created them and which they represented" (Vitali 2002, 19–20). Bonaini's *metodo storico* recognizes the "strong link" between records and the institutions that created them and "follows the order given to the records by their development as archives" (D'Addario 1992; Tamblé 2001, 87).

The Dutch manual may not have been entirely original, but it was enormously influential. The *Manual*'s theories and methods were widely disseminated throughout Europe as it was translated into German in 1905, Italian in 1908, and French in 1910; although an English translation did not appear until 1940, many of its ideas were passed on to English archivists through Hilary Jenkinson's *A Manual of Archive Administration*, published in 1922. In 1910, the International Congress on Archives (ICA), meeting for the first time in Brussels, endorsed a definition of provenance that employed Muller's wording and which was "essentially a condensed summary of the most important sections of the Dutch Manual." The definition read as follows:

> The method of organization by which each archival document has to be brought to the archive (fonds) to which it belongs, and within that archive to the series to which it belonged at the time the archive was still a living organism. (Definition adopted at the First International Congress in Brussels, 1910, quoted in Horsman 2002, 10)

In this definition the principle is described as a "method" for organizing archival material, and while it alludes to the theoretical justification for the method, its practical emphasis is evident. The adoption of this definition, so closely modeled on the Dutch manual, helped contribute to the eventual domination of the Dutch articulation of the principle in general archival discourse. Theo Thomassen describes archival theory as codified in the *Manual* as the "classic paradigm of archival science" and suggests that it was accepted as a "normal science" that for many years inhibited the development of alternate ways of thinking about archival theory and practice (Thomassen 1999, 77).

Despite its status and influence within the archival community, the Dutch manual was not without its detractors. In particular, archivists challenged the Dutch authors' stance on retaining or restoring original order. In the

1930s, for example, Swedish archivist Carl Weibull, who accepted the importance of the principle of *respect des fonds*, questioned whether the original order of a group of records was the order that would best serve researchers (Horsman 1994, 52). At about the same time, Adolf Brenneke argued that contemporary registry systems were not as carefully kept and organized as they had been and asserted that the principle of respect for original order should not be mechanically applied to records kept by inexperienced filing clerks and lacking the "strict, ordered quality" of the registries of the past. Brenneke argued that instead the archivist's arrangement work should be creative, correcting past errors and constructing new orders (Horsman 2002, 2–3). In the English-language archival literature, however, serious challenges to the principle of provenance in both its inward and outward applications were not advanced for several more years. Both Schellenberg and Jenkinson, considered "giants of the profession" by the "English-speaking archival community" (Stapleton 1983–1984, 75), endorsed the principles of *respect des fonds* and respect for original order (although their perspectives differed in certain respects),[2] and it was not until the latter part of the twentieth century that more frequent critiques of the principle of provenance began to be mounted.

PROVENANCE AS PHYSICAL AND CONCEPTUAL CONSTRUCT

It has been widely noted that the European archivists who originally identified and justified the need to respect the external and internal structure of the fonds based their convictions on their own experience working with the closed fonds of long-defunct administrations. One of the most frequent critiques of the classical interpretation of the principle of provenance is that the archives with which modern archivists tend to work are very different from those encountered by nineteenth-century archivists. Archivists in the twentieth and twenty-first centuries must often contend with the records of organizations that continue to function and that frequently undergo considerable changes to their administrative and recordkeeping structures. Furthermore, while the Dutch manual assumes a close correspondence between recordkeeping and administrative structures, in many modern organizations, this is no longer the case (Cook 1993, 22). Therefore, much of modern archivists' criticism and discussion of the principle of provenance (and, therefore, of its subprinciples *respect des fonds* and respect for original order) have focused on how to effectively represent the fluid and changing nature of both the external and internal structure of archival aggregations.

In part, difficulties interpreting the principle of provenance for modern records have arisen because arrangement—which, as Geoffrey Yeo points out, is the means by which the interpretation of the principle is accomplished (see Chapter 7 in this volume)—was originally conceived of as a physical activity. Where an original order was disturbed, records were to be physically arranged so as to reconstruct that order. Similarly, if an original order was not apparent, records were to be physically arranged to reflect the administrative structure of their creator and its activities. This is an approach that the Dutch manual appears to advocate. Despite the assertion of Muller, Feith, and Fruin that their purpose is not to "bring about in any theoretical manner an organization of the archival collection corresponding to the old administrative organization" (Muller et al. 2003, 58), they nevertheless persist in their belief that the structure of the organization will necessarily determine the structure of the *archief*. Archivists have therefore frequently understood the *Manual* as dictating that the records remaining in a fonds or *archief* be physically arranged to restore an "original order" based on the structure of the creating body. As Horsman shows, confusion on this point has led archivists to destroy meaningful physical orders in an effort to establish a preconceived ideal of order. As an example, he describes the case of the Dordrecht town archives, which were rearranged to accord with an ideal order derived from the teachings of the *Manual*. The result, he shows, obscures the records' original legal and administrative functions; if the nature of the record aggregation rather than the nature of the organization that produced it had been respected, the archive's physical arrangement would have told its users much about the original use and significance of different series of records (Horsman 1999, 42).

Horsman's example highlights the disjunction that can exist between a logical order based on administrative structure and the physical order that records assume over time. Recognition of this disjunction has caused archivists to reenvision the archival fonds or aggregation as a conceptual rather than physical entity. For example, at the time when Canadian archivists were "rediscovering" the concept of the fonds and developing national descriptive standards around it, Debra Barr chided the Canadian Working Group on Descriptive Standards for failing to recognize that "a *fonds* can be an abstraction rather than a physical entity." Barr found that the definition of the fonds adopted by the group, and based on Duchein's interpretation,[3] placed too much emphasis on the physical grouping of records, with the result that it gave the impression that any particular document must be "physically and intellectually assigned to only one *fonds*" (Barr 1987–1988, 163). Barr insists that when an archival item or series can be assigned to only one creator, important aspects of the history of its creation, use, and accumulation may be obscured. In her view, "[r]especting provenance means reflecting more than one aspect of the complex history of many records" (168). As a means of respecting and representing a record's history Barr suggests maintaining records physically in accession units and linking them conceptually through cross-referenced descriptions of the various creators with whom they had been associated before arriving at the repository.

Barr was not the only archivist to argue that the fonds should be understood as an abstraction rather than a physical entity and to suggest that to respect provenance meant to respect the multitude of relationships that make up that abstraction. Influenced by their understanding of the complicated nature of modern bureaucracies and administrative and recordkeeping structures and by the opportunities suggested by new automated technologies, archivists began to describe provenance as a conglomeration of many-to-many relationships. In his essay "The Concept of the Archival Fonds: Theory, Description and Provenance in the Post-Custodial Era," Terry Cook, quoting Max Evans, advises archivists to view the fonds "primarily as an 'intellectual construct' "; archivists should focus less on the physical location of archival documents and more on their relationships with their creators and with the functions and activities that generated them. Conceived of as an "intellectual construct," the fonds is equal to the sum of the descriptions of each of these relationships; in other words, the fonds is created through the description of the relationships between records and creators and records and functions. Provenance, Cook argues, is located "at the heart" of these relationships (Cook 1992, 73–74). The focus in defining the principle of provenance therefore shifts; the principle is understood not so much as a method for organizing records but as an intellectual construct created through the archivist's analysis of the numerous relationships that exist between records, creators, and functions.

The efforts of Barr and Cook to conceptualize the fonds address the concerns that earlier had led Australian archivists to propose and adopt the series system as a more effective means of protecting provenance (Scott 1966; Scott et al. 1978–1981). Like Cook, proponents of the series system redefine provenance as the network of relationships between recordkeeping "entities" and context "entities," the latter category of which includes the agencies that create, use, and accumulate records and the functions from which records result (Hurley 1995, 252–53).[4] As we have seen, Muller, Feith, and Fruin's understanding of provenance was endorsed by the international archival community at the 1910 Congress. In a similar fashion, the new view of provenance as a many-to-many system of relationships is sanctioned in *General International Standard Archival Description* (ISAD[G]), which defines *provenance* as:

> The relationship between records and the organizations or individuals that created accumulated and/or maintained and used them in the conduct of personal or corporate activity. (International Council on Archives 2000, 15)

A second effect of the recognition of the disjunction between physical and logical orders can be observed in calls for archivists to respect the integrity of the physical aggregation as it has evolved over time. Both Barr and Horsman stress the significance of found or "received" orders

(Nesmith 2005, 264). Barr describes accession units—or the order in which records arrive at a repository—as akin to "archaeological layers" that must not be "tampered with" if researchers are to understand records in the full "context of their provenance," which includes the history of the records and "its manifestation in their existing order" (Barr 1989, 143). Rather than respecting the administrative structure of the creator, as Muller, Feith, and Fruin appear to advocate, Barr believes in respecting the structure revealed in the records themselves. Maurizio Savoja and Stefano Vitali note a similar shift in thinking about archival structure in Italy. They describe Giorgio Cencetti's influence on Italian archival theory during the mid-twentieth century, explaining that Cencetti held that:

> The archive reflects its creator, or more exactly, is the creator itself, in the sense that the original order of the archive, the order given to the archive by its creator, is the manifestation of the administrative structure, the history, and in some way, the very "essence" of the records creator. (Savoja and Vitali 2007, 123)

However, more contemporary Italian archival thinkers have challenged the notion that archives directly reflect the bodies that create them. Claudio Pavone, for example, distinguishes between the "institutional and archival being," arguing that instead of reflecting the organization of the creator body, archives reflect the way that body "organizes its own memory;" the archives are a mirror not of their creator's history but of their own history as records (Tamblé 2001, 93).

Filippo Valenti challenged Cencetti's ideas in a similar fashion, rejecting the idea that original order could reflect "directly and necessarily, the life and activity of the creator." Valenti contends that archivists rarely work with the "ideal" type of archives envisioned by Cencetti; instead, they encounter most frequently what he calls *aggregazioni archivistiche*, aggregations "shaped by complex processes of transmission" throughout their phases both as active records of the creator body and as historical records in the hands of later custodians and archival repositories. Rather than "original order," Valenti prefers the term *archival structure*, which he felt better represented the found nature of the *aggregazioni*. Original order, he argued, is "something given on purpose to a specific whole," while a "structure is something which is discovered" (Savoja and Vitali 2007, 125). Valenti, like Barr, thus asks archivists to respect the actual organization of a group of records at the time of their transfer to an archive as representative of the records themselves and of their history and development. This idea is echoed by Tom Nesmith who suggests that records be maintained in their "received order," arguing that because it is difficult for anyone to say for certain what the original order of a group of records is, it is better to represent the records in the way that they were received at the archive. Referring to the limitations of the fonds concept identified by Millar

(2002) and Horsman (2002), Nesmith advocates for a notion of a "defensible grouping of records," which may or may not be called a fonds, but which results from a series of "related recordkeeping activities and archival interventions," and whose history as a body of records is respected over any concern for reestablishing an original order tied to the administrative structure of the records' first creators (Nesmith 2005, 264–66).

PROVENANCE AS SOCIOHISTORICAL CONTEXT

Nesmith's recognition of the importance of the history of records' creation, accumulation, and use has led him to propose yet another definition of provenance:

> The provenance of a given record or body of records consists of the social and technical processes of the records' inscription, transmission, contextualization, and interpretation, which account for its existence, characteristics, and continuing history. (Nesmith 1999, 146)

Nesmith agrees with the archivists cited above who argue that traditional interpretations of archival provenance too closely bind records to a single individual, family, or office; however, he further argues that traditional interpretations also fail to recognize the ways in which "societal and intellectual contexts" contribute to the shaping of a body of records (Nesmith 2002, 35). Nesmith and other archivists who advocate expanding the principle of provenance call attention to the social and cultural contexts of record creation and stress that creation exists along a continuum of actions that includes original authorship, custodianship, use, interpretation, representation, and archival intervention. As such, provenance continues to be associated with the context of a record's creation, but that context is broadened considerably.

The first step in broadening the context of creation is to call attention to the social systems in which the identity of a creator and the need of the creator to generate a record are assumed to be embedded. Introducing the term *societal provenance*, Nesmith reminds archivists that people "make and archive records in social settings for social purposes"; the society in which we live necessarily influences "our assumptions, values, ideas and aspirations," and affects how, why, and what information we record (Nesmith 2006, 352). For these reasons, analysis of the provenance of a record ought also to include analysis of the society in which a record was created.

Nesmith illustrates this idea with the example of a journal written by a fur trader named Johann Steinbruck who lived and worked in what are now Canada's northern territories. The journal contains a great deal of information gathered from the First Nations society in which Steinbruck found himself. For this reason, Nesmith argues that the journal "originates" at least in part from "this Aboriginal information." Nesmith also cites Steinbruck's use of birchbark as a medium for his journal as evidence of Aboriginal influence on its creation. He mentions Steinbruck's indigenous wife and children and wonders about the trader's "shifting social identity." Nesmith finds that it is the "complex interaction of the European . . . with Aboriginal society [that] creates this extraordinary document" and insists that the journal's "societal provenance" affects the way it should be read and understood, arguing that a "record created by a man of European origin who is being absorbed into Aboriginal society conveys far different evidence from one made simply by a European'" (Nesmith 2006, 355).

The notion of "societal provenance" asks archivists to recognize that records creators do not operate in isolation but are instead members of a collectivity that influences the choices they make and the ways they behave. Recently, several archivists have examined the impact of various types of collectivities on record creation. For example, Joel Wurl, who carefully points out that creators may identify with or be influenced by membership in any number of social groups or communities, describes ethnicity as a "social construct of group affiliation" and a form of "collective consciousness" that has a deep impact on the creation and preservation of records. Ethnicity, he argues, needs to be understood as a crucial component of a record's provenance rather than as a kind of "subject area" or "theme"; records created within ethnic communities are not *about* ethnicity but are rather created, at least in part, *by* ethnicity (Wurl 2005, 69).

Jeanette Allis Bastian has also examined the effect of "community" on recordmaking and recordkeeping. Noting that prior to the publication of the *Manual for the Arrangement and Description of Archives*, Dutch records were aggregated at the community level,[5] Bastian invites archivists to embrace an "expansive definition of context as community and community as context" (Bastian 2006, 280). In a study of archival practice in colonial and postcolonial U.S. Virgin Islands, she determines that "community" functions "both as a record-creating entity and as a memory frame that contextualizes the records it creates"; she coins the term *community of records* to refer to the "dynamic synergy between a community and its records" (Bastian 2003, 3–4). Within a "community of records," record creation is attributed not only to the literal inscriber of a record but also to the community and each of its members. In the context of the records created by colonial governments in the Virgin Islands, this view of records creation permits the native inhabitants of the Islands and those brought to the Islands as slave labor —that is, the subjects of colonial rule—to lay claim to a part in the creation process and also, as a result, to a right to ownership of colonial records.[6] In a "community of records," therefore, even the subjects of records are viewed as cocreators; as Bastian puts it, "Without the enslaved, there would have been no need for slave lists, without a population, there would be no need for a census" (Bastian 2006, 282–83).

The notion of a "community of records" highlights also the significance of collective memory and the influence of place on record creation. In recent years, a great deal has been written about the significance of archives in the formation of collective memory (Cook 2006; Millar 2006; Piggott 2005a; Piggot 2005b; Upward 2005a; Upward 2005b). Some archivists have also considered how collective memory affects the formation of records (Ketelaar 2005; McKemmish, Gilliland-Swetland, and Ketelaar 2005). Both Eric Ketelaar and Bastian extend the Maurice Halbwach's theory that "every memory is socially framed" to argue that just as records contribute to the formation of society's collective memory, they are also created, at least in part, as a result of the influence of collective memory (Ketelaar 2005, 46). Bastian explores the influence of collective memory on records creation in an article about the archives of the MacDowell Colony, an artists' residence in New Hampshire that houses a large collection of books, artworks, musical scores, and manuscripts created during or inspired by artists' residencies at the colony. She links the development of the colony's collection to the concept of collective memory by showing that each individual creator's contribution is shaped by the creator's relationship to the community and then, in turn, shapes the community by becoming a part of its collective memory and influencing subsequent creations. The provenance of any particular work becomes not only the relationship with the individual creator but also that creator's relationship to the community and repository as cocreators. The physical space of the colony also becomes an important aspect of record provenance, as it is within the space of the MacDowell colony that its collective memory is embodied (Bastian 2003–2004, 15–16).

Looking beyond the social contexts in which records are initially inscribed, archivists have also suggested that full understanding of provenance must include analysis of the ways records are transmitted and used over their lifetime. Laura Millar argues for an understanding of the principle of provenance that would expand it "to include creator history (the story of who created, accumulated, and used the records over time), records history (the story of the physical management and movement of the records over time) and custodial history (the explanation of the transfer of ownership or custody of the records from the creator or custodian to the archival institution and the subsequent care of those records)." A description of these three "histories" would include information about how records have been used, by whom, and when as well as a description of any enhancement or alteration of the records as a result (Millar 2002, 12–13).

As we have seen, the focus on the history of records' use and accumulation is not necessarily new; Barr's call to recognize the fonds as an abstraction was advanced in part to account for records' often complex histories of transmission. What is new is the increasing interest in and emphasis on the narratives of the records themselves as told through their custodial histories. Yeo, for example, traces the "many adventures" (Yeo 2009, 51) of the papers of Sir Richard Fanshawe whose "fluctuating" (53) custodial history creates challenges for archivists seeking to reconstruct a Fanshawe fonds. Fanshawe's papers date from the 1600s, and Yeo relates the history of their transmission from the time of Fanshawe's death in 1666 to the present, describing that history as a "long process of gradual depletion," as parts of the accumulation were sold, reacquired, rearranged, and sold again by a succession of custodians (50). Yeo uses the example of the Fanshawe papers to demonstrate the existence of both a conceptual fonds, which consists of all of the records of one creator, and a physical collection(s), which may or may not correspond at some point in time to the conceptual fonds and which is shaped by its successive custodians; both the physical collection and the conceptual fonds need to be respected and represented through archival description. The key, Yeo warns, is in neither confusing the context of creation with custodial history nor privileging one over the other as well as in recognizing how the eventual interpretation of records is affected by the "previous selection and aggregation decisions" taken by *both* creators and custodians (60). Arguing similarly for the importance of recognizing the role of custodians in shaping groups of records, Heather MacNeil posits the existence of a "custodial bond" and uses the term *archivalterity* to refer to "the acts of continuous and discontinuous change that transform the meaning and authenticity of a fonds as it is transmitted over time and space"; while earlier archival theorists comprehended changes wrought on a group of records by their custodians as "contamination to be eradicated," MacNeil argues that each custodial order is "an embodied argument about the meaning of the archive" and must be understood as part of the history of the records: "the orders given to the records by their various custodians . . . are as relevant to the present meaning and authenticity of the archive as the order given to the records by its creator" (MacNeil 2008, 14, 17).

Concern about the impact of record use and transmission over time on the eventual interpretation of archives is not limited to an investigation into the roles of custodians but also of other users of records and of archivists themselves. Lori Podolski Nordland introduces the term *secondary provenance* to account for the ways in which the meaning and import of records is impacted as they are interpreted, reinterpreted, and represented at different points in time. Referring to a nineteenth-century map known as Ak ko mok ki's map, Nordland suggests that each time the map has been interpreted or reproduced in ethnographic and geographical research publications and Web sites, it has in a sense been re-created and its provenance has "shifted" (Nordland 2004, 153). Provenancial "shifts" also occur as a result of the work of archivists who care for records once they have found their way to repositories, since this work is often of an interpretive and representational nature. Nordland includes archivists among the "reinterpreters" of records, and this view is shared by a long list of archivists influenced by postmodern ideas introduced in to the archival literature by Nesmith, Cook, Verne Harris, and others. Nesmith, for example, describes the creative role played by archivists as they assign value to records by deciding what records should be kept or destroyed and as they determine the context in which researchers will encounter records by determining their arrangement and description and providing reference services.[7] He argues that:

> Some of what makes a record meaningful is inscribed in it by those who literally made it, but most of what makes a record intelligible lies outside its physical boundaries in its context of interpretation. Archivists, who do much to shape this context, therefore share in authoring the record. (Nesmith 2002, 32)

In fact, in Nesmith's opinion, archivists may "make a greater contribution to the creation of a record" than does its original inscriber (Nesmith 2002, 35). In recent years, as archivists have rushed to digitize and make available their most interesting and important holdings, archival "recontextualization" of records has also occurred as archivists select particular records, subject them to digital remediation, and present them within the context of institutional Web sites, often as treasures or as particularly representative remnants of a region or time period (Douglas 2007; Mak 2014).[8] Of course, even those records not selected for digitization are inevitably interpreted within the context of the institution that holds them and/or within the context of their status as archival materials selected by an archive. As Ketelaar explains, the legitimizing power of the archival institution as a space in which the "truth" is contained and history made as well as the policies and rules that researchers must follow will also invariably affect a researcher's experience of the record he or she eventually encounters (Ketelaar 2002). Each of these arguments about the impact of archival intervention or archival power on the representation of records identifies the archivist or archival institution in a creative and authorial capacity and therefore considers the archival role as part of records' provenancial context.

A NOTE OF CAUTION: CAN PROVENANCE ACCOMMODATE INFINITE EXPANSION?

The arguments traced in the previous section of this chapter suggest that any definition of provenance must acknowledge the complexity of archival origins. The archivists cited here locate archival creatorship along a continuum that embraces contexts of original inscription, use, custodianship, archival treatment, and so on. From a narrow definition of provenance as a means to help archivists determine the best arrangement of a group of records, they have extended the scope of the principle to address as well issues of interpretation and representation. Their efforts at expanding the boundaries of the principle have the positive potential to encourage a more inclusive understanding of the various contexts that impact a body of records over time; however, some caution is also advised. In the discussion about provenance as sociohistorical context, the concept of provenance has the potential to become virtually indistinguishable from the notion of context itself: provenance is viewed as the umbrella under which an ever-expanding list of contextual factors is gathered. When provenance grows to include any and all types of action or relationship that impact the nature of a record or a body of records, its boundaries become infinite. There is an inherent difficulty in determining where context ends, and an understanding of provenance that includes any and all contextual factors that influence recordmaking and recordkeeping will have to admit the impossibility of its own endeavor. Inevitably, certain contextual factors will be privileged and others will be left out, depending on the point of view, motives, and position of the archivist doing the describing.

In addition, and perhaps more importantly, meaningful distinctions between the various parties who concur in the formation of a group of records over time and the roles they play may be obscured when they are *all* considered under the umbrella of provenance. As Yeo (2009) and Savoja and Vitali (2007) have discussed with respect to custodial relationships, it can be problematic to equate all types of actions taken by the various actors involved over time in the creation, use, accumulation, and preservation of a body of records. While it seems correct to suggest that the interventions of custodians, archivists, and even, sometimes, researchers result in changes to the way that archives are understood, it might be useful to consider the ways in which each of these types of intervention differs from each other in their motives, methods, and eventual impact. Current descriptive standards such as the Canadian *Rules for Archival Description (RAD)*, the *ISAD(G)*, and the *International Standard Archival Authority Record for Corporate Bodies, Persons and Families (ISAAR [CPF])* include separate areas for the description of initial creators, subsequent custodians, and archival treatment but are not always used to provide robust—or "honest" (Douglas 2016)—description of the many and varied processes that create archives. Calls for an expanded notion of provenance are due in part to recognition of these gaps in description.

In the earlier version of this chapter, I asked whether rather than expanding the concept of provenance to include every contextual aspect of record creation, it might make more sense to differentiate and delineate between different types of context. I suggested that instead of collapsing our increasing understanding of the factors that come to bear on record creation and record preservation in one conceptual category, we need to find more and better ways to analyze and explain to users the often long and complicated stories of how the records they see in front of them have come to exist in their current state. In subsequent research in writers' archives, I made an attempt to distinguish between types of creatorship, identifying in eight writers' archives six layers of archival creation, including (Douglas 2013):

1) contributions made by the individual traditionally identified as the creator of a fonds (in this case, the writer named in each fonds' title);
2) contributions made by communities to which the creator belongs;
3) contributions made by custodians (excluding archivists) of the archive, typically following the end of the archive's active phase;
4) contributions made by archivists as they appraise, acquire, arrange, describe, and make records available;
5) contributions made by subsequent researchers and interpreters of the archive; and
6) contributions made by society, broadly interpreted (Douglas 2013).

This research confirmed that, at least in the cases of the writers' archives I studied, archiving is an "ongoing *process*" (Nesmith 2005, 261) that is affected not only by the named creator of the fonds but also by various other actors and actions over time. These actors could include, as in the case of the poet Sylvia Plath's archives, family members invested in the posthumous reception and reputation of the creator (Douglas 2013, 181–82; see also Douglas 2014). They could also include the writing communities to which individual writers belonged, as for example, in the case of Margaret Laurence and Marian Engel, who were active in the Writers' Union of Canada during the 1970s and 1980s and influenced by the work of the Union's Archives Committee (Douglas 2013, 178–79), or in the case of Alice Munro, who was advised by other prominent Canadian authors and literary agents on what to keep and where to place her archives (Douglas and MacNeil 2009). Communities of writers might work in other ways, as well, to create archives; Christine Faunch, an archivist at the University of Exeter, explains how because the library at Exeter collects the archives of writers working in a relatively small region, many of them know each other well and correspond regularly, "sharing ideas, comments, and encouragement; forming a network of authors, reviewers, agents and friends all involved in shaping a final product." In this way, the authors' participation in a community of writers affects not only the shape of each of their individual archives but also the collective shape of all of their archives in the repository at Exeter (Faunch 2010, 30).

I was also able to identify the creative effects of certain interpretations and readings of an archive on *subsequent* interpretations and readings of the same archive. Plath's archives provide a good example of how some readings can affect those that come next: Plath's husband Ted Hughes's reading of the archive is to a great extent a direct reaction to Plath's mother's reading of it, and over the years, scholars have reacted to both Hughes's and Aurelia Plath's interpretations to produce their own, which continue to affect how new readers approach Plath's papers. It is not an exaggeration to suggest that it has become impossible to approach the Plath archives without being influenced by the array of biographical and psychological readings of it available to researchers.

The most difficult type of creatorship to identify and/or measure in my study of writers' archives was the final type; the "societal dimensions of record creation and archiving" (Nesmith 2006, 352) will necessarily be many and various. Consider the Douglas Coupland fonds and the variety of societal influences that might have had an effect on its nature. Critics and journalists have noted the significance of Coupland's "Canadianness" on his writing and, more specifically, his upbringing in the city of Vancouver: its newness as a city; its proximity to nature; the Asian influences in its physical and cultural development; and its position on the Pacific Rim. They have also asserted the significance of his age and of the period of time during which he came of age (and which he made the subject of his most well-known work, *Generation X: Tales for an Accelerated Culture*) (Coupland 1991). His training as an artist, his submersion in different art cultures, and his role as a public intellectual point to other potential societal influences on his work and life.

My study of the many and various ways in which writers' archives are shaped over time demonstrates empirically that there are a number of agents involved in the creation of archives and that these agents perform different types of roles and have different types of impact on the form and contents of the archive as it accumulates over time. This research, however, focuses on a small number of fonds and a single type of fonds creator; more research is required if archivists want to be able to develop an understanding of provenance that is both more capacious and more nuanced and that can be effectively operationalized through archival description.

Although the need for more research of this particular type has not yet been fulfilled, the principle of provenance continues to be reevaluated in different contexts. In the final sections of this chapter, two of these contexts are briefly discussed.

FROM COMMUNITY ARCHIVES TO SOCIAL JUSTICE: PROVENANCE AND THE RIGHTS OF COCREATORS

In the time since the first version of this chapter was published, ideas associated with the concept of provenance as sociohistorical context have been most suggestively taken up by archivists writing about and/or working with communities that have traditionally been marginalized within and by archives. The growing literature on community archives, which emphasizes the "active participation" of communities in "documenting and making accessible the history of their particular group and/or locality on their own terms" (Flinn, Stevens, and Shepherd 2009, 73; see also Flinn and Stevens 2010), combined with the increasing awareness of the role that recordkeeping and archives play in the pursuit of social justice, has led some archivists to think about how traditional definitions of provenance privilege "the importance of the thing, the record itself" over the people whom the record documents, who are "implicated" in the record, or who have "another stake" in it (Wood et al. 2014, 402). Endorsing Bastian's view that the archive would not exist without those who occupy it as subjects and drawing more broadly on the concept, discussed above, of a community of records, some archivists have recently suggested that especially when working with marginalized communities, the traditional definition of provenance is too narrow and can even at times "be read as a cumulative history of microagressions" (Wood et al. 2014, 401). Livia Iacovino, for example, advocates for the adoption of a "participant model" of provenance (Iacovino 2010, 362) by "expanding the definition of record creators to include everyone who has contributed to the record and has been affected by its action"; such an understanding, she argues, "would support the enforcement of a broader spectrum of rights and obligations" (Iacovino 2010, 367) in and through the records.

Iacovino refers specifically to indigenous rights and to the idea that indigenous peoples documented *in* records, especially in records of colonial governments, should be considered cocreators of those records. This understanding of provenance draws on Chris Hurley's conceptualization of parallel provenance (Hurley 2005a, 2005b) and is supported by the UN Declaration of the Rights of Indigenous People, which affirms the rights of indigenous peoples "to be acknowledged as co-creators" of records and to ensure "that archival description reflects co-creator perspectives, experiences, expressions and ways of knowing" (Gilliland 2012, 342; United Nations 2007).

Recognizing the rights of cocreators and cocreators as part of an archive's provenance is increasingly seen as a means of "decolonizing archival functionality and professional recordkeeping practice" (Upward, McKemmish, and Reed 2011, 218), and potentially, an integral part of a process of "archival reconciliation" (McKemmish, Faulkhead, and Russell 2011, 220).

The rights of cocreators are extended not only to indigenous peoples documented in records of colonizers but also to other marginalized and/or persecuted populations. For example, Michelle Caswell argues for a "survivor-centred approach" to records documenting human rights abuse that recognize "survivor status as a form of provenance" (Caswell 2014; see also Caswell 2013). Although the broader literature on community archives does not always specifically discuss the principle of provenance, implicit in the discussion about the *nature* of community archives (i.e., as collections of material whose "significance," "record-ness," and "archival-ness" are "assured and denoted" by the communities themselves [Flinn 2011, 160]) is the notion that not all claims to archives rest with archivists: there is considerable room yet to explore the implications of cocreation, survivor status, and community-evolved ideas about "archival-ness" on our understanding of provenance.

PROVENANCE IN THE DIGITAL WORLD

A second significant area of discussion about the principle of provenance is in the realm of digital archives. Questions about what constitutes a meaningful aggregation in digital recordkeeping environments (Yeo 2012), who should and who *can* decide (Yeo 2012), and whether archival fonds serve end users (Bak 2012; Lemieux 2014) have prompted some archivists to question the traditional application of the principle of provenance through the representation of a fonds in a hierarchical description. Jefferson Bailey argues that "the affordances of born-digital archives—such as their potential for parallel representation [and] machine-enabled interpretation . . . provoke a reconsideration of the place of privilege" of provenance as the principle underpinning archival arrangement and description (Bailey 2013). Archival practice, Yeo likewise contends, is "no longer constrained by traditional assumptions about stable aggregations and hierarchical systems" (Yeo 2012, 45). Bailey argues for visual rather than "narrative" representation of archives and for emphasis on a "search and query" approach to retrieving records, where context is dynamic, endlessly discoverable, and at least, to some extent, a function of the retriever's approach and needs (Bailey 2013). Yeo points to recent work by computer scientists "who have begun to recognize the importance of context or provenance in their own field and investigate methods of harvesting contextual information" (Yeo 2013a, 23). Provenance, he suggests, "is no longer the sole prerogative of the archival profession"; in the field of e-science, for example, provenance is recognized as a powerful tool for protecting the integrity and trustworthiness of data (Yeo 2013b, 220).

Yeo calls archivists' attention to the work of the Provenance Incubator Group of the W3C, to the Open Provenance Model, and to other similar projects which all aim to ensure that "each piece of data . . . carr[ies] with it some evidence of its history and its original context, to help those who encounter it to form a judgment about its trustworthiness" (Yeo 2013b, 220). While Yeo recognizes that definitions of provenance originating in computer science currently have somewhat limited application to archival work, where the contexts of records are considered to encompass a much broader range of people, functions, and "societal, legal and cultural environments," he suggests, too, that "whatever reservations we have about the limitations of current research, future tools" developed by computer scientists will be "more powerful" and will "eventually help archival institutions meet the challenges of description and contextualization in the world of digital records" (Yeo 2013a, 24).

FUTURE EVOLUTIONS: PROVENANCE AS PRINCIPLE/ PROVENANCE AS METHOD

In her doctoral dissertation, Jennifer Jane Bunn calls attention to the difficulty of "distinguishing the idea (of provenance) from the application" (Bunn 2011, 21). The "most telling characteristic" of the *application* of the principle, Bunn explains, is the "creation of an arrangement," usually a hierarchical one, and meant to reflect an archive's original order (Bunn 2011, 22). However, as Bunn goes on to argue, the application of the principle depends on the context in which it is being made, and this context changes over the years and in different locales: the context in which Muller, Feith, and Fruin worked is different than the context in which twentieth-century archivists worked and different again than the context in which archivists now find themselves, where questions about indigenous rights and the affordances of digital archives suggest new possibilities for the application of the principle. Respecting the fonds—or arrangement by fonds—is one possible application of the principle of provenance; arrangement by series is another; describing cocreators, the adoption of visual representation techniques, and the automatic capture of provenance metadata are others. No doubt there will be many more applications developed as archivists continue to rethink and adapt their work in response to changing societal issues and trends. However, it is useful, and necessary, I think, to keep the distinction Bunn highlights in mind as we continue to evolve in our thinking about the principle of provenance: archivists' traditional, particular focus on the named creator as the provenance of a body of records is *one* application—albeit a tenacious one—of a principle that, broadly interpreted, has to do with what it really means to create an aggregation of records. The various ideas explored in this chapter have grappled with a concept that has variously been understood as a principle or as a method and sometimes muddled up as both; making a clear distinction between the idea and its application will help archivists, as we continue to adapt to changing environments and human needs, to distinguish what are significant acts of archive creation and how best to preserve and represent these over time.

CONCLUSION

The evolution of ideas about provenance traced in this chapter demonstrates that the principle—its interpretation and its application—is continually subject to changes in archival thinking. Initially, the principle was adopted as a practical method for dealing with ancient fonds that found theoretical grounding in contemporary trends in historiography. In the mid- to late twentieth century, responding to the need to deal with open fonds and with the increasing fluidity and complexity of recordkeeping, archivists distinguished between the physical and intellectual boundaries of a record aggregation using the language of new technology to describe provenance as a network of many-to-many relationships. In the late twentieth and early twenty-first centuries, archivists reacted to the focus on sociohistorical context that was characteristic of postmodern trends in the study of history, sociology, literature, and culture and to the particular characteristics and behavior of digital record environments. In the time since then they have continued to rethink and refine what provenance means and what it can do. In 1908, Muller acknowledged that the ideas contained in the Dutch manual were not the invention of him and his colleagues but were circulating in contemporary discourse: they were—as he put it—"just in the air" (Muller quoted in Horsman 2002, 5). Thinking about provenance has evolved significantly in the intervening century, as archivists have responded to intellectual trends, to technological demands, to changes in how the archival mission is perceived; should I be asked again at some future date to revise this chapter, I am certain I will be able to report on more change, as archivists continue to react to and anticipate what they discover "in the air," on the ground, and through our collective conscience.

ENDNOTES

1. Although I acknowledge that there is some debate as to whether the principle of provenance includes both the principles of *respect des fonds* and respect for original order as subprinciples, for the purposes of this discussion, I adopt the view expounded by Horsman, who declares the principle of provenance to be "the only principle of archival theory." He explains, "This principle may have an outward application, which is to respect the archival body as it was created by an individual, a group or an organization as a whole. We call this *Respect des fonds*. The Principle of provenance may also be applied inwardly, respecting the original order given to the documents by the administration which created them" (Horsman 1994, 51). The question of whether the principle of provenance includes the principles of *respect des fonds* and respect for original order as subprinciples is discussed by Shelley Sweeney (2008) and Raimo Pohjola (1994). It is also referred to in Yeo's chapter in this volume. In particular, archivists have questioned whether respect for original order is integral to respect for provenance (Boles 1982; Horsman 1994, 52, 2002, 2–3; Powell 1976).

2. Both Schellenberg and Jenkinson believed that the principle of *respect des fonds* was the most important principle of archival science. Schellenberg, however, was more flexible in his interpretation of the significance of original order, allowing that when an original order was incomprehensible or impeded research, the archivist should feel free to rearrange records within groups. Whereas Jenkinson related both

principles to the integrity of the archive, Schellenberg determined that only the principle of *respect des fonds*, which he termed "provenance" is essential to the integrity of records, while the principle of respect for original order relates more to the "use or convenience" of the archivist and researcher (Schellenberg 1965, 105).

3. The definition of *fonds* adopted in the Working Group on Archival Descriptive Standards Report and to which Barr refers reads: "The whole of the documents of any nature that every administrative body, every physical or corporate entity, automatically and organically accumulates by reason of its function or of its activity." Michel Duchein's article, "Theoretical Principles and Practical Problems of *Respect des fonds* in Archival Science" (1983), had a profound impact on the Canadian Working Group on Archival Descriptive Standards and on the development of national descriptive standards; as Terry Eastwood writes, "the very structure" of such standards, "it came to be assumed, would be dictated by the nature of the fonds along the lines indicated by Duchein" (Eastwood 1992, 3).

4. Yeo's chapter in this book discusses the development of the series system and the evolution of thinking about functions as part of records' provenance and provides useful citations for additional reading.

5. Horsman mentions that prior to the acceptance of the methods advocated by Muller, Feith, and Fruin in the Dutch manual, records within repositories were treated as the records of the entire community (Horsman 2002, 278–79). This point is further elaborated by Thomassen, who explains that the meaningful aggregation of records prior to the publication of the *Manual* was the "whole of the non current records of the *community*," rather than the records of distinct administrative bodies within the community (Thomassen 1999, 78).

6. In "Sharing: Collected Memories in Communities of Records," Ketelaar shares Bastian's opinion that former colonizers and former colonized do, indeed, constitute a "community of records" and suggests that they therefore share a "joint archival heritage."

Ketelaar notes that the ICA distinguishes between "provenance" and "joint archival heritage" as two distinct concepts but ultimately appears to support Bastian's understanding of an entire community, rulers and subjects alike, as constituting the provenance of bodies of records created in colonial societies (Ketelaar 2005, 52).

7. The notion of archival acts of appraisal, selection, arrangement, and description as acts of records creation is discussed in a number of articles, including, but certainly not limited to: Cook (2000, 2001), Ketelaar (2001), Brien Brothman (1991), Elizabeth Yakel (2003), Wendy Duff and Harris (2002), and MacNeil (2005, 2008).

8. The question of how archival provenance ought to be understood in relation to digitized copies of original material is also discussed by Dodge (2002) and Koltun (1999), each of whom questions how digitization affects users' interpretation of records and who suggest some of the many ways in which archivists mediate between users, original records, and digitized copies.

REFERENCES

Bailey, Jefferson. 2013. "Disrespect des Fonds: Rethinking Arrangement and Description in Born-Digital Archives." *Archives Journal* 3. Available at http://www.archivejournal.net/issue/3/archives-remixed/disrespect-des-fonds-rethinking

-arrangement-and-description-in-born-digital-archives/ (last accessed October 31, 2015).

Bak, Greg. 2012. "Continuous Classification: Capturing Dynamic Relationships among Information Resources." *Archival Science* 12 (3): 287–318.

Barr, Debra. 1987–1988. "The *Fonds* Concept in the Working Group on Archival Descriptive Standards Report." *Archivaria* 25: 163–70.

Barr, Debra. 1989. "Protecting Provenance: Response to the Report of the Working Group on Description at the Fonds Level." *Archivaria* 28: 141–45.

Bartlett, Nancy. 1992. "Respect des Fonds: The Origins of the Modern Principle of Provenance." *Primary Sources & Original Works* 1–2: 107–15.

Bastian, Jeanette Allis. 2003. *Owning Memory: How a Caribbean Community Lost Its Archives and Found Its History*. Westport, CT, and London: Libraries Unlimited.

Bastian, Jeanette Allis. 2003–2004. "In a 'House of Memory': Discovering the Provenance of Place." *Archival Issues* 28: 9–19.

Bastian, Jeanette Allis. 2006. "Reading Colonial Records through an Archival Lens: The Provenance of Place, Space and Creation." *Archival Science* 6: 267–84.

Boles, Frank. 1982. "Disrespecting Original Order." *American Archivist* 45: 26–32.

Brothman, Brien. 1991. "Orders of Value: Probing the Theoretical Terms of Archival Practice." *Archivaria* 32: 78–100.

Bunn, Jennifer Jane. 2011. "Multiple Narratives, Multiple Views: Observing Archival Description." PhD Dissertation. University College London.

Caswell, Michelle. 2013. "Rethinking Inalienability: Trusting Nongovernmental Archives in Transitional Societies." *American Archivist* 76 (1): 113–34.

Caswell, Michelle. 2014. "Toward a Survivor-Centred Approach to Records Documenting Human Rights Abuse: Lessons from Community Archives." *Archival Science* 14: 307–22.

Cook, Terry. 1992. "The Concept of the Archival Fonds: Theory, Description and Provenance in the Post-Custodial Era." In *The Archival Fonds: From Theory to Practice*, edited by Terry Eastwood, 31–85. Ottawa: Bureau of Canadian Archivists.

Cook, Terry. 1993. "What's Past Is Prologue: A History of Archival Ideas since 1898, and the Future Paradigm Shift." *Archivaria* 43: 17–63.

Cook, Terry. 2000. "Fashionable Nonsense or Professional Rebirth: Postmodernism and the Practice of Archives." *Archivaria* 51: 14–35.

Cook, Terry. 2001. "Archival Science and Postmodernism: New Formulations for Old Concepts." *Archival Science* 1: 3–24.

Cook, Terry. 2006. "Remembering the Future: Appraisal of Records and the Role of Archives in Constructing Social Memory." In *Archives, Documentation, and Institutions of Social memory: Essays from the Sawyer Seminar*, edited by Francis X. Blouin Jr. and William G. Rosenberg, 169–81. Ann Arbor: University of Michigan Press.

Coupland, Douglas. 1991. *Generation X: Tales for an Accelerated Culture*. New York: St. Martin's Press.

D'Addario, Arnaldo. 1992. "The Development of Archival Science and Its Present Trends." In *Archival Science on the Threshold of the Year 2000: Proceedings of the International Conference, Macerata, 3–8 September 1990*, edited by Oddo Bucci. Ancona, Italy: University of Macerata.

Dodge, Bernadine. 2002. "Across the Great Divide: Archival Discourse and (Re)presentations of the Past in Late-Modern Society." *Archivaria* 53: 16–30.

Douglas, Jennifer (2013). "Archiving Authors: Rethinking the Analysis and Representation of Personal Archives." PhD Dissertation. University of Toronto.

Douglas, Jennifer. 2014. "The Archiving I: A Closer Look in the Archives of Writers." *Archivaria* 79: 53–89.

Douglas, Jennifer. 2007. "Digitization and the Archival Record." Paper presented at the annual meeting of the Association of Canadian Archivists, Kingston, Ontario.

Douglas, Jennifer. 2016. "Toward More Honest Description." *American Archivist* 79 (1): (forthcoming).

Douglas, Jennifer, and Heather MacNeil. 2009. "Arranging the Self: Literary and Archival Perspectives on Writers' Archives." *Archivaria* 67: 25–39.

Duchein, Michel. 1983. "Theoretical Principles and Practical Problems of *Respect des fonds* in Archival Science." *Archivaria* 16: 64–82.

Duff, Wendy, and Verne Harris. 2002. "Stories and Names: Archival Description as Narrating Records and Constructing Meanings." *Archival Science* 2: 263–85.

Eastwood, Terry. 1992. "General Introduction." In *The Archival Fonds: From Theory to Practice*, edited by Terry Eastwood, 1–29. Ottawa: Bureau of Canadian Archivists.

Faunch, Christine. 2010. "Archives of Written Lives: A Case Study of Daphne Du Maurier and Her Biographer, Margaret Forster." *Archives* 35: 28–34.

Flinn, Andrew. 2011. "The Impact of Independent and Community Archives on Professional Thinking and Practice." In *The Future of Archives and Recordkeeping: A Reader*, edited by Jennie Hill, 145–69. London: Facet Publishing.

Flinn, Andrew, Mary Stevens, and Elizabeth Shepherd. 2009. "Whose Memories, Whose Archives? Independent Community Archives, Autonomy and the Mainstream." *Archival Science* 9: 71–86.

Flinn, Andrew, and Mary Stevens. 2010. " 'It Is Noh Mistri, Wi Mekin Histri'; Telling Our Own Story: Independent and Community Archives in the UK, Challenging and Subverting the Mainstream." In *Community Archives: The Shaping of Memory*, edited by Jeannette Allis Bastian and Ben Alexander, 3–27. London: Facet.

Gilliland, Anne J. 2012. "Contemplating Co-Creator Rights in Archival Description." *Knowledge Organization* 5: 340–46.

Horsman, Peter. 1994. "Taming the Elephant: An Orthodox Approach to the Principle of Provenance." In *The Principle of Provenance: Report from the First Stockholm Conference on the Archival Principle of Provenance, 2–3 September 1993*, edited by Kerstin Abukhanfusa and Jan Sydbeck, 51–63. Stockholm: Swedish National Archives.

Horsman, Peter. 1999. "Dirty Hands: A New Perspective on the Original Order." *Archives and Manuscripts* 27: 42–53.

Horsman, Peter. 2002. "The Last Dance of the Phoenix, or the De-discovery of the Archival Fonds." *Archivaria* 54: 1–23.

Hurley, Chris. 1995. "Problems with Provenance." *Archives and Manuscripts* 23: 234–59.

Hurley, Chris. 2005a. "Parallel Provenance: (1) What If Anything Is Archival Description?" *Archives and Manuscripts* 33 (1): 110–45.

Hurley, Chris. 2005b. "Parallel Provenance: (2) When Something Is Not Related to Everything Else." *Archives and Manuscripts* 33 (2): 52–91.

Iacovino, Livia. 2010. "Rethinking Archival, Ethical and Legal Frameworks for Records of Indigenous Australian Communities: A Participant Relationship Model of Rights and Responsibilities." *Archival Science* 10: 353–72.

International Council on Archives. 2000. *ISDG: General International Standard Archival Description*, 2nd ed. Madrid: Subdirección General de Archivos Estatales.

Ketelaar, Eric. 2001. "Tacit Narratives: The Meaning of Archives." *Archival Science* 1: 131–41.

Ketelaar, Eric. 2002. "Archival Temples, Archival Prisons: Modes of Power and Protection." *Archival Science* 2: 221–38.

Ketelaar, Eric. 2005. "Sharing: Collected Memories in Communities of Records." *Archives and Manuscripts* 33: 44–61.

Koltun, Lily. 1999. "The Promise and Threat of Digital Options in an Archival Age." *Archivaria* 44: 114–35.

Lemieux, Victoria L. 2014. "Toward a 'Third Order' Archival Interface: Research Notes on Some Theoretical and Practical Implications of Visual Explorations in the Canadian Context of Financial Electronic Records." *Archivaria* 78: 53–93.

MacNeil, Heather. 2005. "Picking Our Text: Archival Description, Authenticity, and the Archivist as Editor." *American Archivist* 68: 265–78.

MacNeil, Heather. 2008. "Archivalterity: Rethinking Original Order." *Archivaria* 66 (Fall): 1–24.

Mak, Bonnie. 2014. "Archaeology of a Digitization." *Journal of the Association for Information Science and Technology* 65 (8): 1515–26.

McKemmish, Sue, Anne Gilliland-Swetland, and Eric Ketelaar. 2005. " 'Communities of Memory': Pluralising Archival Research and Education Agendas." *Archives and Manuscripts* 33 (May): 146–75.

McKemmish, Sue, Shannon Faulkhead, and Lynette Russell. 2011. "Distrust in the Archives: Reconciling Records." *Archival Science* 11: 211–39.

Millar, Laura. 2002. "The Death of the Fonds and the Resurrection of Provenance: Archival Context in Space and Time." *Archivaria* 53: 1–15.

Millar, Laura. 2006. "Touchstones: Considering the Relationship between Memory and Archives." *Archivaria* 61: 105–26.

Muller, Samuel, J. A. Feith, and R. Fruin. 2003. *The Manual for the Arrangement and Description of Archives*, 2nd ed. Translated by Arthur H. Leavitt. Chicago, IL: Society of American Archivists.

Nesmith, Tom. 1993. "Archival Studies in English-speaking Canada and the North American Rediscovery of Provenance." In *Canadian Archival Studies and the Rediscovery of Provenance*, edited by T. Nesmith, 1–28. Metuchen, NJ: Scarecrow Press.

Nesmith, Tom. 1999. "Still Fuzzy but More Accurate: Some Thoughts on the 'Ghosts' of Archival Theory." *Archivaria* 47: 136–50.

Nesmith, Tom. 2002. "Seeing Archives: Postmodernism and the Changing Intellectual Place of Archives." *American Archivist* 65: 24–41.

Nesmith, Tom. 2005. "Reopening Archives: Bringing New Contextualities into Archival Theory and Practice." *Archivaria* 60: 259–74.

Nesmith, Tom. 2006. "The Concept of Societal Provenance and Records of Nineteenth-Century Aboriginal-European Relations in Western Canada: Implications for Archival Theory and Practice." *Archival Science* 6: 351–60.

Nordland, Lori Podolski. 2004. "The Concept of 'Secondary Provenance': Re-interpreting Ac ko mok ki's Map as Evolving Text." *Archivaria* 58: 147–59.

Piggott, Michael. 2005a. "Archives and Memory." In *Archives: Recordkeeping in Society*, edited by Sue McKemmish, Michael Piggott, Barbara Reed, and Frank Upward, 299–328. Wagga Wagga, New South Wales: Charles Sturt University.

Piggott, Michael. 2005b. "Building Collective Memory Archives." *Archives and Manuscripts* 33: 62–83.

Pohjola, Raimo. 1994. "The Principle of Provenance and the Arrangement of Records/Archives." In *The Principle of Provenance: Report from the First Stockholm Conference on the Archival Principle of Provenance, 2–3 September 1993*, edited by Kerstin Abukhanfusa and Jan Sydbeck, 87–101. Stockholm: Swedish National Archives.

Posner, Ernst. 2006a. "Max Lehmann and the Genesis of the Principle of Provenance." In *Archives and the Public Interest*, edited by Ken Munden, 36–44. Chicago, IL: Society of American Archivists.

Posner, Ernst. 2006b. "Some Aspects of Archival Development since the French Revolution." In *Archives and the Public Interest*, edited by Ken Munden, 23–35. Chicago, IL: Society of American Archivists.

Powell, Graeme T. 1976. "Archival Principles and the Treatment of Personal Papers." *Archives and Manuscripts* 6: 259–68.

Savoja, Maurizio, and Stefano Vitali. 2007. "Authority Control for Creators in Italy: Theory and Practice." *Journal of Archival Organization* 5: 121–47.

Schellenberg, T. R. 1956. *Modern Archives: Principles and Techniques*. Chicago: University of Chicago Press.

Schellenberg, T. R. 1965. *The Management of Archives*. New York: Columbia University Press. Reprint (1988) Washington, D.C.: National Archives and Records Administration.

Scott, P. J. 1966. "The Record Group Concept: A Case for Abandonment." *American Archivist* 29: 493–504.

Scott, P. J., C. D. Smith, and G. Finlay. 1978–1981. "Archives and Administrative Change: Some Methods and Approaches." Parts 1–5. *Archives and Manuscripts*. Part 1 in 7 (August 1978): 115–27; Part 2 in 7 (April 1979): 151–65; Part 3 in 8 (June 1980): 41–53; Part 4 in 8 (December 1980): 51–69; and Part 5 in 9 (September 1981): 3–18.

Stapelton, Rick. 1983–1984. "Jenkinson and Schellenberg: A Comparison." *Archivaria* 17: 75–85.

Sweeney, Shelley. 2008. "The Ambiguous Origins of the Archival Principle of Provenance." *Libraries and the Cultural Record* 43: 193–213.

Tamblé, Donato. 2001. "Archival Theory in Italy Today." *Archival Science* 1: 83–100.

Thomassen, Theo H. P. M. 1999. "The Development of Archival Science and Its European Dimension." In *The Archivist and the Archival Science: Seminar for Anna Christina Ulfsparre 10–11 February 1999 at the Swedish National Archives*, 75–83. Lund, Sweden: Landsarkivets I Lund.

United Nations. 2007. *Declaration on the Rights of Indigenous Peoples*. Available at www.un.org/esa/socdev/unpfii/documents/DRIPS_en.pdf (last accessed September 24, 2016).

Upward, Frank. 2005a. "Continuum Mechanics and Memory Banks: (1) Multi-polarity." *Archives and Manuscripts* 33 (May): 84–109.

Upward, Frank. 2005b. "Continuum Mechanics and Memory Banks: (2) The Making of Culture." *Archives and Manuscripts* 33 (November): 18–51.

Upward, Frank, Sue McKemmish, and Barbara Reed. 2011. "Archivists and Changing Social Information Spaces: A Continuum Approach to Recordkeeping and Archiving in Online Cultures." *Archivaria* 72: 197–227.

Wood, Stacy, Kathy Carbone, Marika Cifor, Anne Gilliland, and Ricardo Punzalan. 2014. "Mobilizing Records: Re-framing Archival Description to Support Human Rights." *Archival Science* 14: 397–419.doi: 10.1007/s10502-014-9233-1.

Wurl, Joel. 2005. "Ethnicity as Provenance: In Search of Values and Principles for Documenting the Immigrant Experience." *Archival Issues* 29: 65–76.

Vitali, Stefano. 2002. "The Archive at the Time of Its Institution: The Central Archive of Francesco Bonaini." In *The Florence State Archive: Thirteen Centuries of Historical Records*, edited by Rosalie Manno Tulo and Anna Bellinazzi, 19–21. Florence, Italy: Nardine Editore.

Yakel, Elizabeth. 2003. "Archival Representation." *Archival Science* 3: 1–25.

Yeo, Geoffrey. 2013a. "Archival Description in the Era of Digital Abundance." *Comma* 2 (2): 15–25.

Yeo, Geoffrey. 2012. "Bringing Things Together: Aggregate Records in a Digital Age." *Archivaria* 74: 43–91.

Yeo, Geoffrey. 2009. "Custodial History, Provenance, and the Description of Personal Records." *Libraries and the Cultural Record* 44 (1): 50–64. doi: 10.1353/lac.0.0062.

Yeo, Geoffrey. 2013b. "Trust and Context in Cyberspace." *Archives and Records* 34 (2): 214–34. doi: 10.1080/23257962.2013.825207.

Yeo, Geoffrey. 2017. "Continuing Debates about Description." In *Currents of Archival Thinking*, edited by Heather MacNeil and Terry Eastwood, 163–92. Santa Barbara, CA: Libraries Unlimited.

3

Archives as a Place[1]

Adrian Cunningham

Recently, when giving a talk on the work of my archives to other public servants within the archives' parent department, I started by explaining that the archives was located 20 kilometres south of the city center and that this location was chosen some 20 years earlier primarily due to financial concerns. Twenty years ago the then government chose to build a large archive repository on relatively cheap land on the suburban fringes rather than invest in expensive real estate in the city center. One of the audience then asked, "Where do you think Archives should be located?" The question was presumably a friendly gesture aimed to incite a lament that the location was neither central nor convenient for staff and clients. However, my response was that in the digital age, the archives should be "everywhere" and that the physical location(s) of its offices and storage facilities should ultimately be a minor consideration.

This anecdote indicates that notions of the physical anchoring of archival holdings and services are undergoing a fundamental rethink. Of course, the physical location of archival holdings and services is not the only aspect that is being challenged and refigured as a result of what many commentators refer to as "digital disruption" (Foreshew 2015). Indeed, digital disruption is driving fundamental rethinks in just about every profession. With many commentators predicting, it will result in certain professions and occupations becoming unrecognizable, if not entirely redundant.

The choice of physical location of an archive says much about society's perceptions about its role and function culturally. Sometimes they are located prominently in the geographic heart of the civic, administrative, and cultural centers of a community. Before the mid-twentieth century, when volumes of archival holdings were relatively small and storage requirements relatively modest, locating an archives on prime real estate was deemed both feasible and desirable. In many cases, this would have reflected utilitarian imperatives associated with enabling easy access to records. Arguably, there were also symbolic reasons for locating archives prominently in administrative and/or cultural precincts—an issue that will be explored further later in the chapter. Later in the twentieth century, as the volume of records expanded considerably, it became common for archival repositories to be built on more affordable and remote "green field" sites. That phenomenon suggests that decision makers viewed archives as primarily places of storage and preservation, with access to and use of the archives being only a secondary consideration. More recently, again there has been a tendency for archives with repositories in noncentral or suburban locations to establish "shop fronts" or access points in central locations, often by colocating with other information services or cultural hubs—usually requiring the shuttling of physical records between the remote repository and the central access point.

Do archives need to be rooted in a physical place to fulfil their mission and to satisfy expectations regarding their role? If so, what does the choice of place tell us about this mission and these expectations and assumptions? If not, what does this tell us about the very nature of archives—most fluidic of constructs? Do the answers to these questions in any given context tell us more about the mutable nature of communities that create and use archives than about any hegemonic laws about the archive and its place in society?

In 1956, American archivist T. R. Schellenberg opened his landmark textbook *Modern Archives: Principles and Techniques* with a quote from Roman emperor Justinian (Schellenberg 1956). Presumably, the irony of opening a book on "modern archives" with a quote from ancient Rome was intended to highlight the immutable continuity of the nature of the archival endeavor. The so-called Justinian Code decreed that every province needed to have a public building for storing records overseen by an archivist with responsibility for ensuring the integrity of those records and enabling their use. Inherent in this code was the notion that records were important physical objects that were vulnerable to corruption and therefore in need of physical protection in a public building.

Such notions still, by and large, receive wisdom in today's archival professional practice—at least in that professional practice that draws its intellectual and cultural roots from Eurocentric origins—albeit with some tentative questioning occurring in the context of digital disruption. Yet, at the same time, a large body of academic literature in philosophy and the humanities positions "the archive" as a metaphor for the accumulated and distributed knowledge of communities and subject disciplines. In these discourses, archives may or may not have tangible form, and in any case, there is usually no expectation that they have to be collected in a particular place—be it a public building or otherwise. In these circles, the archive is a cultural, intellectual, and psychological ecosystem with no fixed boundaries. This metaphorical view of archives may be extended to non-western societies and their oral traditions, where the storage, preservation, and transmission of cultural memory are achieved by huge variety of means, only some of which may be rooted to physical places of preservation.

This chapter provides an overview and comparative analysis of the varied manifestations, roles, and notions of archives throughout time and across the world, with the particular aim of testing the concept place in the archival endeavor. One of the aims of the chapter is to illustrate by example just what mutable creations archives really are. Recognition of this seemingly obvious fact is argued as a counterpoint to any tendency that other authors may have to argue in favor of universal laws and immutable truths about the nature of the archives. While common themes, objectives, and issues can be identified through such a comparative analysis, the main argument of this chapter is that there is no universal law governing the place, form, and mission of archives. All archives fulfil their mission by, as a minimum, controlling and preserving the records that constitute the archive, but the nature of the mission served and the means by which it is pursued can vary from case to case. The ever-shifting, always-contested mission and the form and function of the archive reflect the dynamic nature of human experience, aspiration, and activity in all its infinitely rich variety.

The secondary aim of this chapter is to illustrate not only that all archival programs and institutions are the contingent products of their time and place but also that they are active shapers of such markers. In the words of Verne Harris, archives "at once express and are instruments of prevailing relations of power" (Harris 2002). Indeed, as we shall see, it is the nature of the prevailing power relations and the particular roles archives play as contested sites of power that determine the forms and functions of archival programs—forms and functions that change as the dynamics of societal power relations evolve and/or transform.

THE ARCHIVING IMPULSE AND IMPERATIVE

One of the features that has characterized societies since time immemorial has been an instinct for cultural self-preservation. While culture is contestable and ever-evolving, human beings nevertheless crave that their culture and its achievements endure across generations. This cultural persistence is made possible through the preservation of stories, both orally and in writing and through dance, rituals, art, music, and performance. In many cases, the keeping of these valuable cultural "records" is fostered and institutionalized in an "archive(s)." The forms, functions, and mandates of archival programs and institutions have varied enormously depending on the nature of the society in which they exist and the objectives of those who control the archives.

Records are created as a means of conducting and/or remembering activities. They are created for pragmatic or symbolic purposes—as enablers and evidence of experience and activity, as aids to memory, and/or as artefacts. Some of these records are consciously retained for future reference as archives. As authors such as James O'Toole and Sue McKemmish have argued, human beings throughout the ages have demonstrated impulses to save and to bear witness (McKemmish 1996; O'Toole 1990). Human beings are the sum of their memories. The nature of their interaction with other humans, indeed their very identity, is determined by these memories. While all memories are cognitive, literate individuals learn to rely at least to some extent on the written word to document, express, and supplement cognitive processes. In turn, these cognitive processes give meaning to the archives for, as Jacques Derrida argues, the archive does not speak for itself—users inscribe their own interpretations into it (Derrida 1996).

When these impulses move beyond the purely personal and take on a broader societal purpose, the archives so retained take on a more formal character. One manifestation of this phenomenon is that the records can become part of an archival program or institution. This institutionalization of the record, which Derrida calls *domiciliation*, marks the passage of information from the private to a collective domain (Derrida 1996). For instance, when a novelist offers his or her personal papers to a publicly funded manuscript collecting program and when that program assesses the papers and agrees that they would constitute a worthwhile addition to its collection, the records are simultaneously institutionalized and made public property. The novelist is acting on an individual impulse to pluralize his or her private records for the benefit of current and future generations, while the broader community is acting through its program on an impulse to preserve and provide access to the evidence of the novelist's creative existence.

Records may be institutionalized in this way for a variety of reasons:

- Organisations need to retain their archives in order to meet their legal obligations, to protect and advance their rights, and to retain corporate memory of the activities of the collective over time to support future decision making and organisational continuity;
- Communities, including entire nations, retain archives as a means of remembering and connecting with their pasts. There are numerous factors influencing this kind of institutionalisation of memory. Eric Ketelaar(2002b) describes archives

in this sense as "time machines"—"a bridge to yesteryear." Others describe the need to capture and retain ancestral voices or to listen to the whispers of the souls of long ago (Steedman 2001; Wehner and Maidment 1999). In serving this role archival institutions have much in common with other cultural institutions such as museums;

- Similarly, communities and nations often establish archives to inform, enlighten, educate and sometimes to entertain. Related to this is the collective need to support and control storytelling about the pasts and origins of the community. Often archives are retained as a means of expressing, asserting and preserving a unifying consensus on the nature of its identity, as forged through a shared history—or alternatively to support competing articulations of identity and plurality;
- Organisations and communities retain archives for their symbolic significance. Objects stored in the archives can themselves be invested with and convey enormous symbolic significance (O'Toole 1993, 2002). The creation of a national archives can be symbolically significant as a form of solidification and memorialisation in the context of nation building (Le Goff 1992). The heavy symbolism of the archives and its contents can in turn function as a point of mythology (Echevarria 1990). Powerful rulers or administrators often establish archives as symbolic monuments to their own power and as a means of controlling and directing mythmaking activities concerning their achievements (Harris 2002);
- Powerful rulers create archives not only as symbolic monuments to their greatness, but also to legitimise and perpetuate their power. The deeds, treaties and founding documents in such an archive can legitimise power in a legalistic and evidential sense, while the information on individual subjects in such an archive can provide the information such rulers need to perpetuate their power. Moreover, because archives exercise control over selective memory, they are a source of power that is of enormous utility to autocratic rulers. When endeavouring to control the past, deciding what should be forgotten is just as important as deciding what should be remembered. As Antoinette Burton says, "the history of the archive is a history of loss" (Burton 2001);
- Conversely, in democratic societies archives are meant to enable accountability by providing access that can empower citizens against potential maladministration, corruption and autocracy. In addition to, or perhaps instead of, protecting the entitlements of rulers and governments, such archives are meant to protect the rights of the governed. In the words of John Fleckner, such archives are bastions of a just society where "individual rights are not time bound and past injustices are reversible," where "the archival record serves all citizens as a check against a tyrannical government" (Fleckner 1991).

As it will be seen, these reasons for the existence of archives are not mutually exclusive. Most archives exist for a combination of these reasons. Indeed, many archives struggle either consciously or subconsciously with the ambiguities and contradictions associated with serving these multiple purposes. The ongoing crisis of identity of government archives in democratic countries is a major theme of this chapter. Are archives a part of government or a check on it? How do archival institutions balance the often-competing demands of public and private interests? What is the interplay of symbolic roles with these other functions and mandates? Most importantly, what factors influence responses to these dilemmas in practice, and what are the consequences of the different responses?

ARCHIVAL PLACE, FORM, AND FUNCTION IN ANCIENT AND MEDIEVAL HISTORY

Understanding the origins of archives depends on what one believes an archives to be. One might, for instance, regard prehistoric cave paintings as being archives. Reflecting a more traditional view of archives, Ernst Posner argued that the first archives were created by the Sumerians in the middle of the fourth millennium BCE. The archives were used to support commercial activity and property ownership. Later, ancient societies such as the Hittites, Assyrians, and Mesopotamians all kept archives, although one can only speculate today on just how institutionalized these archives were and what form such institutions took. In at least some of these societies, archives were kept in temples and courts for religious, legal, administrative, commercial, and genealogical purposes (Posner 1972).

During the second and third millennium BCE, the Egyptians developed an extensive system of archives to support their empire, as did the later Persian Empire. These archives existed primarily to serve the legal, administrative, and military purposes of the rulers. An early indication of the perceived role of archives as tools of political oppression occurred in Egypt around 2200 BCE, when, during a revolt, an angry mob destroyed a records office "as the custodians of hated property rights" (Posner 1972). Persian archives often incorporated the captured archives of defeated governments to help establish control over the newly occupied territories.

Archives in China can be traced back almost as far as the Sumerians. These records were inscribed on bones and tortoise shells for religious, administrative, and symbolic purposes. By 700 BCE, bamboo, silk, and stone tablets were in use, with records of military value being stored in secure buildings.

The Greek city-state of Athens began housing its archives in the Metroon, the temple of the mother of the gods next to the courthouse, by around 400 BCE. In what was perhaps the first example of an archival institution fulfilling the function of public access to records and consistent with the democratic principles of Athenian government, private citizens could obtain copies of the records in the archives. The Metroon was also the first instance of an archives being used as a means of protecting records from alteration and as a reliable source of authentic evidence (Sickinger 1999).

The power that resides in the archives is illustrated in the etymology of the word *archives*, which can be traced to this time. The Greek *archeion* referred to the office of the magistrate or *archon* and the records kept by that office. *Archontes* wielded executive power, which in large part was legitimized by the legal documents in the *archeion*. Similarly, the Greek *arkho* meant to command or govern. The Latin *archivum* was likewise the residence of the magistrate and the place where records of official legal and administrative significance were kept.

Rome's first public archives was the Aerarium, or treasury, of the temple of Saturn and housed laws, decrees, reports, and financial records. Like the Metroon, the laws housed in this archives could be consulted by all citizens. When the Aerarium was destroyed by fire in 83 BCE, it was replaced by the Tabularium, a large stone building. In later imperial Rome, the Tabularium adopted a narrower mission as the archives of the Senate. It was supplemented by imperial archives and a network of provincial, municipal, military, and religious archives. Various emperors, most notably Byzantine emperor Justinian I, were keen advocates of archives. The Justinian Code of 529 CE was not only written with the assistance of archives, but it also included a section on the role of archives and archivists. This code, which continued to inform legal systems in post-Roman Europe and Western societies more generally, emphasized the importance of archives as a public place of deposit and as guarantors of the integrity of the records housed therein (Brosius 2003; Culham 1989).

Most medieval European archives were maintained in ecclesiastical settings, often in "muniment rooms." By the middle of the sixth century, a papal archives had been established. Following the collapse of the Roman Empire, a number of municipal archives persisted in Italy and France until the ninth and tenth centuries. Venice and Florence established archives during the eleventh and thirteenth centuries, respectively. It was common practice for royal archives in Europe to have no fixed location but instead to travel with the King's household (Clanchy 1993). Toward the end of the twelfth century, however, there were some moves toward the establishment of a central government archives in England. A century later Exchequer rolls began to be housed in the Tower of London. In time, this archives was expanded to include all of Britain's Chancery records. In 1323, the first inventory of English archives was completed and served as a model for similar initiatives elsewhere in Europe. In 1346, the archives of the kingdom of Aragon was created (Duchein 1992).

In 1524, the archives of the crown of Castille was established by Charles V at Simancas near Valladolid. The archives was greatly expanded by Philip II, who regarded archives as vital for administering and legitimizing an empire and who also viewed archives as symbols of power and prestige. The Simancas archive is now regarded as the classic prototype of a centralized "national archives." Two hundred years later, the Archives of the Indies was established in Seville for the same reasons. When Cortes conquered the Americas, it was considered essential to not only burn the archives of the conquered Incas and Aztecs (Martin 1988) but also ensure legitimate documentation of the occupation by a legally appointed notary, whose records were eventually deposited in archives back in Spain (O'Toole 2002). Between the sixteenth and early eighteenth centuries, royal archives repositories were established in France, Sweden, Denmark, and China. The combined effect of the advent of the printing press and the emergence of the modern administrative state generated a significant growth in records creation and, as a consequence, archives holdings.

The creation and ownership of archives became increasingly important in the context of religious and political power struggles such as the Reformation and parliamentary reform movements, when opposing factions used records to support their arguments. The Renaissance had created demand for access to information for the purpose of supporting scholarly enquiry as opposed to the more common political, financial, legal, administrative, and symbolic purposes. Nevertheless, access to archives was strictly controlled by their owners, usually monarchs or churches, who very often kept them inaccessible to all except themselves and their functionaries.

THE FRENCH REVOLUTION AND THE NINETEENTH CENTURY

The French Revolution provides perhaps the clearest example of the mutable nature and purpose of archives and their tendency to inspire extremes in human emotion. Between 1789 and 1793, much of the archives of the *Ancien Régime* were attacked and destroyed by mobs with the aim of obliterating what the revolutionaries regarded as symbols of their erstwhile oppression. While such actions might sometimes have had the practical benefit of destroying the evidence of feudal debts and obligations, by and large they were cathartic acts of retribution and ritual cleansing of the body politic.

In the midst of this destruction of old archives, there coexisted a desire to create a new archival system for the new society. A legislative repository was provided for by the new assembly just two weeks after the fall of the Bastille. In September 1790, a law was passed establishing a new National Archives that was to be open to the public and which was to report to the assembly. By 1794, the desire to destroy the documentary evidence of the *Ancien Régime* had been replaced by an impetus to preserve and manage those records as nationalized public property, reinvented for the purpose of symbolically highlighting the glory of the new Republic in contrast to the sinful decadence and oppression of the old regime. A decree, issued in June 1794, granted the National Archives jurisdiction over the records of government agencies, provinces, communes, churches, universities, and noble families, thus creating the world's first centrally controlled national archival system. The same decree also proclaimed the right of public access to these records, thus establishing the first modern instance of archives fulfilling a legal role as protectors of the rights and entitlements of the people and as instruments of accountability and transparency in government. The creation of national archives as both symbols of nation building in the midst of turbulent change and ideological—indeed almost mythological—assertions of legitimacy by new orders is a pattern that has been repeated often since. The fate of the archives of the *Ancien Régime* testifies to the fact that no archives can assume an eternal mandate—in the words of Judith Panitch, they are forever "subject to the judgement of the society in which they exist" (Panitch 1996; Posner 1940).

Another implication of the French Revolution was proposed by Luciana Duranti who argues that the 1794 decree created for the first time a dichotomy between administrative and historical archives—the distinction between the archives of the Republic and the archives of the *Ancien Régime*. Duranti considers this an unfortunate development in that it represents a usurpation of the administrative and legal functions of archives by social and cultural functions—a usurpation that has echoes in various places and times since the Revolution (Duranti 1996). However, other commentators like Panitch argue that in the 1790s, the notion of French archives as sites of "historical or cultural scholarship had yet to take hold." While they had acquired the new function of public access for the new purpose of accountability, their essential role as legal, administrative, and symbolic institutions remained unaltered (Panitch 1996).

Nevertheless, Duranti is correct in highlighting the distinction between the administrative/legal and cultural/historical roles of archives, even if the cultural role of French archives did not become apparent until some decades after the Revolution. Duranti's portrayal of one role as being innately superior to another is, however, a position that is far more difficult to sustain, as we shall see. Nor, as we have already seen, is it true that the world had to wait until the late eighteenth century to witness an example of an archives that was established for cultural and historical purposes. While such phenomena were unusual, they were not unprecedented—for example, for hundreds of years China had a Bureau of Historiography that exercised a dual role of controlling both archives and the writing of history (Sharma 2005, 14).

The creation of a centralized national archives in France provided a model for archival development in a number of other countries such as Finland, Norway, the Netherlands, and Belgium during the nineteenth century. Similarly, in Sweden, Denmark, and Prussia, central archives evolved out of preexisting royal or administrative repositories. Forty-eight years after the creation of the French national archives, the English followed suit, but for very different reasons and in much less dramatic circumstances. Between 1800 and 1837, a variety of committees and commissions of inquiry had highlighted the scattered and poorly controlled and preserved state of public records in that country. These efforts culminated in the passage of the Public Records Act in 1838 and the eventual establishment of the Public Record Office during the 1850s by a government concerned to ensure the proper care and preservation of records that guaranteed the legal rights of English people. Lawmakers in Westminster were no doubt aware of the fact that their counterparts in Scotland had beaten not only themselves but also the French in establishing a national archives, when the principal collection of Scottish public records had been assembled in Edinburgh's General Register House as early as 1784.

By the middle of the nineteenth century, the growth in historical scholarship, based on the use of written sources, was becoming an important factor in the evolution of European archival institutions. Selected series of historical documents were published, such as the "Roll Series" and the "Calendars of State Papers" in England. In 1869, the Historical Manuscripts Commission was established in the United Kingdom to identify, describe, and promote the preservation and use of significant historical records that were not otherwise catered for under the Public Records Act. The commission, which existed until April 2003 when it was amalgamated with the Public Record Office to form a rebranded National Archives, is probably the best example of a state-sponsored documentation program for the nationally distributed holdings of historically significant private records.

ARCHIVES IN THE TWENTIETH CENTURY—THE POSTCOLONIAL ERA

Globalization, the spread of modern bureaucracies, and the worldwide interest in history and cultural/national identity together provided the impetus for the emergence of archival systems around the world during the twentieth century. Soon after the Bolshevik Revolution, the Soviet Union established a highly centralized archival system as both a reflection and enabler of centralized state power. In contrast to democratic states, access to archives in totalitarian states was not a guaranteed right of the citizen.

In Asia, Latin America, Africa, and the South Pacific, European colonial powers were responsible for the creation of administrative archives that in turn formed the basis for national archives once independence was achieved (Alexander and Pessek 1988; Stoler 2002). For instance, the National Archives of Malaysia was established in 1957 and was based on the model of the Public Record Office in London (Nor 1994). In Vietnam, the French colonial administrators established an archives in 1917. This was eventually superseded by the State Archives Department in 1962, which in turn was consolidated by the 1982 Decree on the Protection of National Archives Documents. The scope of this decree was, however, limited to government records (Hai 1996). In many such territories, archival development has also benefited from a strong precolonial archival tradition. Thailand, which was never colonized by a European power, inherited an impressive system of royal, legal/administrative, and cultural archives of palm leaf manuscripts and bark paper stretching back many hundreds of years. This system was overlaid with a more Western approach, including the adoption of a registry system, during the late nineteenth century. In the early twentieth century, records retention schedules were introduced and a National Archives was established in 1952 (Prudtikul 1999).

A common feature of archival institutions in the postcolonial developing world is that institutions established with the best of intentions on a European model have often struggled to fulfil expectations in the harsh economic and political reality of independence. Just as these nations have struggled to consolidate inherited democratic institutions, so too have inherited archival institutions often failed to establish themselves as robust organic components of postcolonial societies (Papadopoulis 1996). Not only have administrators often been inclined to view archives as at best luxuries and at worst irrelevant, but also citizens living in predominantly oral cultures have often been slow to develop attachments with institutions primarily associated with preservation of the written word (Wehner and Maidment 1999). Indeed, an interesting variant on the traditional archival institutional model has been the emergence of alternative forms of memory institutionalization such as so-called keeping places and memory institutions that deal primarily with orality in preference to written records (McIver, Best, and Hutchinson 1994).

Archives in these territories have to develop flexible new conceptions of indigenous knowledge ownership, control, and access in response to a rejection of the inappropriate aspects of Eurocentric archival theory, which support the systematic marginalization and dispossession of the indigenous by dominant global discourses. The more successful of these have been able to demonstrate the potential of archives to support the rediscovery of suppressed cultural identities and the redressing of past injustices (Harris and Cunningham 2003). Indeed, the often-tenuous place of archives in oral societies tells us much about the mutable and contingent nature of such institutions. While many have endeavored to increase their relevance by instituting oral history programs, others argue that such activities fail to comprehend the difficulties involved in converting fluid orality into fixed material custody, without destroying the very thing that the archives is trying to capture. In the words of Harris, there exists “a reluctance to engage indigenous conceptualisations of orality not as memory waiting to be archived, but as archive already” (Harris 2000; Hatang 2000).

ARCHIVES IN NORTH AMERICA

Contrary to the more usual pattern of legal/administrative archives gradually acquiring a cultural/historical role, in North America, the primary impetus for the creation of archival institutions were cultural/historical imperatives. The Public Archives of Canada was established in 1872, only five years after confederation, following a petition to government by the Quebec Literary and Historical Society. Of particular concern to Canadian historians was the desire to have access to records of Canadian historical interest held in Britain and France. Driving the cultural/historical interest was a perceived need to build national unity through the study of the origins of the Canadian people. Although the Public Archives of Canada lacked both proper facilities and a legislative mandate, these shortcomings were rectified in 1906 with the construction of an archives building and in 1912 with the passage of archival legislation. This legislation was informed exclusively by the need to preserve records for historical rather than for legal/administrative purposes.

From its outset, the Canadian archival endeavor encompassed both public and private records, a concept later articulated as "total archives" (Millar, 1998, 1999). The total archives concept reflects a long-standing social consensus that public funds should be used to preserve a wide range of Canadian documentary heritage, regardless of its origins and format, and that this preservation effort should be pursued via a planned national system. As a result, Canada has not experienced the emergence of separate (and sometimes warring) archival tribes or traditions for public records and historical manuscripts, as has been the case in the United States and Australia. With Canadian national identity constantly at risk of being swamped by the more dominant identity of its southern neighbor, recognition of the need to take coordinated action to preserve something distinctly Canadian has compelled generations of Canadians to take a holistic approach to the management of their archival heritage. The National Archives of Canada (since 2004, Library and Archives Canada) has, at least in theory, always given equal priority to the preservation of records regardless of their origin. Nevertheless, it was not until the 1950s that the then Public Archives of Canada began to exert authority over public records and perform the legal/administrative role that provided the original basis for its counterpart institutions in Europe (Atherton 1979; Wilson 1982/1983).

Like Canada, it was cultural/historical concerns that led to the creation of a national archives in the United States. Unlike Canada, which wasted little time in establishing a central archives, the United States had to wait until 1934—over 150 years after the Declaration of Independence—before its national archives was established. This represented the culmination of many decades of agitation by historians, most notably the American Historical Association. By that time, the desire to rescue, preserve, and provide access to historical records had manifested itself in the emergence of the so-called historical manuscripts tradition. This tradition, which dated back to the earliest years of the nation, had been shaped by an antiquarian collecting instinct and had become institutionalized in organizations such as state historical societies and the Library of Congress, where the main focus was the collecting, researching, and publishing of the private papers of prominent individuals.

Why did the United Statestake so long to establish a national archives despite the fact that a number of state governments had already established government archives? In 1939, Posner argued that a major contributing factor was American ambivalence, if not hostility, toward centralized state bureaucratic power. So, while manuscript collecting endeavors pursued for scholarly purposes were considered laudable, proposals to create an archival institution as an integral part of the federal bureaucracy was regarded, at least subconsciously, with suspicion (Posner 1967). H. G. Jones, in contrast, blames bureaucratic indifference and in some cases outright opposition. Faced with the loss of records in regular fires in government buildings in Washington, during the late nineteenth and early twentieth centuries, the bureaucrats responded by establishing a "hall of records," which was nothing more than a reasonably fireproof warehouse. Through the lobbying efforts of John Franklin Jameson and Waldo Gifford Leland, Congress finally started to take a serious interest in establishing a national archives on the European model during the 1910s, but many years and much momentum were lost as a result of the distractions of World War I and its aftermath (Jones 1969).

Interestingly, the initial decision to establish a national archives was primarily a decision to allocate funds for the construction of an archives building on Pennsylvania Avenue. Only later did legislators determine that any agency operating out of this building would need a legislative mandate outlining its powers and functions—an instance of notions of "archives as a place" preceding notions of the role of the entity that would occupy that place. At the ceremony for the laying of the cornerstone of the National Archives building in 1933, President Hoover emphasized the commemorative role of archives in nation building, binding the "State and the hearts of all our people in an indissoluble union" (Jones 1969). Americans had to wait until the latter part of the twentieth century before there was a clear articulation of the role of archives as guarantors of the democratic rights of citizens and as means of holding public officials to account—a role that, while recognized as an ideal, is yet to be fully realized both in practice and in public perception.

Just as the Public Archives of Canada was established for historical purposes and had to wait until the 1950s to acquire an administrative/legal role, so too the U.S. National Archives had to wait until 1950, with the passage of the Federal Records Act, before it acquired a role as a supporter and enabler of public administration. Public records archivists such as Margaret Cross Norton from Illinois pursued a campaign to articulate and assert an administrative and legal accountability role for archives in the face of the primacy of the historical/cultural role (Norton 1975). While Norton had very good reasons for pursuing these efforts, they had the unfortunate effect of creating a polarization of the American archival community—a polarization that persists to this day in a profession that struggles to attain a comfortable and balanced view of the dual role of archival institutions (Berner 1983; Gilliland-Swetland 1991).

The American experience highlights in sharp relief the tensions and contradictions that have emerged in the roles of archives worldwide since the nineteenth century and which represent contested ground everywhere. Arguably, the polarization is more pronounced in the United States because there is more at stake. Archives in Europe were initially established for legal and administrative purposes, thus conferring on them a valuable legitimacy in the eyes of government that has enabled them to acquire a cultural/historical role from a position of strength. In contrast, at the time of their establishment, American archives had no such legal/administrative legitimacy and have had to struggle ever since to attain such a role and the government support and funding that it could attract. The addition of democratic accountability to the legal/administrative role by proponents such as Norton merely helped the struggle to work against itself. So, while the general public may be suspicious of the legal/administrative role of archives and supportive of the accountability role, the reverse is very often the case from the perspective of those that control the corridors of power in government.

ARCHIVES AS A PLACE AND AS A TRADITIONAL ORTHODOXY

A common trope over many decades in Western culture has been the architectural use of archival buildings to make symbolic statements about the role and significance of archives in society. Many archival buildings throughout the ages have architectural features suggestive of solidity, impenetrability, durability, and authority. The temple motif has been a particularly common theme in archival architecture over many decades (Ketelaar 2002a; McCausland 2013). Indeed, such featurism is so common as to be almost a cliché—something which itself speaks volumes about perceptions of archives (O'Toole 1993). Recent, more imaginative architectural representations of the form and function of archives, such as the Gatineau Preservation Centre in Canada, have attempted to convey an image of archives as "the epitome of liberal-humanist and objective-scientific activity" but perhaps unwittingly reflect instead the ultimately indeterminate and mutable nature of the archival pursuit (Koltun 2002).

We have seen that throughout the ages one of the regularly recurring functions of archival institutions is to provide a secure place for the safekeeping of valuable records to guarantee their ongoing legal authenticity. This is especially common for archives that serve solely or primarily a legal/administrative role, where control of the records is recognized as a source of power. Duranti has highlighted the importance of this function in archives stretching back to the days of the Justinian Code and the Tabularium in ancient Rome, while Michel Duchein has identified the same issue as being important to archives in Flanders and Hungary. One of Sir Hilary Jenkinson's more influential contributions to the archival discourse is the related notion of the need to guarantee an uninterrupted transmission of custody from records creator to archival institution—the physical and moral defence of the record (Jenkinson 1922). Duranti has argued that when records "cross the archival threshold," they are attested to be authentic and henceforth guaranteed to be preserved as such by an archives that is independent from the records creating office and for which the preservation of the authenticity of its holdings is its raison d'être (Duchein 1992; Duranti 1996).

While this is a common theme in the history of archives, it is nevertheless not a universal one. Duchein has argued that there are many countries in which the notion has never existed, including France "where the fact of its being preserved in a public archival repository does not give a document any guarantee of authenticity" (Duchein 1992). Similarly, while the preservation of authenticity is undoubtedly an objective of most collecting/historical archives programs, it cannot be said to be their raison d'être. More recently, archivists who agree with Duranti and Jenkinson about the absolute importance of guaranteeing the authenticity of records have disagreed with Duranti's argument that this can only be achieved by means of archival institutions taking physical custody of the records. To these critics, adequate control of records to guarantee authenticity in the digital age can be achieved without the need for archives to provide a physical place of safekeeping. In the digital age, the very physicality of records is superseded by a virtual concept or "performance" where the idea of a record having a set physical location becomes meaningless. These critics also object to the notion of records crossing an "archival threshold" at some point in time after their creation. They argue that the "archival bond" (Duranti 2015) and subsequent guarantees of authenticity should commence at the point of records creation which, by definition, cannot be physically in the archives. If the archival bond is achieved and guaranteed at the point of records creation, the decision when or whether to perform a physical act of custodial transfer to an archives becomes a minor administrative consideration, not a matter of central significance (Cook 1994; Hedstrom 1991; Upward and McKemmish 1994).

THE POST-CUSTODIAL CHALLENGE

Since the early 1980s, a growing number of archival writers and practitioners have subscribed to the philosophy of post-custodialism. The philosophy asserts that the archival mission should not be limited to traditional notions of managing archival holdings in custodial arrangements but should embrace a much wider and more proactive range of programs involving outreach, collaboration, and documentation of and support for records in distributed custody. Sometimes conflated with noncustodialism, the philosophy does not in fact reject centralized custody as a valid archival strategy.

In 1980, F. Gerald Ham presented a set of archival strategies for what he called "the post-custodial era" (Ham 1981). He characterized archives in the custodial era as being passive and introspective and almost exclusively concerned with the management of archival holdings. He argued that archives and archivists could not afford to persist with this narrow custodial mindset, especially if they were to both survive the challenges of, and take advantage of the opportunities presented by, automation and the growth of born-digital information and online networks.

Ham characterized the post-custodial era as featuring a decentralized computer environment where every individual will become his or her own records manager. In such an environment, archivists would need to be much more active and interventionist if they were to have any hope of fulfilling their mission. He called for much greater levels of interinstitutional cooperation between archives programs, the development of strategies for providing easy and centralized access to increasingly complex and decentralized archives, and for greater archival involvement in the process of information creation and management.

Importantly, Ham did not argue that archives should stop managing custodial holdings, but rather that archives needed to expand their repertoire of strategies in order to navigate the increasingly complex realities of the late twentieth century. This expansion of archival strategies was not a renunciation of custody, but rather a recognition that custody on its own was insufficient to ensure future archival success. Ham was not recommending a "non-custodial era," but a "post-custodial era" where archival programs and archivist self-image would not be defined by custody alone.

How does the vision of the post-custodial archive sit with resilient notions of archives as a place of secure deposit? Sceptics argue that it is naïve for post-custodialists to assert that technological change has made it possible, much less essential, for digital records to be archivally captured, described, and controlled in such a way as to guarantee the long-term integrity of the records from the instant of creation onward. Perhaps the closest archivists have come to achieving this vision is with the "VERS encapsulated objects" (VEOs) of the Victorian Electronic Records Strategy (VERS). VEOs are versions of records captured (ideally at or close to the moment of records creation in the creating office) into a standardized archival file format and locked with a digital signature to guarantee authenticity. The vision, however, remains an unproved—though appealing—hypothesis. The problem is convincing creating agencies to capture all of their records as VEOs at the point of records creation, as only a small proportion of the records of an agency need to be retained for long-term archival purposes. The overheads for this commitment are high and may often be viewed as a case of "the archival tail wagging the business dog."

DAVID BEARMAN'S "INDEFENSIBLE BASTION" AND RESPONSES FROM AUSTRALIA AND ELSEWHERE

During the 1990s, in the midst of a fevered discourse on electronic records, Ham's post-custodial vision reemerged as a divisive fault line in the archival community. In this context, there was no figure more divisive than American commentator David Bearman. Bearman reshaped Ham's call to arms as a visceral polemic that reverberated for years to come. Bearman (1991) argued that not only should archives adopt strategies based on distributed custody but they should also avoid (except as a last resort) taking any custody at all of electronic records. According to Bearman, there were "few imaginable advantages and considerable disadvantages to the archival custody of electronic records." He argued that in a networked world "if archives have intellectual control over the records that are deemed archival, it doesn't matter much where records or users are."

In a commentary published simultaneously with Bearman's polemic, Margaret Hedstrom (1991) demurred. While agreeing with Bearman's call for an expanded role for archival programs and that there would be many circumstances where custody of records by archives would be "unnecessary and even ill-advised," she did not agree that custodianship was always going to be incompatible with these broader imperatives and strategies. Hedstrom presented some criteria to help archives decide whether or not it was best to take custody of electronic records. There will be times, Hedstrom argued, when creating agencies will be much better prepared than any archives to take physical custody of archival records in electronic form, for example, agencies whose primary mission is data collection and analysis. In any case, until archives develop the requisite technical capacity, the archival mission would be better served by temporarily leaving electronic records in the custody of the creating agency. To Hedstrom, such issues ultimately were trivial matters of implementation and timing. What was more important was for archival institutions to become sources of expertise in digital media, formats, management, preservation, and dissemination.

Hedstrom's rejoinder to Bearman's provocative paper should probably have been an end to the matter. Instead, however, Bearman's "non-custodial" arguments gained significant traction in Australia, traction that served largely as a distraction in the context of the broader post-custodial discourse. In 1994, the then Australian Archives (now National Archives of Australia [NAA]) announced a distributed custody policy for electronic records that was, for all intents and purposes, Bearman's indefensible bastion paper in the guise of official archival policy. Many other commentators joined the fray, with much of the mid-1990s archival literature being shaped along battle lines on either side of this schism (Eastwood 1996; Henry 1998; O'Shea and Roberts 1996).

Within seven years, the NAA officially moved on from its policy of non-custody of electronic records, when it established a digital preservation project and an accompanying custody policy, which argued that archival value digital records should ideally be transferred to archival custody sooner, rather than later. In retrospect, the NAA was simply doing what Hedstrom had recommended in 1991, namely to leave electronic records in the custody of creating agencies until such time as the archives had the necessary technical capacity to receive and preserve digital records. Had the NAA said clearly in 1994 that "distributed custody" was merely an interim measure, few would have objected. Instead, its 1994 announcement was accompanied by elaborate and contentious justifications for a policy regime that had the appearance of being a long-term commitment and in retrospect may be seen as a misguided attempt to make a virtue out of a necessity. As such, "post-custodial" became confused with "non-custodial" in the minds of many observers and participants in the discourse. Significantly, almost 20 years later, when the heat generated by this debate had largely dissipated, a new director-general of the NAA announced that his organization was once again intending to pursue distributed custody strategies for digital records (Fricker 2012).

At the same time as the NAA found itself embroiled in a largely sterile debate about custody during the 1990s, it and many other Australian archival programs, educators, and practitioners were exploring the broader "post-custodial" terrain first envisaged by Ham. For some years, Frank Upward and Sue McKemmish of Australia's Monash University had been endeavoring to reconcile the emerging new paradigm with Jenkinsonian principles. Jenkinson's requirements for unbroken chains of custody and the physical and moral defense of records had, according to Upward (1993), been honored by the Australian Archives during the 1960s, when it attempted to implement a universal system of documentation for all Australian government records, "without regard to location or the designation of permanency." The father of the Australian "series system" for intellectual control and archival description, Peter Scott, and his colleague and mentor Ian Maclean were acclaimed as the first post-custodialists. Scott's groundbreaking 1966 article on the series system argued crucially that the archivist is essentially "a preserver and interpreter of recordkeeping systems" and that "series registration may be extended to cover series not yet in archival custody" (Scott 1966). According to Upward

(1993), "Jenkinson's concept of custody is that of guardianship, not imprisonment, and can be readily extended out from the archival institution." While the realities of limited resources meant that this brave experiment was only ever-partially successful, it nevertheless pointed the way ahead toward a truly post-custodial recordkeeping paradigm.

Validation of emerging Australian post-custodial thinking came from the Canadian archivist Terry Cook (1994). According to Cook, archivists needed to "stop being custodians of things and start being purveyors of concepts" and to reorient themselves from "records to the acts of recording." Cook argued that the future of archives was as access hubs and "virtual archives without walls." In prefiguring the following decade's dominant archival discourse about the power relationships that are integral to all information systems and related social and organizational systems, Cook managed to simultaneously applaud Australian post-custodial thinking while at the same time question some of its neo-Jenkinsonian foundations.

TODAY'S POST-CUSTODIAL REALITIES IN ARCHIVAL PROGRAMS AND "VIRTUAL" ARCHIVES

To what extent has the vision of post-custodial archives been realized? From the comfort of 2015, there seems little doubt that what once was a radical new vision is now almost the new archival orthodoxy. The functions of many archival programs have expanded greatly since Ham added the phrase "post-custodial" to our professional lexicon. Most larger archival programs now allocate significant resources to interinstitutional co-operation, including the development of cooperative online access services for distributed holdings, and to "front-end" engagement with records creators (often through influencing the design and implementation of recordkeeping systems). While traditional custodial functions have been retained, albeit often with proportionately fewer resources, archives are now usually far more proactive and outwardly engaged—with records creators, with other archives and documentation programs, and with an expanding base of users in cyberspace.

Archives and archivists are far less introspective and holdings-focused than was the case a generation ago. For most archives user services, access and public outreach are at least as important as the physical and moral defense of records. Digitization programs abound and users vote with their fingers in cyberspace in far greater numbers than has ever been the case with users voting with their feet in visiting reading rooms. The community expects its information sources to be available online and increasingly regards anything that is not online as being irrelevant.

Nevertheless, despite the explosion in online access to archives, physical custody of holdings remains the stated preference of the overwhelming majority of archival programs, both for traditional format and for digital records. Why has a preference for old-fashioned archival custody proved to be so resilient? In recent years, the notion of "trusted digital repositories" has achieved widespread acceptance in the so-called digital curation community that extends well beyond archives to include digital libraries, digital museums, and statistical and scientific data management. This reflects recognition of the fragility of digital information objects and the need for reliable infrastructure and professional curation skills to ensure the authenticity, integrity, accessibility, and longevity of those objects. Digital curation is emerging as a specialist field in its own right, partly perhaps as a reaction against the notoriously short-term perspectives of the great majority of information and communications technology (ICT) professionals. Experience has taught archivists that, except for a small minority of exceptional cases, creating agencies cannot be relied upon to manage born-digital archival value records over the long term. Agencies may maintain legacy systems for a certain period of time or may export or migrate business's critical data from such systems into replacement systems, but it is not their core business to ensure the long-term preservation of records that have broader societal or historical value but little or no ongoing legal/administrative value. That is the core business of archives—core business that is usually most effectively carried out by transferring archival value digital records into archival custody at the earliest possible convenience, when the archives in question has the technical capacity to preserve those records.

None of which means that archives should be disconnected from current recordkeeping in records creating environments, or that archives should not maintain a strong interest in documenting and assisting the sound management of records that are in the custody of creating agencies. Nor does it mean that archives should not support those creating agencies that have good business reasons for retaining and preserving digital records over the medium to long term, when they can be relied upon to do so. The U.K. National Archives' Digital Continuity Service is an example of post-custodial innovation, expert outreach, and cooperation by an archival institution that nevertheless remains committed to taking archival value digital records into archival custody at the earliest possible opportunity.

The archival paradigm shift into the post-custodial era, envisaged by Ham a generation ago, has occurred. Archives are very different institutions nowadays and archivists, by and large, think and operate in very different ways. Archives have different priorities, different partnerships and use very different tools and processes. Archivists are less inclined to see themselves and their role as being passive and objective defenders of records created by other people, and, instead, they recognize the significance of their own role in shaping records. Being flexible, open-ended, and post-custodial is seen as a more attractive orientation for archives than being rigid, narrow-minded, and passively focused on custodial considerations and operations.

Over the past 30 years, archivists worldwide have come to recognize this and have been busy putting the new outlooks and mindsets into operation.

Ultimately, different archives will make their own choices as to how important guarantees of authenticity are and, if they are considered vital, which strategies they feel will give them the best chance of achieving that objective. Certainly, the post-custodialists argue for a more proactive and virtual "archives without walls" as an antidote to the traditional passive custodial view, although there is no reason why a custodial approach could not also be combined with a more proactive role. Jeannette Bastian has recently argued that (distributed) custody and authenticity should not be ends in themselves, but rather means to a more important end—that of facilitating use of the archives by those who stand to benefit from such activity (Bastian 2002). As Upward has argued, "The externalities of place are becoming less significant day-by-day . . . the location of the resources and services will be of no concern to those using them . . ." (Upward 1996).

A significant trend in the archival discourse over recent years has been the growing acceptance of the value of regarding archival resources as the national or indeed supranational collective property of humanity. Such views transcend the narrow concerns, mandates, and places of individual institutions or archival programs, instead focusing on the archival whole being greater than the sum of its component parts—enabled by a coherent, overarching system informed by common humanistic values and a sense of shared or collective purpose. In short, archivists are being encouraged to "think global, act local." The spread of digital technology is making this view of virtual collective archives not just relevant but indeed consistent with the default expectations of users and society in general (Cunningham 2014; Gilliland 2015; Millar 2013).

In the online world, the development of virtual archives is not only desirable but also essential for continued relevance and survival. Users will wish to be assured of authenticity but will be unlikely to care about the existence of or necessity for places of custody. It will be interesting to watch as archival institutions respond to new user expectations of 24-hour online virtual access and the opportunities offered by digitization programs for transforming and democratizing archival access programs. Already, though, the signs are that archives are more interested in being participatory platforms rather than places (Theimer 2014); ubiquitous access enablers and ecosystems rather than geospatially bound symbolic temples (Ketelaar 2002a); active documenters of living/evolving records rather than passive custodians and arsenals of arcane relics (Cook 1994); and agents of empowerment and democracy rather than places and instruments of control and oppression.

ARCHIVES AS A METAPHOR IN PHILOSOPHY AND SOCIOCULTURAL DISCOURSE

Over the past 20–30 years, while many archivists were busy arguing over custody and authenticity, scholars in other disciplines have discovered that the notion of "the archive" provides fertile ground for academic debate. For the most part, these two separate discourses have proceeded in blissful ignorance of each other, with one being essentially practical in nature ("much ado about shelving," as one commentator dismissed derisively—[Roberts 1987]) and the other being deeply philosophical. Where they have intersected, it has tended to be in the context of grappling with postmodernism and its relevance to archives, although the discourse in philosophy and sociocultural studies has been about much, much more than mere postmodernism. More significant crossovers have influenced archival thinking about the power wielded by or through archives and archivists (Schwartz and Cook 2002).

At the forefront of the philosophical discourse on archives were French cultural theorists Michel Foucault and Derrida (Manoff 2004, 2010). "The archive" has been used as a vehicle for digging into the meaning of human knowledge, memory, and power. According to Wolfgang Ernst (2015), the archive has become "a universal metaphor for all conceivable forms of storage and memory." He speaks about notions of archives shifting from being spatial to being time-based, in which the key feature is the dynamics of the permanent transmission of data. In a similar vein, Thomas Richards regards the archive as "a utopian space of comprehensive knowledge ... not a building, nor even a collection of texts, but the collectively imagined junction of all that was known or knowable" (Richards 1993). In more concrete terms, Boris Groys sees the archive as "a machine for the production of memories, one that fabricates history out of the material of unassimilated reality" (Groys as discussed in Ernst 2015, 11). Ernst describes archives as both places of temptation and places of silence as well as "bastions of memory," "history's arsenal," and "fortresses that speak to us." Yet, in cyberspace, according to Ernst, traditional notions of the archive are an anachronistic and hindering metaphor. Philosophy, it seems, is not immune from the impact of digital disruption, with Ernst endeavoring to show how archives need to find a new narrative in this disrupted future.

To Derrida, the archive is a constant source of tension between the competing impulses of memory and forgetting. Constantly evolving methods of knowledge transmission and consignation shape the nature of that knowledge, with recordmaking and archiving processes not just recording events but actually helping to produce them. If the archive cannot or will not—for whatever reason—accommodate a particular kind of information, that knowledge is excluded and therefore forgotten. Unlike Richards and Ernst, for whom the sites or places of archiving seem largely irrelevant, to Derrida such matters (and who gets to decide such matters) may be key in determining what will and will not be remembered (Derrida 1996).

The grandfather of this discourse is undoubtedly Foucault, who first started pushing open the floodgates as early as 1969 in his book *The Archaeology of Knowledge* (Foucault 1969). To Foucault, the archive is a "system of discursivity." The silences in archives are determined by the rules for what cannot be said. Who makes these rules, how they are made, and for what purpose can provide endless fodder for speculation, theorizing, and conjecture. Dutch archivist Ketelaar has picked up this baton and carried it into the heart of archival discourse, for instance, with his writings on "archivalization" (Ketelaar 1999). South Africa's Harris has been more confrontational, interpreting Derrida and Foucault through his personal political prism of growing up in apartheid South Africa to challenge the cosy, positivist assumptions of traditional archivists who cleave to notions of the impartial third-party archivist guaranteeing the authenticity of the record through the provision of secure places of custody and deposit. Channelling Derrida and Foucault, Harris asks—what records are you guaranteeing and for whose benefit?

CONCLUSION

Such complex and nuanced ruminations on the meaning of archives might seem far removed from the prosaic concerns of practicing archivists and their debates about archives as a place and the place of archives. But just as digital disruption is causing practitioners to rethink the place of archives in cyberspace, so too is the philosophical disruption of Derrida and Foucault causing us to rethink the place of archives in society.

We have seen in this chapter how, over the course of human history, archives have meant many different things to different societies—and as such taken many different mutable and dynamic manifestations. How societies choose to carry their cultural memory forward through time—and how archives in turn help to shape those societies—is subject to many contextual and contingent variables. To really understand the place of archive and archives as a place, one has to start by understanding the social, cultural, and political context in which archives operate at any given time and in any given place.

ACKNOWLEDGMENT

Many thanks are due to my colleague Andrew Patch for his insightful comments and suggestions on earlier drafts of this chapter.

ENDNOTE

1. Parts of the text of this chapter reuse in revised form text by the author that was previously published in a chapter titled "Archival Institutions" in Sue McKemmish, Michael Piggott, Barbara Reed, and Frank Upward (eds.), *Archives: Recordkeeping in Society* (Wagga Wagga, New South Wales: Charles Sturt University, 2005). The author thanks The Recordkeeping Institute for permission to reuse this text.

REFERENCES

Alexander, Philip, and Pessek Elizabeth. 1988. "Archives in Emerging Nations: The Anglophone Experience." *The American Archivist* 51: 121–29.

Atherton, Jay. 1979. "The Origins of the Public Archives Records Centre, 1897–1956." *Archivaria* 8: 35–60.

Bastian, Jeanette A. 2002. "Taking Custody, Giving Access: A Postcustodial Role for a New Century." *Archivaria* 53: 76–93.

Bearman, David. 1991. "An Indefensible Bastion: Archives as a Repository in the Electronic Age." Technical Report. *Archives and Museum Informatics* 13: 14–24.

Berner, Richard C. 1983. *Archival Theory and Practice in the United States: A Historical Analysis*. Seattle: University of Washington Press.

Brosius, Maria. 2003. *Ancient Archives and Archival Traditions: Concepts of Record-Keeping in the Ancient World.* Oxford, England: Oxford University Press.

Burton, Antoinette. 2001. "Thinking beyond the Boundaries: Empire, Feminism and the Domains of History." *Social History* 26 (1): 60–71.

Clanchy, M. T. 1993. *From Memory to Written Record, England 1066–1307*, 2nd ed. Oxford, England: Wiley-Blackwell.

Cook, Terry. 1994. "Electronic Records, Paper Minds: The Revolution in Information Management and Archives in the Post-Custodial and Post-Modernist Era." *Archives and Manuscripts* 22 (2): 300–28.

Culham, Phyllis. 1989. "Archives and Alternatives in Republican Rome." *Classical Philology* 84: 100–15.

Cunningham, Adrian. 2014. "Eternity Revisited: In Pursuit of a National Documentation Strategy and a National Archival System."*Archives and Manuscripts* 42 (2): 165–70.

Derrida, Jacques. 1996. *Archive Fever: A Freudian Impression*. Chicago, IL: University of Chicago Press.

Duchein, Michel. 1992. "The History of European Archives and the Development of the Archival Profession in Europe." *The American Archivist* 55: 14–25.

Duranti, Luciana. 1996. "Archives as a Place." *Archives and Manuscripts* 24 (2): 242–55.

Duranti, Luciana. 2015. "The Archival Bond." In *Encyclopedia of Archival Science*, edited by Luciana Duranti and Patricia C. Franks, 28–29. Lanham, MD: Rowman & Littlefield.

Eastwood, Terry. 1996. "Should Creating Agencies Keep Electronic Records Indefinitely?" *Archives and Manuscripts* 24 (2): 256–67.

Echevarria, Roberto. 1990. *Myth and Archive: A Theory of Latin American Narrative*. Cambridge, England: Cambridge University Press.
Ernst, Wolfgang. 2015. *Stirrings in the Archives: Order from Disorder*. Lanham, MD: Rowman & Littlefield.
Fleckner, John. 1991. " 'Dear Mary Jane': Some Reflections on Being an Archivist." *The American Archivist* 54: 8–13.
Foreshew, Jennifer. 2015. "Australian Companies Tackling the Digital Disruption Era." *Australian Business Review*, May 19. http://www.theaustralian.com.au/business/technology/australian-companies-tackling-the-digital-disruption-era/story-e6frgakx-1227359403603 (accessed October 10, 2015).
Foucault, Michel. 1969. *The Archaeology of Knowledge*. Paris: Gallimard.
Fricker, David. 2012. "Archives—What Is Our Business Model for the Digital Age?" Paper presented to International Congress on Archives, Brisbane, August 23. http://www.naa.gov.au/about-us/media/speeches/ica-director-generals-speech.aspx (accessed October 10, 2015).
Gilliland, Anne. 2015. "Permeable Binaries, Societal Grand Challenges, and the Roles of the Twenty-First-Century Archival and Recordkeeping Profession." Paper presented at the annual conference of the Archives and Records Association of New Zealand, Footprints in Space and Time, Auckland, New Zealand, September. http://escholarship.org/uc/item/90q5538g.
Gilliland-Swetland, Luke J. 1991. "The Provenance of a Profession: The Permanence of the Public Archives and Historical Manuscripts Traditions in American Archival History." *The American Archivist* 54: 160–75.
Hai, Pham thi Bich. 1996. "Professional Identity of the Archivist in Vietnam." In *Archivists—The Image and Future of the Profession: 1995 Conference Proceedings*, edited by M. Piggott and C. McEwen, 142–48. Canberra: Australian Society of Archivists.
Ham, F. Gerald. 1981. "Archival Strategies for the Post-Custodial Era." *The American Archivist* 44: 207–16.
Harris, Verne. 2000. *Exploring Archives: An Introduction to Archival Ideas and Practice in South Africa*, 2nd ed. Pretoria: National Archives of South Africa.
Harris, Verne. 2002. "The Archival Sliver: Power, Memory, and Archives in South Africa." *Archival Science* 2: 63–86.
Harris, Verne, and Adrian Cunningham, eds.. 2003. "Archives and Indigenous Peoples." Theme issue of *Comma, International Journal on Archives*: 1.
Hatang, Sello. 2000. "Converting Orality to Material Custody: Is It a Noble Act of Liberation or Is It an Act of Incarceration?' *ESARBICA Journal* 19: 61–68.
Hedstrom, Margaret. 1991. "Archives: To Be or Not to Be: A Commentary." *Archival Management of Electronic Records, Archives and Museum Informatics Technical Report* 13: 25–30.
Henry, Linda J. 1998. "Schellenberg in Cyberspace." *The American Archivist* 61 (2): 309–27.
Jenkinson, Hilary. 1922. *A Manual for Archive Administration*. London: Percy Lund, Humphries and Co.
Jones, H. G. 1969. *The Records of a Nation: Their Management, Preservation and Use*. New York: Atheneum.

Ketelaar, Eric. 1999. "Archivalisation and Archiving." *Archives and Manuscripts* 27 (1): 54–61.

Ketelaar, Eric. 2002a. "Archival Temples, Archival Prisons: Modes of Power and Protection." *Archival Science* 2: 221–38.

Ketelaar, Eric. 2002b. "Is Everything Archive?" Seminar presentation at Monash University, Melbourne, August 5.

Koltun, Lilly. 2002. "The Architecture of Archives: Whose Form, What Functions?" *Archival Science* 2 (3–4): 239–61.

Le Goff, Jacques. 1992. *History and Memory*. New York: Columbia University Press.

Manoff, Marlene. 2004. "Theories of the Archive from across the Disciplines." *Libraries and the Academy* 4 (1): 9–25.

Manoff, Marlene. 2010. "Archive and Database as Metaphor: Theorizing the Historical Record." *Libraries and the Academy* 10 (4): 385–98.

Martin, Henri-Jean. 1988. *The History and Power of Writing*. Chicago, IL: University of Chicago Press.

McCausland, Sigrid. 2013. "Temporary or 'Temple'? Archives Buildings and the Image of Archives in Australia." *Australian Library Journal* 62 (2): 90–99.

McIver, Glenys, Ysola Best, and Fabian Hutchinson. 1994. "Friends or Enemies? Collecting Archives and the Management of Archival Materials Relating to Aboriginal Australians." In *Archives in the Tropics: Proceedings of the Australian Society of Archivists Conference Townsville, 9–11 May 1994*, edited by June Edwards, 135–40. Canberra: ASA.

McKemmish, Sue. 1996. "Evidence of Me ..." *Archives and Manuscripts* 24 (1): 28–45.

Millar, Laura. 1998. "Discharging Our Debt: The Evolution of the Total Archive Concept in English Canada." *Archivaria* 46: 103–46.

Millar, Laura. 1999. "The Spirit of Total Archives: Seeking a Sustainable Archival System." *Archivaria* 47: 46–65.

Millar, Laura. 2013. "Coming up with Plan B: Considering the Future of Canadian Archives." *Archivaria* 77: 103–39.

Nor, Zakiah Hunum. 1994. "The National Archives of Malaysia—Its Growth and Development." In *Archives in the Tropics: Proceedings of the Australian Society of Archivists Conference, Townsville 9–11 May 1994*, edited by June Edwards, 94–98. Canberra: ASA.

Norton, Margaret Cross. 1975. *Norton on Archives*. Chicago, IL: Society of American Archivists.

O'Shea, Greg, and David, Roberts. 1996. "Living in a Digital World: Recognising the Electronic and Post-Custodial Realities." *Archives and Manuscripts* 24 (2): 286–311.

O'Toole, James. 1990. *Understanding Archives and Manuscripts*. Chicago, IL: Society of American Archivists.

O'Toole, James. 1993. "The Symbolic Significance of Archives." *The American Archivist* 56: 234–55.

O'Toole, James. 2002. "Cortes's Notary: The Symbolic Power of Records." *Archival Science* 2: 45–61.

Panitch, Judith M. 1996. "Liberty, Equality, Posterity? Some Archival Lessons from the Case of the French Revolution." *The American Archivist* 59 (1): 30–47.

Papadopoulis, Sophie. 1996. "The Image and Identity of Africa's Archivists." In *Archivists—The Image and Future of the Profession: 1995 Conference Proceedings*, edited by M. Piggott and C. McEwen, 149–56. Canberra: Australian Society of Archivists.

Posner, Ernst. 1940. 'Some Aspects of Archival Development Since the French Revolution.' *The American Archivist* 3 (1940): 159–172.

Posner, Ernst. 1967. "Archival Administration in the United States." In *Archives and the Public Interest: Selected Essays by Ernst Posner*, edited by Ken Mundsen, 114–30. Washington, D.C.: Public Affairs Press.

Posner, Ernst. 1972. *Archives in the Ancient World*. Cambridge, MA: Harvard University Press.

Prudtikul, Somsuang. 1999. "Records and Archives Management in Thailand." Paper presented at the Annual Congress of the International Federation of Library Associations, Bangkok.

Richards, Thomas. 1993. *The Imperial Archive: Knowledge and the Fantasy of Empire*. London: Verso.

Roberts, John W. 1987. "Archival Theory: Much Ado about Shelving." *The American Archivist* 50 (1): 66–74.

Schellenberg, T. R. 1956. *Modern Archives: Principles and Techniques*. Melbourne: Cheshire.

Schwartz, Joan M., and Terry Cook. 2002. "Archives, Records and Power: The Making of Modern Memory." *Archival Science* 2 (1–2): 1–19.

Scott, Peter J. 1966. "The Record Group Concept: A Case for Abandonment." *The American Archivist* 29 (4): 493–504.

Sharma, Tej Ram. 2005. *Historiography: A History of Historical Writing*. New Delhi: Concept Publishing.

Sickinger, James P. 1999. *Public Records and Archives in Classical Athens*. Chapel Hill: University of North Carolina Press.

Steedman, Carolyn. 2001. *Dust*. Manchester, England: Manchester University Press.

Stoler, Ann Laura. 2002. "Colonial Archives and the Arts of Governance." *Archival Science* 2: 87–109.

Theimer, Kate. 2014. "The Future of Archives Is Participatory: Archives as a Platform, or a New Mission for Archives." ArchivesNext blog post, April. http://www.archivesnext.com/?p=3700 (accessed October 10, 2015).

Upward, Frank. 1993. "Institutionalising the Archival Document: Some Theoretical Perspectives on Terry Eastwood's Challenge." In *Archival Documents: Providing Accountability through Recordkeeping*, edited by Sue McKemmish and Frank Upward, 41–54. Melbourne: Ancora Press.

Upward, Frank. 1996. "Structuring the Records Continuum Part One: Post-Custodial Principles and Properties." *Archives and Manuscripts* 24 (2): 268–85.

Upward, Frank, and Sue McKemmish. "Somewhere beyond Custody." *Archives and Manuscripts* 22 (1): 136–49.

Wehner, Monica, and Ewan Maidment. "Ancestral Voices: Aspects of Archival Administration in Oceania." *Archives and Manuscripts* 27 (1): 22–31.

Wilson, Ian. 1982/1983. "A Noble Dream: The Origins of the Public Archives of Canada." *Archivaria* 15: 16–35.

PART II

Functions

4

Managing Records in Current Recordkeeping Environments

Gillian Oliver

The purpose of this chapter is to explore the issues, controversies, and debates relating to theory and professional practice in current recordkeeping environments. The focus is on the management of current records as defined within the Western tradition, particularly North American, British, and Australasian environments, and does not necessarily reflect realities in other parts of the world.

Managing current records is a contested and confusing area, where internationally there are some fundamental philosophical differences with regard to the primary goals and responsibilities of those concerned with creating and managing recordkeeping systems. On the other hand, the stakes are high—while the debates continue, the risks of not charting and understanding the environment exponentially rise. The complexity of the environment increases on a daily basis: cloud computing, social media, and big data in conjunction with regulatory and legislative frameworks addressing privacy, confidentiality, and freedom of information provide a challenging terrain to navigate. The discipline of records management is relatively new, and thus, perhaps, some of the issues faced are characteristic of an immature field of study, underpinned by relatively little research and development.

Practice relating to the management of records in current environments predates the development of theory by decades, if not centuries. Historical context provides the foundation necessary to understand how and why relevant theories have developed and consequent influences on the shaping of practical systems and tools. The chapter begins therefore by providing a historical overview of the evolution of the concept of current recordkeeping, which led to the development of the occupation of records management. This is followed by a discussion of the main models and theories that are applicable to this area: the life cycle, the continuum, recordkeeping informatics, diplomatics, and rhetorical genre studies. The next section describes the professional landscape, including professional associations, the development of standards, and technological tools. The chapter concludes by highlighting future directions, signaling the need to broaden the view of current recordkeeping environments beyond organizational and workplace concerns.

HISTORICAL FRAMEWORK

The internationally agreed definition of records management, as it appears in the international standard on records management, is as follows: "[The] field of management responsible for the efficient and systematic control of the creation, receipt, maintenance, use and disposition of records, including the processes for capturing and maintaining evidence of and information about business activities and transactions in the form of records" (International Organization for Standardization 2015). In order to clarify the evolution of this concept and current attempts at reconceptualization, this section provides a chronological outline of relevant theoretical and practical matters.

It is generally claimed that records management, if understood as the need to be concerned with the totality of information that needs to be managed for evidential purposes, emerged as a distinct occupation in the United States in the twentieth century. Nevertheless, this should not detract from awareness of the requirement to be concerned about records in current environments that has been reflected in civilizations through the ages. Luciana Duranti provides an overview of the evidence in this regard in her two-part chronicling of the "odyssey of records managers" (Duranti 1989a, 1989b). Duranti draws a comparison between the functions and responsibilities of the keepers of records in the ancient world and those of today's records managers. She states that "the profession of keeper of records is as old as the first societal groups because the need of a memory arises naturally in any organization" (Duranti 1989a, 3) and traces the need for memorializing skills from the earliest oral cultures through to the development of textual systems and their associated manifestations and infrastructures. In this chapter, the focus is on the evolution of records management in Great Britain, North America, and Australia, where the two world wars in the twentieth century motivated some key developments in archival theory, which in turn influenced the practice of managing records in current environments.

Problems associated with records created in World War I prompted the first major contribution from archival theory in Great Britain. In 1922, Sir Hilary Jenkinson, then lecturer at University College, London, published *A Manual of Archive Administration Including the Problems of War Archives and Archive Making*. Part IV of this manual, "Archive Making," considers much that is relevant to recordkeeping today, for instance, the influence of new technologies on the making of records. Jenkinson's consideration of the problems of contemporary office work and communications technology resulted in specifying the need for control procedures, which were formulated as new functions for a Central Registry (Jenkinson 1922, 143–44). These new functions included being responsible for determining documentary form, with rules regarding dating and authentication, and "the most difficult work" of assuming responsibility for determining preservation and destruction decisions (144).

During the 1930s and 1940s, increased attention was paid to the challenges associated with the management of current records as a result of massive increases in the volume of records being created in the course of World War II. In the United States, Margaret Cross Norton, state archivist of Illinois, published papers and reports that have been said to represent "the first American manual of archives administration" (Posner 1975, viii). Writing in 1945, Norton highlighted the importance of the evidential nature of records and their role as memory devices. Many of her ideas continue to be very relevant today, for example, emphasizing the need to understand functions in order to identify where records need to be created and the importance of the person with records responsibility having an understanding of organizational activities. She was critical of what she perceived as a preoccupation with files, which she considered obscured the importance of being cognizant of records (Norton 1975).

The newly established National Archives and Records Administration (NARA) in the United States played a key role in developing records management. Concerns about the increasing volume of wartime records led to NARA's development of disposal schedules for the records created by federal agencies, stipulating how long records needed to be kept and whether they were destined for destruction or transfer to archival custody (Ross 1985, 46). These new ideas were put into practice when senior staff members of NARA took up records management administration responsibilities for both the navy and the army (47).

In these early days of records management, in the United States, it was not long before concerns began to be expressed about the absence of involvement of archivists in the initial stages of recordkeeping. In calling for archivists to be concerned with the creation of records and their existence before transfer to archival custody, American archivist Philip Brooks declared that no stage in the existence of records could be ignored, issuing a strongly worded warning to the effect that "it is inevitable that the iniquity of omitting care for records as they accumulate shall be visited upon the third and fourth generations of later administrators, archivists, research students, and society as a whole" (Brooks 1943, 164).

Experience at NARA had a direct influence on the development of records management in Australia. In 1954, a senior NARA official, T. R. Schellenberg, went to Australia as a Fulbright scholar. The lectures on public records that he presented there formed the basis of his book *Modern Archives: Principles and Techniques* (Schellenberg 1956, ix), which was dedicated to Australian archivists. Of particular interest here is the differentiation between the registry systems prevalent in Australia at the time, which were based on the methods established by the British Colonial Office, and the so-called American Filing Systems (Schellenberg 1956, 71–93).

A key figure involved in organizing Dr. Schellenberg's visit to Australia was Ian Maclean, who was later to become the chief archives officer of the Commonwealth Archives Office (CAO), the predecessor of National Archives of Australia. The CAO was responsible for the Australian Commonwealth Government recordkeeping program, which included the appointment of departmental registrars. These registrars were responsible for developing comprehensive records management systems and procedures (Maclean 1959).

It is in the writings of Maclean that we can see signs of divergence in the North American and Australian approaches to recordkeeping. In North America, records management, with duties and responsibilities associated with the creation and management of records in office environments, was emerging as an occupation in its own right. Maclean, writing for an American audience, noted that archivists and records managers "... are or should be the same people, all with similar training but dealing according to personal inclination and aptitude with different problems and periods" (1959, 417).

Australia from the 1960s onward was a fertile ground for the emergence of new thinking about the fluidity of relationships between records and their contexts of creation. The contributions of Peter Scott (a colleague of Maclean at the CAO) articulated a clinical rather than forensic approach to archival description, reflecting the realities of managing records in current environments where organizational structures and relationships are constantly changing (Scott 1966). This tradition of innovation provided a receptive environment for the emergence of ideas that were to lead to the conceptualization of the major Australian contribution to theory, the continuum.

The increasing proliferation of digital technologies and electronic records in the late twentieth century led to realization of the by now urgent need for common ground to be recognized by what had become two separate occupations: one concerned with current records, the other with archives. Recognition of this common purpose was not new and was not limited to Australia. In North America, Charles Dollar discussed the premise that records managers and archivists do not share common theories and methodologies (Dollar 1993). In exploring the notion that North America "reinvented" the occupation of records manager in the 1940s, he stresses the shared historical origins of records management and archival endeavor, as recounted by Duranti (1989a, 1989b). Dollar attributes the "reinvention" not only to the failure to recognize the shared history but also to the fact that "... there was very little of practical benefit that could be learned from European archival experience and tradition" (1993, 39).

The 1990s saw the start of much research into managing records in digital environments. The first major undertakings were the Pittsburgh and University of British Columbia (UBC) projects. The Pittsburgh research resulted in the definition of functional requirements for recordkeeping in information systems and raised awareness of the need for metadata (Bearman 1993, 1994). The UBC project focused on specifying the methods for ensuring the reliability and authenticity of electronic records and related management issues (Duranti, Eastwood, and MacNeil, n.d.). Both projects provided the basis for subsequent standards, in some cases leading to certification and audit regimes for electronic recordkeeping systems. A further outcome from the UBC project was the influential InterPARES series of projects (www.interpares.org).

This concise history of the development of ideas and practices relating to managing current records provides the backdrop to consider features in more detail, beginning with consideration of the main conceptual models and theories.

CONCEPTUAL MODELS AND THEORIES

Subsequent to the emergence of records management as a specialist occupation, two conceptual models have been developed. Fundamental differences in North American and Australian approaches are reflected in these two models, the life cycle and the continuum. The models tend to polarize discussion with proponents of each often seeing them as representing oppositional viewpoints. However, their development is intertwined, and there are some areas of common ground which tend to be lost sight of. Also discussed is recordkeeping informatics, which seeks to expand on the implementation of the continuum in current records environments and in so doing to reconceptualize records management. The section concludes by noting two theories that are particularly relevant to current environments: diplomatics and rhetorical genre studies.

The Life Cycle

The life cycle provides a linear, sequential approach to the actions deemed necessary to manage records at specific points of their existence. The Canadian archivist Jay Atherton describes the concept as having two distinct phases, the first being a records management one, the second archival (Atherton 1985–1986).

The records management stages will include, but not necessarily be limited to, the following points in the "life" of a record: the point of creation; the "active" period (when records are needed to support current operational working needs); the "inactive" period (when records are no longer needed for current use but still have to be kept for a designated period of time); and finally disposition. "Disposition" includes destruction or transfer to archival custody for preservation (see Figure 4.1).

From a practical perspective, the life cycle analogy provides a clear and easily understood framework that can be associated with key records management responsibilities. For instance, at the point of creation, the context of the record must be documented. At subsequent maturity stages, the storage of records can be determined to facilitate different frequency of access requirements in the most cost-effective and efficient manner. Finally, at the end of life, records must be disposed of at the appropriate point of time in accordance with legal and operational requirements.

The implementation of formal retention and disposal schedules has been described as imposing the life cycle model on records by establishing definite time periods for when things happen and how long records should be retained at the different stages of their existence (Dingwall 2010, 143). This is an interesting proposition, which perhaps sheds some light on the reluctance to engage with alternative theoretical approaches. It suggests that the life cycle is the only model that recognizes the significance and need for retention periods, which is not the case.

The origins of the concept of the records life cycle can be traced to American archivist Brooks, who explored what he called the life history of records in a paper emphasizing the need for an awareness of the critical nature of appraisal (Brooks 1940). The notion of a life history of records is not unique to the life cycle model (continuum proponents refer to the "life span" of records) but is often regarded as such, because the critical stages of a record's "life" are the dominant features of the model.

Figure 4.1 Records Management Life Cycle Stages

Although the life cycle model provides a very clear framework that enables the specification of actions, awareness of complications arising from the split of responsibilities between records managers and archivists have been expressed from the outset. Brooks identified the different perspectives involved, noting the dependency of the archivist on those active in the management of records prior to transfer to archival custody:

> The administrator looks upon records positively as he needs to use them and negatively as they represent a space problem and a task of serving outsiders who wish to consult them. The archivist looks upon current records as future archives, and it is a legitimate part of his function to make available counsel on how they can best be handled. The archivist in his own custodial and service functions is dependent upon the creator and the filer of the records for the kind of material he must deal with and the character of his problems. (Brooks 1940, 223)

Brooks called for cooperation between the originating agency and the archivist as early as possible in the life history of records. Several decades later, Atherton proposed that the model in itself was detrimental to collaboration between archivists and records managers, thus hindering awareness of common goals and interests. Furthermore, he argued that with the advent of the computer, it was no longer possible to stipulate such clear and fixed points in time when things happen. So, "creation, for example, is an ongoing process rather than an event in time," and "the formal differentiation between the active, dormant, and dead stages in the life of a record is becoming decidedly fuzzy" (Atherton 1985–1986, 47). Atherton proposed the alternative concept of a continuum as a means of addressing these issues.

In 2015, Duranti argued that Brooks's "life history" model is very similar to Atherton's continuum and that although North America has embraced the life cycle model, in practice it is "... moving toward Atherton's concept of the continuum, primarily because of the need to acquire control of 'machine readable,' 'electronic,' and today 'digital,' records of enduring value as soon as possible after creation ..." (Duranti 2015a, 344). Confusingly, this should not be read as acceptance of the Australian conceptualization of the continuum, as Duranti differentiates between Atherton's proposal and what she terms the "Australian circular concept of records continuum" (344). Henceforth, the term *continuum*, if not otherwise stated, is used to refer to the records continuum model as developed by Australians Frank Upward and colleagues.

The Continuum

The records continuum is an alternative conceptual model that encompasses the totality of recordkeeping, thus including activities occurring in the two life cycle phases relating to current records and archives. In contrast to the life cycle model, the emphasis in the continuum is on activities, the recordkeeping processes, rather than records as objects. The recognition of the complexity of what had previously been regarded as fixed, stable, and immutable points in time when the very nature and use of a record suddenly changed is a key point which the records continuum model attempts to address.

Nevertheless, different stages in a record's existence are also acknowledged and referred to as the record's lifespan rather than life cycle. These two points alone begin to indicate the considerable complexity of the continuum model, which is in sharp contrast to the simplicity of the life cycle model. In itself, this complexity has proved to be a major stumbling block in promoting understanding of the implications of continuum thinking.

In a paper written for the records management community at the beginning of the millennium, Upward, the main architect of the continuum, commented on polarized reactions to the records continuum model (Upward 2000, 116). He attributed these polarized reactions to the need for a fundamental change in thinking and perceiving the very nature of the recordkeeping environment: "You cannot have an easy discussion across a paradigm shift" (116). Despite the undoubted influence of the model, extreme reactions either of acceptance or rejection continue to be evident today. The impetus for the records continuum model was the need to provide "new rules for a new game" (119) for recordkeeping in an age when the accessibility of records was more important than their location. The main inspiration for the model was sociologist Anthony Giddens's structuration theory. Giddens discussed time-space distantiation and identified four interacting "layers of distancing" rippling outward from the immediate locus of action (Giddens 1986, 298). Giddens's notions of space and time are represented in the four dimensions of create, capture, organizes, and pluralize, which in the most familiar "target" graphic of the continuum appear as four concentric circles (see Figure 4.2).

It can be readily acknowledged that the circles may hinder rather than help interpretation of the model. The intention of the diagram was not to suggest circular processes or systems, rather a rippling out of movements from the center—by no means an easy task using only two-dimensional tools.

The innermost point of the model is the "create" dimension. Giddens's locus of action, where information is formed, and some degree of communication take place. From the perspective of an individual, a messy desktop with randomly named and hastily saved electronic files can be considered as a digital representation of activities occurring in the create dimension. However, it should be noted that creation can also occur at a workgroup, organizational, or even societal level. The second or "capture" dimension assesses how that information is captured and made a part of the corporate memory. Activities in this dimension occur when

> . . . communications are brought into a framework that enables consistent and coherent use of information by groups of people. This involves the addition of information about the recorded information and its communication, metadata,

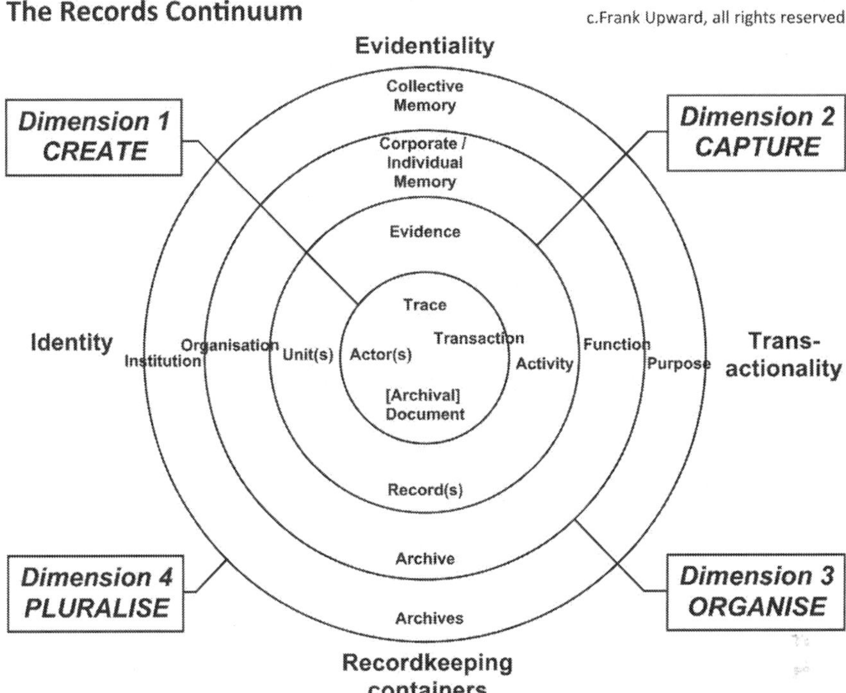

Figure 4.2 The Target Graphic of the Continuum (Reproduced by permission from Frank Upward)

> which disembeds information from the immediate contexts of its creation. (Upward 2000, 122)

The "organize" dimension is where information is organized so that it can be accessed and used within an organization.

> Organise equates with the need to marshal information across a range of participants who do not share the same frameworks of the group interaction. Commonly navigable structures and understandings have to be set up within systems so that the information can be shared in different spacetime. (Upward 2000, 122)

The "pluralize" dimension is where information is deployed beyond the organization.

> Pluralise equates with taking information out to points beyond organisational contexts into forms of societal totalities, still more distant from the organisations, community totalities, and whole of person views of the individual, within which the creation and capture processes took place. (Upward 2000, 122)

The foreground consists of four continua, or axes, as described by Upward:

- The recordkeeping axis addresses the containers for the storage of recorded information, its co-ordinates are those of the document, the record, the archive and the archives.
- The evidence axis consists of the trace of actions, the evidence which records can provide, and their role in corporate and collective memory.
- The transactional axis reflects an emphasis on records as records of activities undertaken in the conduct of business. Its co-ordinates are the act, activities, functions and purposes.
- The identity axis represents the actor, the work unit which the actor is associated with, the organisation which the unit is a part of and the manner in which the identity of these are institutionalised by broader social recognition. (Upward 1996)

Another very important aspect to the continuum model is that the records continuum was not developed in isolation but was one of several continua which had been developed by Frank Upward and other colleagues. These other models are complementary and have been developed to provide views of other domains. They include but are not limited to the information continuum (Oliver 2010; Upward 2000), the information systems continuum (Upward 2000), and the cultural heritage continuum (most recently explored and modified by Leisa Gibbons [2015]). The existence of a dynamic suite of models, which continue to be explored and developed, provides a rich and fertile backdrop appropriate for our dynamic and constantly changing information environment. It is tempting to attempt to take a very narrow and concentrated focus on an entity that can be labeled "record," but this approach will ultimately result in recordkeeping concerns being out of step with the ways in which information is created, used, and reused and thus recordkeeping being perceived as irrelevant.

Records continuum thinking has been and continues to be enormously influential. It was the prime motivator for the development of the world's first standard on records management (the Australian AS4390), which in turn led to the development of an ongoing suite of international standards. More recently, continuum thinking is providing the underpinning for an attempted reconceptualization of records management as "recordkeeping informatics" (Upward et al. 2013).

Recordkeeping Informatics

Recordkeeping informatics is work in progress to reconceptualize records management. The principals involved are an Australasian group all with strong connections to Monash University, Melbourne (Upward, Barbara

Reed, Joanne Evans, and Gillian Oliver). Use of the term *recordkeeping* in conjunction with informatics signifies acknowledgment of societal, technological, and cognitive aspects of information processing, specifically in recordkeeping contexts. Recordkeeping informatics is an attempt to take a much more holistic view of the problems, issues, and challenges inherent in current recordkeeping environments —the people, the broader environment as well as the information and communication technologies—than has hitherto been the case. It is hoped that the term *recordkeeping informatics* in itself will provide a bridge between recordkeepers (both records managers and archivists) and information systems professionals (Upward et al. 2013).

One clear goal of this recordkeeping informatics endeavor is to pursue a single-minded (i.e., recognition of a unified purpose for records managers and archivists as called for by Brooks, Dollar, Duranti, and Atherton) approach to recordkeeping while positioning the call in today's environment where there are many more occupations competing for jurisdiction over recorded information.

The constituent parts of recordkeeping informatics are divided into facets for analysis and building blocks. The identified facets are: information culture, business processes, and access or dissemination of information. Underpinning these facets are the two main building blocks or pillars of continuum thinking and metadata. The practical implementation of the facets and building blocks to recordkeeping by a scientific community is documented by Evans et al. (2014), who clearly demonstrate the utility of a recordkeeping informatics approach to a complex and challenging recordkeeping environment in which big data plays a prominent role.

Members of the recordkeeping informatics group have been working together since 2008, producing several conference and journal papers (Oliver et al. 2009, 2010, 2014; Upward et al. 2013) in the course of compiling a book, *Recordkeeping Informatics for a Networked Age* (Upward et al., in press), that at the time of writing has just been completed. The book is not regarded as an end in itself but rather a precursor to action and thus includes many suggestions for research and development.

Another body of theory that is highly relevant to current recordkeeping environments is concerned with e documentary form. Diplomatics and rhetorical genre theory represent different ontological perspectives and thus are discussed separately.

Diplomatics

Diplomatics, or the science of the diploma, has traditionally been part of the education for archivists in many European countries (Duranti 1989c, 8). The principles and methodology of diplomatics come from seventeenth-century France, formulated from the examination of about 200 mediaeval charters focusing on specific features such as the materials used, linguistic elements, and so on (13). This analysis resulted in the codification of explicit rules that could be applied as a test to prove authenticity. Diplomatics is not purely of historical interest, however, and it has been argued that the discipline provides the theoretical basis for records management (Duranti 1999). More recently, a special issue of the *Records Management Journal* has been devoted to digital diplomatics. By focusing on metadata, digital diplomatics can provide ways to identify digital records and furthermore determine what metadata needs to be captured and managed (Rogers 2015). In the introduction to that special issue, Duranti provides a concise history of the role played by diplomatics in research into authenticity of records in the digital environment, noting linkages with the new field of digital forensics (2015b). Digital forensics is concerned with developing techniques to identify and examine digital information that can no longer be accessed using current software and operating systems.

Heather MacNeil (2004) provides another view of diplomatics in her discussion of the challenges faced in applying diplomatic principles to current recordkeeping environments. Most notably, she highlights the post-positivist nature of diplomatics, that is, representing a view of the world that points to objective and measurable rules about a distinct reality. Reflecting on the application of diplomatics in the InterPARES 1 Project, she points out that although diplomatic analysis could identify what was missing or wrong in particular systems, crucially "it could not identify alternative, new, or unanticipated ways in which records were being created and managed in those systems" (222). Current recordkeeping environments are characterized by new and unanticipated ways of creating records, an inevitability given the ongoing development of new and unanticipated technologies. It is necessary therefore to seek other explanatory theories to illuminate the unexpected.

Rhetorical Genre Studies

In contrast to diplomatics, rhetorical genre studies is a late twentieth-century development, initiated by the reconceptualization of traditional genre (focused on determining distinct textual formats) to genre as social action (Miller 1984). Rhetorical genre studies therefore approach documentary form from a very different perspective to diplomatics, namely as being embedded in social action, shifting, and changing in response to societal needs while at the same time influencing and shaping those needs, for example, the use of e-mail in organizations. E-mail is one of the predominant means of communication for businesses and individuals, and the functionality of e-mail clients reflects rapidly changing and sometimes conflicting requirements. Fiorella Foscarini is the leading proponent of genre theory and recordkeeping. In applying a rhetorical genre lens to records and recordkeeping, she notes that "... the records generated in the course of the 'acting together' of specific groups of records creators are shaped by unwritten, local rules of communication and embody conflicting motives—that is, they are 'rhetorical in the sense of being persuasive, directed to produce some effects on the outside world, while at the same time being a product of that world" (Foscarini 2014, 2–3).

Interestingly, Foscarini identifies an aspect of cocreation (a concept discussed further in the concluding section of this chapter) in her surfacing of the multiauthored nature of corporate records. She notes that the ways in which writing is performed by multiple actors has not been explored in records management (2014), and yet, understanding this activity is fundamental for insight into records creation. Furthermore, analysis of this activity and indeed other manifestations of genres will provide insight into the organizational cultures in which recordkeeping systems are constructed. Failure to understand the nuances of these cultures and the multitude of forces and influences at play will be detrimental in terms of achieving recordkeeping goals. In particular, applying a genre lens for analysis will identify the new and unexpected deviations from social and organizational norms for recordkeeping, the workarounds and creative approaches people utilize to achieve their goals. Rhetorical genre studies thus have an important contribution to make to analyzing information cultures, one of the facets for analysis identified in recordkeeping informatics.

Comparing diplomatics with rhetorical genre studies, Foscarini contrasts the static Platonic perspective of the former with the dynamic Darwinian view of the latter. She argues, however, that it is possible to combine both approaches, with each providing a different view of the object under investigation (2012, 405).

Much of the debate relating to the theoretical basis for the management of records in current environments centers on the two conceptual models, the life cycle and the continuum. Given that the two models have such a fundamental difference in terms of focus (the former on record as objects, the latter on recordkeeping processes) and are at opposite extremes on a simplicity-complexity scale, comparative analysis is difficult and of questionable value. Recordkeeping informatics may provide a way of demonstrating the practical utility of the continuum. Theories relating to documentary form are undoubtedly relevant to recordkeeping in current environments; further research into combining diplomatic and rhetorical genre studies analysis would be beneficial.

In summary, the theoretical landscape relating to the management of records in current environment can best be described as fragmented and divisive. Those characteristics are reflected in the professional practice landscape too.

THE PROFESSIONAL LANDSCAPE

A number of facets to the professional landscape or infrastructure encompassing the management of current records are instrumental in terms of influencing directions and the future of the discipline. With regard to the development of records management in North America, the contrast in the mission and aims articulated for records managers as opposed to archivists is worth making explicit. The origins of records management can be found in office administration and are reflected in the life cycle model, which emphasizes actions at specific points in time. In the paper world, being able to free up expensive office space was undoubtedly a dramatic achievement for the new records managers, which would have been much appreciated and highly valued by management. Atherton quotes Gerald Brown, a records manager of the U.S. corporate sector as saying:

> The archivist serves the needs of the scholar, the historian, and posterity, whereas, the records manager serves the needs of business which is usually profit motivated and which is interested only in information that contributes to or protects that profit or the goals of the organization. To put it another way, the records manager is basically a business administrator and the archivist is basically a historian. (Brown 1971, cited in Atherton 1985–1986, 43)

These origins with their focus on cost savings are undoubtedly still very influential in determining the current priorities of records managers. In a digital environment, however, it can no longer be sufficient or may not even be possible to demonstrate cost savings on the basis of freeing up expensive office real estate. Concerns about the need for quantifiable data and metrics have recently been raised by Steve Bailey in an attempt to demonstrate the return on investment represented by records management (Bailey 2011). He argues that in times of economic crisis, records managers must be able to demonstrate improved cost efficiencies as a result of the implementation of their systems and services (47). However, it can also be argued that a professional ethos driven primarily by cost efficiency concerns has resulted in an occupation that now finds it challenging to articulate or conceptualize their reason for existence in any other way. This restricted worldview poses significant risks for the future of records managers when the environment in which they work is populated by other specialists, all competing for jurisdiction over the same problem area.

This section considers the key drivers in the professional and practice environment, namely the role of professional associations and groups, the development of records management standards, and the impact of technological tools.

Professional Associations

The development of records management as a distinct occupational group in the English-speaking world is marked by the formation of professional associations in various countries. From the early twentieth century, associations concerned with "filing" started to form in the United States (Scanlan 2011). Eventually, two large groups were established around the same time in the mid-1950s: the Association of Records Executives and Administrators (AREA) and the American Records Management Association. In 1975, both groups merged to become the Association of Records Managers and Administrators (ARMA) (ARMA International Education Foundation, n.d.). Kathryn Scanlan (2011) provides a detailed account of the attempts to retain records management under the auspices of the Society of American Archivists (SAA) (noting her personal view that the primary motivator was the desire to maintain membership numbers rather than any more altruistic or theoretical concern). She describes the eventual formation of the association as follows:

> While the professionalization of records management stemmed from archivists in the federal government, ARMA International originated from pre-existing paraprofessional groups that focused on filing and clerical work, primarily in the business realm. ARMA International found its niche, borrowing from the public-sector rise of the records management professional while maintaining an otherwise neglected focus on private-sector business needs, from the earliest days of its existence. (Scanlan 2011, 440)

ARMA has published a journal since 1967. Initially entitled *Records Management Quarterly* (from 1975, the *ARMA Records Management Quarterly*), in 1998, there was a move toward a more comprehensive label when the publication was renamed the *Information Management Journal*. The association describes itself as "... the authority on governing information as a strategic asset" and has over 25,000 members in the United States, Canada, and elsewhere (ARMA International 2015a). Its stated mission is "to provide information professionals the resources, tools, and training they need to effectively manage records and information within an established information governance framework" (ARMA International 2015b). Accordingly, the association has an extensive publishing cataloge of guides, technical reports, manuals, and training materials, in addition to the professional journal mentioned earlier.

ARMA International is undoubtedly the largest and best resourced professional association representing records managers, which perhaps is not surprising given the North American genesis of the occupation. Associations with similar aims and goals exist in other Anglophone countries, notably the U.K. Information and Records Management Society, and in the Southern Hemisphere, the Records and Information Management Professionals Australasia. As with ARMA International, both associations publish journals and hold conferences.

The communication channels for all three associations show the participation of vendors to a far greater extent than the corresponding archival associations, which can only raise questions about the objectivity of the advice and guidance that are provided to members. For instance, despite widespread doubts about the success of electronic recordkeeping solutions (see "Technological Tools" later), in the years since the first systems were implemented, a whole industry has developed consisting of developers, marketing teams, and consultants. There are therefore strong commercial interests at stake in the continued implementation and upgrading of these systems. In the light of this, the availability of disinterested advice becomes of prime importance.

Despite repeated calls for a single voice and mind (from both life cycle and continuum proponents) to be applied to current recordkeeping environments, the continued existence of specialist professional associations differentiates between the work of archivists and the work of records managers and in so doing perpetuates the lack of focus that recordkeeping professionals can bring to bear on addressing the immense challenges characterizing this environment. The merger between the Society of Archivists and the Records Management Association to form a single Archives and Records Association for the United Kingdom and Ireland (http://www.archives.org.uk/) could be viewed as providing a glimmer of hope for a new direction, but as noted earlier, the United Kingdom still has a specialist "homegrown" records management association in the form of the Information and Records Management Society. In addition, ARMA International has recently established a U.K. chapter (http://armaeurope.org/), so the situation is by no means clear-cut.

Standards

A prominent characteristic of the current recordkeeping environment is represented by the development of a number of high-level, principle-based standards. As noted earlier, the first ever records management standard was an Australian initiative, based very firmly on records continuum understandings. AS4390 was issued in 1996 and in response to international endorsement was proposed as an international standard. The fraught process that ensued to finally publish the international standard on records management, ISO15489, not to mention its subsequent revision, has been documented elsewhere (Oliver 2014). It is clear that achieving consensus on internationally agreed principles for the management of records in current environments is no easy task, and part of the reasons for this must lay with differing theoretical perspectives. Nevertheless, achievements of the standards-setting community are impressive. The scale and scope of standards work could not have been envisaged in the early years of the twentieth century, when Brooks rather plaintively expressed a longing for filing systems to incorporate retention decisions in their design: "How fine it would be if in preparing such [filing] schemes the eventual fate of the records were always borne in mind!" (Brooks 1940, 224).

Continuum thinking is also very evident in the metadata standards (ISO23081 parts one to three). The points indicated on the four axes of the records continuum (namely evidentiality, transactionality, recordkeeping containers, and identity) are all codified as metadata elements within the standard. The ISO23081 three-part series represents the practical application of research undertaken in Australia from the late 1990s at Monash University (Evans, McKemmish, and Bhoday 2005; McKemmish et al. 2006).

In addition to the international standards, a raft of national and professional association standards have also been developed, sometimes derived from the international standards or developing principles further in particular national or regional contexts. Alternatively, new initiatives may be developed which subsequently form the basis of new international standards, for example, ISO 13028: 2012 *Information and Documentation—Implementation Guidelines for Digitization of Records* began life as a national standard developed for New Zealand.

As yet largely unexplored and undocumented is the impact of all these standards on our current recordkeeping environments. Regardless though of this missing information, the body of work represented by the standards that currently exist indicates recognition of the complexity of the requirements that are inextricably intertwined and associated with managing records in current environments.

Technological Tools

The main technological tool that up until recently has been seen as the "solution" to digital recordkeeping by the professional records community is the electronic records and document management system (EDRMS). EDRMS, a virtual repository approach to the challenges of digital recordkeeping, first started to emerge in Australia in the 1990s. The repository nature of these systems meant that records needed to be consciously filed (however, that was accomplished, by dragging and dropping or simply assigning some additional metadata), with the process becoming another task for users.

By 2005, John McDonald was pointing out the sluggish nature of change, highlighting the ongoing characterization of the modern office environment as the wild frontier, just as he had described it a decade earlier (1995, 2005). This vivid indictment of the lack of progress was the inspiration for research into ways in which real improvement could be made in terms of managing digital records (McLeod, Childs, and Hardiman 2011). Findings from this research indicated that people issues were significant in achieving recordkeeping outcomes and that technology alone could not address the issues that arose. A subsequent issue that has only become clear in recent years as organizations, particularly governments, have restructured is that merging entities with preexisting EDRMS have resulted in nightmare scenarios with the new organizational body having multiple digital repositories, which cannot be connected at all. "Information silos" takes on a whole new meaning when considered from this perspective, as the ability to break down or influence them can only be achieved with substantial commitment of resources.

Problems experienced and reported internationally with user acceptance and uptake of EDRMS have prompted doctoral research, one conclusion being that even when digital recordkeeping is legislatively mandated, the values assigned by individuals to records are instrumental in influencing their behaviors (Lewellen 2015). In other words, if people do not regard recordkeeping as necessary and important, then they are unlikely to fulfill their responsibilities with regard to EDRMS usage.

In the new wave of systems and tools, increased attention is being paid to developing strategies that take into account cultural and people issues (see, for instance, Oliver and Foscarini 2014) in tandem with increasing emphasis on developing technological tools to automate recordkeeping functions. Rather than requiring people to follow what may appear as arcane and bureaucratic rules to fulfill recordkeeping requirements in the course of their daily activities, attention has turned toward making sure those requirements are performed invisibly, behind the scenes (see, for example, Bailey 2009; Reed 2008).

In 2010, James Lappin commented on the failure of EDRMS and the consequences of this for records managers and records management. He concluded that if there was not another "orthodoxy" to replace the failed EDRMS, that is, a concept or tool that could be believed in as providing a solution, records management would be in crisis (Lappin 2010, 262). As discussed earlier, research is attempting to address this crisis, but the extent to which research is influencing practice is a moot point.

Professional associations, standards setting, and technological tools are entities or activities which are not mutually exclusive but are manifestations of the current recordkeeping environment. They are instrumental in shaping directions and priorities. They are each worthy of consideration, as analysis may help shed light on motivators and directions for the current environment.

CONCLUSIONS AND FUTURE DIRECTIONS

Despite all the impressive progress since the emergence of concern for the management of current records in the first part of the twentieth century, it remains to be seen what the consequences are of two main problem areas. Firstly, the paraprofessional nature of records management. A significant feature that still persists relates to the unique nature of records management as an occupation and its separation from the archival endeavor. In the United States, Scanlan points to the absence of any recognition of records management as a formal occupation by the U.S. Department of Labor's

Bureau of Statistics and states, "The lack of professional recognition reveals lingering evidence of records managers' ancestry in paraprofessional endeavors and stands as an obstacle to the advancement of the records management field" (Scanlan 2011, 450). The historical development of the occupation of records management (as recounted earlier) allows insight into how and why these tensions exist.

The second problem area relates to the theoretical divergence and disagreements. As we have seen, there does appear to be at least some common ground in terms of perspectives from proponents of life cycle and continuum models. This is most apparent in the calls for a single-minded approach to the challenge of recordkeeping in current environments, in other words, a distancing from the records management/archival division of responsibilities, which perhaps can be regarded as being perpetuated by professional associations. However, alignment with what are generally represented as polarizing or binary oppositional views can only lead to considerable confusion among practitioners. The situation is challenging and the way forward unclear. Considerable responsibility lies with educators to explain and discuss differing perspectives, to encourage critical reflection of the issues and challenges inherent in current recordkeeping environments and the developments that have resulted in today's contested understandings. Similarly, with diplomatics and rhetorical genre studies, a mature discipline will allow for the combination of multiple perspectives, but at present, it seems we have to pick sides, to be a proponent of one or the other.

Most of the research and thinking to date has been firmly positioned in an organizational or workplace environment, reflecting the origins of the emergence of records management as a distinct occupation. However, concerns for social justice and reconciliation that have emerged in the archival literature (see, for instance, the *Archival Science* special issue on "Archives and Human Rights," October 2014) have very major implications for current recordkeeping. For example, the concept of cocreation of records sets out to acknowledge the rights of the subject of the record. Cocreation recognizes in a very unique way multiple roles, voices, and perspectives in records, granting the same status to the subject of records as to the agency traditionally regarded as creator, which could be, for example, a government department. Jacqui Wilson and Frank Golding provide an eloquent and moving personal account of the impact of the contents of the records documenting their years in the "care" of institutions (Wilson and Golding 2016) and in doing so contribute considerable insight into the need to broaden thinking about ownership and creation of records.

Anne Gilliland has called our attention to the Universal Declaration on Archives that emphasizes the need to protect citizens' rights, to establish individual and collective memory in order to understand the past and document the present to guide future actions (Gilliland 2015, 3). The critical role that records managers could play with regard to citizens' rights becomes starkly apparent in a time when society is characterized by shifting populations and displaced peoples. The day-to-day functioning of civil societies (voting, entitlement to educational opportunities, health care, welfare benefits, even shopping) is predicated by identities that are documented, providing "proof" of people being who they claim to be.

The records that are required to enable people to establish and reconstruct their identities, families, and lives are "often still maintained in non-digital and frequently haphazard or idiosyncratic ways by a range of different government records offices and regimes" (Gilliland 2015, 7) or in other words, in current recordkeeping environments. For outsiders to our professional community, locating and understanding the systems creating and maintaining these records, which are so instrumental in their current and future existence, is a Herculean task. The records professionals responsible for these services may take on the role of gatekeeper and be reluctant to perceive the subjects of those records as their clients.

In thinking about current recordkeeping environments, therefore, we have to be aware of the personal dimensions as well as the organizational needs and drivers. It will require a fundamental shift in thinking for records managers to broaden their awareness beyond the goals of corporate or government organizational structures. After all, powerful drivers for the emergence of records management as a distinct occupation in the United States were economic and aimed at reducing business costs (Dollar 1993). The potential for cost savings has persisted as one of the major tenets of records management, even if much of the evidence of this has traditionally been anecdotal rather than proven (Bailey 2011).

Absence of this awareness of personal rights will be a moral failure, and the need to recognize the personal should be reflected in ethical codes for recordkeepers. Solutions and strategies to the problems of displaced peoples and the absence of records will require creativity and new ways of thinking but are a question of urgency that is situated very clearly in current recordkeeping environments. The consequences of not addressing these issues are not only severe for the day-to-day living of diasporic peoples but will also deny future generations their abilities to trace their ancestors and understand their past. One clear direction that is becoming apparent from professional discourse considering the needs of refugees and migrant communities (such as Gilliland's 2015 paper) relates to recordkeeping literacy as a means of empowerment. Information literacy has been acknowledged by UNESCO as being a fundamental human right (UNESCO 2005), yet specific recordkeeping aspects of information literacy (the power and significance of records in day-to-day life) have not been addressed. Concern with recordkeeping literacy of individuals, beyond the traditional parameters of records management practice within organizational settings, will require significant broadening of vision and interpretation of professional responsibilities.

REFERENCES

ARMA International. 2015a. "Who We Are." http://www.arma.org/who-we-are/vision-mission-who-we-are (accessed September 2, 2015).

ARMA International. 2015b. "Vision and Mission: Who We Are." http://www.arma.org/who-we-are/vision-mission-who-we-are (accessed September 2, 2015).

ARMA International Education Foundation. n.d. "In the Beginning . . ." http://www.armaedfoundation.org/history.html (accessed September 2, 2015).

Atherton, J. 1985–1986. "From Life Cycle to Continuum: Some Thoughts on the Records Management–Archives Relationship." *Archivaria* 21: 43–51.

Bailey, Steve. 2009. "Forget Electronic Records Management, It's Automated Records Management that We Desperately Need." *Records Management Journal* 19 (2): 91–97.

Bailey, Steve. 2011. "Measuring the Impact of Records Management: Data and Discussion from the UK Higher Education Sector." *Records Management Journal* 21 (1): 46–68.

Bearman, David. 1993. "Record-Keeping Systems." *Archivaria* 36 (Autumn): 16–36.

Bearman, David. 1994. "Managing Electronic Mail." *Archives and Manuscripts* 22 (1): 28–50.

Brooks, Philip C. 1940. "The Selection of Records for Preservation." *American Archivist* 3 (4): 221–34.

Brooks, Philip C. 1943. "The Archivist's Concern in Records Administration." *American Archivist* 6 (3): 158–64.

Brown, Gerald. 1971. "The Archivist and the Records Manager: A Records Manager's Viewpoint." *Records Management Quarterly* 5: 21.

Dingwall, Glenn. 2010. "Life Cycle and Continuum: A View of Recordkeeping Models from the Postwar Period." In *Currents of Archival Thinking*, edited by Terry Eastwood and Heather MacNeil, 139–61. Santa Barbara, CA: Libraries Unlimited.

Dollar, Charles M. 1993. "Archivists and Records Managers in the Information Age." *Archivaria* 36: 37–52.

Duranti, Luciana. 1989a. "The Odyssey of Records Managers Part I: From the Dawn of Civilisation to the Fall of the Roman Empire." *Records Management Quarterly* 23 (3): 3–11.

Duranti, Luciana. 1989b. "The Odyssey of Records Managers Part II: From the Middle Ages to Modern Times." *Records Management Quarterly* 23 (4): 3–11.

Duranti, Luciana. 1989c. "Diplomatics: New Uses for an Old Science." *Archivaria* 28: 7–27.

Duranti, Luciana. 1999. "Concepts and Principles for the Management of Electronic Records, or Records Management Theory Is Archival Diplomatics." *Records Management Journal* 9 (3): 149–71.

Duranti, Luciana. 2015a. "Records Lifecycle." In *Encyclopedia of Archival Science*, edited by Luciana Duranti and Patricia C. Franks, 342–46. Lanham, MD: Rowman and Littlefield.

Duranti, Luciana. 2015b. "Guest Editorial." *Records Management Journal* 25 (1). doi: http://dx.doi.org/10.1108/RMJ-01-2015-0004.

Duranti, Luciana, Terry Eastwood, and Heather MacNeil. n.d. *The Preservation of the Integrity of Electronic Records*. http://www.interpares.org/UBCProject/index.htm (accessed September 13, 2016).

Evans, Joanne, Barbara Reed, Henry Linger, Simon Goss, David Holmes, Jan Drobik, Bruce Woodyat, and Simon Henbest. 2014. "Winds of Change: A Recordkeeping Informatics Approach to Information Management Needs in Data-Driven Research Environments." *Records Management Journal* 24 (3): 205–23.

Evans, Joanne, Sue McKemmish, and Karuna Bhoday. 2005. "Create Once, Use Many Times: The Clever Use of Recordkeeping Metadata for Multiple Archival Purposes." *Archival Science* 5 (1): 17–42.

Foscarini, Fiorella. 2012. "Diplomatics and Genre Theory as Complementary Approaches." *Archival Science* 12: 389–409.

Foscarini, Fiorella. 2014. "A Genre-Based Investigation of Workplace Communities." *Archivaria* 78: 1–24.

Gibbons, Leisa M. 2015. "Culture in the Continuum: YouTube, Small Stories and Memory-Making." Doctoral Dissertation. Monash University, Faculty of Information Technology, Caulfield School of Information Technology.

Giddens, Anthony. 1986. *The Constitution of Society*. London: Polity Press.

Gilliland, Anne. 2015. *Permeable Binaries, Societal Grand Challenges, and the Roles of the Twenty-First Century Archival and Recordkeeping Profession*. Available at http://escholarship.org/uc/item/90q5538g (accessed September 13, 2016).

International Organization for Standardization. 2015. *Information and Documentation—Records Management*. Final Draft International Standard ISO/FDIS 15489-1:2015(E), Geneva.

Jenkinson, Hilary. 1922. *A Manual of Archive Administration Including the Problems of War Archives and Archive Making*. Oxford, England: Clarendon Press.

Lappin, James. 2010. "What Will Be the Next Records Management Orthodoxy?" *Records Management Journal* 20 (3): 252–64.

Lewellen, Matthew J. 2015. "The Impact of the Perceived Value of Records on the Use of Electronic Recordkeeping Systems." Doctoral Thesis. Victoria University of Wellington.

Maclean, Ian. 1959. "Australian Experience in Record and Archives Management." *The American Archivist* 22 (4): 387–418. Society of American Archivists.

MacNeil, Heather. 2004. "Contemporary Archival Diplomatics as a Method of Inquiry: Lessons Learned from Two Research Projects." *Archival Science* 4: 199–232.

McDonald, John. 1995. "Managing Records in the Modern Office: Taming the Wild Frontier." *Archivaria* 39 (Spring): 70–79.

McDonald, John. 2005. "The Wild Frontier Ten Years On." In *Managing Electronic Records*, edited by J. McLeod J and C. Hare, 17. London: Facet Publishing.

McKemmish, Sue, Glenda Acland, Nigel Ward, and Barbara Reed. 2006. "Describing Records in Context in the Continuum: The Australian Recordkeeping Metadata Schema." *Archivaria* 48: 3–37.

McLeod, Julie, Sue Childs, and Rachel Hardiman. 2011. "Accelerating Positive Change in Electronic Records Management—Headline Findings from a Major Research Project." *Archives and Manuscripts* 39 (2): 66–94.

Miller, Carolyn R. 1984. "Genre as Social Action." *Quarterly Journal of Speech* 70 (2): 151–67.

Norton, Margaret C. 1975. "Making and Control of Administrative Records." In *Norton on Archives: The Writings of Margaret Cross Norton on Archival and Records Management*, edited by Thornton W. Mitchell, 132–56. Carbondale: Southern Illinois University Press.

Oliver, Gillian. 2010. "Transcending Silos, Developing Synergies." *Information Research* 15 (4): 23.

Oliver, G. 2014. "International Records Management Standards: The Challenges of Achieving Consensus." *Records Management Journal* 24 (1): 22–31.

Oliver, Gillian, and Fiorella Foscarini. 2014. *Records Management and Information Culture: Tackling the People Problem.* London: Facet.

Oliver, Gillian, Frank Upward, Barbara Reed, and Joanne Evans. 2014. *Recordkeeping Informatics: Building the Discipline Base. DLM 2014: Making the Information Governance Landscape in Europe/7th Triennial Conference of the DLM Forum*, edited by José Borbinha, Zoltán Szatucsek, Seamus Ross. Livro eletrónico. Lisboa: Biblioteca Nacional de Portugal. ISBN 978-972-565-541-2. Available at http://purl.pt/26107/1/DLM2014_PDF/02%20-%20Recordkeeping%20Informatics%20Building%20the%20Discipline%20Base.pdf (accessed September 13, 2016).

Oliver, Gillian, Joanne Evans, Barbara Reed, and Frank Upward. 2009. "Achieving the Right Balance: Recordkeeping Informatics, Part 1." *IQ* 25 (4): 18–21.

Oliver, Gillian, Joanne Evans, Barbara Reed, and Frank Upward. 2010. "Achieving the Right Balance: Recordkeeping Informatics, Part 2." *IQ* 26 (1): 42–44; 52.

Posner, Ernst. 1975. "Foreword." In *Norton on Archives: The Writings of Margaret Cross Norton on Archival and Records Management*, edited by Thornton W. Mitchell, vii–viii. Carbondale: Southern Illinois University Press.

Reed, Barbara. 2008. "Service-Oriented Architectures and Recordkeeping." *Records Management Journal* 18 (1): 7–20.

Rogers, Corinne. 2015. "Diplomatics of Born Digital Documents—Considering Documentary Form in a Digital Environment." *Records Management Journal* 25 (1): 6–20.

Ross, Rodney A. 1985. "The National Archives: The Formative Years 1934–1949." In *Guardian of Heritage: Essays on the History of the National Archives*, 33–49. Washington, D.C.: Smithsonian Institution Press. Available at http://www.archives.gov/about/history/sources/ross.pdf (accessed September 13, 2016).

Scanlan, Kathryn. 2011. "ARMA v. SAA: The History and Heart of Professional Friction." *American Archivist* 74 (2): 428–50.

Schellenberg, Theodore R. 1956. *Modern Archives: Principles and Techniques.* Melbourne: Cheshire.

Scott, Peter J. 1966. "The Record Group Concept: A Case for Abandonment." *The American Archivist* 29 (4): 493–504. Society of American Archivists.

UNESCO. 2005. *Information Literacy.* http://portal.unesco.org/ci/en/ev.php-URL_ID=27055&URL_DO=DO_TOPIC&URL_SECTION=201.html.

Upward, Frank. 1996. "Structuring the Records Continuum—Part One: Postcustodial Principles and Properties." *Archives and Manuscripts* 24 (2): 268–85.

Upward, Frank. 2000. "Modelling the Continuum as Paradigm Shift in Recordkeeping and Archiving Processes, and Beyond—A Personal Reflection." *Records Management Journal* 10 (3): 115–39.

Upward, Frank, Barbara Reed, Gillian Oliver, and Joanne Evans. 2013. "Recordkeeping Informatics: Re-Figuring a Discipline in Crisis with a Single Minded Approach." *Records Management Journal* 23 (1): 37–50.

Upward, Frank, Barbara Reed, Gillian Oliver, and Joanne Evans. In press. *Recordkeeping Informatics for a Networked Age*. Clayton, Victoria: Monash University Press.

Wilson, Jacqueline Z., and Frank Golding. 2016. "Latent Scrutiny: Personal Archives as Perpetual Mementos of the Official Gaze." *Archival Science* 16 (1): 93–109.

5

Archival Appraisal in Four Paradigms

Fiorella Foscarini

Archival appraisal for the purpose of identifying the records and archives that are worthy of continuous preservation started to emerge as a crucial demand and a major intellectual challenge in the writings of the archivists of the last century. In ancient and medieval times and until the watershed of the French Revolution, those who were capable of documenting their transactions through written records (e.g., courts, chanceries, churches, and a few privileged literate individuals and families) used to retain and transmit to their successors what they tacitly adjudged useful for their own continuity as legal entities and for the accomplishment of their political and administrative goals. The motivation to keep records as "self-documentation-memory," which rested primarily, though not exclusively,[1] on legal-judicial grounds, preceded a collective awareness that the same records might be used as "source-memory" for the writing of history and other cultural purposes (Zanni Rosiello 1987).[2] With the collapse of the *ancien régime*, the rising nation-states of Europe felt the need to provide their citizens with a common "heritage" that would sustain and promote the development of national identities. The creation of centralized repositories for select older records as "national archival patrimony" (Ketelaar 2007, 353) was accompanied, in the course of the nineteenth century, by the issuing of archival laws for the legal destruction of records. We have to wait until the period between the two world wars and the transformation of relatively simple societies into increasingly complex organizational apparatuses to witness an explosion in the production of records in both the private and the public sector and the parallel surge of attention to questions that had never been seriously addressed before, such as: What constitutes the lasting value of records? Who should decide on that? And why and for whom should we keep archives in the first place?

This chapter will highlight a few stages in the evolution of the discourse about archival appraisal from the early twentieth century until today. Because any attribution of value is time-bound and culturally conditioned, different approaches to appraisal can only be fully appreciated by considering them within the "archival paradigms" in which those approaches had been forged. How archivists look at themselves and how they are perceived by society, the ways in which they articulate the properties of records and archives and the goals of recordkeeping, and their participation in broader intellectual currents and societal contexts, all these factors have direct bearing on the divergent views of the controversial subject of appraisal that have emerged over time. In order to frame my overview, I will refer to the "four shifting archival paradigms" (i.e., evidence, memory, identity, and community) as identified by Canadian archivist Terry Cook (2013) in one of his last articles. In that work, Cook, one of the most influential and original thinkers of all time about appraisal, was not writing specifically on appraisal. Rather, his purpose was to offer a comprehensive reading of the development of the "archival mindset" or "ways of imagining archives and archiving" shared by various generations of archivists over time (2013, 97). Applying his idea of the four paradigms to this discussion of the appraisal discourse will provide a lens that will help us understand how and why certain themes, connections, and discontinuities have occurred throughout the history of the theory and methodology of appraisal. However, Cook cautions us that cultural paradigms are always "porous" (97), cumulative, and partially coexisting: "they do not entirely replace each other" (105). This attempt to systematize the rich literature on appraisal according to the lines drawn by Cook will thus reveal the "discursive tension" (105) that necessarily characterizes any history of ideas and practices, especially when such ideas and practices are driven by weak "technical imperatives" (Hofstede 2001, 382), as it is the case with appraisal.

APPRAISAL IN THE EVIDENCE PARADIGM

Early representations of the archival function portray it as a function of the state. With the establishment of national archives all over Europe, archival laws started to set parameters for the content and structure of public archives, their regulating policies, and the roles and responsibilities of the professionals taking care of them. At this time, it is appropriate to view the archivist as a "guardian or keeper of the juridical evidence of government agencies" (Cook 2013, 106). The first archival writers consolidated in their manuals that which "was in the air" (Horsman 2002, 5), that is, they devised principles and methods for arranging, describing, and preserving archives that focused on the centrality of the administrative activity, which was conceived as a rational and impartial, almost scientific, endeavor. Appraisal was not contemplated in the Dutch manual of 1898. In his *Manual of Archive Administration*, first published in 1922, the father of archival studies in the English language, Sir Hilary Jenkinson, rejected the idea that archivists had a role in appraisal, because of its being fundamentally "un-archival," as Cook (2013, 106) puts it. Jenkinson's arguments reflect his rigorous interpretation of the nature of records as natural, unique, and impartial phenomena and of the moral duty of the archivist as neutral custodian to defend the record's characteristics. Assessing value cannot be part of an archivist's skill set, simply because "to destroy a document because he [*sic*] thinks it useless is to import into the collection under his charge what we have been throughout most anxious to keep out of it, an element of his personal judgement" (Jenkinson 1966, 149). Following Jenkinson's stringent logic, the "Administrator," as "Archive maker," is the only agent allowed to sift through his or her records and to decide what to pass on to his or her successors, "provided always that the Administrator proceeds only upon those grounds upon which alone it is competent to make a decision: the needs of its own practical business" (149). The "disagreeable necessity" (Jenkinson 1980, 341) to select records is only permissible so long as it is a "natural" activity, seamlessly ingrained in the usual and ordinary course of business. Thus, archivists, and even less so historians, have no say in the process.

The "evidence paradigm" of the premodern times, so perfectly championed by Jenkinson, "dominated the professional discourse until the 1930s and continues to the present as an important archival concern" (Cook 2013, 107). Although in modern and postmodern times, evidence has become a more complex and contested notion, the relationship between recordkeeping and accountability is still a guiding idea for archivists, especially those embedded in some organizational context, where protecting the authenticity and integrity of the records remains a fundamental aspiration.

APPRAISAL IN THE MEMORY PARADIGM

More than just an acceptable practice, appraisal is the "defining characteristic" of Cook's second paradigm (2013, 107), the "memory paradigm," which thrived from the 1930s to the 1970s. The sheer bulk of records produced by modern organizations, mostly without any plans to guide accumulation, on the one hand, and the growing demand of historians to access archival materials, on the other, convinced archivists—often trained as historians themselves—that they could not shun their responsibility to decide which sliver of the vast amount of records sitting in creating agencies should be kept and which archives should be added to the holdings of an institution. European and North American archivists provided different answers to what Robert-Henri Bautier described as "*le problème-clef de l'archivistique moderne*" (quoted in Booms 1987, 71), European archivists being more concerned about maintaining the evidentiary value of records and North American archivists being more oriented toward the cultural aspects of their job and more pragmatic in their approach.[3]

In his 1956 manual, *Modern Archives: Principles and Techniques*, American archivist Theodore R. Schellenberg formulated an "Appraisal Standard" that, by placing the archivist and his or her subjective judgment at the center of the appraisal process, contradicted each and every "Golden Rule" established by Jenkinson (1966, 153). Schellenberg had little interest in the "values [of the records] for the originating agency itself," which he called "primary values." Rather, he emphasized the role of archival institutions as storehouses for a select portion of public records that have "lasting, secondary values," that is, "values for others than the current users" (1956, 133) or, in other words, records that historians (and Schellenberg was especially referring to academic historians) can draw on as authoritative sources of public memory. The archivist's primary responsibility is to identify those records that either contain "evidence ... of the functioning and organization of the government body that produced them" or provide "information ... on persons, corporate bodies, problems, conditions, and the like, with which the government body dealt" (Schellenberg 1956, 139). Although his notion of "evidential value" has been subject to misinterpretations (see, e.g., Menne-Haritz 1994), Schellenberg explains clearly that it has nothing to do with the Jenkinsonian "sanctity of the evidence in archives that is derived from 'unbroken custody' " (1956, 139). Instead, he refers, "and quite arbitrarily" (139), to the archivist's assessment of the importance of the records as source for understanding how an organization used to work.

Schellenberg cautions archivists about the "careful analytical work" (1984, 57) that his methodology entails. The "test of evidential values" (59–62), in particular, requires a thorough examination of "1) the position of each office in the administrative hierarchy of an agency, 2) the functions performed by each office, and 3) the activities carried out by each office in executing a given function" (Schellenberg 1956, 142). In this way, he tried to mitigate the obvious subjectivity of his approach. However, in relation to "informational values," Schellenberg concedes that "in applying the test of importance, the archivist is in the realm of the imponderable" (1984, 66).

Good training in historical methods, in-depth analyses of the records creator, a comprehensive approach to the documentation (which may also involve cooperation with archivists of other institutions), and "moderation and common sense" (68) are some of the basic precepts that should guide the appraiser. Rather than aiming at as objective and impartial an appraisal outcome as possible, Schellenberg admits that "complete consistency" in appraisal is an unattainable and "undesirable" goal. Actually, he concludes, "diverse judgments" may result in a more adequate record of human activity (Schellenberg 1984, 68).

Although Schellenberg's focus was on public records, his taxonomic, content-based approach also influenced the private manuscript tradition, which flourished in the United States especially in the 1960s and 1970s, with the establishment of new social history programs, the emergence of alternative cultural movements, and the founding or expansion of several nongovernmental archives (Trace 2010, 51). The collecting practices of university archives, libraries, museums, and various public and private special documentation centers were based on the assessment of different kinds of values (both inherent and external to the records), cost-benefit analyses, and the knowledge archivists/librarians had of their thematic collections and of the needs of their users (see Boles and Young 1985; Brichford 1977). In Canada, acquiring private papers has traditionally been part of the mandate of public archival institutions. The "total archives" concept was intended to build a distributed system of publicly funded archives, which would be responsible for collecting the totality of the records, "no matter what their media, age, or source" (Millar 1998, 115) that were considered significant to the history of Canada. Still today, nearly all Canadian archives at all levels of government preserve both public and private records. It may be appropriate to introduce here a common distinction between appraisal for selection and appraisal for acquisition, as two distinct decision-making approaches that influence the building of archival holdings in different ways. While in order to select what to retain within specific bodies of records, archivists tend to apply analytical methods that ideally respect the organic nature of the fonds; planning what to collect or acquire from sources that are external to the acquiring institution (e.g., private collections, personal papers) often implies making high-level choices about subjects or typologies of records of interest (e.g., photographs, maps, literary papers, architectural records) that follow more pertinence- or content-based ideas than provenance-based ones.

If the building of planned collections characterized both the Canadian total archives and the American historical manuscript traditions, planning was also the driver behind the first records management programs that started to be developed in the 1940s in the United States. As mentioned earlier, Schellenberg did not elaborate on the issue of how the record creators would go about selecting their own records (primary values). On the contrary, Philip Brooks thought that the problem of the enormous and undisciplined accumulation of records in the creator's office could only be solved if the appraisal function was conceived as "one undertaking" that would begin as early in a record's life cycle as possible. "The earlier in [the] life history [of the records] the co-operation between the agency of origin and the archivist can be established, the easier will be the work of all" (Brooks 1940, 226). Brooks envisioned the "filing scheme" as the tool through which "the eventual fate of the records" (224) could be decided right at creation so that "appraisal [could be] made when the records are filed" (225).

While the practice of assigning "retention periods" to certain typologies of routine records so that those having no further value for the administration would be periodically eliminated was already known in some offices since the end of the previous century (Frost 1991–1992, 78), combining records scheduling with records filing or classification, as suggested by Brooks, became common records management practice only in the late 1980s. It should be noticed that in the taxonomy of values proposed by Brooks (1948) for the identification of the records that are worthy of longer retention, one finds both administrative and historical values, and the latter basically coincide with Schellenberg's secondary values. However, as seen in the next section, records scheduling developed into a method primarily oriented toward safeguarding the interests of the creating agency and the records' evidentiary value (though not exactly in the same sense as expressed by Jenkinson) and is, in today's records management practice, not so much concerned with the potential memory value of records.

Going back to Europe, the Jenkinsonian idealism of the previous paradigm continued to exercise a strong influence on archival theory and practice in the United Kingdom until well into the twentieth century. In the mid-1950s, the so-called Grigg Report, from the name of the chairman of the committee appointed to "review the arrangements for the preservation of the records of the Government Departments" (Great Britain 1954, 5), devised an "administratively workable" (7) method that would satisfy the Public Record Office's (PRO) mandate to ensure the continuous maintenance of "all valuable Public Documents . . . as Public Muniments" (13) and to facilitate any "non-administrative uses" (20) of the records. The two-tier review system that the committee recommended enabled an "indirect" application of the "historical criterion" (29). It was based on the assumption that the records retained by a department for its own purposes would include those that a historian of the future may wish to have preserved. One may say that Sir James Grigg, who, like Brooks, believed that the problem of selection was primarily an administrative problem, attempted to "modernize" Jenkinson by making concrete proposals to improve the records creator's management of its own records before the latter would undergo the first review (five years after the closing of the relevant file), including the appointment of departmental record officers. At the second review (when the file is 25 years old), the decision of which of the surviving records should be further retained would take into consideration both historical and administrative factors. Archivists from the PRO were given a role in this second review—with the blessing of Jenkinson, who was still deputy keeper. It is noteworthy that the report did not dwell on the historical criterion, once more confirming that talking about memory values or user needs was still a taboo in the legalistic British context.

In Germany, the "evidence-memory tension" that Cook (2013, 105) describes as an irreducible characteristic of the archival profession, unfolded as a "provenance-pertinence tension" in the period under consideration, with some writers clearly siding with the *Provenienzprinzip* in their elaborations of an appraisal methodology (e.g., Mueller, Sante and Rohr, and Booms) and others being inclined toward content-based criteria (e.g., Meisner, Zimmerman, Zachel, and the early Booms) (see Booms 1987; Kolsrud 1992; Schellenberg 1956, 135–37). The major contribution of most of these writers (leaving aside Booms, who will be discussed in the next section) was the idea that the level of authority and independence of an administrative body could be used as an indicator of the significance of its records. Sante and Rohr (quoted in Booms 1987, 99; see also Kolsrud 1992, 31–32), in particular, articulated a top-down approach (a sort of macro-appraisal *ante litteram*) that involved the structural and functional analysis of agencies for the purpose of ranking them according to their importance. Top-ranked record creators would then be assumed to be those who produce the most valuable records. A certain idea of the state as a rational, predictable machine encompassing all possible societal needs and of historical research as scientific and formalistic investigation, relying on the "objectivity inherent in the sources" (Pabst, quoted in Booms 1987, 80), was the driver of all these appraisal approaches. Although most German archivists self-identified with historians, their strong "scientific imperative" would not allow them to let intuition (*Fingerspitzengefuehl* in German) guide the appraisal process.

In this second archival paradigm, the evidence or accountability dimension is still quite central, especially in relation to the development of modern business tools to manage records selection or the amount of research required to analyze a record's content and context. Nevertheless, historian-archivists of this period saw their mission as supporting research into the archives as "cultural memory resources rather than guarding an inherited juridical legacy of evidence" (Cook 2013, 109). Memory—which in this second paradigm, is primarily conceived of as institutional memory—is evidence of human and organizational activity. Yet, it is a kind of evidence that does not require a passive custodian to be preserved. Appraisal is now seen as the process that enhances the value or quality of the records, both as evidence and as memory. "A reduction in the quantity of ... public records is essential to both the government and the scholar"

(Schellenberg 1984, 57), and archivists reckoned that they could not refrain from taking the lead in this crucial matter.

APPRAISAL IN THE IDENTITY PARADIGM

Cook interprets the last quarter of the twentieth century as the time when the "imagined community"[4] of archivists suffered from an identity crisis, which would eventually result in the emergence of "the archivist as a professional expert" (2013, 109). The domain of appraisal is exemplary in this sense. From the mid-1970s onward, we may witness a continuous sequence of critical self-reflections on the archivists' accomplishments as appraisers and the adequacy of their methods, the exploration of innovative selection and acquisition models (often by drawing insights from other disciplines), and new attempts to delineate a theory of appraisal in the wake of Jenkinson and Schellenberg's incompatible standards. These are all symptoms of a profession that was struggling to find a justifiable rationale for a function, appraisal, that had started to be perceived as very powerful, profoundly political, and entrenched in many important societal processes, including the construction and de(con)struction of collective and individual identities. Postmodernism played a significant role in this process of "revisionism" through questioning traditional assumptions about the nature and purposes of archives and archiving and destabilizing any truth-value propositions and professional certainties. At the same time, the advent of computerization and digital communication networks changed radically the way people work and the characteristics of the objects (records and systems) they work with, thus contributing, perhaps from a more tangible perspective than any postmodern idea, to challenge long-standing principles and beliefs.

An alternative name for this third archival mind-set could be "the society paradigm," as implicitly suggested by Cook (2013, 111–12), in that archivists began to realize that they belong to and serve something larger than the institutions in which they are embedded. By looking at "archives as a societal resource" (112), the key issues for the appraiser become: How can we represent society more completely and directly, in all its colors and shades, beyond the monohierarchical and monochromatic picture provided by the official files? What features of current and past societies are worth preserving as our shared documentary heritage, not just for those who occupy positions of power but, as Cook puts it, as "a societal foundation for identity and justice" (112)?

The first wake-up call to archivists in relation to their responsibilities toward society came from Gerald Ham. In his 1974 Society of American Archivist's (SAA) presidential address, Ham reproached his audience for their "passivity and perceptions [which would] produce a biased and distorted archival record" (1975, 5). He urged the profession not only to forgo its custodial attitude but also to keep the "vogue of the academic marketplace" (329) at a distance (in this way criticizing both Jenkinsonian and Schellenbergian approaches). He envisioned "imaginative acquisition guidelines or comprehensive collecting strategies" (328), based on collaboration and coordination of efforts (rather than the present reality of competition among institutions), which would allow a "representative record of human experience in our time" (326) to be handed over to the next generations. Ham went as far as to suggest that archivists should "fill in the gaps" (330) by, for instance, resorting to creating oral history, photographic records, and survey data when the extant record was incomplete or insufficient. "Documenting culture" (334): this, he argued, should become the archivists' prime mission. In order to meet such ambitious goal, he launched the slogan: "Conceptualization must precede collection" (333).

Helen Samuels, head of Special Collections and Archives at the Massachusetts Institute of Technology (MIT), seized the opportunity and offered the archival community a new acquisition model, which her librarianship training as well as her experience with discipline-based history centers (see Elliott 1983; Haas, Samuels, and Simmons 1985) had been instrumental in developing. "Our modern, complex, information-rich society," writes Samuels (1986, 110–12), characterized by the "integration" of information resources and the "integration" of institutions, requires "integrated appraisal decisions." Her "documentation strategy" was conceived as "a plan formulated to assure the documentation of an ongoing issue, activity, or geographic area" (115). Her "recipe" involved choosing a topic to be documented and a suitable site (not necessarily a physical one) where to conduct the documentation activity and, most importantly, investigating the topic chosen across institutions and across any kinds of borders, by paying more attention to "what should exist" (120) than what already existed on a given topic.

Samuels's initial article on documentation strategy —powerfully entitled "Who Controls the Past" and opening with the relevant epigraph from George Orwell's book *1984*—shook archivists' consciousness, especially outside the United States, in countries where her document-based terminology was not common currency. For instance, she speaks of "documentation" as a thematic concept, the "active documenter" as a substitute for custodian or keeper, and "to document" as the verb describing what archivists do rather than verbs such as to maintain, to preserve, or to keep. However, it also intrigued the international archival community, which was in search of a new identity, better aligned with the electronic age and with an archives' user base that had progressively become more diverse and thus demanded different kinds of services. The dissatisfaction with existing appraisal methods was, once again, "in the air," and any new ideas that would relieve archivists from the impossible task of managing an enormous and unstable mass of records "at the bottom" were welcome.

In her subsequent works, Samuels (1991–1992, 1992) smoothed out some of the most "un-archival wrinkles" of her approach—particularly the "thematic or subject focus" (Cook 1992a, 181; see also Bailey 1997, 93) of her documentation projects—and positioned the analysis of organizational functions at the core of her strategy. In her book, *Varsity Letters: Documenting Modern Colleges and Universities*, archivists are portrayed as "documenters of their institutions" (Samuels 1992, 12), with a "documentary mission" requiring that they gain "knowledge of what is to be documented and the problems of gathering the desired documentation" (1). The method for accomplishing this mission is a variation of the documentation strategy labeled "institutional functional analysis." However, Samuels explains, this is not the same as the "traditional hierarchical analysis" (5) archivists usually apply within their organizational structures. The "integrated functions" of modern institutions call for a broader notion of context, one encompassing all sites and situations where the functions we are aiming to document are carried out. Although some commentators pointed out that Samuels did not articulate in her study how she identified the seven functions making up the mandate of higher education institutions (Bailey 1997, 93), her planned and cooperative approach (Cox 1994), together with her suggestion that the scope of appraisal should be expanded to embrace the "universe of documentation" (Bearman 1989) and that the appraiser's focus should shift from the actual records to their functional context (Cook 1992a, 1992b), have been, and continue to be (see Cook 2011), an inspiration to several generations of archivists.

Cook is among those authors with whom Samuels's ideas have had the strongest and longer lasting appeal. His immersion in critical and postmodern thinking, combined with insights he gained from Giddens's theory of structuration and his reading of German archivists on appraisal, enabled him to define, refine, and situate Samuels's generic documentation approach in a more "archival," that is, provenance-based, frame of reference. His macro-appraisal model, which in 1991 became the official appraisal methodology of the then National Archives of Canada, is an innovative analytical framework aiming to "document governance rather than the structures and functions of government *per se*" (Cook 2004, 16). In the term *governance*, Cook subsumes the "societal context in which the record is created" (1992b, 46), a context that is dynamic and pluralistic, as it is not only made of functions or structures, but rather it occurs in the "interaction" between the record creators (structures), the programs they enact (functions), and the citizens (clients) "upon whom both function and structure impinge, and who in turn influence both function and structure" (40).

As a postmodernist, Cook recognizes that archives are "contested sites of power in society" (2004, 16). One of the purposes of macro-appraisal is to allow the voice of marginalized groups to emerge so that the resulting body of selected records would not just represent the official narratives of the state and other powerful entities (as was the case within the evidence and memory paradigms), but it would rather offer a more comprehensive and ambiguous "'image' of society" (42). Through archival appraisal, the archivist, as a "conscious mediator aiding society in forming its own multiple identities" (Cook 2013, 113), becomes a non-neutral interpreter of the "societal values" that emerge at the "points of sharpest interaction of the structure, function, and client." These are the points where "the best documentary evidence will be found" (Cook 1992b, 50).

In practice, Cook's macro-appraisal model involves a top-down approach starting with a ranking of record creators based on an assessment of the impact made by government agencies and their programs on society.[5] The identification of "hot spots of the societal image" (Cook 1992b, 55) is followed by the generation of an "appraisal hypothesis suggest[ing] where the records of highest archival value should be found" (Bailey 1997, 105). All of this macro-level analysis should be completed before any actual record of the creating agency is examined for the purpose of confirming or modifying the hypothesis formulated. This final phase of the methodology is called "micro-appraisal" (Cook 1992b, 47). One of the practical advantages of the macro-appraisal model is that archivists apply their "traditional appraisal methods" to a substantially reduced portion of an otherwise unmanageable information universe and only after getting an idea of what they expect to find. The major disadvantage consists in the great amount of time and efforts archivists are supposed to invest in extensive, detailed, and potentially never-ending research into processes, communication patterns, organizational cultures, information systems, and the many other factors involved in the citizen-state interaction, which is their object of analysis (Bailey 1997). In fact, one may infer that the maturation of the archival profession and their growing accountability toward society, which Cook (2013) discusses in his later essay, stem from the knowledge, experience, and intellectual rigor that archivists have over time accumulated through exercises like the macro-appraisal one.

In line with the total archives proposition, Cook (1992a, 2004) suggested that Samuels's documentation strategy could usefully complement macro-appraisal by bringing private sector archives under the purview of the appraiser. He also posited that his approach could be adapted so as to be applicable to any organizational environment (Cook 1992b, 66). It should, however, be emphasized that Cook developed his approach having the appraisal of public records as his priority, and the National Archives of Canada de facto never used the macro-appraisal methodology for the acquisition of private records. It is only in the second half of the 1990s that archivists in Canada and anywhere else in the world start to be openly critical about the inherent bias (toward government records) of their institutional repositories. Despite the declared inclusiveness of some programs, "the 'place' of the personal archive in the collective archives"

(McKemmish 1996, 184) did not seem to be well understood, or at worst, was completely neglected by the professional literature, to the detriment of the practice of appraising and acquiring private records (see Pollard 2001). Turning now to the influence of German archivists on the appraisal discourse of the 1990s (including, as mentioned earlier, Cook's ideas) will help contextualize the discussion on the role of private archives in shaping memories and identities, a discussion that will fully unfold within the fourth paradigm.

Hans Booms, in particular, through an article written in 1972 that was translated into English only in 1987, opened archivists' eyes on the "societal significance of appraisal" and the responsibility they have in "the formation of the documentary heritage" through the act of appraisal, an act that "dictates what kind of cultural representation of society . . . will be handed down to future generations" (Boom 1987, 78). Booms's contribution to the "post-institutional" thinking about appraisal lies more in his reflections on the "connection . . . between societal values and archival standards" and the effects of the "ideological context" on such a connection (73) than in his methodological insights. Due to historical circumstances (Germany was at that time a politically and physically divided country) and perhaps also Booms's lack of procedural clarity, no implementation of both instantiations of his "documentation plan" (initially articulated in 1972 and then revised in his 1991–1992 article) produced the results he might have expected. However, his interpretation of the societal process and the components of his appraisal method deserve to be examined; they somehow anticipate the character of the paradigm that will be discussed in the next section.

Because "individuals . . . are unable to separate themselves from the socio-historical conditions of their existence," it follows that our behaviors and values are inescapably captive of the "dominant values of society" (Booms 1987, 74), whether we are aware of it or not. Reducing these values to those that emanate from the "institutional or formal public realm at the expense of the informal" (90) is, according to Booms, an unwarranted simplification. Booms's understanding of society and social dynamics was rooted in the *Annales* School of historiography. This was at opposite poles with most of his colleagues' ideas, which were based on an idealistic and state-centered view of history (in line with Hegel's philosophy and Marx's dialectical materialism). Booms was certainly reacting to their formalistic appraisal approaches relying on the analysis of government functions and hierarchical structures (see, e.g., Sante and Rohr), when he rejected the *Provenienzprinzip* as a suitable basis for appraisal—a position that he would later retract (Booms 1991–1992). Given the premise that "the sum of activities of government offices does not equal the sum of historical-political life" (Booms 1987, 100), Booms turned to the methods of the social sciences and the new social history trend, known as "history from the bottom up" (see Wingen and Bass 2008), as a way to get a comprehensive picture of the "societal process" (Booms 1987, 100). Eventually, he operationalized his view by means of "conceptual grids of history"—later reshaped into "chronicles of important dates" (Booms 1991–1992, 31)—which he envisaged to obtain by interrogating the "public opinion" of the time, that is, any available published sources through which the voice of the contemporaries to the events represented in the records could emerge (Booms 1987, 104). This approach would prevent archivists from applying today's values to material that was created in different sociohistorical circumstances. He also suggested that any documentation plans formed in this way should be "sanctioned by society at large" (107). As mentioned earlier, Booms's methodology did not succeed as intended. His principle of contemporary value as an objective standard for appraisal, in particular, was at odds with his belief that archivists cannot escape from being bound to the temper of their own times and soon revealed its limitations. However, his insight that society is something broader and richer than any representations that can possibly be derived from analyzing official institutions and that "all society should contribute to the development and implementation of methods for appraising the documentary heritage" (107) will get renewed attention as the twenty-first century approached.

Within the third archival paradigm, dominated by the notion of societal memory and identity formation, a large number of archivists continue to be concerned with the protection of the essential properties of records as evidence of transactions. Authors who align with the Jenkinsonian school and therefore reject appraisal as attribution of value tend to consent to appraisal for acquisition and selection as long as it respects "the internal functionality of the documents and the documents' aggregations" (Duranti 1994, 341), or in other words, as a tool that facilitates the transmission of evidence in a clear and transparent manner so that it can serve as foundation for future decision making (Menne-Haritz 1994).

Records scheduling as a prospective appraisal method (in the sense that it applies to records that are still in use by their creators, and it may be devised even before the actual records are created) is also primarily associated with evidence-based or legalistic considerations. Legal, fiscal, regulatory, and business requirements are the main needs that a records or retention schedule aims to satisfy, as an administrative mechanism supporting organizational accountability and operations. Societal or "community expectations" are part of the picture as well; however, they are mainly understood as the "rights and interests of all stakeholders" (ISO 2001, 11) that any decisions to create, keep, or destroy records should strive to respect.

The coming into force of privacy and freedom of information legislation, together with the advent of electronic recordkeeping, placed new demands on the records scheduling exercise. Some commentators have expressed doubts about the ability of these tools, which had been conceived for the paper world, to control the management of today's current records effectively. The effectiveness of an old-fashioned method such as records survey to develop the schedules had also been questioned (see Bailey 1999; Diers 1992; Frost 1991–1992). By the end of the 1990s, the functional approach, which had in the meantime become a pillar of archival methodology, had transformed traditional schedules into more sophisticated retention plans, usually integrated with function-based records classification systems (see Shepherd and Yeo 2003). The era of records management standards, which also started in the 1990s, placed retention and disposition, as well as deciding what to capture into a records system, at the core of recordkeeping. In line with the records continuum approach, which emphasizes the iterative and nonlinear nature of all archival functions, the international standard ISO 15489:2001-1 specifies that all assessments and decisions can be "made at any time in the existence of records, including during the design stage of records systems" (ISO 2001, 10). One of the characteristics of these standards is their business-driven approach. Records management is understood as a set of administrative techniques to help organizations contain costs, improve efficiency, and mitigate business risks. Appraisal, or records retention, is consequently described as a "consistent, systematic and logical" (Man 2005, 25) method to allow for the authorized and, where possible, "automatic" (ISO 2001, 10) disposal of records that the organization no longer needs for the accomplishment of its goals, the maintenance of its accountability, and the building of its "corporate memory" (28), the latter being conceptualized as an organizational knowledge base to inform decision making. Retaining evidence of business activities and ensuring that such evidence is created in the first place are the main goals of a robust recordkeeping system. It is important to acknowledge that the kind of evidence that records management standards and models advocate is now miles away from the non-interventional context in which Jenkinson conceived his idea of evidence. As Cook put it, these "ever more sophisticated and complex modernist techniques for evidence protection," which attest to the growing professionalization of records managers and archivists, "ultimately involved an imposition of the archivist's expertise on records, records creators, and records users" (2013, 111). By defining what a record is, in what format it should be saved, how long it should be kept in the creator's office or system, what functional contexts produce records worthy of retention, and other similar "impositions," the records professionals of the "identity paradigm," in collaboration with information technology (IT) specialists, constructed a new kind of "engineered evidence."

A brief excursus on the impact of computerization on the thinking around appraisal will confirm the trends highlighted previously. From the end of the 1970s and throughout the 1980s, machine-readable records were generally regarded as a different "species" of records. For this reason, Harold Naugler was tasked by UNESCO to write a "RAMP Study" for the appraisal of that specific kind of records. Naugler (1984) dealt with the issue as an information problem and came up with an extensive taxonomy of values that took into consideration the technical characteristics of the new medium (e.g., manipulability, readability, level of data aggregation) and a few legal factors (e.g., admissibility in court, copyright). In the 1990s, each and every project concerning electronic recordkeeping tried to demonstrate that, on the contrary, all records, independently of their medium or format, have a common nature. The appraisal of electronic records should not therefore be substantially different from that of paper records, except for the fact that with the former, archivists do not have the "luxury" of time. If storage space, and any correlated costs, apparently is no longer a problem—to the point that some authors have argued that "universal retention" (Bailey 2008, 100) might now be an option—"the volatile nature of computer records requires [placing] the appraisal decision at an early stage of the records' life cycle" (Duranti 1996, 499). Electronic records should also be reassessed periodically, as their properties may change over time, particularly when migrations or other processes for overcoming technological obsolescence occur. We have already seen that records scheduling may be used to enact some forms of preemptive and recurrent appraisal. However, research on appraisal in the digital world has shown that our current methods are inadequate to address some of the most pressing issues concerning the long-term preservation of the evidentiary quality of electronic records. The first iteration of the International Research on Permanent Authentic Records in Electronic Systems (InterPARES 1) Project produced a model for the "selection function" that highlighted how much contextual information about the records, including the technology employed to make them, should be captured, and then continuously monitored, in order to prepare the basis for an informed appraisal decision. Besides assessing value, the appraiser must "establish the grounds for the presumption of authenticity" (InterPARES 2001, 9) of the records, which involves highly specialized identity and integrity checks, and may influence the final disposition decision. The latter also depends on "feasibility" considerations. Can the "preserver" guarantee the appropriate preservation of the records (i.e., their digital components and metadata) that it decided to retain? This determination requires "knowledge of the preserver's current and anticipated capability" (10) to preserve the records (e.g., adequacy of IT equipment, staff expertise, financial resources). Finally, the project reaffirmed the importance of producing, maintaining, and providing access to detailed documentation concerning the decision-making process behind any appraisal decision.

Terry Eastwood, who was instrumental in the preparation of the InterPARES selection model, positioned himself in a particular line of thought in the heated debate on appraisal that characterizes the 1990s. Besides adhering to the organic theory of the archives, he also pragmatically acknowledged that "archives are utilitarian things," and as such, they "require utilitarian appraisal, that is, appraisal based ultimately but not exclusively on an assessment of use" (Eastwood 1992, 83). "Use," Eastwood (1993, 117) submits, is more concrete than "need" and provides a measurable expression of "value." The "need for evidence," typical of the archival approach, is different from a generic "need for information" and leaves empirical traces of use that should be tracked down, as they represent the memory-evidence of how we valued archives. This knowledge of past uses of archives should serve as the grounds on which the appraiser can make a prediction of their future usefulness. Although Eastwood recognized that "archivists are unavoidably participants in the process of documentary memory-making" (119), he did not go so far as to embrace the postmodernist understanding of archivists as interpreters and cocreators of archives (see Brothman 1991; Cook 2004; Harris 1998). Preserving the integrity of the body of records entrusted to their custody should remain their highest goal. At the same time, providing citizens with well-documented appraisal decisions is of the essence in order to enable them to participate in and scrutinize those decisions so that they can eventually trust the process and its outcome. "Appraisal of archival documents in a democratic society must somehow serve the need of citizens to know how they have ruled themselves" (Eastwood 2002, 66).

Ensuring that collective memory making is a rational and accountable process is Eastwood's answer to the cry for social justice that characterizes the appraisal discourse of this third paradigm from both an intellectual and a practical standpoint. Verne Harris is among the authors who have most vividly illustrated why we should *not* trust the appraiser, especially, but not exclusively, when the "sliver of the documentary record" (Harris 2002a, 64) that constitutes any archives is "constructed" under regimes that openly violate human rights. Following Jacques Derrida's critique of the archive, but also his own reflections as a practitioner archivist who experienced South Africa's transition from apartheid to democracy, Harris unveiled the power that archivists wield when they decide "which stories will be consigned to the archive and which will not." As this power "is ultimately a political power," democratic societies must find "ways of holding archivists accountable for their appraisal decisions" (Harris 1998, 50). This, however, does not affect the basic consideration that the past is continuously reconstructed, and the "political act" of appraisal adds a "very substantial layer of construction" (49). We should, in other words, be mindful that "beyond the dynamics of remembering and forgetting, a more profound characterization of the struggle in social memory is one of narrative against narrative, story against story" (Harris 2002b, 205).

From the awareness of multiple narratives and of the political dimension of appraisal that postmodernist thinkers injected in the archival consciousness, new interpretations of documenting who we are, the role of archivists in society, archival accountability, and archiving beyond and independently of the institution have emerged and continue to evolve in the first decades of our century.

APPRAISAL IN THE COMMUNITY PARADIGM

In his analysis of the evolution of archivists' behaviors, values, and (self-representations), Cook glimpses a new paradigm that has begun to emerge in the early twenty-first century in our Western world, partly thanks to the affordances offered by the Internet. "Archivists ... have the exciting prospect of being able to document human and societal experience with a richness and relevance never before attainable" (Cook 2013, 113). Contemporary telecommunication technologies have also contributed to shift the focus from the bureaucratic and official to the individual and private dimensions of life. In the previous paradigms, the appraiser was still firmly embedded in some formal context and even when attempting to document society, would in fact act on behalf of his or her institution. Today, archiving has become a ubiquitous, pervasive phenomenon, where "every person [is] his or her publisher, author, photographer, film-maker, music-recording artist, ... archivist" (113)—and appraiser, we may add. At the center of this new framework, Cook places the notion of "community" as both an actual and a virtual entity, in which evidence, memory, and identity coalesce in particular, distinctive ways, not necessarily aligned with the "orthodox historical narratives" (Flinn and Stevens 2009, 4) created by traditional power structures.

Archivists dealing with materials from private corporations, families, and individuals have always been concerned with "unorthodox," non-mainstream issues, whether they worked for government institutions, local communities, or independent grassroots organizations; however, their experiences have hardly been reported (see Craig 2004, 157). Consideration of appraisal for private archives has for long been neglected by the literature compared to that for public records (Fisher 2009). Only in the past two decades, one may find theoretical reflections on the nature of personal records and personal recordkeeping, spanning from their assimilation to business records and relevant recordkeeping models to recognition of the specific "personality" (Hobbs 2001, 134) and idiosyncratic processing of the records created and maintained by individuals in their private capacity.[6] The roles played by symbolic, emotional, and other subconscious values in our choices to keep or purge our documentary traces (see Craig 2004, 7–12; Hobbs 2001, 2010) as well as the "intimacy" (Hobbs 2001, 127) that may develop in the relationship between donors and archivists are just a few aspects of appraisal and acquisition characterizing the private sphere. The analysis of actual appraisal and acquisition practices has helped demystify certain assumptions concerning, for instance, the effectiveness of "proactive acquisition" (Fisher 2015, 105) and collection planning. However, as Fisher warns us, we are still far from fully understanding what actually goes on in the "negotiated, perhaps even contested, ground" (2015, 118) where the appraisal of private records takes place.

While in the third paradigm, archivists were primarily concerned with their own professional identity and strove to build quasi-scientific models and systems meant to support concerted actions and try to contain the uncontrollable factors of life, the "community paradigm" acknowledges the "agency" of the others (i.e., "creators, stewards, and donors") (Fisher 2015, 109) and is wary of any attempts to rationalize the acquisition of private collections within or among institutions. Private fonds have traditionally been sought after and acquired only when their cultural or "heritage value" (Fisher 2009, 23) was evident (i.e., when the archivist could vouch for some form of subsequent use of the records) and/or "the materials pursued [fell] within the collecting policy and scope of the institution" (Pollard 2001, 143). The "institutional filter," made of deliberate and systematic acquisition or collection policies and strategies and including all the "logistical aspects of carrying [them] out" (143), did not allow a truly representative image of society to arise. Even within the more inclusive approaches, such as macro-appraisal, the citizens' activities that had no interaction with the government would not fall under the appraiser's radar.

In order to extend the representativeness of their collections, archivists would look for documentary gaps, missing traces, or "archival silences" (Carter 2006) and would try to remedy them, for instance, by resorting to some documentation strategy exercise. [7] Within today's paradigm, there is growing recognition that "not everyone wishes to be heard" (226) and that removing evidence, memory, and identity from the originating communities can be "problematic and undesirable for several reasons" (Cook 2013, 13). By "appropriat[ing] the histories of marginalized communities," the "active documenters" of the second half of the twentieth century "creat[ed] archives *about* rather than *of* the communities" (Shilton and Srinivasan 2007, 89; italics in original). By "seeking to balance the record, to incorporate authentic voices, to resolve the problem of the underdocumented, or even, sometimes, to celebrate diversity, [they] reif[ied] identity, thereby making cultural differences immutable" (Kaplan 2000, 148). How can this tendency be corrected? "Participatory appraisal" where "archival activism" does not occur "on behalf of groups ... but alongside groups" (Shilton and Srinivasan 2007, 92) is one answer. In this form of "immersive collaboration," archivists take on the role of "mentors, facilitators, coaches" (Cook 2013, 114) and work together with the communities of records creators through, for instance, teaching them methods for assessing the materials they hold. In this way, the communities are able to decide autonomously what best represents what they are. At the same time, archival professionals learn something very precious and essential to a successful appraisal process, that is, "the value of particular narratives and records to a community" (Shilton and Srinivasan 2007, 93)—an approach that resonates with Booms's suggestion that one should appraise according to values that are "contemporary" to the creators of the records. "Participatory archiving," Shilton and Srinivasan conclude, "asks that [all] choices be made explicit and transparent, . . . to let the creator own the choices they have made, ensuring that they speak with their own voices, and empowering their representations into the future" (2007, 101).

A new, more transparent notion of accountability can be distinguished within the emerging paradigm. "The challenge," Cook summarizes, "is to achieve a more democratic, inclusive, holistic archives, collectively, listening much more to citizens than the state, as well as respecting indigenous ways of knowing, evidence and memory, than occurred in the first three paradigms" (2013, 116). Are the state, the institution, and the citizen, the people, necessarily irreconcilable opposites? Some authors argue that even mainstream institutions, usually portrayed as impersonal sites of bureaucratic production, could be reimagined and made the subject of introspective analyses. Rather than appraising institutions for what they "*do*," from a distant, top-down perspective, archivists should try to understand what institutions "*mean*" to those who inhabit them (Hughes 2014, 281; italics in original). In line with the bottom-up approach of social history, cultural studies scholars invite archivists to stop "think[ing] of institutions as monoliths where all productive and relevant activity is devoted solely to achieving the aims of the institution" and start "documenting institutional culture" (Hughes 2014, 281–82). One such scholar, Kit Hughes, suggests "mapmaking" as a "multiperspectival" method that would allow the "everyday experience . . . of those fulfilling the functions of the organization [emerge] as a significant part of the appraisal process" (2014, 283). We should not forget that institutions are communities too, and as such, they are shaped by multiple, local microcultures and social practices, as much as they embody mandates, functions, and other legally defined contexts.[8]

Putting communities and people at the center is the hallmark of the archival paradigm in which we are immersed. The "cyberspace [as well] is not about geography and national borders. It is about communities" (Werf and Werf 2014). The amount of digital materials that we all accumulate on the Web, and that may potentially become part of our digital heritage, is simply too huge, too dynamic, and too fragmented for any of our existing memory institutions to acquire. Cook envisages the creation of "a virtual, inclusive, 'total' archive for a country, province or state, or similar jurisdiction, one held by many archives and libraries, including community archives, but unified in conception and comprehensiveness" (2013, 115). However, for his vision to become reality, established institutions must count on individuals' awareness of their digital footprint and on their commitment to identify and actively select what should be preserved for future generations. Basically, rather than delegating the appraisal function to experts, each of us should be enabled to "filter" our own digital products and by-products (Mayer-Schoenberger 2009; Werf and Werf 2014).[9]

In line with the main features characterizing the fourth paradigm, the digital preservation literature, which is obviously dominated by technological considerations, has lately started to recognize the need to include "people-centric" perspectives in its "data-centric" models in order to "address properties that are important for maintaining meaning over time" (Faniel and Yakel 2011, 159). This is to say that any assessment of which digital objects, metadata, or "significant properties" must be the focus of our preservation efforts should be regarded as an appraisal decision and as such cannot eschew some human judgment. The field of digital preservation is tightly linked to ideas of authenticity and integrity that resonate with the Jenkinsonian view of evidence (Cook's first paradigm) and that involve micro-level analyses of the records' digital components. This may suggest that in the future, archivists might more and more be concerned with devising strategies for the appraisal of metadata and other kinds of information at a level lower than the record. In general, however, the current landscape seems to be split between those who believe that archival appraisal methods must be integrated in digital preservation and curation practices (Harvey 2007) and authors who deny the need for appraisal in the digital age altogether. The latter stress that "keeping everything better supports new research modes and enfranchises a greater diversity of user groups and uses" (Gilliland 2014, 54). Methods such as "visualization" have been advocated to aid in making sense of large digital collections (Xu, Esteva, and Dott 2010).

The archival paradigm characterizing our time is still evolving and defining itself. It seems, however, that an emphasis on participation, local practices, the inclusion of multiple narratives, and above all, the dimension of keeping records as "human remains" (Kirk and Sellen 2010) has fostered a bottom-up perspective that, initially, the volume of modern information appeared to deny but that might in fact be supported thanks to the capabilities of today's technologies.

CONCLUSION

Reviewing how archival appraisal has been articulated through time by means of Cook's four shifting paradigms has revealed discontinuities and variations, persistence and continuities. The fact that, in a little more than a century, archivists could not come up with a broadly shared, unified theory of appraisal should not be a disappointing finding. Appraisal is indeed like "mapmaking": a single terrain can be mapped in "infinite ways," and every map we create by selecting this or that element "has a distinct agenda and purpose" and "positions its user in a unique relationship with its various elements" (Hughes 2014, 282). It is important to be aware of the possible consequences of choosing the legalistic approach rather than—or together with—the memory-based one, of setting as the goal of appraisal identity building as a societal function rather than—or together with—the empowerment of individual communities. Awareness of the archival frameworks in which archivists operate should have a "liberating" effect, not a paralyzing one. Instead of defending one single view, we should feel authorized to take all the knowledge we have accumulated about ourselves and our methods as well as about records and archives institutions, society, and individuals. Only in this way, we will be able to "develop new directions" (Cook 2013, 117) as a community.

ENDNOTES

1. By examining the archiving practices of old Dutch, English, and German families and cities, Eric Ketelaar (2007) demonstrates that besides using records as "muniments" for the defense of their rights and privileges, private individuals have been keeping records as "monuments" to celebrate themselves and their power, or simply as cherished treasures, from as early as the seventeenth century. This is confirmed by Cook when he suggests that "in reality, archives long before 1789 were themselves hardly a legal-juridical enclave jealously guarding evidence" (2013, 102).

2. I am here referring to the distinction made by Italian archivist Isabella Zanni Rosiello (1987) between "self-documentation-memory" (*memoria-autodocumentazione*), characterizing the initial archival impulse linked to the need to preserve evidence of titles of authority, property, rights, and obligations, and "source-memory" (*memoria-fonte*), as a more recent, cultural view of the archives that emerged with the establishment of the first national archives in Europe between the end of the eighteenth and the beginning of the nineteenth century. In my opinion, the most interesting aspect of Zanni Rosiello's terminology is that the notion of "memory" is included in both expressions so as to suggest that even when records were exclusively used for administrative-political purposes, they already had some inherent cultural-historical potential.

3. This broad distinction into two main schools of thought—one which may be called "idealistic" and the other one, "pragmatic" school—reflects the different origins of archival institutions in the old and the new world. Adrian Cunningham (2005) reminds us that archival institutions in Europe were initially established for legal and administrative purposes, while in North America and in Australia, they had no such legitimacy. Thus, the development of a "collecting tradition" was natural in the latter group of countries, while the former had permanently to justify their cultural-historical role in the face of their sanctioned juridical role.

4. Cook borrows the notion of an "imagined community" from political scientist Benedict Anderson, who described it as the shared sense of belonging that holds together the citizens of a nation. Despite the fact that the members of a nation will never meet most of their fellow members, despite the differences and inequalities among them, "yet in the minds of each lives the image of their communion" (quoted in Cook 2013, 98). Anderson's idea can also be extended to the members of smaller communities. Cook applies it to the professional community of archivists, which should be understood as a historical phenomenon in part, but still having an "emotional legitimacy" in the present (98).

5. The National Archives of Canada's document, "Appraisal Methodology: Macro-Appraisal and Functional Analysis. Part B: Guidelines for Performing an Archival Appraisal on Government Records" (NA 2001), written by Terry Cook in 2001, offers a detailed, step-by-step description of the methodology, including some of the questions that may be asked during the research phase of macro-appraisal. This phase requires thorough investigations into administrative structures, business processes, information systems, and the records themselves in order to gain an understanding (which will always be partial and biased) of the nature and the *loci* of citizens' interactions with the state, which would in turn allow establishing the significance of the record creators under examination. For a detailed description of the suite of National Archives' documents that formed the basis for government records appraisal in Canada from 2001 onward, see C. Bailey (2006).

6. Australian archivist Sue McKemmish is among the first authors who felt the need to fill the personal recordkeeping gap in the archival literature. Her (1996) article, in which she tried to demonstrate that "evidence of me" could be captured and interpreted through the same models used for government recordkeeping, raised a heated debate within the archival community in the late 1990s to early 2000s (see Cunningham 1996; Harris 2001; Hobbs 2001; McKemmish and Upward 2001).

7. The notion of a "gap" in the archives and that of "silence" may only partly coincide. Missing or dispersed documentation often is the result of the complex, meandering ways in which records are created, handed over, and cared for. Legal and illegal destructions, intentional and unintended losses, floods, fires, wars, and the like cause absences in the archives that may be revealing of significant events, besides offering insights into the pre-custodial and custodial histories of the records. Silences, instead, refer to the lack of information about certain events, groups of people, and aspects of life that the record did not capture because of the purposes for which it was created. Identifying silences may provide hints about the political, economic, and sociocultural circumstances in which the records were created.

8. According to Hughes, "The top-down nature of functional analysis—and by association, macro-appraisal—assumes that individual records creators are relevant to the appraisal process insomuch as they are vessels that carry out and institution's key aims and functions" (2014, 283). If "Cook ... may [have] overly rationalize[d] organizational activities due to a desire to rationalize the system of appraisal itself" (284), such tendency had been emphasized even further in the PIVOT project. The "Project for the Implementation of the Reduction of the Transfer Period" (PIVOT in Dutch), which was launched in the Netherlands in the early 1990s, was based on a macro-appraisal methodology that explicitly embraced a notion of bureaucracy as a system "rationally controlled by laws, regulations, procedures," rather than a "social system ... with its own unwritten laws ... [and self-]defined goals" (Horsman 1997, 41; see also, Hol 1996).

9. Internet expert Viktor Mayer-Schoenberger (2009) has written about the unintended consequences of digital technology, highlighting that it is preventing society from forgetting, as nothing is ever really erased in cyberspace. While forgetting has traditionally been easier than remembering, and the ability to recall only that which was considered important allowed human beings to survive and advance, in the digital age, forgetting has become the exception and remembering the default.

REFERENCES

Bailey, Catherine. 1997. "From the Top Down: The Practice of Macro-Appraisal." *Archivaria* 43 (Spring): 89–128.

Bailey, Catherine. 2006. "Turning Macro-aAppraisal Decisions into Archival Holdings: Crafting Function-Based Terms and Conditions for the Transfer of Archival Records." *Archivaria* 61 (Spring): 147–79.

Bailey, Stephen. 1999. "The Metadatabase: The Future of the Retention Schedule as a Records Management Tool." *Records Management Journal* 9 (1): 33–45.

Bailey, Stephen. 2008. *Managing the Crowd: Rethinking Records Management for the Web 2.0 World*. London: Facet Publishing.

Bearman, David. 1989. "Archival Methods." *Archives and Museum Informatics Technical Report* 9. Pittsburgh, PA: Archives and Museum Informatics.

Boles, Frank, and Julia Marks Young. 1985. "Exploring the Black Box: The Appraisal of University Administrative Records." *The American Archivist* 48 (April): 121–40.

Booms, Hans. 1987. "Society and the Formation of the Documentary Heritage: Issues in the Appraisal of Archival Sources." *Archivaria* 24 (Summer): 69–107.

Booms, Hans. 1991–1992. "Uberlieferungsbildung: Keeping Archives as a Social and Political Activity." *Archivaria* 33 (Winter): 25–33.

Brichford, Maynard J. 1977. *Archives and Manuscripts: Appraisal and Accessioning*. Chicago, IL: Society of American Archivists.

Brooks, Phillip C. 1940. "The Selection of Records for Preservation." *The American Archivist* 3 (October): 221–34.

Brooks, Phillip C. 1948. "Archival Procedures for Planned Records Retirement." *The American Archivist* 11 (October): 308–15.

Brothman, Brian. 1991. "Orders of Values: Probing the Theoretical Terms of Archival Practice." *Archivaria* 32 (Summer): 78–100.

Carter, Rodney G. S. 2006. "Of Things Said and Unsaid: Power, Archival Silences, and Power in Silence." *Archivaria* 61 (Spring): 215–33.

Cook, Terry. 1992a. "Documentation Strategy." *Archivaria* 34 (Summer): 181–91.

Cook, Terry. 1992b. "Mind over Matter: Towards a New Theory of Archival Appraisal." In *The Archival Imagination: Essays in Honour of Hugh A. Taylor*, edited by Barbara L. Craig, 38–70. Ottawa: Association of Canadian Archivists.

Cook, Terry. 2004. "Macro Appraisal and Functional Analysis: Documenting Governance rather than Government." *Journal of the Society of Archivists* 25 (Spring): 5–18.

Cook, Terry, ed. 2011. *Controlling the Past: Documenting Society and Institutions*. Chicago, IL: Society of American Archivists.

Cook, Terry. 2013. "Evidence, Memory, Identity, and Community: Four Shifting Archival Paradigms." *Archival Science* 13 (2): 95–120.

Cox, Richard. 1994. "The Documentation Strategy and Archival Appraisal Principles: A Different Perspective." *Archivaria* 38 (Fall): 11–36.

Craig, Barbara L. 2004. *Archival Appraisal: Theory and Practice*. Munich, Germany: Saur Verlag.

Cunningham, Adrian. 1996. "Beyond the Pale? The 'Flinty' Relationship between Archivists Who Collect the Private Records of Individuals and the Rest of the Archival Profession." *Archives and Manuscripts* 24 (May): 20–26.

Cunningham, Adrian. 2005. "Archival Institutions." In *Archives: Recordkeeping in Society*, edited by Sue McKemmish, Michael Piggott, Barbara Reed, and Frank Upward, 21–50. Wagga Wagga, New South Wales: Centre for Information Studies, Charles Sturt University.

Diers, Fred V. 1992. "The Bankruptcy of the Records Retention Schedule." *Records Management Quarterly* 26 (April): 3–10.

Duranti, Luciana. 1994. "The Concept of Appraisal and Archival Theory." *The American Archivist* 57 (Spring): 328–45.

Duranti, Luciana. 1996. "The Thinking on Appraisal of Electronic Records: Its Evolution, Focuses, and Future Directions." *Archivi e Computer* 6: 493–518.

Eastwood, Terry. 1992. "Towards a Social Theory of Appraisal." In *The Archival Imagination: Essays in Honour of Hugh A. Taylor*, edited by Barbara L. Craig, 71–89. Ottawa: Association of Canadian Archivists.

Eastwood, Terry. 1993. "How Goes It with Appraisal?" *Archivaria* 36 (Autumn): 111–21.

Eastwood, Terry. 2002. "Reflections on the Goal of Appraisal in Democratic Societies." *Archivaria* 54 (Fall): 59–71.

Elliott, Clark A., ed. 1983. *Understanding Progress as Process: Documentation of the History of Post-War Science and Technology in the United States: Final Report of the Joint Committee on Archives of Science and Technology* (a.k.a. *JCAST Report*). Chicago, IL: Society of American Archivists.

Faniel, Ixchel M., and Elizabeth Yakel. 2011. "Significant Properties as Contextual Metadata." *Journal of Library Metadata* 11 (3–4): 155–65.

Fisher, Rob. 2009. "In Search of a Theory of Private Archives: The Foundational Writings of Jenkinson and Schellenberg Revisited." *Archivaria* 67 (Spring): 1–24.

Fisher, Rob. 2015 "Donors and Donor Agency: Implications for Private Archives Theory and Practice." *Archivaria* 79 (Spring): 91–119.

Flinn, Andrew, and Mary Stevens. 2009. " 'It Is Noh Mistri, Wi Mekin Histri.' Telling Our Own Story: Independent and Community Archives in the UK, Challenging and Subverting the Mainstream." In *Community Archives: The Shaping of Memory*, edited by Jeannette Bastian and Ben Alexander, 3–27. London: Facet Publishing.

Frost, Eldon. 1991–1992. "A Weak Link in the Chain: Records Scheduling as a Source of Archival Acquisition." *Archivaria* 33 (Winter): 78–86.

Gilliland, Anne. 2014. "Archival Appraisal: Practising on Shifting Sands." In *Archives and Recordkeeping: Theory into Practice*, edited by Caroline Brown, 31–63. London: Facet Publishing.

Great Britain. 1954. *Committee on Departmental Records Report*. Parliament, Cmnd. 9163. London: Her Majesty's Stationary Office.

Haas, Joan K., Helen W. Samuels, and Barbara Trippel Simmons. 1985. *Appraising the Records of Modern Science and Technology: A Guide*. Cambridge: Massachusetts Institute of Technology.

Ham, Gerald F. 1975. "The Archival Edge." *The American Archivist* 38 (January): 5–13.

Harris, Verne. 1998. "Postmodernism and Archival Appraisal: Seven Theses." *South African Archives Journal* 40: 48–50.

Harris, Verne. 2001. "On the Back of a Tiger: Deconstructive Possibilities in 'Evidence of Me.' " *Archives and Manuscripts* 29 (May): 8–22.

Harris, Verne. 2002a. "The Archival Sliver: Power, Memory, and Archives in South Africa." *Archival Science* 2 (1–2): 63–86.

Harris, Verne. 2002b. " 'They Should Have Destroyed More.' The Destruction of Public Records by the South African State in the Final Years of Apartheid, 1990–1994." In *Archives and the Public Good: Accountability and Records in Modern Society*, edited by Richard Cox and David Wallace, 205–28. Westport, CT, and London: Quorum Books.

Harvey, Ross. 2007. "Installment on 'Appraisal and Selection.' " In *DCC Digital Curation Manual*, edited by Seamus Ross and Michael Day. HATII, University of Glasgow; University of Edinburgh; UKOLN, University of Bath; Council for the Central Laboratory of the Research Councils: Digital Curation Centre. http://www.dcc.ac.uk/resource/curation-manual/chapters/appraisal-and-selection (last accessed January 26, 2016).

Hobbs, Catherine. 2001. "The Character of Personal Archives: Reflections on the Value of Records of Individuals." *Archivaria* 52 (Fall): 126–35.

Hobbs, Catherine. 2010. "Reenvisioning the Personal: Reframing Traces of Individual Life." In *Currents of Archival Thinking*, edited by Terry Eastwood and Heather MacNeil, 214–22. Santa Barbara, CA: Libraries Unlimited.

Hofstede, Geert. 2001. *Culture's Consequences. Comparing Values, Behaviors, Institutions, and Organizations across Nations*. Thousand Oaks, CA: Sage Publications.

Hol, Roelof C. 1996. "PIVOT's Appraisal of Modern Records: A 'Floody' Tale from the Dutch Experience." *South African Archives Journal* 38: 5–15.

Horsman, Peter. 1997. "Appraisal on Wooden Shoes. The Netherlands PIVOT Project." *Janus* 2: 35–41.

Horsman, Peter. 2002. "The Last Dance of the Phoenix, or the Re-Discovery of the Archival Fonds." *Archivaria* 54 (Fall): 1–23.

Hughes, Kit. 2014. "Appraisal as Cartography: Cultural Studies in the Archives." *The American Archivist* 77 (Spring–Summer): 270–96.

International Organization for Standardization (ISO). 2001. *ISO 15489-1:2001 Information and Documentation—Records Management. Part 1: General*. Geneva, Switzerland: ISO.

InterPARES Project. 2001. "Appraisal Task Force Final Report." http://www.interpares.org/book/interpares_book_e_part2.pdf (last accessed January 26, 2016).

Jenkinson, Hilary. 1966. *A Manual of Archive Administration*. London: Percy Lund, Humphries & Co.

Jenkinson, Hilary. 1980. "Modern Archives: Some Reflections on T.R. Schellenberg: Modern Archives: Principles and Techniques." In *Selected Writings of Sir Hilary Jenkinson*, edited by Roger H. Ellis and Peter Walne, 338–42. Gloucester, England: Alan Sutton Publishing Ltd.

Kaplan, Elizabeth. 2000. "We Are What We Collect, We Collect What We Are: Archives and the Construction of Identity." *The American Archivist* 63 (Spring–Summer): 126–51.

Ketelaar, Eric. 2007. "Muniments and Monuments: The Dawn of Archives as Cultural Patrimony." *Archival Science* 7 (4): 343–57.

Kirk, David S., and Abigall Sellen. 2010. "On Human Remains: Values and Practice in the Home Archiving of Cherished Objects." *ACM Transactions on Computer-Human Interaction* 17 (July): 1–43.

Kolsrud, Ole. 1992. "The Evolution of Basic Appraisal Principles: Some Comparative Observations." *The American Archivist* 55 (Winter): 26–39.

Man, Elizabeth. 2005. "A Functional Approach to Appraisal and Retention Scheduling." *Records Management Journal* 15 (1): 21–33.

Mayer-Schoenberger, Viktor. 2009. *Delete: The Virtue of Forgetting in the Digital Age*. Princeton, NJ: Princeton University Press.

McKemmish, Sue. 1996. "Evidence of Me." *Archives and Manuscripts* 24 (May): 28–45. Reprint, *The Australian Library Journal* (August): 174–87.

McKemmish, Sue, and Frank Upward. 2001. "In Search of the Lost Tiger, by Way of Sainte-Beuve: Re-constructing the Possibilities in 'Evidence of Me.' " *Archives and Manuscripts* 29 (May): 23–43.

Menne-Haritz, Angelika. 1994. "Appraisal or Documentation: Can We Appraise Archives by Selecting Content." *The American Archivist* 57 (Summer): 528–42.

Millar, Laura. 1998. "Discharging Our Debt: The Evolution of the Total Archives Concept in English Canada." *Archivaria* 46 (Fall): 103–46.

National Archives of Canada (NA). 2001. "Appraisal Methodology: Macro-Appraisal and Functional Analysis. Part B: Guidelines for Performing an Archival Appraisal on Government Records." http://www.bac-lac.gc.ca/eng/services/government-information-resources/disposition/records-appraisal-disposition-program/Pages/appraisal-methodology-part-b-guidelines.aspx (last accessed January 26, 2016).

Naugler, Harold. 1984. *The Archival Appraisal of Machine-Readable Records: A RAMP Study with Guidelines*. Paris: UNESCO.

Pollard, Riva A. 2001. "The Appraisal of Personal Papers: A Critical Literature Review." *Archivaria* 52 (Fall): 136–50.

Samuels, Helen W. 1986. "Who Controls the Past." *The American Archivist* 49 (Spring): 109–24.

Samuels, Helen W. 1991–1992. "Improving Our Disposition: Documentation Strategy." *Archivaria* 33 (Winter): 125–40.

Samuels, Helen W. 1992. *Varsity Letters: Documenting Modern Colleges and Universities*. Metuchen, NJ: Society of American Archivists and Scarecrow Press.

Schellenberg, Theodore R. 1956. *Modern Archives: Principles and Techniques*. Chicago, IL: University of Chicago Press.

Schellenberg, Theodore R. 1984. "The Appraisal of Modern Public Records." In *A Modern Archives Reader: Basic Readings on Archival Theory and Practice*, edited by Maygene F. Daniels and Timothy Walch, 57–70. Washington, D.C.: National Archives and Records Service.

Shepherd, Elizabeth, and Geoffrey Yeo. 2003. *Managing Records: A Handbook of Principles and Practice*. London: Facet Publishing.

Shilton, Katie, and Ramesh Srinivasan. 2007. "Participatory Appraisal and Arrangement for Multicultural Archival Collections." *Archivaria* 63 (Spring): 87–101.

Trace, Ciaran B. 2010. "On or Off the Record? Notions of Value in the Archive." In *Currents of Archival Thinking*, edited by Terry Eastwood and Heather MacNeil, 47–68. Santa Barbara, CA: Libraries Unlimited.

Werf, Titia (van der), and Bram van der Werf. 2014. "The Paradox of Selection in the Digital Age." Paper presented at the International Federation of Library Associations and Institutions (IFLA) World Library and Information Congress (WLIC), Lyon, August. IFLA Library. http://library.ifla.org/1042/1/138-vanderwerf-en.pdf (last accessed January 26, 2016).

Wingen, Melissa (van), and Abigail Bass. 2008. "Reappraising Archival Practice in Light of New Social History." *Library Hi Tech* 26 (4): 575–85.

Xu, Weijia, Maria Esteva, and Suyog Jain Dott. 2010, May. "Visualization for Archival Appraisal of Large Digital Collections." In *Proceedings of Archiving 2010. Preservation Strategies and Imaging Technologies for Cultural Heritage Institutions and Memory Organizations*, 157–62. The Netherlands: imaging.org.

Zanni Rosiello, Isabella. 1987. *Archivi e Memoria Storica*. Bologna, Italy: Il Mulino.

6

Digital Preservation: From Possible to Practical

Glenn Dingwall

Although analog methods of records creation are still thriving, when considered relative to the rate of creation of digital records, a trend quickly emerges. Most of the analog records that will be created in the course of human history have already been created. The implication for archives is that, within a generation, the overwhelming majority of the records they acquire will be digital. With this in mind, the most urgent task for the current generation of archivists is to develop digital preservation capacity at both the institutional and personal level. There is perhaps some comfort to be taken in the recognition that while this issue is colossal in both size and importance, archivists have been addressing it in some manner for at least the past 40 years, and it has been recognized by those educating archivists as "the most pressing concern in equipping individuals to function as archivists" since the 1990s (Cox 2010, 180). This is of particular importance to those archivists who are just beginning their careers, as knowledge of the skills, problems, and issues specific to the digital preservation landscape is no longer seen by employers as a specialized knowledge but part of the expected competencies of archival professionals.[1]

Although archivists have long been aware of the disruptive effect that the proliferation of digital information objects would have on institutions and the profession, it is only within the past decade or so that the capacity to do something about the unique problems associated with the preservation of digital records has been realizable for the majority of archivists not working in the archives of major governments or research institutions. Previous generations of archivists were successfully able to delineate the fundamental challenges posed by the digital environment, address the problems of digital preservation within the framework of archival theory, and extend existing theory and develop new theory to address novel situations. However, absent the tools, community support networks, and interdisciplinary collaboration that have emerged since the start of the century, sustainable digital preservation programs were simply not achievable for most archives. Happily, this is no longer the case.

DIGITAL PRESERVATION—THE EARLY YEARS

Digital preservation, necessarily, does not appear as a discipline until the introduction of computers and digital technology to society after World War II. The use of computers by government and businesses became increasingly common in the 1960s, and it is then that archivists began to have their first contact with the digital environment. Meyer Fishbein identifies 1960 as the year when the U.S. National Archives and Records Service (NARS) began to investigate "the problems relating to the disposition of data in machine language form" (Fishbein 1972, 37). Similarly, Catherine Bailey identifies the late 1960s as the time when archivists first became concerned with the preservation of digital information in digital form. Prior to then, digital information was perceived as being essentially transitory in nature; the paper documents generated from the information in those systems were viewed as being the true archival record. The precedent for this predates digital technology; it first appears in the NARS treatment of data on punched cards in the 1930s (Fishbein 1972, 36). Archivists at the Public Archives of Canada had similar reservations about the status of computer data and records, particularly in cases where their content was available elsewhere in human readable form (Baldwin 2006, 175–77). Archivists of that era eventually reached the conclusion that computer records were not necessarily transitory, but that they could in fact be distinct records in themselves, which led them to undertake investigations as to how to preserve digital information (Bailey 1989–1990, 181). This period, according to Terry Cook, is when the first generation of archivists interested in digital preservation appeared. This first generation was concerned with the immediate conceptual and technical problems introduced by what were called at the time "machine readable records." Their approaches were influenced by the types of objects they sought to preserve, typically financial, statistical and similar data, usually tabulated into large, flat-file data structures (Cook 1991–1992, 203–04).

A second generation of digital archivists appeared in the late 1980s (Cook 1991–1992, 208).[2] This was a time when desktop computing began to infiltrate office environments. The information objects produced by desktop computers—so called unstructured records[3]—were similar in form and function to familiar paper record types and often existed in parallel with paper recordkeeping systems. Building upon the work of their predecessors, this generation moved beyond the consideration of the preservation of simpler types of digital objects that often existed in isolated or unique contexts, to investigate digital objects that were more integrated into recordkeeping systems and the subsequent relationships of these systems to archival systems (Cook 1991–1992, 205–06). Archivists of this generation attempted to establish the implications of the properties of electronic records and recordkeeping systems on the larger body of archival theory. Debate arose as to whether electronic records were merely another form of record, the preservation of which could be addressed with minor adaptions to existing archival theory on appraisal, arrangement, and description, or whether they were a sufficiently distinct class of object to necessitate a separate body of theory (Bailey 1989–1990, 180–81).

By the late 1990s, a number of significant research projects emerged that sought to investigate problems related to preserving electronic records. Whereas the first generation of digital archivists were primarily concerned with matters related to the preservation of the electronic record singular, the research interests of these projects were of broader scope, examining not only the nature of the record itself but also the types of systems used for creating, maintaining, and using records. Notable among these were the University of Pittsburgh Electronic Records Project (1993–1996) and the two projects based at the University of British Columbia (UBC): Preservation of the Integrity of Electronic Records (1994–1997) and its intellectual successor, InterPARES (1998–2001).[4] The Pittsburgh and UBC projects differed in their theoretical foundation and overall approaches. The UBC project was grounded in a life cycle-based custodial approach wherein records were formally created through registration in a recordkeeping system, whereas the Pittsburgh project was grounded in a continuum-based post-custodial approach that used the transmission of the record as the point of its creation. Looking retrospectively at the two projects, David Bearman suggests that despite the differences in the methodological approaches of the two projects, there was considerable agreement in their overall conclusions—namely the role of metadata[5] in preservation and the need to create a persistent link between the record and its metadata, that records should be preserved under archival control (though, in the case of the Pittsburgh findings, this need not be an archival institution), and that the trustworthiness of the record depended on having trusted recordkeeping systems and authorities (Bearman 2006, 18–19). The research undertaken by these projects and others[6] in the 1990s was very important for developing awareness among archivists of the kinds of challenges posed by digital preservation and the enormous scale of these challenges. Their research products were useful for providing guidance on how to create records that would be preservable and systems that would be capable of generating and maintaining preservable records. However, it is fair comment to say that relatively few examples exist of findings from these projects being directly applied to practical digital preservation implementations.

WHAT IS DIGITAL PRESERVATION?

The question that should be addressed in more detail before continuing is: "what is digital preservation?" Within the context of archives, preservation is understood to mean the prevention or minimization of damage to an information object, particularly the damage that would otherwise result in the loss of information from the object (Pearce-Moses 2005, 304–05). The goal of preservation is to allow the communication of information into the future in a way that it remains accessible and usable. For records to be preserved, it is also important that future users of the records have confidence in the reliability[7] and authenticity[8] of the records or at least have the ability to assess these attributes of the records. The reliability of a record—the trustworthiness of its content—is a product of the circumstances of the record's creation. For digital systems, this includes the technological environment that the record was created in. The authenticity of a record is linked to how the record was managed while in use by the creator and, importantly, to the preservation methods applied to it after it passes outside of the creator's custody.

In the analog world, prevention of the physical degradation of the record is accomplished through a combination of activities such as controlling environmental conditions, halting or limiting destructive chemical and physical processes, and limiting opportunities for accidental or intentional alterations to the content. The authenticity of a record is protected by maintaining it in the continuous custody of the records creator and its legitimate successors (e.g., an archives) and through archival practices such as accessioning, arrangement, and description, which aim to "stabilize and perpetuate the relationships between and among those records at the point at which they enter archival custody" (MacNeil 2005, 272). The means by which the goals of protection against physical degradation and safeguarding authenticity are accomplished in the digital environment is substantially different from that in the analog. Most obviously, the modes of information loss from digital objects are very different from physical objects. These are too numerous to provide a comprehensive list here, but some of the primary concerns are discussed in the following paragraphs.[9]

The frailty of digital media and media failure issues were among the first digital preservation issues to be recognized. The physical media on which digital information is written are information dense and give little or no warning of imminent failure. Their actual longevity and degradation characteristics are not as well understood as those for analog media.[10] Their relative newness and the rate at which physical information carriers tend to get replaced with new technology mean that long-term studies (as opposed to studies using an accelerated life-testing methodology) of the reliability of digital media are few. Media that is in good physical condition can still be unreadable as playback devices become obsolete. Individual bits can become corrupted while sitting on the original media or during migration from one physical carrier to another. Bit corruption is an inevitability for magnetic media. Some file formats are more resilient to the effects of bit corruption than others (Heydegger 2008), and the consequences can range from trivial to catastrophic. Intentional alterations can also be made to the record. Regardless of whether they are accidental or intentional, alterations to the record are much more difficult to detect in the digital environment unless appropriate measures are taken to actively monitor them.

The risk of file format obsolescence that would prevent the digital file from being capable of being rendered into a meaningful message has been a major concern and the focus of much research. File format obsolescence occurs when the ability to access the content of files of a particular format is lost. This occurs as new formats and new versions of existing formats replace the older formats, and the tools for reading a particular format disappear (Pearson and Webb 2008, 91). Obsolescence is seen as a major risk for digital preservation, as it is assumed that almost all formats will eventually become obsolete—some gradually, some suddenly (94).

Capturing and maintaining metadata about digital records is seen as essential to their preservation. Metadata can relate to technical details about the file format or how the file was created, its provenance and contextual relationship to other records and digital components necessary to properly interpret its content, identifiers used to locate and retrieve the file, and fixity information used to establish integrity (CCSDS 2012, sec. 2.2.2). Metadata is also critical for establishing the authenticity of digital records, as it documents the processes by which records were created, used, and maintained, the persons that participated in the records' creation and use, contextual links to other records, and the chain of custody. In many cases, recordkeeping metadata that would be an intrinsic part of an analog record exists separately from the record in the digital world, introducing the risk that the metadata might become dissociated from the record and compromise its authenticity, reliability, or readability. This metadata needs to be perpetually linked to the record as part of the preservation process.

Several core strategies have been used to address these central problems. Redundancy is an important method for dealing with problems related to media failure and obsolescence, by making sure that there are multiple copies of the digital object in the event that any single copy becomes compromised. Redundancy can also be used as a tool to protect the integrity of a digital record, as is done with the LOCCKS[11] approach (Rosenthal et al. 2005, sec. 4.5.3), which keeps multiple copies of digital records and can compare the distributed copies to detect changes in any one copy of the record. Recently, the potential use of blockchain technology, known for its application within Bitcoin, has been proposed to address authenticity issues through the use of a distributed ledger (Findlay 2015).

Format migration and normalization have been used to address the problem of format obsolescence. David Pearson and Colin Webb suggest that obsolescence exists in a continuum; all formats are at risk of obsolescence, but to varying degrees, and within differing timescales (Pearson and Webb 2008). Migration is the conversion of a file from a format at risk of becoming obsolete to a more current format. Normalization is a related concept wherein files are converted to standardized formats, usually at the time they enter the archive, selected based on considerations about longevity and openness and a corresponding presumption of a lower risk of obsolescence. These strategies involve transforming the original object into something else, and it is rare that the transformation can be done in a way that creates a derivative that is functionally equivalent, in both form and content, to the original. Consequently, target formats must be selected and transformation parameters set appropriately so as to preserve essential elements of form that are critical to the accurate and authentic representation of the content of a digital object. These may be elements such as sampling frequency and bit depth for audio files, color space for raster images, page layout markup for textual documents, and so on, which are commonly referred to as *significant properties*. These are not a fixed set of properties for a given format or class of digital objects. Rather, they must be determined by the preserver based on an understanding of how the creator of the content intended for it to be represented in order to communicate the intended message (Cedars Project 2002, 24). Furthermore, the viability of the target's format must be monitored over time and migration undertaken again if that format becomes at risk of obsolescence.

The severity of the risk posed by format obsolescence is beginning to be reconsidered. David Rosenthal (2010) believes that format obsolescence is not the risk that it was once presumed to be. He argues that assumptions about the inevitability of obsolescence that seemed valid in the 1990s no longer hold. Market maturity within the technology sector, the level of interoperability required by the Web, the proliferation of open source products, and the increasing ease of emulating the original software stack have combined to make format obsolescence much less of a risk than once believed. Consequently, there may be considerable wasted resources, in terms of both cost and effort, dedicated to processes undertaken to guard against obsolescence, such as format validation, metadata capture, and migration and normalization at the time that the files are brought into the preservation system. The risk obsolescence poses may be more of a financial one for archives rather than an existential one for the record. Pearson and Webb recognize that an obsolete format can be made accessible with effort and resources; it is only a question of the magnitude of resources required. It is possible that obsolescence may be a local issue for institutions with insufficient resources rather than a problem that affects that format universally (Pearson and Webb 2008, 94).

When trying to establish what is meant by digital preservation, the first question that must be addressed is: what are you actually trying to preserve? This is clear in the analog environment where the information content is inextricably fixed to the physical medium. In the digital environment, the medium is not part of the message. A bit stream looks the same to a computer regardless of the media it is read from. A physical carrier is necessary, but as long as the source media can be read, bit-perfect copies can be made cheaply and easily on other devices, making the preservation of the original carrier of diminishing importance. As the physical media that carry digital information are quite frail relative to most analog media, it is expected that digital information will necessarily need to be migrated from one physical carrier to another as part of the ongoing preservation process. It is not the media itself but the information on the media that needs to be preserved.

Preservation of digital information therefore involves not only the preservation of the information itself but also the ability to render the information in a meaningful way. Many information objects have external dependencies on metadata about those objects and on relationships to other information objects that are necessary for accurately representing their content. Web pages, for example, may depend not only on the HTML source code but also on links to external files, browser plug-ins, local settings, and so on. Digital objects are often dynamic—changing in content and structure over time. They can also be interactive—possessing defined behaviors that are dependent on user inputs. The users' experience interacting with a digital object in turn influences their perception and interpretation of it. At the same time, that interaction is often fragmented across time and space and is constituted from interrelated and interdependent sources that are themselves constantly changing (Owen 2007, 47–48).

Of particular concern to archivists seeking to preserve *records*, as opposed to documents or data, is that, to be meaningful as a record, information about the context of creation and the relationship to other records must be kept. Often this contextual information exists outside of the record in the form of metadata about the record and about the system it was created and kept in. This contextual metadata is more abstract, in the sense that it is not technical information about the record or dependencies on other information objects required to render the record properly and make it readable. Rather, it is about contextual links to other records that make the record understandable within the context of the whole and contribute to the establishment of the authenticity of the record.

Preservation of digital records means not only providing meaningful access to the record but also ensuring that records are capable of communicating the message that the author of the record intended to convey. This requirement does not change the basic strategies used to preserve digital records. It does necessitate that, when applying these strategies to the preservation of archives, requirements specific to archives be taken into account. When records are removed from their original systems, it must be done in a way that preserves their contexts of use within those systems. Metadata that establishes authenticity, provenance, and contextual relationships with other records, actors, and activities must be collected, maintained, and preserved together with the records. And any migration or transformation of a record must take into account how that transformation could potentially affect the significant properties of the record and its ability to communicate the author's intended message. Representation of a digital record to users must not only render the digital object in a way that makes its information content meaningful, but also it must be done in a way that makes it meaningful as a record.

RECENT TRENDS

Despite an ever-increasing grasp on the nature of the problem and the solutions required, actually undertaking digital preservation has been problematic for archives and archivists, particularly those with limited resources. There is little overlap between the infrastructure required for analog and digital preservation. Analog preservation requires controlled storage environments, preservation facilities and supplies, and space for physically accessing the records. Digital preservation requires redundant digital storage, hardware and software for processing records, and servers and networks for providing access to the preserved digital materials. To commit to a digital preservation program, archives need to acquire both the necessary technological infrastructure and staff with the appropriate knowledge base for conducting digital preservation activities and managing a digital preservation program.

The outlook for those archives seeking to establish digital preservation programs began to improve substantially in the early 2000s. There was a noticeable increase in educational opportunities for both new and currently practicing archivists. These archivists were able to seek support from a growing community of practice within the archival community itself and within a much larger interdisciplinary digital preservation community. The research products of earlier generations from multiple disciplines helped to create a shared body of standards. The ability of the community to come to some general agreement about the content of these standards gives support to Bearman's musings that the results of the research projects of the 1990s had more similarities than were commonly realized at the time. Christopher A. Lee posits that the development of the *Open Archival Information System* (OAIS)[12] facilitated increased interactions among different communities of digital preservation researchers that were emerging in the 1990s (Lee 2005, 4–6). Many terms and concepts within the OAIS, such as those present in the functional model, which describes the five primary functions that an OAIS must perform,[13] were important for facilitating interdisciplinary collaboration in digital preservation by standardizing meanings across disciplines. Terms such as *ingest*—the OAIS function responsible for accepting content from outside of the archive and transforming it into something that can be more readily preserved, through processes such as file integrity validation, format identification, metadata extraction, and format conversions—have become ubiquitous within the body of digital preservation literature. Undoubtedly, the emergence of generally agreed upon standards was critical for the development of the many software tools for preservation that were developed after the turn of the century.

Despite the wealth of research products generated from the digital preservation research projects of the 1990s, transforming the recommendations present in these research products into actual preservation activities was out of reach for all but the largest institutions, such as government archives at the national level and large research universities. Some success had been achieved incorporating research findings into the activities of making and keeping records—the issuing of the DOD 5015.2[14] standard for records management software and its subsequent endorsement by the U.S. National Archives and Records Administration (NARA) in 1998 (Miller 1998) being a prime example. Examples of archival digital preservation programs from this era are at best sparse among large national archives and nonexistent among smaller archives. In part, this can be attributed to the fact that there were still only a handful of archival professionals fully versed in the problems and solutions of digital preservation. Educational institutions had yet to institute digital preservation as part of their core curricula. More significantly, there was a lack of tools with which to undertake the work.

Digital Preservation in Practice

The preservation problems that differentiate digital records from their analog cousins are fundamentally technological in nature. Consequently, the preservation solutions required for the digital environment are also technological. This is not to say that the specific challenges present in digital preservation can be overcome solely through technological means—they are a necessary, though not sufficient, component of any digital preservation program. Although early research into digital preservation helped to make archivists familiar with appropriate methodologies and the requirements necessary to implement those methodologies, few archivists had the requisite skills to transform those requirements into actual code. The development of software tools was, given the budgetary constraints of most archives, unfeasible for all but the largest institutions.

The practicability of digital preservation began to change in the early 2000s, not because of a sudden increase to the budget of a typical archives but because large institutions—chiefly national libraries and archives and major research universities—began to develop their own tools. Most of the tools were intended to facilitate ingest processes like file format identification and validation, metadata extraction, and normalization. Importantly, they shared them with the community by releasing them under open source licenses.[15] These tools allowed archivists to apply automation to critical preservation tasks. Although none of these tools provided a comprehensive set of preservation capabilities, the emergence of products demonstrating that at least some of the tasks required for digital preservation could be undertaken by small and medium-sized institutions was an encouraging development for the large number of archivists who were aware of the issues of digital preservation but until then had felt powerless to address the problems in any material way. In recent years, several software packages that integrate multiple open source tools have appeared. Many of the existing tools that perform ingest-related services were assembled into the Archivematica software package, released in 2012.[16] Archivematica connected the tools in a workflow derived from the OAIS functional model, with particular emphasis on the ingest component of that model, performing the necessary tasks to make digital records preservable. The same year saw the release of BitCurator,[17] an assembly of open source digital forensic tools intended for use in digital preservation. These two products are part of a growing trend to provide software tools for digital preservation that integrate multiple preservation services and distribute them using a software-in-a-box model that aims to reduce the complexity of installation and setup, with the goal of making the products accessible to a broader user base.

Institutional Repositories

Digital preservation tools did not come solely from the archival community. In many respects, the library community was well ahead of the archival community in developing tools to address their digital preservation needs. Academic libraries in particular were forced to address their need to manage and provide access to increasing amounts of research output in digital form being generated by their parent institutions as well as digital content purchased or licensed from other sources. These materials included electronic theses and dissertations (ETDs), journal articles, preprints, books, and research data sets. To address this need, several universities developed institutional repository (IR)[18] software—tools designed to store, index, and provide permanent and persistent access to these and other works—and made them available to the community under open source licenses. Some of the most popular and well-known open source IR platforms include EPrints, developed by the University of Southampton in 2000 (EPrints for Open Access 2015); DSpace, currently the most widely used platform,[19] developed at MIT in 2002 (DSpace 2016); and Fedora, created by Cornell University and the University of Virginia in 2004 (DuraSpace 2015).[20] The core functionality performed by an IR is to ingest digital content and its associated metadata, manage access rights to the content in the repository, facilitate discovery through search engines and metadata harvesting, and preserve and distribute the content (Gibbons 2004, 7–8)—functions closely aligned with the core functional entities present in the OAIS model (CCSDS 2012, sec. 4.1).

Although initially developed to manage the more formal scholarly outputs of academic institutions, the use of IRs quickly expanded in scope beyond their original intended use to include materials such as faculty and staff records, teaching materials, student products, and contributions from diverse groups and organizations associated with the sponsoring institution's community. IRs do many things well, but certain aspects of their functionality, based on their original intended purpose, make them less than ideal for the preservation of archival records. In particular, they are not adept at representing the complex web of relationships that occur within archival collections that link records to other records, persons, and organizations. This is problematic because of the role that context plays in establishing the authenticity of archival records. Contextual relationships among the predominant types of digital objects present in IRs[21] are generally limited to structural relationships that link multiple objects constituting a single work or flat relationships that link multiple works to a series, collection, or topical grouping. The relationships among archival records constitute important representation information, without which it is impossible to understand how an individual record is positioned within the whole. Preserving these relationships and accurately representing them to the user are therefore critical to preserving a body of records as an archives. This is not to say that IRs are not capable of preserving archives, only that to do so requires additional effort. Successful instances exist where an IR's functionality has been extended to better address the requirements of archives. For example, the Bentley Historical Library at the University of Michigan is working to integrate ArchivesSpace and Archivematica with the university's DSpace IR (Shallcross 2015). It can make sense for archives to take advantage of an IR hosted by an affiliated institution by sharing some services using the IR to manage storage of digital objects, manage discovery metadata, and provide access and implementing other tools to address gaps in functionality related to the particular needs of archival materials.

Open Source and Open Standards

Although they certainly receive the most attention from the digital preservation community, the available selection of digital preservation tools is not limited solely to open source products. Several proprietary software products have emerged that claim to address the requirements of the OAIS functional model. The fact that commercial vendors see marketplace opportunities for digital preservation software is indicative that enough of a consensus has emerged among members of the preservation community about what their requirements are and that sufficient demand exists to make commercial preservation products viable. There seems to be agreement however within the digital preservation community that open source standards and solutions are preferable. Open source standards are thought to be at less risk of obsolescence and to require fewer resources to rescue from obsolescence. Furthermore, black box type tools are seen as undesirable. Although not every archivist needs to know the details of every line of code involved in a preservation activity, it is desirable that source code be available for analysis should the need arise. Open source software also increases opportunities for sharing resources and collaborating on further development, allowing institutions to leverage limited financial resources more effectively by allocating funds to projects that share development costs and by reducing licensing costs. There are risks associated with relying on open source products. Institutions are required to provide their own support or contract out for software support services. Until open source projects reach a critical mass and are associated with a community that supports the project, develop a governance structure, and establish sustainability, they are at risk of becoming orphaned. These are some of the reasons that organizations, instead of using open source solutions, prefer the cost certainty and ability to externalize risks associated with licensed proprietary software products.

The availability of preservation tools alone is not enough to account for increasing numbers of archives implementing digital preservation programs. Paul Conway (1996) suggests that technology is not the chief impediment to implementing digital preservation solutions; rather, it is a lack of appropriate organizational contexts for undertaking and managing preservation programs. One of the risks to preservation presented by its technological component is that it becomes too easy to get bogged down in the technological details of preservation and lose sight of the other components. Due attention needs to be paid to the other aspects of a preservation program. This is addressed within standards such as the OAIS and *Trustworthy Repositories Audit and Certification: Criteria and Checklist* (TRAC),[22] which describe the organizational responsibilities that preservers have.

Archives have to negotiate relationships with those generating records as well as those seeking to use the archives. The technological solutions need to be supported by appropriate policy frameworks and resource commitments that demonstrate the overall viability of the archives and the sustainability of a digital preservation program. This is the essence of what it means to be called a trusted digital repository. At the same time that tools for digital preservation were becoming increasingly available, initiatives to implement the findings of digital preservation research projects began to form.

Digital Curation

Since 2001, the label *digital curation*[23] has been used by some to describe the set of programs, activities, tools, and knowledge base identified with digital preservation. *Digital curation* can be defined as the active management of digital data throughout its life cycle in order to maintain, preserve, and add value to the data (DCC 2015, para. 1). The seeds of the digital curation movement can be found within the body of digital preservation research that took place in the 1990s, not solely from within the library and archives community but from a broader set of stakeholders with an interest in digital preservation (Higgins 2011, 79–80). The prime contributor was the scientific community, which extended concepts associated with data curation (Beagrie 2006, 4) and informatics (Zorich 1995, 431) into the digital preservation realm.

The material differences between archival understandings of digital preservation that developed in the 1990s and those concepts embodied in digital curation are those of scope and the level of interaction between the preserver and the community—community meaning both creators and consumers of the record. Many fundamental principles of traditional archival preservation are echoed within the core concepts of digital curation. Digital curation holds that digital resources should be managed throughout their life cycle in a manner that makes them discoverable, accessible, and understandable by those that use them and that custodial measures should be in place to establish access restrictions, security procedures, document preservation processes, and open processes and procedures to audit (Committee on Future Career Opportunities and Educational Requirements for Digital Curation et al. 2015, sec 1.5.2). However, one concept that is unique to digital curation is that preservers acting consistently with the principles of digital curation should seek to enhance or provide added value[24] to preserved objects. Through activities such as cleaning noise within data sets, correcting errors, and repackaging and presenting objects with regard to the needs of specific user communities, digital curators not only preserve information but also improve it by making it more usable and therefore of greater relevance to a broader set of users.

Digital curation emphasizes the importance of interacting and collaborating with the user community in ways that traditional archives perhaps value less or have been slow to embrace. This can manifest in many ways. Institutions can employ initiatives like crowdsourcing additional metadata and enabling tag content to enhance discoverability. Metadata can also be supplied to enhance the usability of content—for example, adding user-supplied geospatial metadata for maps in library collections to permit different maps to be used together more effectively (Fleet, Kowal, and Přidal 2012). Institutions can also facilitate user interaction within virtual exhibit spaces to allow researchers to share their knowledge about the collections among themselves (Cannon 2015, 66).

Sue Kunda and Mark Anderson-Wilk argue that value can be added to digital holdings through community engagement and that the role of the digital curator is akin to a broker, mediating the space between the digital resources and the user community (Kunda and Anderson-Wilk 2011, 904–05). Value may also be added through economic and other benefits that accrue to society such as cost efficiencies for researchers, new opportunities for interdisciplinary collaboration, and by promotion of previously unavailable or underused resources (Committee on Future Career Opportunities and Educational Requirements for Digital Curation et al. 2015, ch. 2). Benefits from enhancing the use of holdings can be realized by preserving institutions as well, as there is often a strong link between the extent to which a repository's holdings are being used and its ability to secure resources for continuing preservation (Kunda and Anderson-Wilk 2011, 896).

There may be reticence among some archivists, particularly those who tie their professional identities to Jenkinsonian ideals of objectivity and impartiality, to see themselves as curators, due to the interpretative role of selection and framing for the purpose of constructing a narrative or channeling usage implicit in curation. However, the ready adoption of the term across multiple member communities within the greater digital preservation community suggests a need for a unifying umbrella term to serve as a convenient proxy for the multiple and complex sets of activities it embodies. Although curation has suffered from recent overuse in the media in a wide variety of contexts, within the specific context of digital preservation, its use can be representative of a do-it-yourself sprit that is more inclusive than that projected by institutionalized, custodial preservation models.

Cloud Computing

It is impossible to consider recent trends in digital preservation without considering the transformative effect the advent of cloud computing has had not only on digital preservation but also on computing in general. Cloud computing is not a single technology. Rather, it is a catchall term for a variety of combinations of deployment models, wherein organizations do not maintain local computing infrastructure but instead rely on remote storage, processing power, platforms, and software. The frequently cited

National Institute of Standards and Technology's (NIST) definition describes cloud computing in terms of essential characteristics, deployment models, and service models. NIST characterizes cloud computing as on-demand services delivered over a network, in a way that is elastic and scalable. Cloud resources are pooled and shared among multiple users and monitored and controlled in a way that allows the shared resources to be used efficiently while at the same time allocating resources appropriate to the current demand. The resources may be deployed as a private, community, public, or hybrid cloud and may consist of infrastructure, platforms, or software applications (Mell and Grance 2011).

Cloud computing has many attractive features. The scalable, elastic nature of cloud computing means that resources can be added as necessary with relatively little effort. It can introduce simplicity to workflows by abstracting complex details that are not pertinent to the typical user (Venters and Whitley 2012, 187–88); it offers access to state-of-the-art technology that might not otherwise be available (Oliver and Knight 2015); it can reduce variability in costs and provide access to economies of scale that would not be achievable with locally maintained systems (Aitken et al. 2012) and improve overall transparency of costs (Oliver and Knight 2015). Many of these perceived benefits are particularly attractive to smaller institutions with limited resources that are unable or unwilling to maintain their own infrastructure and can lower barriers to entry associated with the costs and complexities of digital preservation.

Cloud computing emerged relatively recently. As such, initial cloud options for digital preservation were limited to infrastructure as a service —providers of storage and computing power like Amazon, Google, and Rackspace. More options have begun to appear recently, particularly within the software as a service space. Examples listed by the Digital Preservation Coalition include storage providers such as DuraCloud and Arkivum (Digital Preservation Coalition 2016). DuraCloud provides brokered third-party storage, while Arkivum operates its own storage. Both provide additional preservation services such as the management of backups, synching of files, and file integrity monitoring. Both of these providers also offer integration with Archivematica[25] to apply ingest preservation services to digital objects before they are stored. Preservica Cloud Edition is a similar service that offers preservation workflows and third-party storage (Preservica 2016).

Cloud computing is not without risks. Abstracting complexity and entrusting services to third parties necessarily involve a reduction in the level of control that an institution has over the objects in its holdings and the operations performed on them (Venters and Whitley 2012, 187). While costs are frequently lower, they are complex to assess and may not always be lower than a local solution[26] or may contain hidden or unforeseen costs such as bandwidth charges (Leinwand 2009). There are also risks and uncertainties beyond financial considerations. Cloud computing increases the number of potential attack vectors, making systems more vulnerable unless security is adequately addressed (Jansen and Grance 2011). If data is transmitted through or stored in foreign jurisdictions, it may be subject to the laws of those jurisdictions; the transmission of data to third parties may have consequences under the data protection laws of the jurisdiction that the client operates in (Bushey, Demoulin, and McLelland 2015, 143). Disruptions affecting service providers or Internet connectivity can interrupt access to data. This is to name only a few. Cloud computing involves swapping financial risks associated with procuring and maintaining computing infrastructure locally, with a different set of risks related to security, access, availability, and the trustworthiness of third-party service providers.

ONGOING CHALLENGES AND WAYS FORWARD

A decade ago, digital preservation was an inconceivable undertaking for all but the largest institutions. High entry costs and infrastructure maintenance costs, the need to attract professionals with the requisite knowledge and experience to operate digital preservation programs, and the need to dedicate time to research and development in what was, at the time, a newly emerging field simply placed digital preservation out of reach for small and medium-sized institutions. In the time since then, there has been a dramatic increase in options and opportunities for these institutions to build their own digital preservation programs, facilitated to a large extent by the availability of preservation tools, more flexible infrastructure configurations permitted by cloud computing, and the emergence of a marketplace for preservation services. Despite the abundance of tools and options now available, there are still obstacles. Technology, though essential, is only one component of a digital preservation program. To function, a preservation program also requires skilled staff to do the work and adequate and predictable funding streams to sustain the program.

Skills

The perception among current practitioners is that the most desirable qualifications, other than a general knowledge of digital preservation standards, are project planning, communications and analytic skills, and, most importantly, passion for the work (NDSA Standards and Practices Working Group 2013, 17). Despite this, current and future archivists involved with digital preservation (i.e., virtually all archivists) would benefit greatly by expanding their technical skill set beyond what it now typical for members of the profession. Archivists are not expected to be IT experts or have computer science degrees to do their work, just as motorists are not expected to be certified mechanics in order to drive a car. But someone who is not afraid to look under the hood of their car and get their hands dirty and has the skills to do so competently has a better sense of when their vehicle is working properly and when it is not and can often fix minor problems themselves. All other things being equal, the digital archivist who has competent technical skills—who understands the underlying architecture of their systems, who can read and understand code, who can run their own SQL queries, who knows how to resolve file permission issues—and is confident enough to apply them when appropriate and to seek more knowledgeable assistance when the situation calls for it will have a much better understanding of preservation processes and the tools that are performing them. This becomes even more important in the cloud environment as services are entrusted to third parties. Simplifying workflows by abstracting detail does not absolve the people ultimately responsible for those workflows from understanding those details. If anything, technical understanding becomes more important when archivists are contracting with a third party to provide preservation or storage services for objects in their custody, in which case they have an obligation to understand the details of how those services will be provided.

Providing digital preservation skills has largely been the responsibility of graduate library and archives programs, which have been expanding the digital component of their curricula for many years. Doing so, however, has required those schools to strike a balance between providing their students with an appropriate grounding in core archival theory, which was almost entirely developed in the pre-digital world, and providing them with an adequate exposure to an ever-expanding set of technologies, practices, and newly emerging forms of content in the digital world. This can be challenging to do within the constraints of their available course offerings and faculty expertise and within the time limits of a two-year graduate program (Cox 2013). Some have risen to the challenge better than others. Ultimately, it is the responsibility of individual professionals to seek and acquire the skills they need to undertake digital preservation. Fortunately, there are many post-appointment educational opportunities, in the form of workshops and professional certification programs,[27] available outside of graduate programs to improve digital preservation skills.

Funding

Digital preservation programs require reliable funding sources in order to ensure that preservation efforts can continue into the future. Decreasing prices for computing hardware and the availability of open source software have helped to lower costs to the point that preservation programs are viable for institutions with limited resources. Nevertheless, it seems as if institutions are constantly struggling to secure funds for digital preservation activities. Inevitably, doing so requires convincing stakeholders that digital preservation is necessary and that the benefits received from preservation are proportional to the resources spent on it. Getting sufficient resources requires communicating preservation methods and goals to stakeholders, particularly resource users, both current and potential (Corrado and Moulaison 2014, 89). Outreach efforts need to dissuade stakeholders of the notions that storage is essentially free, that backups are equivalent to preservation, and therefore digital preservation requires only minimal resources. This can be difficult when the average person is accustomed to seeing constantly decreasing prices for consumer electronics and has expectations that both content and software should be free or almost free. Commercial providers of free content, apps, and services are able to do so, because they have other ways to monetize their products. Archives have less ability to do so, though some have tried.[28] Furthermore, storage costs may only be half of the lifetime costs of digital preservation; acquisition and ingest costs make up the other half (Rosenthal et al. 2012, 2). With digital content, the labor costs associated with these activities are more closely tied to the complexity of the material—which is ever increasing—rather than the volume. Diminishing costs on one side of the equation are balanced by increasing costs on the other. It remains a major challenge, particularly for small and medium-sized institutions, to secure permanent program funding, as opposed to periodic, project-based grant funding.

Analog Theory in a Digital World

The archival theory that forms the foundation of professional education and training contains fundamental concepts that are rooted in the analog world. However, as technology progresses, records seem less like their analog ancestors. Similarly, the constraints that drove the development of prior archival theory were also artifacts of the analog world. It seems reasonable to question the appropriateness of relying on a body of theory developed to a world that is increasingly diverging from that of the twentieth century.

One of the main drivers of the development of appraisal theory was a perceived need to reduce the volume of records being preserved, in order to reduce costs, while simultaneously enhancing discoverability and usability—the oft repeated argument of separating the wheat from the chaff. The costs associated with preservation in the digital environment are not the same as in the analog environment. Digital records can be subjected to analytic techniques that are not feasible for analog records. These techniques are not restricted to only structured data in their application; some, such as text mining, sentiment analysis, and other natural language processing techniques, are suitable for use with unstructured data, including many of the documents and records that exist in archival fonds. Regardless of the type of data (i.e., structured, semi-structured, or unstructured) being analyzed, these techniques work better with larger data sets. Reducing the sample size creates multiple avenues through which biases can be introduced to the results (Gray 2015) and places limits on the kinds of analysis that can be performed (Henning 2014). The economics of the digital environment and the new modes of analysis that can be applied to records call into question whether the assumptions underlying past appraisal practices continue to hold for digital records.

The concept of arrangement becomes problematic within the digital environment. With paper records, storage is necessarily linear—a record can only exist in one folder, that folder can only be in a single box, and that box can only be on one shelf. Traditional arrangement either assumes or imposes a privileged view of the records by preserving or attempting to re-create the original order or by imposing an order if none exists. This privileged arrangement is associated with and therefore reflective of the intent of the records creator, the archivist, or, more frequently, both. With digital records, physical limitations on the number and complexity of relationships among the records disappear. Users of a recordkeeping system impose their own view on the records in the system, and context is defined through sets of pointers to records, not by physical proximity. Imposing traditional hierarchical arrangements on such records inevitably privileges a particular context while denying others. Bailey remarks that "in a database, objects are related but not ordered. The database logic is nonlinear and there is no original order because order is dependent upon query" (Bailey 2013, para 34). This can be extended to digital systems in general. The goal of arrangement in the digital environment should be to preserve all of the orderings of the records, not just a single privileged view. How this should be done is an open question.

CONCLUSIONS

Technology, being what it is, will continue to change. New types of information objects will continue to emerge, as will the practices used to make, and distribute and consume those objects and perceptions about how they should be interpreted and consumed. Throughout its brief existence, digital preservation has always been a discipline that is constantly trying to catch up to the current state of technology and is likely to continue in this vein for some time to come.

A shift in current recordkeeping practices is reminiscent of changes to organizational recordkeeping that occurred when computer technology first achieved significant penetration in the office environment in the 1980s. That era saw a decentralization of recordmaking and keeping, as desktop computing allowed organizations to push those responsibilities out to a broader class of workers. This led to the flattened organizational and relational hierarchies and the creation of silos of information. Until relatively recently, digital records were made and managed locally on one or a small number of devices. Those records are now distributed across multiple devices and applications and stored in the cloud using complex set of rules to coordinate synching of content among all of the components of an individual's recordkeeping. It is difficult, sometimes impossible, to know now where records actually reside. Contextual relationships that link records are moving away from hierarchical structures and becoming more weblike, and boundaries between systems are blurring as the same content gets used by different people for different purposes in different contexts.

The biggest challenge for those trying to preserve records, not just so that their content can be used but so that they can be used as evidence of past activities, is to understand the patterns of use and the dynamic contextual relationships present in the modern recordkeeping environment and to find ways to communicate this information into the future via the methods used to preserve records and present them to users in the future. This is what archivists have always done and is what digital archivists must continue to do.

ENDNOTES

1. At the time of writing, 25 of 35 job opportunities posted on the SAA Online Career Center identified duties or qualifications that could be considered to fall within the realm of digital preservation (Society of American Archivists 2015).

2. In particular, the RAMP study prepared by Harold Naugler in 1984 (Naugler 1984) is a significant marker of the boundary between the first and second generations. The study summarizes much of what was learned about the problems unique to the preservation of digital records and information and asks many of the theoretical questions that the second generation would seek to address.

3. "Unstructured records" is taken to mean records where the data does not reside in fixed fields, as contrasted with structured records, where data resides in defined fields, and semi-structured records, where data does not reside in fixed fields, but are tagged or marked up in some way (Manyika et al. 2011, 33).

4. International Research on the Preservation of Permanent Authentic Records in Electronic Systems (InterPARES Project 2015): this was the first of four projects to bear the name, including InterPARES 2 (2002–2007), InterPARES 3 (2007–2012), and InterPARES Trust (2013–2018).

5. Metadata is "a characterization or description documenting the identification, management, nature, use, or location of information resources (data)," or, more simply, "data about data" (Pearce-Moses 2005, 248–49). Metadata is a ubiquitous entity in digital preservation, being involved with virtually all digital preservation processes.

6. Other noteworthy projects of the era, to name only a few, and from only the archival community, include: the Indiana University Electronic Records Project, 1995–1997 (http://www.indiana.edu/~libarch/summary.html); CEDARS, 1998–2002 (http://www.ukoln.ac.uk/metadata/cedars); and CAMiLEON, 1999–2003 (http://www.webarchive.org.uk/ukwa/target/113954/source/alpha).

7. Reliability is "the quality of being dependable and worthy of trust" (Pearce-Moses 2005, 340–41). A record is reliable if its content can be trusted as factual. It is important to note, however, that because the content of a record is trusted to

be factual does not mean that the content *actually* is factual. Countless decisions are made every day based on false information contained in a record that is presumed to be truthful because of the circumstances of the record's creation—that is, because the record was created using the appropriate procedures, in the usual and ordinary course of business.

8. Authenticity is "the quality of being genuine ... and free from tampering" (Pearce-Moses 2005, 41–42). Authenticity has two components: *identity* and *integrity*. Identity means that a record is what it purports to be, that is, it is not a counterfeit or otherwise fraudulent. Integrity means that a record has not been altered either accidentally or by intentional tampering. Authenticity should not be confused with the truthfulness of the records content. For example, a report can have false content and conclusions but still be authentic if it is the report that it claims to be and has not been altered.

9. For a more detailed list, see "Information Loss Wiki" on the Saving the Digital World website (Information Loss Wiki—Saving the Digital World, n.d.).

10. Most digital storage media in use at present are magnetic, optical, or solid state. Each type has its own set of failure modes and metrics for predicting failures. Optical media have an expected lifespan on the order of a few decades (NIST 2007), depending on the metrics used and other variables; conventional hard disk drives have a median lifespan of around six years (Beach 2013; Schroeder and Gibson 2007); solid state drives are relatively new and unknown but may have much longer lifespans than anticipated when the first consumer versions appeared (Gasior 2014); magnetic tape has a lifespan estimated up to 30 years (Bigourdan et al. 2006).

11. Lots of Copies Keeps Stuff Safe (LOCKSS 2013).

12. OAIS is a very influential reference model first released in 2003 that defines responsibilities for an archive and models the functional entities and information objects found within the archive (CCSDS 2012).

13. Ingest, data management, archival storage, administration, and access (CCSDS 2012, sec 4).

14. The full title is Design Criteria Standard for Electronic Records Management Software Applications.

15. Examples include, in 2003, JSTOR and Harvard University Library released JHOVE (JSTOR/Harvard Object Validation Environment 2009), a tool for performing file format identification, validation, and characterization. The same year (though not released as open source until 2007), the National Library of New Zealand released the NLZL Metadata Extraction Tool (National Library of New Zealand 2010). In 2005, The National Archives of the United Kingdom (TNA) released DROID (The National Archives 2014), an automated tool for file format identification using the PRONOM file format registry developed by TNA in 2002 (The National Archives 2011).

16. The beta release of Archivematica was in September 2012; v1.0 was released in January 2014 (Artefactual Systems 2015).

17. The beta release of BitCurator was in 2012; v1.0 was released in September 2014 (BitCurator Consortium 2015).

18. *IR* can refer specifically to a software implementation used to store, index, and deliver digital content or more broadly to the program and related services within an institution responsible for acquiring, preserving, and disseminating content (Burns, Lana, and Budd 2013). It is the first use that applies here.

19. Based on reporting by the Registry of Open Access Repositories (ROAR 2015) and by the Directory of Open Access Repositories (OpenDOAR—Charts—Worldwide 2016).

20. Fedora has been incorporated with Drupal, an open source content management system, into Islandora (Islandora 2015), another example of the trend toward integration and software-in-a-box distribution.

21. OpenDOAR provides statistics on the most frequent content types (OpenDOAR—Charts—Worldwide 2016); see also the survey of content types present in (Burns et al. 2013).

22. Often referred to as both the *Trustworthy Repositories Audit Checklist* and the *Trustworthy Repositories Audit and Certification.* TRAC was developed from *Trusted Digital Repositories: Attributes and Responsibilities* (TDR), issued by Research Libraries Group in 2002, and formed the basis for the CCSDS *Audit and Certification of Trustworthy Digital Repositories* (CCSDS 2011), which was also released as ISO 16363:2012.

23. The term was first used at the Digital Preservation Coalition seminar held in London in 2001 (Beagrie 2006, 4).

24. *Preparing the Workforce for Digital Curation* defines *digital curation* as "the active management and enhancement [emphasis added] of digital information assets for current and future use" (Committee on Future Career Opportunities and Educational Requirements for Digital Curation et al. 2015, sec. 1.5.1); "adding value" is present in the DCC definition cited previously.

25. As ArchivesDirect for the integrated DuraCloud instance (ArchivesDirect 2016) and Arkivum/Perpetua for the Arkivum instance (Arkivum 2016).

26. Rosenthal presents such an argument with regard to storage (Rosenthal 2012).

27. Standout examples include the Digital Preservation Management Workshop series initially developed at Cornell University and currently hosted by MIT Libraries (Digital Preservation Management Workshops 2016); the DigCCurr Professional Institute based out of the University of North Carolina Chapel Hill (DigCCurr 2016); and the Society of American Archivists Digital Archives Specialist Certificate Program (Society of American Archivists 2016).

28. In 2008, Library and Archives Canada (LAC) contracted with Ancestry.ca to digitize frequently used records held by LAC, wherein the digitize records were, for a limited time, only available through Ancestry (Library and Archives Canada 2010).

REFERENCES

Aitken, Brian, Patrick McCann, Andrew McHugh, and Kerry Miller. 2012. "Digital Curation and the Cloud." Technical report, JISC/Digital Curation Centre. http://eprints.gla.ac.uk/60659/ (accessed October 29, 2015).

ArchivesDirect. 2016. http://www.archivesdirect.org/about (accessed February 25, 2016).

Arkivum. 2016. "Arkivum/Perpetua." http://arkivum.com/arkivum-perpetua (accessed September 16, 2016).

Artefactual Systems. 2015. *Archivematica—Release Notes.* July 20. https://wiki.archivematica.org/Release_Notes (accessed September 9, 2015).

Bailey, Catherine. 1989–1990. "Archival Theory and Electronic Records." *Archivaria* (Winter, 29): 180–96.

Bailey, Jefferson. 2013. "Disrespect des Fonds: Rethinking Arrangement and Description in Born-Digital Archives." *Archive Journal* (Summer, 3). http://www.archivejournal.net/issue/3/archives-remixed/disrespect-des-fonds-rethinking-arrangement-and-description-in-born-digital-archives/ (accessed March 1, 2016).

Baldwin, Betsey. 2006. "Confronting Computers: Debates about Computers at the Public Archives of Canada during the 1960s." *Archivaria* (Fall, 62): 159–78.

Beach, Brain. 2013. "How Long Do Disk Drives Last?" November 12. https://www.backblaze.com/blog/how-long-do-disk-drives-last (accessed September 10, 2015).

Beagrie, Neil. 2006. "Digital Curation for Science, Digital Libraries, and Individuals." *International Journal of Digital Curation* 1 (Autumn, 1): 3–16. http://www.ijdc.net/index.php/ijdc/article/view/6/2 (accessed October 28, 2015).

Bearman, David. 2006. "Moments of Risk: Identifying Threats." *Archivaria* (Fall, 62): 15–46.

Bigourdan, Jean-Louis, James M. Reilly, Karen Santoro, and Gene Salesin. 2006. "The Preservation of Magnetic Tape Collections: A Perspective." National Endowment for the Humanities Division of Preservation and Access.

BitCurator Consortium. 2015. "BitCurator Consortium—History." https://bitcuratorconsortium.org/history (accessed December 9, 2015).

Burns, C. Sean, Amy Lana, and John M. Budd. 2013. "Institutional Repositories: Exploration of Costs and Value." *D-Lib Magazine* 19 (January/February, 1/2). http://www.dlib.org/dlib/january13/01contents.html (accessed March 20, 2016).

Bushey, Jessica, Marie Demoulin, and Robert McLelland. 2015. "Cloud Service Contracts: An Issue of Trust." *Canadian Journal of Information and Library Science* 39 (June, 2): 128–53.

Cannon, San. 2015. "Content Curation for Research: A Framework for Building a 'Data Museum.' " *International Journal of Digital Curation* 10 (2): 58–68. http://www.ijdc.net/index.php/ijdc/article/view/10.2.58/408 (accessed March 14, 2016).

Cedars Project. 2002. "Cedars Guide to Digital Collection Management." http://www.webarchive.org.uk/wayback/archive/20050410120000/http://www.leeds.ac.uk/cedars/guideto/collmanagement/guidetocolman.pdf (accessed February 25, 2016).

Committee on Future Career Opportunities and Educational Requirements for Digital Curation, Board on Research Data and Information, Policy and Global Affairs, and National Research Council. 2015. *Preparing the Workforce for Digital Curation.* Washington, D.C.: National Academies Press.

Consultative Committee for Space Data Systems (CCSDS). 2011. *Audit and Certification of Trustworthy Digital Repositories.* Washington, D.C.: CCSDS Secretariat. http://public.ccsds.org/publications/archive/652x0m1.pdf (accessed April 16, 2016).

Consultative Committee for Space Data Systems (CCSDS). 2012. *Reference Model for an Open Archival Information System (OAIS).* Washington, D.C.: CCSDS

Secretariat. http://public.ccsds.org/publications/archive/650x0m2.pdf (accessed August 22, 2015).

Conway, Paul. 1996, March. *Preservation in the Digital World.* http://www.clir.org/pubs/reports/reports/conway2/index.html (accessed October 25, 2015).

Cook, Terry. 1991–1992. "Easy to Byte, Harder to Chew: The Second Generation of Electronic Records Archives." *Archivaria* (Winter, 33): 202–16.

Corrado, Edward M., and Heather Lea Moulaison. 2014. *Digital Preservation for Libraries, Archives, and Museums.* Lanham, MD: Rowman and Littlefield.

Cox, Richard. 2010. *The Demise of the Library School: Personal Reflections on Professional Education in the Modern Corporate University.* Duluth, MN: Library Juice.

Cox, Richard. 2013. "Archival Education: Past the Crossroads, But Where?" *Mid-Atlantic Regional Archives Conference Spring 2013 Conference.* Erie, PA. http://d-scholarship.pitt.edu/18782 (accessed March 22, 2016).

DigCCurr. 2016. http://ils.unc.edu/digccurr/institute.html (accessed April 3, 2016).

Digital Curation Centre (DCC). 2015. "What is Digital Curation?" http://www.dcc.ac.uk/digital-curation/what-digital-curation (accessed October 20, 2015).

Digital Preservation Coalition. 2016. "Cloud Services." http://www.dpconline.org/advice/preservationhandbook/technical-solutions-and-tools/cloud-services (accessed February 25, 2016).

Digital Preservation Management Workshops. 2016. http://www.dpworkshop.org (accessed March 24, 2016).

DSpace. 2016. http://www.dspace.org/ (accessed April 4, 2016).

DuraSpace. 2015. History | Fedora Repository. http://fedorarepository.org/about (accessed September 16, 2016).

EPrints for Open Access. 2015. http://www.eprints.org/uk/index.php/openaccess (accessed September 10, 2015).

Findlay, Cassie. 2015. "Decentralised and Inviolate: The Blockchain and Its Uses for Digital Archives." January 23. http://rkroundtable.org/2015/01/23/decentralised-and-inviolate-the-blockchain-and-its-uses-for-digital-archives (accessed December 3, 2015).

Fishbein, Meyer H. 1972. "Appraising Information in Machine Language Form." *American Archivist* 35 (1): 35–43.

Fleet, Christopher, Kimberly C. Kowal, and Petr Přidal. 2012. "Georeferencer: Crowdsourced Georeferencing for Map Library Collections." *D-Lib Magazine* 18 (November/December, 11/12). http://www.dlib.org/dlib/november12/fleet/11fleet.html (accessed October 28, 2015).

Gasior, Geoff. 2014. "The SSD Endurance Experiment: Casualties on the Way to a Petabyte—The Tech Report." June 16. http://techreport.com/review/26523/the-ssd-endurance-experiment-casualties-on-the-way-to-a-petabyte (accessed September 10, 2015).

Gibbons, Susan. 2004. "Defining an Institutional Repository." *Library Technology Reports* (July–August, 4): 6–10.

Gray, Alexander. 2015. *Big Data's Small Lie—The Limitation of Sampling and Approximation in Big Data Analysis.* July 20. http://www.datanami.com/2015/07/20/big-datas-small-lie-the-limitation-of-sampling-and-approximation-in-big-data-analysis (accessed November 20, 2015).

Henning, Jeffery. 2014. *The N in Text Analytics: Text Mining with Different Sample Sizes*. December 20. http://researchaccess.com/2014/12/the-n-in-text-analytics (accessed December 9, 2015).

Heydegger, Volker. 2008. "Analysing the Impact of File Formats on Data Integrity." *Proceedings of Archiving 2008*, Bern, Switzerland. Springfield, VA: Society for Imaging Science and Technology.

Higgins, Sarah. 2011. "Digital Curation: The Emergence of a New Discipline." *The International Journal of Digital Curation* 6 (2): 78–88. http://www.ijdc.net/index.php/ijdc/article/view/184/251 (accessed October 14, 2015).

Information Loss Wiki—Saving the Digital World. n.d. http://www.savingthedigitalworld.com/data-loss-wiki (accessed September 18, 2015).

InterPARES Project. 2015. http://www.interpares.org (accessed October 19, 2015).

Islandora. 2015. "Islandora—About." http://islandora.ca/about (accessed December 9, 2015).

Jansen, Wayne, and Timothy Grance. 2011. *Guidelines on Security and Privacy in Public Cloud Computing*. Gaithersburg, MD: National Institute of Standards and Technology.

JSTOR/Harvard Object Validation Environment. 2009. http://jhove.sourceforge.net (accessed September 16, 2015).

Kunda, Sue, and Mark Anderson-Wilk. 2011. "Community Stories and Institutional Stewardship: Digital Curation's Dual Roles of Story Creation and Resource Preservation." *Libraries and the Academy* 11 (4): 895–914.

Lee, Christopher A. 2005. "Defining Digital Preservation Work: A Case Study of the Development of the Reference Model for an Open Archival Information System." Unpublished dissertation. University of Michigan. Available at: https://ils.unc.edu/callee/dissertation_callee.pdf (accessed December 10, 2015).

Leinwand, Allan. 2009. "The Hidden Cost of the Cloud: Bandwidth Charges." July 17. https://gigaom.com/2009/07/17/the-hidden-cost-of-the-cloud-bandwidth-charges (accessed March 28, 2016).

Library and Archives Canada. 2010. "Library and Archives Canada Agreement with Ancestry.ca." March 3. https://www.collectionscanada.gc.ca/about-us/012-215.01-e.html (accessed March 31, 2016).

LOCKSS. 2013. http://www.lockss.org (accessed November 25, 2015).

MacNeil, Heather. 2005. "Picking Our Text: Archival Description, Authenticity, and the Archivist as Editor." *American Archivist* 68 (Fall/Winter, 2): 264–78.

Manyika, James, Michael Chui, Brad Brown, Jacques Bughin, Richard Dobbs, Charles Roxburgh, and Angela Hung Byers. 2011. *Big Data: The Next Frontier for Innovation, Competition, and Productivity*. McKinsey Global Institute.

Mell, Peter, and Timothy Grance. 2011. *The NIST Definition of Cloud*. Gaithersburg, MD: National Institute of Standards and Technology.

Miller, Michael L. 1998. "NWM 03.99." November 19. http://www.archives.gov/records-mgmt/memos/nwm03-99.html (accessed October 25, 2015).

The National Archives. 2011. "The National Archives | PRONOM | About." http://www.nationalarchives.gov.uk/aboutapps/pronom (accessed September 9, 2015).

The National Archives. 2014. "DROID—Digital Record and Object Identification." http://digital-preservation.github.io/droid (accessed September 16, 2015).

National Institute of Standards and Technology (NIST). 2007. "NIST/Library of Congress (LC) Optical Disc Longevity Study." Library of Congress and National Institute of Standards and Technology. https://www.loc.gov/preservation/resources/rt/NIST_LC_OpticalDiscLongevity.pdf (accessed September 21, 2015).

National Library of New Zealand. 2010. "Metadata Extraction Tool." http://meta-extractor.sourceforge.net (accessed September 9, 2015).

Naugler, Harold. 1984. *The Archival Appraisal of Machine-Readable Records: A RAMP Study with Guidelines*. Paris: UNESCO.

NDSA Standards and Practices Working Group. 2013. "Staffing for Effective Digital Preservation." National Digital Stewardship Alliance: 17. http://www.digitalpreservation.gov/documents/NDSA-Staffing-Survey-Report-Final122013.pdf (accessed November 17, 2015).

Oliver, Gillian, and Steve Knight. 2015. "Storage Is a Strategic Issue: Digital Preservation in the Cloud." *D-Lib Magazine* 21 (March/April, 3/4). http://www.dlib.org/dlib/march15/oliver/03oliver.html (accessed March 24, 2016).

OpenDOAR—Charts—Worldwide. 2016. http://www.opendoar.org/find.php?format=charts (accessed March 31, 2016).

Owen, John Mackenzie. 2007. "Preserving the Digital Heritage: Roles and Responsibilities for Heritage Repositories." In *Preserving the Digital Heritage*, edited by Yola de Lusenet and Vincent Wintermans, 45–49. Amsterdam: Netherlands National Commission for UNESCO.

Pearce-Moses, Richard. 2005. *A Glossary of Archival and Records Terminology*. Chicago, IL: The Society of American Archivists.

Pearson, David, and Colin Webb. 2008. "Defining File Format Obsolescence: A Risky Journey." *The International Journal of Digital Curation* 3 (July, 1): 89–106. http://www.ijdc.net/index.php/ijdc/article/view/76/44 (accessed November 15, 2015).

Preservica. 2016. http://preservica.com (accessed February 25, 2016).

Registry of Open Access Repositories (ROAR). 2015. http://roar.eprints.org/view/software/ (accessed November 30, 2015).

Rosenthal, David S. H. 2010. "Format Obsolescence: Assessing the Threat and the Defenses." http://lockss.stanford.edu/locksswiki/files/LibraryHighTech2010.pdf (accessed November 20, 2015).

Rosenthal, David S. H. 2012. "Cloud Storage Pricing History." *DSHR's Blog*. February 17. http://blog.dshr.org/2012/02/cloud-storage-pricing-history.html (accessed February 18, 2016).

Rosenthal, David S. H., Daniel C. Rosenthal, Ethan L. Miller, Ian F. Adams, Mark W. Storer, and Erez Zadok. 2012. "The Economics of Long-Term Digital Storage." In *The Memory of the World in the Digital Age: Digitization and Preservation*, edited by Luciana Duranti and Elizabeth Shaffer, 513–28. Vancouver, BC: United Nations Educational, Scientific and Cultural Organization.

Rosenthal, David S. H., Thomas Robertson, Tom Lipkisii, Vicky Reichi, and Seth Morabitoiii. 2005. "Requirements for Digital Preservation Systems:

A Bottom-Up Approach." *D-Lib Magazine* 11 (November, 1). http://www.dlib.org/dlib/november05/rosenthal/11rosenthal.html (accessed November 10, 2015).

Schroeder, Bianca, and Garth A Gibson. 2007. "Disk Failures in the Real World: What Does an MTTF of 1,000,000 Hours Mean to You?" FAST '07: 5th USENIX Conference on File and Storage Technologies, San Jose, CA.

Shallcross, Mike. 2015. "Hello World!" April 8. http://archival-integration.blogspot.ca/2015/04/hello-world.html (accessed December 9, 2015).

Society of American Archivists. 2015. "SAA Online Career Center." http://www2.archivists.org/groups/saa-online-career-center (accessed November 6, 2015).

Society of American Archivists. 2016. "Digital Archives Specialist (DAS) Curriculum and Certificate Program." http://www2.archivists.org/prof-education/das (accessed April 1, 2016).

Venters,Will, and Edgar A. Whitley. 2012. "A Critical Review of Cloud Computing: Researching Desires and Realities." *Journal of Information Technology* 27 (3): 179–97.

Zorich, Diane M. 1995. "Data Management: Managing Electronic Information: Data Curation in Museums." *Museum Management and Curatorship* 14 (4): 430–32.

7

Continuing Debates about Description

Geoffrey Yeo

This chapter is a lightly revised and updated version of the essay entitled "Debates about Description" that appeared in the first edition of this book. Like its precursor, it reviews different strands in professional thinking about description—as both a process and a product—in English-language writings of the late twentieth and early twenty-first centuries and explores some of the controversies that have been subjects of debate.

Why do we describe archival records? Some archivists consider accessibility—assisting users in locating records—the primary or only purpose of description (Haworth 2001, 11): an emphasis implicit in the term *finding aids*, often used as a generic label for products of the descriptive process. But others see this perspective as too limited and expound further purposes. Descriptive products act as inventories to counter possible misplacement or loss. They serve a preservation role, reducing handling of original paper documents. Above all, they capture and collate information about context. Such information is needed to aid interpretation, because records do not usually bear their wider context on their faces but can be elucidated by understanding their interrelationships. Because creators and immediate recipients of records normally have shared cultural assumptions, they can communicate effectively without leaving "social context cues"

(Sproull and Kiesler 1986); to later users, however, record *content* may mean little without explanation of *context*.

Some writers also affirm that contextual description establishes or safeguards the authenticity of records "by documenting their chain of custody, their arrangement, and the circumstances of their creation and use" (CUSTARD 2002). To others (Bearman and Sochats 1996; Evans 2014), descriptions, or metadata, are essential and innate components of "recordness"; they do not merely allow records to be retrieved, interpreted, or authenticated but are integral to the construction of the record itself.

These distinct perceptions of the role of description reflect different worldviews. Writers emphasizing context or authenticity largely focus on records, their evidentiality, and the actions that generate them; those emphasizing access and retrieval are more interested in users and their information needs. User-focused professionals typically see archival description as analogous to library cataloging. Some assert the "benefits of integrating archival material with the rest of the bibliographic universe" (Hensen 2001, 78). To records-focused professionals, archival material is not part of that universe at all; records and archives are not simply pieces of information content describable using quasi-bibliographic techniques but representations of activities in the real world, intimately bound to the business processes that generated them. In continuum thinking, *archival* description is a subset of a wider range of description embracing agents and activities as well as records of any age irrespective of custodial status (Australian Society of Archivists ca. 2007). Continuum thinkers disparage their opponents for subordinating descriptive systems to custodial arrangements (Cunningham 2005, 90) and for failing to comprehend how records differ from book collections (Hurley 1998, 66–67), but, equally, the records focus can be criticized for showing little interest in accessibility.

PROVENANCE

All parties agree that description should follow the principle of provenance. At its broadest, this principle requires records to be managed in ways that secure and preserve knowledge of their origins and contexts. From its nineteenth-century genesis in continental Europe, the principle of provenance came to be accepted in the United Kingdom in the early twentieth century and in North America from the 1940s or 1950s onward. Its methodological interpretation varies, and the purity of its implementation has sometimes been questioned, but its theoretical validity has been almost universally accepted.

Its accomplishment, in the paper world of the twentieth century, was not just through description but through *arrangement*. Respecting provenance demanded that records having the same origin be kept together and records of different origins not be intermixed. The order of records established by their creator was to be preserved (the principle, or subprinciple, of "original order"). If disturbances had already occurred, the original arrangement was to be reconstituted where possible. Original arrangements could be reconstituted on paper rather than on shelves but were not to be lost. Arrangement, rather than description, was said to be the bulwark protecting the authenticity of archives (Cook 1986, 80).

In the new millennium, "arrangement" strongly suggests a physical ordering of tangible objects, and we may wonder whether it needs to be reinvented or abandoned in digital environments where physical orders seem to have little or no meaning. Even in the paper world, there was something odd about the notion of arrangement. Archivists were advised to arrange archives before describing them (Cook 1993, 59), but was not the arrangement, at least implicitly, already present when archives arrived in an archival institution? Arguably, following the principle of original order, no arranging work by archivists could be allowed.

In fact, the principle of original order had been under scrutiny in Europe since at least 1930, when Swedish archivist Carl Gustaf Weibull argued for rearrangement by subject matter for the supposed convenience of researchers and because few original orders reflected "a well-thought-out system" (Schellenberg 1956, 188–89). The view that original order might be susceptible to improvement was also expressed in prewar Germany by Adolf Brenneke (Menne-Haritz 1994, 111–12) and in the United States by Ernst Posner (1940, 169), in some measure anticipating the arguments of Graeme Powell (1976) and Frank Boles (1982). Others, less radically, pointed out that difficulties arise when original orders have been disturbed or lost or when records creators impose different orders at different times. Archivists often find it unclear how far the orders they encounter were imposed by the creators of records and how far any particular ordering may have been affected by later interventions.

All this raises the question of why original order matters. In the 1930s, Giorgio Cencetti argued that it manifests the structure and history of the records creator (Savoja and Vitali 2007, 123). Others have suggested that it reflects sequences of record-creating events or logical associations between records. But structures and events have relationships beyond the merely sequential, and logical associations can be very complex. It seems unlikely that physical ordering of papers could truly capture such intricate phenomena. Kjeld Schmidt and Ina Wagner (2004) demonstrated some of the elaborate interrelationships between records and the diverse actors and activities in architectural practice—more elaborate than any single ordering of records could manifest. Original order can certainly give vital clues to this underlying complexity and perhaps show how creators or records managers tried to represent it within the constraints of a hierarchical filing system. In the paper world, original order is the best approach we have; however, archivists are increasingly aware that we cannot make excessive claims for its efficacy.

In digital environments, where juxtaposition of records seems insignificant, even the limited contextual clues provided by physical ordering are often largely missing, and several writers have affirmed a need to rethink the principle of original order in terms of identifying, interpreting, or re-creating multiple logical relationships among records rather than preserving their physical groupings (Cook 1997, 48; Eastwood 2000, 93; Meehan 2010, 35–37; Niu 2015, 71). David Bearman (1996) suggested that we can employ metadata to document these relationships, thus shifting the emphasis from arrangement to description.

Nevertheless, archivists have long believed that records have a collective significance and that knowledge of their meaning and context is lost or diminished if their collective nature is not protected. In many countries, the traditional linchpin of archivists' understanding of collective provenance is the *fonds*, defined as "the whole of the records . . . created and/or accumulated and used by a particular person, family, or corporate body" (International Council on Archives 2000, 10). Even in countries where the word *fonds* is not used in description, *respect des fonds* is usually recognized as a guiding principle for arrangement, although its implementation is sometimes compromised by the application of arbitrary "record groups" (Fenyo 1966; Gorzalski 2014) notionally based on provenance but tempered by perceived requirements for groupings of a "convenient size" for administration.

Within a fonds or record group, archivists traditionally identify a number of subordinate collective levels: possibly *subfonds* or *subgroups*, usually record *series*, and other levels such as *files* within series. The assembly of elementary records into files and series is normally determined by their origins, and these collective levels play important roles in documenting context. With organizational records, archivists generally assume that records creators have made these collective levels explicit and that the archivist's role is to preserve the physical files and series that creators construct; with personal papers, creators' recordkeeping systems may be less meticulous, but collective structures are often presumed to be implicit and realizable by archivists to support the papers' future management and use. Descriptions of archives are expected to reflect these structures.

Archivists have also assumed that these structures constitute hierarchies, in which no file belongs to more than one series and no series to more than one fonds or record group (Holmes 1964, 27). But this monolithic view often creates difficulties, especially with organizational records. When organizational changes occur, responsibilities for particular business functions or processes frequently move from one agency or department to another; a record series whose life extends across such changes may have records added to it by several different creators over time and is therefore a candidate for membership of several different fonds, subfonds, or record groups. The traditional solution is to assign a multicreator series to just one of a number of possible fonds, but this "provides a partly false administrative context" (Scott 1966, 495). It "distorts provenance and thereby undermines a central purpose of description" (Cook 1992, 65).

The Australian "Series System," which emerged from Peter Scott's work in the 1960s, deals with these challenges by separating what Scott called "context control" from "record control" (Cunningham 2010; Scott 1966). Its separate description of creators and series abandons assumptions that relationships between series and record-creating entities are hierarchical and allows a series to be linked to as many record-creating entities as context documentation requires. Despite some initial dissent (Duchein 1983; Fischer 1973), most writers now acknowledge that, for archives of dynamic organizations, the Series System provides truer representations of provenance than traditional monohierarchical approaches.

Debra Barr (1987–1988) and Terry Cook (1992) argued convincingly that the fonds is primarily a conceptual abstraction and that the error of the traditional approach lies in perceiving it as a physical entity. When the fonds is viewed as an intellectual construct, we can readily acknowledge that fonds may overlap (Hurley 2008, 4), that their borders may be open to variable interpretation (Yeo 2012a, 66–68), and that a single series may be seen to belong to multiple fonds (Eastwood 2000, 114). Although conceptual fonds with shared membership cannot easily be isolated on repository shelves, their membership can be documented and descriptions of the series associated with each fonds can be generated (Cunningham 2000, 8); in digital environments, the perceived components of a conceptual fonds can be assembled virtually if required.

Scott's Series System and Cook's acknowledgment that fonds are conceptual supplied a framework for describing multiple relationships between records and creators. Subsequent development of the Series System in Australia led to deeper exploration of relationships between records and context entities, including identification of *functions* as a further type of context entity (Hurley 1995). The SPIRT project (McKemmish et al. 1999) developed a model of interrelationships among records, agents, mandates, functional (or "business") entities, and recordkeeping entities to provide a basis for descriptive systems that would map the evolving relations among these entities and thus more closely reflect the richness of provenance. The SPIRT model is far removed from traditional approaches to description that, as Bearman and Richard Lytle (1985–1986, 20) noted, retain the intellectual constraints of physical shelf-order; instead, it employs relational techniques from computer science to support understandings that evidential contexts are dynamic and multifaceted.

Scott's system assumed that series may have multiple contexts but that items, files, and folders within a series have single, stable contexts and can be managed collectively using traditional hierarchical methods. In practice, however, physical components of series may be fluid, and logical contexts of elementary or item-level records may not be straightforward. Physical and conceptual series do not always coincide. Records creators may move items between folders or folders between series. Logically, a single item can often be attributed to multiple series or even multiple fonds (Yeo 2012a, 65–66, 2012b, 62–64). Moreover, aggregation of items into files, folders, and series is a common but not an essential feature of recordkeeping; some records systems do not employ these levels. Ultimately, every elementary record has its own contexts and (especially in digital environments) requires its own metadata, both to document its contexts and to ensure its continuing accessibility over time. As Bearman (1996) foresaw, the transition to digital recordkeeping is shifting much of the descriptive focus onto the elementary record, and recent Australian work no longer privileges the series. Once thought to be a natural unit of control, the series, too, may need to be deconstructed. Even at the lowest level of decomposition, records have complex networks of relationships.

WHY DESCRIBE RETROSPECTIVELY?

Descriptions are traditionally created retrospectively, after records have been transferred to archival repositories. Bearman (1989) asserted that retrospective description fails on many counts; it demands resources unavailable to archivists, leads to huge processing backlogs, is unable to capture critical contextual information, and neglects to take advantage of existing data stores from which much of the requisite information could be obtained. Organizations need metadata about their current records, and Bearman and other opponents of retrospective description claim that these metadata serve broadly similar purposes to the descriptions traditionally created by archivists later in the records' life. Especially when archivists recognize that digital records are unlikely to remain accessible in the long term without appropriate intervention at an early stage, there appear to be strong arguments for "integrating the previously separate control regimes for records management and archives" (Cunningham 2001, 279) and for archivists reusing metadata rather than re-creating them.

Bearman associated these ideas with life cycle management, but, like many of his ideas, they were adopted in Australia and realigned to the records continuum model, which eschews binary divisions between current and archival records. But retrospective description also has its defenders. While some writers dismiss it as "a postponement of what could have been documented at creation" (Hurley 1998, 60) or, at best, an expedient contrivance in repositories that collect archives from individuals or organizations lacking rigorous recordkeeping systems, others affirm a distinctive role for retrospective description in attesting to authenticity or providing a broader and more considered contextual perspective (Gilliland et al. 2005,

66; MacNeil 1995; Nesmith 2007, 6). Later discourse moved away from the simple view that all or most descriptive needs can be met by capturing metadata at record creation (Wallace 1995) to an understanding that descriptive information can be added progressively throughout a record's life (McKemmish 2001, 336) and, ideally at least, reused or repurposed as necessary over time (Evans, McKemmish, and Bhoday 2005).

Archival theory affirms that the records generated by a single creator constitute a fonds, but such a fonds is rarely reified in practice (Horsman 2002, 21–22). Some records are intentionally destroyed, others lost through accident or neglect. According to Laura Millar (2002, 6), "Archivists manage the residue, not the entirety," and although such residues are often referred to as "fonds" in Canada and the United Kingdom, both Millar and I have argued that they are more appropriately labeled with the American term *collection*. Even commentators who affirm that fonds are purely conceptual recognize the existence of physical aggregations of records; in the digital world, too, records creators, custodians, and users assemble record aggregations (Yeo 2012a, 78) and frequently impose orders on these aggregations in directory systems and user interfaces (Niu 2015, 65; Zhang 2012, 185). All such aggregations can be viewed as collections, because they result from human decisions about selection, grouping, ordering, or custodianship as well as from the chances of survival and loss. Whether digital or analog, large or small, collections often have complex histories, passing from one custodian to another and sometimes acquiring additions as well as suffering losses. A conceptual fonds or series may be distributed across several collections; over time, parts of it may move from one collection to another (Yeo 2012a, 2012b).

A particular benefit of retrospective description is its ability to provide overviews of record aggregations. Users often find such overviews helpful, not only for contextual interpretation but also for pragmatic use in assessing the scope of available resources (Kooyman 1994; Prom 2004, 259–60). Here retrospective description seems inevitable; it is difficult to circumscribe aggregate groupings in their earliest stages of formation (MacNeil 1996, 241–42).

In practice, retrospective description has remained the norm in most countries. For archival services handling records generated in past centuries and for those lacking influence over the early life of records, it is usually the only option. Most retrospective description employs hierarchical structures, but relational methods can also be used retrospectively, provided they are flexible enough to accommodate lower levels of certainty (because full information about past contextual relationships is unavailable for many older archives). Relational systems could document not only the links among records, agents, and business activities in controlled organizational environments but also the more fragmented histories of physical collections and their changing memberships over time (Yeo 2012a, 71–77).

STANDARDS

Since the 1980s, increasing numbers of descriptive standards have been promulgated. Many reflect particular national traditions, and global agreement remains conspicuously absent; despite its name, *ISAD(G): General International Standard Archival Description* (International Council on Archives 2000) has not been fully accepted internationally. Nevertheless, some convergence has occurred, with the American *Describing Archives: A Content Standard (DACS)* (Society of American Archivists 2004, 2013) and the third edition of the British *Manual of Archival Description (MAD)* (Procter and Cook 2000) both seeking closer alignment to *ISAD(G)* than their predecessors. Because early standardization initiatives in North America largely arose from desires to contribute data to bibliographic networks, their models were adapted from library practice, but later developments moved away from bibliographic implementations and sought to provide structures in fuller accord with archival principles.

Promotion of these standards has been successful in many countries. For example, in a 2007 "self-assessment exercise" for English and Welsh local government archival services, 92 percent of respondents claimed at least some level of compliance with *ISAD(G)* (Haunton 2008); in a 2013 survey of American archivists, 90.2 percent of respondents stated that they were familiar with *DACS* (Gracy and Lambert 2014, 108). In Canada, compliance with the *Rules for Archival Description (RAD)* is a requirement for all institutions wishing to participate in the national archival network (Bureau of Canadian Archivists 2008; Dancy 2012, 8). To varying extents, these standards have helped ensure consistency in descriptive practice, made descriptions easier to use, provided quality assurance benchmarks, and acted as indicators of professionalism (Davis 2003, 293). They have facilitated systems development, data sharing, remote access, and the construction of some remarkably successful cross-institutional online services (Stockting 2005; Van Camp 2001). Encoded Archival Description (EAD), developed in the United States and adopted in many other countries, provides a platform independent of proprietary software—thus offering some safeguards against technological obsolescence (Pitti 2012)—and is associable with a larger family of standards and frameworks based on Extensible Markup Language (XML).

Nevertheless, these standards have not been immune from criticism. It has been claimed that they confuse conceptual and physical groupings of records (Yeo 2012a, 69–71), underestimate the importance of custodial histories (MacNeil 2009, 95–99), and focus excessively on data sharing while paying insufficient regard to records' evidential meanings (Bunn 2013, 243–44). To Bearman (1992) and Chris Hurley (2000), they fail because they are designed for retrospective description of physical objects rather than capture of process-centric information at the time when records are created. Of course, description at the point of creation was never these standards' intended role, and subsequent revisions have not altered their retrospective standpoint. But Australian criticisms that *ISAD(G)* did not allow separation of context description from records description (McKemmish 1994, 193) elicited a response. American archivists in the 1980s had already begun to explore possible roles for authority records derived from library science, and Bearman and Lytle (1985–1986) and Max Evans (1986) had recommended using them to maintain discrete provenance information. In 1996, *ISAAR(CPF): International Standard Archival Authority Record for Corporate Bodies, Persons and Families* adopted these ideas. *ISAAR(CPF)* recognized that information about creators is logically separate from information about records and opened the way to establishing collaborative databases of creator descriptions (Ottosson 2006).

ISAAR(CPF) sought to combine terminology control with structured descriptions of creators. Its first edition was not widely used, and its second edition (International Council on Archives 2004) moved closer to a relational model, emphasizing relationships between creators and records, in addition to the provision of information about creators themselves. *ISDF: International Standard for Describing Functions* (International Council on Archives 2007) also takes a more explicitly relational approach, documenting relationships as well as functions and functional components. *ISDF* is not labeled as a standard for "authority records," but, like *ISAAR (CPF)*, it includes both terminology control and descriptive elements.

In separating description of records and contexts, *ISAAR(CPF)* and *ISDF* can also be seen as tentative responses to the challenges of multicreator and multifunctional records (Cunningham, Millar, and Reed 2013, 128). But in contrast to Australian strategies, international standards have generally remained ambivalent about multiple contextual relationships; the earliest proponents of *ISAAR(CPF)* often preferred to stress its role in linking records from the same creator held in different archival institutions (Cook 1996, 260). Some archivists remain doubtful whether authority systems can adequately represent complex contexts of origin (Hurley 2005), but others argue that they model them effectively (Peters 2005; Savoja and Vitali 2007). Among published guidelines, only *Describing Archives in Context* (Australian Society of Archivists ca. 2007) gives full support to the Series System as a solution to these challenges.

The past two decades have also seen the issue of various standards—mostly, but not exclusively, Australian—for recordkeeping or records management metadata. Many have been influenced by the SPIRT model and some also by ISO23081:*Metadata for Records*, a high-level standard employing the SPIRT framework. The most advanced of the Australian standards propose complex multientity relational systems. All are rigorously designed for use in controlled records-creation environments, but there are many unresolved questions about the willingness of records-creating organizations to adopt them. Although the Australian standards are ostensibly continuum based, their hospitality to cultural domains and to records kept outside formal organizational contexts remains open to debate.

The archival standards in commonest use in Europe and North America have been widely criticized on the grounds that they remain rooted in custodial mind-sets and monohierarchical descriptive practices inappropriate for a digital era. But growing numbers of voices are raising questions, not just about the standards currently most popular but also about the implications of *any* attempt at standardization and the cultural baggage it brings. Standards require us to divide descriptions into discrete elements, to segment reality into neat packages (Light 2007, 51), but critics are increasingly aware that such rigidity makes it "difficult to tell stories that cut across one's data structures" (Bowker 2005, 140). To social commentators, the desire to categorize and codify is one of the "impulses of . . . expert occupations" (Dandeker 1990, 145) and a leitmotif of modernist rationality. Underlying it are assumptions that objects and understandings can be systematically classified and analyzed using explanatory schemas, assumptions firmly rejected by postmodernism. Archivists aim at standardized, consistent descriptions, but records are multifarious, and the stories to be told about them are not simple ones. Critics argue that standardized description imposes semblances of order or uniformity where none exist, simplified views where reality is complex, or single perspectives where multiple perspectives are required (Nesmith 2005, 267–69).

Knowledge of context is crucial, yet context is limitless. How can archivists presume to reduce it to definable categories? Boundaries must be invented, and archivists emphasize those aspects of context they consider essential or desirable for interpreting or authenticating records: creators' histories or biographies, organizational structures and functions, and, increasingly, the histories of other stakeholders besides creators. *ISAAR (CPF)*, *ISDF*, and Australian multientity metadata standards attempt to capture these contexts by surrounding descriptions of records with descriptions of other discrete objects and with specified relationships among these objects. They assume that organizations, functions, and agents are intermittently stable entities, subject to definable changes at identifiable moments in time. But postmodern organization theory suggests that these are not isolable objects but fluid "accomplishments," ceaselessly evolving and constantly emerging (Chia 1995). Process models, for example, are seen as social constructions, not as units of analysis existing independently of the analyst (Crabtree, Rouncefield, and Tolmie 2001). From these perspectives, standards such as *ISDF*, for all their merits in attempting richer views of context than *DACS* or *ISAD(G)*, are based on illusory assumptions about the possibility of reducing complex and ever-changing realities to defined stages and formalized elements of data. Wendy Duff and Verne Harris (2002, 284–85) have advocated development of a "liberatory standard" that would "offer optimal flexibility and permeability" and allow descriptions to be continually reinvented over time. Others might argue that no standards-based approach could achieve this and that only unsystematized description can provide the flexibility to respond creatively to heterogeneous realities.

According to Anthony Giddens (1984, 25), "Structure . . . is always both constraining and enabling," and this certainly seems true of the categorized data structures of descriptive standards, which confine modes of expression but facilitate information sharing and the development of online access tools. Like any structural system, a descriptive standard may be experienced as predominantly enabling by some (such as archivists seeking to maximize remote user accessibility) and predominantly constraining by others (such as those wishing to emphasize the fluidity of archival materials and contexts). But it may be doubted how far wholly unstructured descriptions would be intelligible. Standardized descriptions offer users "a stable point of departure and return" (MacNeil 2005, 277), and it seems we must accept a degree of structure, at least until we have computer systems as yet unimagined.

VOICES

Description is necessarily of its time and place. Despite erstwhile claims that archival principles or descriptive standards can ensure accurate and definitive representations (CUSTARD 2002, Introduction; Duff and Haworth 1990–1991, 32; Haworth 1992, 97), archivists increasingly recognize that representation is never perfect; that compromises must be made; and that standards are not universal but are localized products of particular societies. Some would argue that descriptions merely impose our own cultural perceptions onto phenomena that can never be described objectively.

Growing numbers of critics affirm that descriptions reflect the worldview of the describer, or that they reveal as much about the minds of archivists as about the records themselves (Duff and Harris 2002, 275–76; Hedstrom 2002, 39). The structures and functionalities of the descriptive systems archivists employ also impact the descriptions they create (Evans 2014, 15). Descriptions, and archivists who compile them, are not impartial or neutral. For example, archivists often seem biased against irrationality or disorder, preferring to present a "well-organized . . . view of a record collection that may never have existed that way in operational reality" (Cook 2006, 173). They describe the origins of records and the actions of the initial creators but often fail to document losses from subsequent neglect or alterations at the hands of later custodians (Yeo 2009) or the transformative effects of their own appraisal and arrangement decisions (Cox 2004, 249–65; Nesmith 2005).

These biases may be inadvertent or shaped by training or tradition rather than conscious individual preference. But because descriptive work has to be selective, archivists also make conscious decisions about what to include in their descriptions, what to emphasize, and what to ignore (Nesmith 2002, 36). Such decision making necessarily privileges some aspects while diminishing others and is increasingly being questioned: How far do traditional approaches to description perpetuate the value systems of individual and corporate records creators, who often occupy positions of authority, power, and influence? How far do they perpetuate the value systems of archival institutions, which may be equally unrepresentative of a wider society? Do archivists consciously or unconsciously exclude other views or other meanings? Can records be described in ways that not only reflect administrative or personal contexts of creation but also accommodate the voices of others, including those who are mentioned in the records or those who have shaped or used the records at different times? These questions—raised in writings by Duff and Harris (2002), Randall Jimerson (2009, 309–14), and Michael Piggott and Sue McKemmish (2002, 9–12), among others—owe much to the postmodernist agenda.

One set of proposed solutions lies in recognizing that holdings of archival institutions are not pristine but have usually undergone many vicissitudes. Descriptions should give credit not just to original creators but also to collectors, custodians, and others who have intervened in shaping collections over time (MacNeil 2008; Millar 2002; Yeo 2009). Archivists should also acknowledge their own mediating role and provide information about appraisals in which they participated, appraisal criteria they applied, and assumptions they made in processing and describing records as well as details of records they decided *not* to keep (Cook 2001, 34; Duff and Harris 2002, 278). Tom Nesmith (2011) recommends overlaying descriptions with reports or essays on topics such as the societal contexts that shape records creation and the evolution of records through recordkeeping processes, custodial histories, and appraisal decisions. Cook (2001, 34) and Nesmith (2011, 42) suggest making biographical sketches of appraisers publicly accessible. Jennifer Meehan (2009, 86–89) calls for archivists to supply explicit documentation of their arrangement work, and Jennifer Douglas (2013, 24) urges them to be more "honest" about the ordering activities they undertake. Such measures would help fulfil their obligations for accountability and transparency (MacNeil 2009; Millar 2006).

Other approaches seek ways of increasing the hospitality of description, especially to those on the margins of society. In forwarding this cause, several writers aspire to transform older understandings of provenance. Nesmith (1999, 147, 2006, 352) argues for "societal provenance" embracing "all of those people, organizations, and entities whose decisions and actions account for the records' existence, characteristics and continuing history." Jeannette Bastian (2003, 82) wants to understand provenance as encompassing "the entire society ... so that the voiceless population is ... full partner in the record-creating process." Hurley (2005, 138) proposes the term *parallel provenance* to accommodate the narratives of those "involved in the events or circumstances which the records document." All three authors reinterpret provenance as a way of acknowledging complexity and the range of stakeholders involved in records creation. They see the people mentioned in records—those whose lives were affected by the activities the records represent—as more than mere subject content; their lives also form part of the record's *context*. In this way, content and context meet (Bastian 2006, 282–83). As McKemmish and Piggott (2013, 137) note, "By expanding the definition of record creators to include everyone who has contributed to a record's creative process or has been directly affected by its action, the notions of co-creation and parallel or simultaneous multiple provenance reposition 'records subjects' as 'records agents.' "

The implications of these ideas have not yet been fully explored. Some critics may argue that, in reinventing description to redress the balance of power and privilege, we endanger our understanding that the form, language, and structure of records are all determined by the immediate circumstances of their origin. Should we (as Douglas suggests in Chapter 2 of this book) develop descriptive methods in which the persons, objects, and events to which records pertain can be fully represented as contextual entities, without necessarily labeling all of them as provenance? For many commentators, however, the move from simple to complex provenances is an opportunity rather than a risk. Postmodernist writers, dedifferentiating archives from other "texts," insist that the voices of "authors" must not be privileged over other voices and suggest that traditional approaches are authoritarian attempts to diminish diversity, privilege dominant social groups, and silence alternative interpretations (Brothman 1999, 78–80). Advocates of archival activism in support of social justice argue that, where human rights are at issue, the traditional conception of provenance can perpetuate repressive behaviors and asymmetries of power (Wood et al. 2014, 401–04).

One practical means of acknowledging these concerns and bringing other voices to description is by engaging users, or individuals affected by records, to generate descriptive content. In the early twenty-first century, inviting users to contribute to description has become increasingly popular, because it aligns not only with social justice and inclusivity agendas but also with current developments in technology. User contributions can be made in face-to-face settings (Newman 2012) but are now more frequently associated with online interaction in a "Web 2.0" environment. Growing numbers of archival institutions offer online venues where users can take part in description by tagging, commenting, or adding substantive new information. Instead of being passive consumers of finding aids prepared by archivists, users are invited to become active contributors to descriptive work, a shift that is often seen as part of a wider movement toward increased user participation in archival enterprise (Evans 2007; Theimer 2011; Yakel 2011).

Web 2.0 is widely perceived as a democratizing environment that enables collaborative knowledge sharing and breaks down barriers of exclusion. Some proponents of radically democratic approaches affirm that user-contributed descriptions should be independent of control or moderation by archivists and that users should not only be empowered to participate but should also "decide … the forms and frameworks of participation" (Huvila 2008, 30). However, other commentators argue that concerns about the reliability and traceability of user contributions necessitate a degree of institutional control (Grannum 2011, 119–23). Further issues that still need explicating include ownership of contributions, relationships between user-generated and institutionally authored descriptions, and reports indicating low levels of user interest (Gorzalski 2013, 12; Yakel 2011, 272), which may suggest a need for more research into methods of identifying and reaching potential contributors. Although often seen as a means of advancing social inclusion, use of Web 2.0 tools may still exclude those who are less comfortable with or lack easy access to computer technology. In moving beyond assumptions that archivists are the sole or best mediators, a participatory culture also gives rise to potentially controversial questions about the role of professionalism in archival work (Flinn 2010). As Heather MacNeil (2012, 495) suggests, blurring the boundaries between creators and consumers of description opens a debate about how closely "the generic identity of finding aids [is] linked to the professional identity of archivists."

Inviting contributions from users is not wholly new. In the past, archivists undertaking description have sometimes sought assistance from users with specialist knowledge, recognizing that they can bring levels of understanding and sensitivity that might otherwise be lacking (Newman 2012, 62). However, many new participatory models and practices depend not on specialists but on the so-called wisdom of crowds: the assumption that a large quantity of contributions will compensate for any bias or lack of expertise on the part of any individual contributor. Sporadic user participation cannot offer the safeguards on which such "crowdsourcing" normally relies, and it remains uncertain whether archival description projects can attract user contributions in sufficient numbers. Equally, it can be argued that continued reliance on a small number of expert users will tend to promote established identities rather than cultural pluralism.

In practice, user contribution initiatives differ in the extent to which they rely on experts or a larger "crowd," just as they vary in their emphasis on supporting existing archival infrastructures or aspiring to transform them (Eveleigh 2014). Nevertheless, they are frequently heralded as opportunities to build collaborative communities and promote wider engagement with archives. Opening description to user participation can counterbalance finding aids that seem to privilege the value systems of the powerful, by enabling minority groups to supply alternative narratives and additional points of view. It also recognizes that final or definitive descriptions are never possible. Descriptions are, or should be, "always beta," always responsive to new understandings and further development.

SERVING USERS

Over the past three decades, technology has simplified the dissemination of descriptive information. Users now have instant remote access to thousands of descriptions that were previously dispersed and difficult to access. But standardization initiatives have concentrated on intellectual structures for description and rules for content; little has been done to identify best practices for presenting descriptive work to users. It is arguable that presentation may have mattered less when finding aids were almost always consulted in reading rooms with archivists on hand to offer assistance but becomes critical when descriptions are rendered digitally for remote use. In the absence of agreed standards, users consulting a variety of online resources often have to learn a new interface and retrieval syntax for each Web site they visit.

Studies have also shown that many display formats present barriers to accessing, navigating, and understanding descriptions (Chapman 2010; Daniels and Yakel 2010; Gerhold 2013). Users, especially novice users, often find interaction with online finding aids bewildering. Moreover, when descriptions are exposed to Web search engines, they are likely to be found by people who have little or no knowledge of archives; while this provides opportunities to bring archives to new audiences, it also means that descriptions must be adequately self-explanatory. However, in the early years of the digital era, archivists have tended to prioritize delivery of large quantities of descriptive information rather than research and development of effective methods of online presentation.

As yet, we do not fully understand how technology affects the usability of descriptions. Browsing, for example, has the potential to become more sophisticated in digital environments, using navigational techniques unknown in the paper world. But archivists remain uncertain how best to render online finding aids browsable and navigable. Many Web sites display them as single scrollable documents, offering little advance from the paper paradigm. Other archivists have been swept up in enthusiasm for search tools, and, despite Stefano Vitali's (1998, 42) assertion that "navigation within the system must be regarded as more important than . . . query-based retrieval," offer Web sites designed on the assumption that search technology should provide the main, or only, access route.

These different approaches are reminiscent of the debate, in the era of paper-based descriptions, about the relative merits of "provenance access" and "subject access" (Lytle 1980). Very broadly, provenance access would appear to correspond to use of browsing and navigation functions in online systems, and subject access to search. The earlier debate was never fully resolved, but most writers concluded that both were necessary. Yet, in the online world, subject access often has primacy, as computer scientists develop ever more powerful search techniques. On the Web, search is ubiquitous, and users increasingly "expect to be able to find archives ... using the same techniques they use to find other things" (Schaffner 2009, 4). However, search tools are usually more suited to well-defined queries that seek precise results than to the "complex, open-ended tasks" (Whitelaw 2012, 124) that often characterize the more speculative kinds of research in which archives are employed. Some critics have recently argued that descriptive finding aids may be unnecessary in a world where digitization and text-recognition software can make archival records discoverable using full-text search (Katz and Gandel 2011, 228; Miller 2013, 523–24), but comments of this kind assume that description serves no purpose beyond fulfilling retrieval needs that can be reformulated as specific search queries. In their traditional guise, finding aids also act as orientational tools that allow for situations of uncertainty and help users evaluate the range and utility of archives when planning their research. Reliance on full-text search alone cannot do this, nor can it offer interpretative assistance or supply contextualization for archival materials.

Further questions arise concerning online presentation of descriptive metadata. How can contextual information be provided when users are presented with sets of search results listing items from different provenances or fragments from different finding aids? How can multiple levels of description best be incorporated into screen displays? In Burt Altman and John Nemmers's study (2001, 126–27), users insisted on the importance of seeing the overall shape of a collection and expressed concern that presenting extensive finding aids on screen might lead to confusion. Robin Darwall-Smith and Michael Riordan (2012, 116–18) suggest that when online systems display so-called hit lists or show only selected parts of finding aids, the results are not always adequately contextualized. Dorian Gerhold (2013) and Jane Stevenson (2008) draw attention to concerns about the difficulties of ascertaining whether online search results are comprehensive and understanding what they represent. Research is still needed to discover what kinds of interface are most effective.

These challenges will become even more demanding if archivists adopt standards like *ISDF* or models influenced by ISO23081 or if they seek to reposition their finding aids "as part of a complex network of hyperlinked ... documentation" (MacNeil 2005, 276). Such moves would introduce even more intricate structures for users to navigate and interpret. Measures to enhance the transparency of descriptions or endow them with diverse voices would probably also increase their length and thus complicate their presentation. Archives are rich and multifaceted, but the further we elaborate their richness in our descriptions, the greater the challenge of presenting them effectively. If we think that there are "many provenances, multiple voices, hundreds of relationships . . . all needing to be documented" (Duff and Harris 2002, 274), interfaces more sophisticated than those currently on offer would seem to be required. Visualization techniques (Lemieux 2012; Whitelaw 2012) offer intriguing possibilities; they can assist comprehension of complex data and provide ways of displaying and navigating multidimensional relationships that cannot easily be presented in linear text.

An important element of any solution must be a better understanding of how users seek archival materials and how they interact with descriptions or visualizations. Although such understanding is a prerequisite for planning effective finding aids, few projects are known to have undertaken user consultation to inform system development and interface design. Moreover, different user groups may require different approaches. For example, academic users of finding aids can be suspicious of indexes and may prefer browse facilities; nonacademics and novice users are often content to use search functions (Sexton et al. 2004, 194–95). Although technological tools can provide different interfaces for different audiences, archivists will need fuller knowledge of how user communities are composed (Yeo 2005) and how they seek to interact with digital resources (Johnson 2008; Prom 2011) if customized presentation of descriptions is to be explored.

DIGITAL ARCHIVES: FUTURE DIRECTIONS

Digital records bring new descriptive challenges. It is widely argued that they need significantly more metadata than their paper counterparts, particularly at item level (Daines 2013, 96; Dow 2009, 4–5; Zhang 2012, 188–90). Preservation and long-term access concerns have led to calls to connect digital records with a range of technical and structural information that cannot be accommodated by current descriptive standards for archives and that necessitates using a separate standard for preservation metadata, such as the *PREMIS Data Dictionary* (PREMIS Editorial Committee 2015).

User expectations have also expanded in the digital world. Increasingly, users expect finding aids to be associated with digitized images or transcripts of analog originals, born-digital records, and perhaps digital materials from other domains and assume that they will be able to access all of these through a single interface. Users may also seek the ability to download their own copies of images or born-digital records, manipulate or annotate them, or assemble them into personal digital collections. Digital environments that empower users to recombine items dynamically and build temporary collections within and across the boundaries of formal provenance will offer enhanced capabilities for research and intellectual discovery (Westbrook 2002, 77–78; Yeo 2014, 174–76).

It is easy to imagine environments of this kind offering items from other domains alongside archival materials, but interoperability is impeded when standards for archives, libraries, and museums (and for audiovisual media and the like) remain largely domain-specific and descriptions are not reusable across domains. I have argued elsewhere (Yeo 2008) that domain boundaries are fuzzy, that many items are "boundary objects," transcending the boundaries with membership in more than one domain, and that questions arise about the appropriateness of practices that oblige us to assign items to a single domain for descriptive purposes.User expectations will make it increasingly difficult to justify such "silos" of resources, particularly where boundary objects are concerned, but the issue extends beyond retrieval to wider questions of management, use, and interpretation. We need integrated systems that permit multiple contributions to the descriptive process and inclusion of bibliographic, curatorial, and recordkeeping metadata in a single environment and support shared management of boundary objects to meet the requirements of different stakeholders.

How such systems might be developed, and how they might be presented in ways that offer appropriate interfaces and access routes, await investigation. In Geoffrey Bowker's words (2005, 199), "The ordering of data across multiple disciplines is not simply a question of finding a commonly accepted set of spatial and temporal units and naming conventions, though this is the way that it is often portrayed in the literature." Nor should it be seen merely as a matter of developing crosswalks or mappings between existing discipline-specific standards, an exercise that often leads to false equations between differently nuanced concepts (Duff 2001, 293). Instead, we should recognize that different communities bring different concerns and perceptions to the same objects or to overlapping sets of objects (Yeo 2008, 131), and the challenge will be to develop systems that effectively accommodate various frames of reference.

Personal letters provide a simple example. Letters are filed by their recipients; in archival worldviews, they form part of the recipients' fonds. However, to biographers and linguists, a letter forms part of the literary output of its author. Archivists have had good reason to complain that "autograph letter collections" assembled by librarians or antiquarians conceal or destroy the integrity of the fonds, yet authorship is also part of context and a wish to bring together an author's works is legitimate (Hurley ca. 2004, sec. 7). Other players may have little interest in letters or in these aspects of context but may want to bring together a range of items across traditional domain boundaries on the basis of form, content, techniques, materials, cultural associations, or other criteria. Such diverse requirements are often difficult to meet in analog environments, but digital items can be grouped and regrouped at will. In the digital world, it should be possible to design systems that accommodate different groupings and different interpretations of boundary objects (Yeo 2012b, 66–70). If such systems were relational, documenting the relationships of individual objects and entities across domains, they could provide rich evidential contexts for objects with record characteristics while also supporting the alternative perspectives of other communities.

Such systems could be envisaged as spanning the boundaries, not only of professional domains but also of social and cultural groups outside the professional arena. Besides expressing relationships that support evidentiality and document creation contexts and custodial histories, their relationality could incorporate a variety of "relationships divined from other points of view" (Hurley ca. 2004, sec. 7), while their granularity could underpin access to digital materials and provide the capacity for individuals and communities to form their own digital collections, offering new possibilities for scholarly and popular research and encouraging users to engage with archives in innovative ways.

In the years since the earlier version of this chapter was published, its comments about the relevance and value of relational approaches have been echoed in a number of calls to rethink or transform descriptive frameworks for records and archives (Bailey 2013; Evans 2014; Higgins, Hilton, and Dafis 2014; Yeo 2012b). The writers who advocate such rethinking all question hierarchical descriptive practices, and most propose a shift toward networked models that can transcend predetermined collective structures and offer richer representations of complex contexts. Recent projects using the Encoded Archival Context (EAC-CPF) standard also evince a growing interest in networks of relationships, particularly agent relationships that influence records creation (Pitti et al. 2014; Wisser 2015). The "international conceptual model" that the International Council on Archives' Experts Group on Archival Description has begun to formulate (Gueguen et al. 2013) is expected to emphasize the use of relational modeling.

Many professionals now conclude that, in digital realms, description requires relational and granular rather than hierarchical and purely collective approaches. Relational systems, perhaps used in conjunction with linked data technologies or visualization tools, will allow archival resources to be presented in many different ways. Records-focused thinkers have recognized that relational approaches can extend documentation of context beyond the single creator of the traditional model, beyond Scott's multiple creators, to the functional and societal context of the act of creation, and to actors and actions involved in the record's subsequent adventures. Some also acknowledge that every single record object may have its own contexts, overlapping with, but ultimately distinct from, the contexts of its neighbors. For those whose main focus is on users, relational systems bring concerns about ease of use but also have the potential to provide users with new and more powerful means of engagement. Those seeking democratization should also welcome a relational approach, since it can support descriptions of a record's relations to multiple agents so that perceptions of the roles of all parties can be documented without insisting that any single role should have a privileged status. Relational methods offer opportunities to build on the interconnectivity and remixability afforded by digital materials (Bailey 2013). They align archival practices with a number of technological developments, including the movement away from rigid hierarchical file systems, the shift from centralized repositories to federated metadata, and the growing use of discovery and semantic analysis techniques. At the same time, they need to be flexible enough to accommodate uncertainty and diversity of interpretation and to respond to understandings that contextual relationships evolve over time (Yeo 2014, 177–79).

Relational systems require a fundamental shift away from collective description. Archival practice has long emphasized collective description, but many archivists have begun to ask whether this emphasis has been driven by theory or practical necessity. Context is crucial, and contextual knowledge is often captured in high-level descriptions, but relying *exclusively* on high-level descriptions is not easily justified as a matter of principle. According to Bearman (1996, 200–01), it is merely pragmatism elevated to the level of ideology, and "we manage paper records collectively because it is too expensive to manage them individually." Despite evidence that users would welcome more information at item level (Allison-Bunnell, Yakel, and Hauck 2011, 86; Altman and Nemmers 2001, 129; Anderson 2004, 100), few archival institutions have the resources to undertake much item-level description. Many have large backlogs that they have been unable to describe at *any* level. Mark Greene and Dennis Meissner (2005, 253) have asserted that archivists should "avoid ... descriptive work on an item level" to achieve increased productivity, and many archivists in the United States have adopted their "More Product, Less Process" (MPLP) methodology, which deprecates item-level orientation. In other countries, most archivists have long acknowledged the practical constraints that preclude the creation of large numbers of item-level descriptions using traditional methods.

How can this conundrum be resolved? First, while it may be desirable for relational or other descriptive systems to operate at item level (Bak 2012; Bearman 1996), it is not essential. The Australian Series System is a relational system where the series is the basic unit of control. Newer relational models are hospitable to levels lower than series, but an orientation to file or folder level may sometimes be adequate; cost-benefit arguments suggest that item-level control is not always necessary (Gilliland-Swetland 2001, 222), at least for paper records. Nevertheless, relational systems are most powerful when they function at item level, and most preservation and access strategies for digital records require item-level metadata, captured alongside or within the records. In digital environments, an orientation to manipulable items will overcome many of the constraints imposed by traditional fixed hierarchies, while modeling of relationships and use of appropriate metadata will supply the wider contextualization that item-level systems would otherwise lack (Yeo 2012b).

Given the modest staffing levels of most archival institutions, few archivists can expect to achieve these outcomes unaided, but sharing responsibility may help to lighten the load. Organizational employees and other individuals at the start of a record's life, and users at later stages, all have roles to play. Creators of records have firsthand knowledge of their work and its setting, and reuse of item-level metadata generated by creators can avoid the need for arduous reconstruction of information that was more readily available at an earlier time. However, organizational records creators are often reluctant to devote themselves to metadata gathering if it impinges on business activity (Wallace 2001, 262). If archivists call on users to describe records at item level, the burden of capture can be shared further (Evans 2007), although engaging users in description requires time and effort (Gorzalski 2013, 19; Newman 2012, 70); some critics argue that the objectives of user participation initiatives should be social, not economic, and should emphasize community building rather than acquisition of metadata at minimal cost (Yakel 2011, 258).

As archives become increasingly digital, automated capture of descriptive information can be expected to offer the most promising economic solutions. Archivists can use automated tools to identify and extract technical metadata from digital records (Daines 2013, 96–97). They may be able to employ natural language processing, data mining, and textual analysis tools to create visualizations or determine the content of records; they may also be able to use newly emerging techniques for automated generation of contextual metadata and automated or semi-automated documentation of relationships (Yeo 2013a, 22–24, 2013b, 221–23). All these tools operate at low levels of granularity. They are in their infancy at present and are unlikely to supply all the information—particularly broader contextual information—that archival institutions and users may require, but it seems almost certain that they will eventually perform the more mundane aspects of description and representation at item level, thus allowing archivists to focus resources on aspects that require human understanding.

CONCLUSION

Describing archives is rarely a straightforward task. While future automated tools will substantially reduce the burden, archival institutions will continue to meet challenges in fashioning and populating their descriptive systems. Description is sometimes derided as "expediency chasing theory" (Gilliland-Swetland 2001, 209), and in a world of restricted budgets, ever-growing volumes of digital archives, and substantial quantities of legacy paper records, archivists will undoubtedly experience tensions between what seems theoretically desirable and what can be practically achieved.

But resource limitations will not be the only source of difficulty or disagreement. Conflicts will continue to arise between those perceptions and practices that emphasize accessibility and those that give priority to authentication and "recordness"; between objectivized standards and multiple subjective realities; and between traditional understandings of provenance and attempts to open description to other voices and broader ranges of interests.

It is not wholly clear how such conflicts might be resolved or even how far their resolution is desirable. Indeed, it could be argued that the most critical tension lies between individual practitioners seeking unambiguous guidance on "best practice" for particular descriptive projects and the need for the wider profession to acknowledge that description can never be reduced to simple certainties and to continue its exploration of different modes of thought. The complexity of the issues surrounding description is an inevitable consequence of the intricacy and diversity of archival materials and the world in which they are created, kept, and used.

REFERENCES

Allison-Bunnell, J., E. Yakel, and J. Hauck. 2011. "Researchers at Work: Assessing Needs for Content and Presentation of Archival Materials." *Journal of Archival Organization* 9: 67–104.

Altman, B., and J. R. Nemmers. 2001. "The Usability of Online Archival Resources: The Polaris Project Finding Aid." *American Archivist* 64: 121–31.

Anderson, I. G. 2004. "Are You Being Served? Historians and the Search for Primary Sources." *Archivaria* 58: 81–129.

Australian Society of Archivists. ca. 2007. *Describing Archives in Context: A Guide to Australian Practice*. Dickson, Australian Capital Territory: Australian Society of Archivists.

Bailey, J. 2013. "Disrespect des Fonds: Rethinking Arrangement and Description in Born-Digital Archives." *Archive Journal* 3. http://www.archivejournal.net/issue/3/archives-remixed/ (accessed June 1, 2016).

Bak, G. 2012. "Continuous Classification: Capturing Dynamic Relationships among Information Resources." *Archival Science* 12: 287–318.

Barr, D. 1987–1988. "The Fonds Concept in the *Working Group on Archival Standards* Report." *Archivaria* 25: 163–70.

Bastian, J. A. 2003. *Owning Memory: How a Caribbean Community Lost Its Archives and Found Its History*. Westport, CT: Libraries Unlimited.

Bastian, J. A. 2006. "Reading Colonial Records through an Archival Lens: The Provenance of Place, Space and Creation." *Archival Science* 6: 267–84.

Bearman, D. 1989. *Archival Methods*. Pittsburgh, PA: Archives and Museum Informatics.

Bearman, D. 1992. "Documenting Documentation." *Archivaria* 34: 33–49.

Bearman, D. 1996. "Item Level Control and Electronic Recordkeeping." *Archives and Museum Informatics* 10: 195–245.

Bearman, D., and R. H. Lytle. 1985–1986. "The Power of the Principle of Provenance." *Archivaria* 21: 14–27.

Bearman, D., and K. Sochats. 1996. *Metadata Requirements for Evidence*. http://www.archimuse.com/papers/nhprc/BACartic.html (accessed June 1, 2016).

Boles, F. 1982. "Disrespecting Original Order." *American Archivist* 45: 26–32.

Bowker, G. C. 2005. *Memory Practices in the Sciences*. Cambridge, MA: MIT Press.

Brothman, B. 1999. "Declining Derrida: Integrity, Tensegrity, and the Preservation of Archives from Deconstruction." *Archivaria* 48: 64–88.

Bunn, J. 2013. "Developing Descriptive Standards: A Renewed Call to Action." *Archives and Records* 34: 235–47.

Bureau of Canadian Archivists. 2008. *Rules for Archival Description*, revised version. http://www.cdncouncilarchives.ca/archdesrules.html (accessed June 1, 2016).

Chapman, J. C. 2010. "Observing Users: An Empirical Analysis of User Interaction with Online Finding Aids." *Journal of Archival Organization* 8: 4–30.

Chia, R. 1995. "From Modern to Postmodern Organizational Analysis." *Organization Studies* 16: 579–604.

Cook, M. 1986. *The Management of Information from Archives*. Aldershot, England: Gower.

Cook, M. 1993. *Information Management and Archival Data*. London: Library Association Publishing.

Cook, M. 1996. "The International Descriptive Standards: New Departures." *Archivi & Computer* 6: 259–66.

Cook, T. 1992. "The Concept of the Archival *Fonds*: Theory, Description, and Provenance in the Post-Custodial Era." In *The Archival Fonds: From Theory to Practice*, edited by T. Eastwood, 31–85. Ottawa: Bureau of Canadian Archivists.

Cook, T. 1997. "What Is Past Is Prologue: A History of Archival Ideas since 1898, and the Future Paradigm Shift." *Archivaria* 43: 17–63.

Cook, T. 2001. "Fashionable Nonsense or Professional Rebirth: Postmodernism and the Practice of Archives." *Archivaria* 51: 14–35.

Cook, T. 2006. "Remembering the Future: Appraisal of Records and the Role of Archives in Constructing Social Memory." In *Archives, Documentation, and Institutions of Social Memory: Essays from the Sawyer Seminar*, edited by F. X. Blouin and W. G. Rosenberg, 169–81. Ann Arbor: University of Michigan Press.

Cox, R. J. 2004. *No Innocent Deposits: Forming Archives by Rethinking Appraisal*. Lanham, MD: Scarecrow Press.

Crabtree, A., M. Rouncefield, and P. Tolmie. 2001. "There's Something Else Missing Here: BPR and the Requirements Process." *Knowledge and Process Management* 8: 164–74.

Cunningham, A. 2000. "Dynamic Descriptions: Recent Developments in Standards for Archival Description and Metadata." *Canadian Journal of Information and Library Science* 25 (4): 3–17.

Cunningham, A. 2001. "Six Degrees of Separation: Australian Metadata Initiatives and Their Relationships with International Standards." *Archival Science* 1: 271–83.

Cunningham, A. 2005. Review of *Describing Archives: A Content Standard. Journal of Archival Organization* 3 (1): 87–90.

Cunningham, A., ed. 2010. *The Arrangement and Description of Archives amid Administrative and Technological Change*. Brisbane: Australian Society of Archivists.

Cunningham, A., L. Millar, and B. Reed. 2013. "Peter J. Scott and the Australian 'Series' System: Its Origins, Features, Rationale, Impact and Continuing Relevance." *Comma* 2013 (1): 121–44.

CUSTARD. 2002. *Statement of Principles for the CUSTARD Project*. http://www.archivists.org/news/custardproject.asp (accessed June 1, 2016).

Daines, J. G. 2013. "Processing Digital Records and Manuscripts." In *Archival Arrangement and Description*, edited by C. J. Prom and T. J. Frusciano, 87–143. Chicago, IL: Society of American Archivists.

Dancy, R. 2012. "*RAD* Past, Present, and Future." *Archivaria* 74: 7–41.

Dandeker, C. 1990. *Surveillance, Power and Modernity*. Cambridge, England: Polity Press.

Daniels, M. G., and E. Yakel. 2010. "Seek and You May Find: Successful Search in Online Finding Aid Systems." *American Archivist* 73: 535–68.

Darwall-Smith, R., and M. Riordan. 2012. " 'Bad and Dangerous Work': Lessons from Nineteenth- and Early-Twentieth-Century Oxford Archives." *Archivaria* 74: 93–118.

Davis, S. E. 2003. "Descriptive Standards and the Archival Profession." *Cataloging and Classification Quarterly* 35: 291–308.

Douglas, J. 2013. "What We Talk about When We Talk about Original Order in Writers' Archives." *Archivaria* 76: 7–25.

Dow, E. H. 2009. *Electronic Records in the Manuscript Repository*. Lanham, MD: Scarecrow Press.

Duchein, M. 1983. "Theoretical Principles and Practical Problems of *Respect des Fonds* in Archival Science." *Archivaria* 16: 64–82.

Duff, W. M. 2001. "Evaluating Metadata on a Metalevel." *Archival Science* 1: 285–94.

Duff, W. M., and K. M. Haworth. 1990–1991. "The Reclamation of Archival Description: The Canadian Perspective." *Archivaria* 31: 26–35.

Duff, W. M., and V. Harris. 2002. "Stories and Names: Archival Description as Narrating Records and Constructing Meanings." *Archival Science* 2: 263–85.

Eastwood, T. 2000. "Putting the Parts of the Whole Together: Systematic Arrangement of Archives." *Archivaria* 50: 93–116.

Evans, J. 2014. "Designing Dynamic Descriptive Frameworks." *Archives and Manuscripts* 42: 5–18.

Evans, J., S. McKemmish, and K. Bhoday. 2005. "Create Once, Use Many Times: The Clever Use of Recordkeeping Metadata for Multiple Archival Purposes." *Archival Science* 5: 17–42.

Evans, M. J. 1986. "Authority Control: An Alternative to the Record Group Concept." *American Archivist* 49: 249–61.

Evans, M. J. 2007. "Archives of the People, by the People, for the People." *American Archivist* 70: 387–400.

Eveleigh, A. 2014. "Crowding Out the Archivist? Locating Crowdsourcing within the Broader Landscape of Participatory Archives." In *Crowdsourcing Our Cultural Heritage*, edited by M. Ridge, 211–29. Farnham, England: Ashgate.

Fenyo, M. D. 1966. "The Record Group Concept: A Critique." *American Archivist* 29: 229–39.

Fischer, G. L. 1973. "Letting the Archival Dust Settle: Some Remarks on the Record Group Concept." *Journal of the Society of Archivists* 4: 640–45.

Flinn, A. 2010. "An Attack on Professionalism and Scholarship? Democratising Archives and the Production of Knowledge." *Ariadne* 62. http://www.ariadne.ac.uk/issue62/flinn (accessed June 1, 2016).

Gerhold, D. 2013. "Record Office Online Catalogues." *The Local Historian* 43: 57–63.

Giddens, A. 1984. *The Constitution of Society: Outline of the Theory of Structuration*. Berkeley: University of California Press.

Gilliland, A., N. Rouche, L. Lindberg, and J. Evans. 2005. "Towards a 21st Century Metadata Infrastructure Supporting the Creation, Preservation and Use of Trustworthy Records: Developing the InterPARES2 Metadata Schema Registry." *Archival Science* 5: 43–78.

Gilliland-Swetland, A. J. 2001. "Popularizing the Finding Aid: Exploiting EAD to Enhance Online Discovery and Retrieval in Archival Information Systems by Diverse User Groups." *Journal of Internet Cataloging* 4 (3–4): 199–225.

Gorzalski, M. 2013. "Examining User-Created Description in the Archival Profession." *Journal of Archival Organization* 11: 1–22.

Gorzalski, M. 2014. "Reimagining Record Groups: A Case Study and Considerations for Record Group Revision." *Provenance* 32: 28–48.

Gracy, K. F., and F. Lambert. 2014. "Who's Ready to Surf the Next Wave? A Study of Perceived Challenges to Implementing New and Revised Standards for Archival Description." *American Archivist* 77: 96–132.

Grannum, G. 2011. "Harnessing User Knowledge: The National Archives' *Your Archives* Wiki." In *A Different Kind of Web*, edited by K. Theimer, 116–27. Chicago, IL: Society of American Archivists.

Greene, M. A., and D. Meissner. 2005. "More Product, Less Process: Revamping Traditional Archival Processing." *American Archivist* 68: 208–63.

Gueguen, G., V. M. M. da Fonseca, D. V. Pitti, and C. Sibille-de Grimoüard. 2013. "Toward an International Conceptual Model for Archival Description: A Preliminary Report from the International Council on Archives' Experts Group on Archival Description." *American Archivist* 76: 567–84.

Haunton, M. 2008. E-mail from Melinda Haunton, The [U.K.] National Archives, to the author, April 30.

Haworth, K. M. 1992. "The Principles Speak for Themselves: Articulating a Language of Purpose for Archives." In *The Archival Imagination: Essays in Honour of Hugh A. Taylor*, edited by B. L. Craig, 90–104. Ottawa: Association of Canadian Archivists.

Haworth, K. M. 2001. "Archival Description: Content and Context in Search of Structure." *Journal of Internet Cataloging* 4 (3–4): 7–26.

Hedstrom, M. 2002. "Archives, Memory, and Interfaces with the Past." *Archival Science* 2: 21–43.

Hensen, S. L. 2001. "Archival Cataloging and the Internet: The Implications and Impact of EAD." *Journal of Internet Cataloging* 4 (3–4): 75–95.

Higgins, S., C. Hilton, and L. Dafis. 2014. "Archives Context and Discovery: Rethinking Arrangement and Description for the Digital Age." http://www.girona.cat/web/ica2014/ponents/textos/id174.pdf (accessed June 1, 2016).

Holmes, O. W. 1964. "Archival Arrangement: Five Different Operations at Five Different Levels." *American Archivist* 27: 21–41.

Horsman, P. 2002. "The Last Dance of the Phoenix, or the De-Discovery of the Archival Fonds." *Archivaria* 54: 1–23.

Hurley, C. 1995. "Problems with Provenance." *Archives and Manuscripts* 23: 234–59.

Hurley, C. 1998. "The Making and the Keeping of Records: (1) What Are Finding Aids For?" *Archives and Manuscripts* 26: 58–77.

Hurley, C. 2000. "The Making and the Keeping of Records: (2) The Tyranny of Listing." *Archives and Manuscripts* 28 (1): 8–23.

Hurley, C. ca. 2004. *Relationships in Records.* http://www.infotech.monash.edu.au/research/groups/rcrg/publications/relationships-in-records-rev-3b.rtf (accessed June 1, 2016).

Hurley, C. 2005. "Parallel Provenance: (1) What, if Anything, Is Archival Description?" *Archives and Manuscripts* 33 (1): 110–45.

Hurley, C. 2008. *Documenting Archives and Other Records.* http://www.infotech.monash.edu.au/research/groups/rcrg/publications/ch-documenting-archives.pdf (accessed June 1, 2016).

Huvila, I. 2008. "Participatory Archive: Towards Decentralised Curation, Radical User Orientation, and Broader Contextualisation of Records Management. *Archival Science* 8: 15–36.

International Council on Archives. 2000. *ISAD(G): General International Standard Archival Description*, 2nd ed. http://www.ica.org/sites/default/files/CBPS_2000_Guidelines_ISAD%28G%29_Second-edition_EN.pdf (accessed June 1, 2016).

International Council on Archives. 2004. *ISAAR(CPF): International Standard Archival Authority Record for Corporate Bodies, Persons and Families*, 2nd ed. http://www.ica.org/sites/default/files/CBPS_Guidelines_ISAAR_Second-edition_EN.pdf (accessed June 1, 2016).

International Council on Archives. 2007. *ISDF: International Standard for Describing Functions.* http://www.ica.org/sites/default/files/CBPS_2007_Guidelines_ISDF_First-edition_EN.pdf (accessed June 1, 2016).

Jimerson, R. C. 2009. *Archives Power: Memory, Accountability, and Social Justice.* Chicago, IL: Society of American Archivists.

Johnson, A. 2008. "Users, Use and Context: Supporting Interaction between Users and Digital Archives." In *What Are Archives? Cultural and Theoretical Perspectives*, edited by L. Craven, 145–64. Aldershot, England: Ashgate.

Katz, R. N., and P. B. Gandel. 2011. "The Tower, the Cloud, and Posterity: Documenting in a Digital World." In *Controlling the Past: Documenting Society and Institutions*, edited by T. Cook, 217–38. Chicago, IL: Society of American Archivists.

Kooyman, S. M. 1994. "*RAD* and the Researcher." *Archivaria* 37: 104–10.

Lemieux, V. L. 2012. "Using Information Visualization and Visual Analytics to Achieve a More Sustainable Future for Archives: A Survey and Critical Analysis of Some Developments." *Comma* 2012 (2): 55–70.

Light, M. 2007. "Moving beyond the Name: Defining Corporate Entities to Support Provenance-Based Access." *Journal of Archival Organization* 5 (1–2): 49–74.

Lytle, R. H. 1980. "Intellectual Access to Archives: I. Provenance and Content Indexing Methods of Subject Retrieval, and II. Report of an Experiment Comparing Provenance and Content Indexing Methods of Subject Retrieval." *American Archivist* 43: 64–75, 191–207.

MacNeil, H. 1995. "Metadata Strategies and Archival Description: Comparing Apples to Oranges." *Archivaria* 39: 22–32.

MacNeil, H. 1996. "The Implications of the UBC Research Results for Archival Description in General and the Canadian *Rules for Archival Description* in Particular." *Archivi & Computer* 6: 239–46.

MacNeil, H. 2005. "Picking Our Text: Archival Description, Authenticity, and the Archivist as Editor." *American Archivist* 68: 264–78.

MacNeil, H. 2008. "Archivalterity: Rethinking Original Order." *Archivaria* 66: 1–24.

MacNeil, H. 2009. "Trusting Description: Authenticity, Accountability, and Archival Description Standards." *Journal of Archival Organization* 7: 89–107.

MacNeil, H. 2012. "What Finding Aids *Do*: Archival Description as Rhetorical Genre in Traditional and Web-Based Environments." *Archival Science* 12: 485–500.

McKemmish, S. 1994. "Are Records Ever Actual?" In *The Records Continuum: Ian Maclean and Australian Archives First Fifty Years*, edited by S. McKemmish and M. Piggott, 187–203. Clayton, Victoria: Ancora Press.

McKemmish, S. 2001. "Placing Records Continuum Theory and Practice." *Archival Science* 1: 333–59.

McKemmish, S., G. Acland, N. Ward, and B. Reed. 1999. "Describing Records in Context in the Continuum: The Australian Recordkeeping Metadata Schema." *Archivaria* 48: 3–43.

McKemmish, S., and M. Piggott. 2013. "Toward the Archival Multiverse: Challenging the Binary Opposition of the Personal and Corporate Archive in Modern Archival Theory and Practice." *Archivaria* 76: 111–44.

Meehan, J. 2009. "Making the Leap from Parts to Whole: Evidence and Inference in Archival Arrangement and Description." *American Archivist* 72: 72–90.

Meehan, J. 2010. "Rethinking Original Order and Personal Records." *Archivaria* 70: 27–44.

Menne-Haritz, A. 1994. "Appraisal or Selection: Can a Content Oriented Appraisal Be Harmonized with the Principle of Provenance?" In *The Principle of Provenance: Report from the First Stockholm Conference on Archival Theory and the Principle of Provenance, 2–3 September 1993*, edited by K. Abukhanfusa and J. Sydbeck, 103–26. Stockholm: Riksarkivet.

Millar, L. 2002. "The Death of the Fonds and the Resurrection of Provenance: Archival Context in Space and Time." *Archivaria* 53: 1–15.

Millar, L. 2006. "An Obligation of Trust: Speculations on Accountability and Description." *American Archivist* 69: 60–78.

Miller, L. K. 2013. "All Text Considered: A Perspective on Mass Digitizing and Archival Processing." *American Archivist* 76: 521–41.

Nesmith, T. 1999. "Still Fuzzy but More Accurate: Some Thoughts on the 'Ghosts' of Archival Theory." *Archivaria* 47: 136–50.

Nesmith, T. 2002. "Seeing Archives: Postmodernism and the Changing Intellectual Place of Archives." *American Archivist* 65: 24–41.

Nesmith, T. 2005. "Reopening Archives: Bringing New Contextualities into Archival Theory and Practice." *Archivaria* 60: 259–74.

Nesmith, T. 2006. "The Concept of Societal Provenance and Records of Nineteenth-Century Aboriginal–European Relations in Western Canada: Implications for Archival Theory and Practice." *Archival Science* 6: 351–60.

Nesmith, T. 2007. "What Is an Archival Education?" *Journal of the Society of Archivists* 28: 1–17.

Nesmith, T. 2011. "Documenting Appraisal as a Societal-Archival Process: Theory, Practice, and Ethics in the Wake of Helen Willa Samuels." In *Controlling the Past: Documenting Society and Institutions*, edited by T. Cook, 31–50. Chicago, IL: Society of American Archivists.

Newman, J. 2012. "Revisiting Archive Collections: Developing Models for Participatory Cataloguing." *Journal of the Society of Archivists* 33: 57–73.

Niu, J. 2015. "Original Order in the Digital World." *Archives and Manuscripts* 43: 61–72.

Ottosson, P. 2006. "Authority File Information in Archives." *International Cataloguing and Bibliographic Control* 35: 57–58.

Peters, V. 2005. "Developing Archival Context Standards for Functions in the Higher Education Sector." *Journal of the Society of Archivists* 26: 75–85.

Piggott, M., and S. McKemmish. 2002. *Recordkeeping, Reconciliation and Political Reality*. http://www.infotech.monash.edu.au/research/groups/rcrg/publications/piggottmckemmish2002.pdf (accessed June 1, 2016).

Pitti, D. 2012. "Encoded Archival Description (EAD)." In *Understanding Information Retrieval Systems*, edited by M. J. Bates, 685–97. Boca Raton, FL: CRC Press.

Pitti, D., R. Hu, R. Larson, B. Tingle, and A. Turner. 2014. "Social Networks and Archival Context: From Project to Cooperative Archival Program." *Journal of Archival Organization* 12: 77–97.

Posner, E. 1940. "Some Aspects of Archival Development since the French Revolution." *American Archivist* 3: 159–72.

Powell, G. T. 1976. "Archival Principles and the Treatment of Personal Papers." *Archives and Manuscripts* 6: 259–68.

PREMIS Editorial Committee. 2015. *PREMIS Data Dictionary for Preservation Metadata*, version 3.0. http://www.loc.gov/standards/premis/v3/premis-3-0-final.pdf (accessed June 1, 2016).

Procter, M., and M. Cook. 2000. *A Manual of Archival Description*, 3rd ed. Aldershot, England: Gower.

Prom, C. J. 2004. "User Interactions with Electronic Finding Aids in a Controlled Setting." *American Archivist* 67: 234–68.

Prom, C. J. 2011. "Using Web Analytics to Improve Online Access to Archival Resources." *American Archivist* 74: 158–84.

Savoja, M., and S. Vitali. 2007. "Authority Control for Creators in Italy: Theory and Practice." *Journal of Archival Organization* 5 (1–2): 121–47.

Schaffner, J. 2009. *The Metadata Is the Interface: Better Description for Better Discovery of Archives and Special Collections, Synthesized from User Studies.* http://www.oclc.org/research/publications/library/2009/2009-06.pdf (accessed June 1, 2016).

Schellenberg, T. R. 1956. *Modern Archives: Principles and Techniques*. Melbourne, Victoria: F. W. Cheshire.

Schmidt, K., and I. Wagner. 2004. "Ordering Systems: Coordinative Practices and Artifacts in Architectural Design and Planning." *Computer Supported Cooperative Work* 13: 349–408.

Scott, P. J. 1966. "The Record Group Concept: A Case for Abandonment." *American Archivist* 29: 493–504.

Sexton, A., G. Yeo, C. Turner, and S. Hockey. 2004. "User Feedback: Testing the LEADERS Demonstrator Application." *Journal of the Society of Archivists* 25: 189–208.

Society of American Archivists. 2004. *Describing Archives: A Content Standard.* Chicago, IL: Society of American Archivists.

Society of American Archivists. 2013. *Describing Archives: A Content Standard*, 2nd ed. Chicago, IL: Society of American Archivists.

Sproull, L., and S. Kiesler. 1986. "Reducing Social Context Cues: Electronic Mail in Organizational Communication." *Management Science* 32: 1492–1512.

Stevenson, J. 2008. " 'What Happens if I Click on This?' Experiences of the Archives Hub." *Ariadne* 57. http://www.ariadne.ac.uk/issue57/stevenson/ (accessed June 1, 2016).

Stockting, W. 2005. " 'A Flexible Friend': The Role of Encoded Archival Description (EAD) in the Promotion of Access to Archives in the United Kingdom." *Comma* 2005 (2): 1–11.

Theimer, K., ed. 2011. *A Different Kind of Web*. Chicago, IL: Society of American Archivists.

Van Camp, A. 2001. "Providing Unified Access to International Primary Resources in the Humanities." *Journal of Internet Cataloging* 4 (3–4): 137–45.

Vitali, S. 1998. "Surfing without Going Off Course: An Archival Description System for the Internet." In *Electronic Access: Archives in the New Millennium Conference Proceedings 3–4 June 1998*, 39–45. London: Public Record Office.

Wallace, D. A. 1995. "Managing the Present: Metadata as Archival Description." *Archivaria* 39: 11–21.

Wallace, D. A. 2001. "Archiving Metadata Forum: Report from the Recordkeeping Metadata Working Meeting." *Archival Science* 1: 253–69.

Westbrook, B. D. 2002. "Prospecting Virtual Collections." *Journal of Archival Organization* 1 (1): 73–80.

Whitelaw, M. 2012. "Towards Generous Interfaces for Archival Collections." *Comma* 2012 (2): 123–32.

Wisser, K. M. 2015. "Investigating the Small World of Literary Archival Collections: The Impact of EAC-CPF on Archival Descriptive Practices—Part 1: Relationships, Description and the Archival Community." *Journal of Contemporary*

Archival Studies 2. http://elischolar.library.yale.edu/jcas/vol2/iss1/1/ (accessed June 1, 2016).

Wood, S., K. Carbone, M. Cifor, A. Gilliland, and R. Punzalan. 2014. "Mobilizing Records: Re-Framing Archival Description to Support Human Rights." *Archival Science* 14: 397–419.

Yakel, E. 2011. "Who Represents the Past? Archives, Records, and the Social Web." In *Controlling the Past: Documenting Society and Institutions*, edited by T. Cook, 257–78. Chicago, IL: Society of American Archivists.

Yeo, G. 2005. "Understanding Users and Use: A Market Segmentation Approach." *Journal of the Society of Archivists* 26: 25–53.

Yeo, G. 2008. "Concepts of Record (2): Prototypes and Boundary Objects." *American Archivist* 71: 118–43.

Yeo, G. 2009. "Custodial History, Provenance, and the Description of Personal Records." *Libraries and the Cultural Record* 44: 50–64.

Yeo, G. 2012a. "The Conceptual Fonds and the Physical Collection." *Archivaria* 73: 43–80.

Yeo, G. 2012b. "Bringing Things Together: Aggregate Records in a Digital Age." *Archivaria* 74: 43–91.

Yeo, G. 2013a. "Archival Description in the Era of Digital Abundance." *Comma* 2013 (2): 15–25.

Yeo, G. 2013b. "Trust and Context in Cyberspace." *Archives and Records* 34: 214–34.

Yeo, G. 2014. "Contexts, Original Orders, and Item-Level Orientation: Responding Creatively to Users' Needs and Technological Change." *Journal of Archival Organization* 12: 170–85.

Zhang, J. 2012. "Original Order in Digital Archives." *Archivaria* 74: 167–93.

8

Archival Interaction

Wendy Duff and Elizabeth Yakel

Over the past century, archival reference services have evolved from facilitating an elitist pastime in which a few high-status and expert users received preferential treatment to welcoming all people who wish to use records, either on-site or online. Today, the competencies of the reference archivist should include not only an understanding of the content of the archives but also an understanding of interpersonal interactions online and in person, contemporary learning and instructional theory and practice, archival retrieval systems, archival processes, and search strategies across disparate repositories. Instead of focusing on reference services, which imply a pointing out or pointing to, this chapter reconceptualizes archival reference service as an interaction, a two-, three- or, even four-way interaction among some combination of researchers, reference archivists, archival records, and archival systems. We discuss the core functional elements of reference services as practiced in archives today. These elements highlight the pressing demand for archivists to design iterative and flexible interactions that not only respond as researchers refine their information behaviors but also address new questions that arise from a researcher's exposure to archival records.

DEFINITION AND SCOPE

The Society of American Archivists' glossary of archival terminology defines *reference* as a "service to aid patrons in locating materials relevant to their interests" (Pearce-Moses 2005). The glossary defines *reference interview* as a "conversation between an archivist and a researcher designed to give the researcher an orientation to the use of the materials, to help the researcher identify relevant holdings, and to ensure that research needs are met" (Pearce-Moses 2005). Although on the surface the reference process might appear relatively simple, involving a conversation between an archivist and a researcher, these definitions obscure the complex, multifaceted, and challenging nature of this service.

Furthermore, some authors have indicated that reference services include more than identifying information sources. Bruce Dearstyne (2000) and Ellen Gartrell (1997) have both called for an expanded view of the reference process, one that encompasses not only helping patrons locate records but also doing research and preparing answers for them. Elizabeth W. Adkins and Karen Benedict (2011) point out that business archives normally conduct research for their users rather than just identifying relevant records. In discussing reference services at the advertising firm J. Walter Thompson, Gartrell (1997, 59) states, "We found that business inquirers most often need the answer, they need it now, and [they] want it in 'packaged' form. They are not, as a rule, much interested in where the answer came from or in the interesting twists in the process of finding it." Certainly at J. Walter Thompson a majority of users wanted answers, not citations to records that might have the answers.

In this chapter, we consider information delivery and analysis as part of the reference process. Furthermore, although traditional reference services assume synchronous or asynchronous human contact (e.g., in person, on the telephone, on live electronic chat, or through e-mail), reference service has often involved indirect rather than direct human contact. Wendy Duff and Catherine Johnson (2001, 47–48) note that reference requests can be "either in person or over the telephone, to a reference librarian or archivist, or to an information retrieval system." This type of service (archival access or retrieval systems) moves reference into an area traditionally considered the purview of arrangement and description. Thus, in this chapter, we use the concept of archival interaction as the overarching concept and adopt an expanded definition of archival reference that includes new services and venues. We broaden the discussion to include the social and behavioral processes associated with reference services, the venues for interaction, and concepts traditionally considered to be part of these services. For the purposes of our discussion, we define *archival interaction* as *any social or technical interaction by an archivist or archival system that aids patrons in locating the materials or evidence or information relevant to their interests in a form that is meaningful and actionable to the patron.*

We adopt the interaction framing for several reasons. First, we draw this framing from interaction design, "the practice of designing interactive digital products, environments, systems, and services" (Cooper et al. 2007, 610). The reference process is first and foremost focused on interaction among people (researchers and archivists); digital and analog records and manuscripts; online and physical environments or systems; and services. Second, interaction design primarily concentrates on practice and behavior. The reference process includes online and face-to-face behaviors and practices from search interactions to question negotiation. Third, this framework has been successfully adapted in mixed environments. For example, service interaction has emerged as a subfield focused on improving customers' interactions with services and increasing the value customers get from service interactions (Patricio et al. 2011). Interaction design has also been adapted to redesign social interactions between government and citizens. Citizen interaction design redesigns government functions to make them more accommodating as well as accountable to citizens (Citizen Interaction Design [School of Information. University of Michigan 2016]). Finally, interaction is crucial in archival reference; few people come to the archives without first having interacted with a system or a person. Normally, archival researchers interact with numerous systems and many individuals to solve their information needs. A goal of reference service, then, is to design seamless movement and interaction among the social systems (e.g., reference archivist to researcher, researchers among themselves), the technical systems (within archives, between archives), and the records.

MODES OF INTERACTION

Interaction with People

Reference Knowledge and Skills

Reference archivists skillfully interact with people in face-to-face or remote situations. Yet, this skill is often de-emphasized. Reference archivists must have a combination of *know that* (factual knowledge) and *know how* (tacit knowledge about archival processes, collections, and systems). The Society of American Archivists (n.d.) "Core Archival Knowledge" document delineates 14 subject areas comprising core archival knowledge, one of which is reference and access, in which archivists should know "[t]he policies and procedures designed to serve the information needs of various user groups, based on institutional mandates and constituencies, the nature of the materials, relevant laws and ethical considerations, and appropriate technologies." Additionally, instruction should include "the study of user behavior, user education, information retrieval techniques and technologies, user-based evaluation techniques, and the interaction between archivist and user in the reference process" (Society of American Archivists, n.d.).

However, in examining the syllabi of archival courses, Ciaran Trace and Carlos Ovalle (2012) found that the most popular type of reference and access assignment provided the students with only indirect experience. They also identified little evidence of simulated experiences or role-playing in the syllabi. In separate research building on Elizabeth Yakel and Deborah Torres's (2007) model of archival intelligence, Duff, Yakel, and Helen Tibbo (2013) developed an Archival Reference Knowledge (ARK) model drawing on interviews with 64 users of archives and an online survey of archivists conducted by the Society of American Archivists' Reference and Outreach Section. The model identified three broad types of reference knowledge: collection knowledge, research knowledge, and interaction knowledge. Interaction knowledge includes knowledge of people, access systems, and institutions; collection knowledge comprises knowledge of holdings and contextual knowledge about the collection; and research knowledge consists of knowledge of research methodologies, artifactual literature, and domain knowledge. Archival reference knowledge helps the reference archivist answer patrons' questions.

Specific disciplinary knowledge underlies all of these areas of reference knowledge. Question negotiation requires psychology and communication skills. Instruction requires knowledge of learning theories (educational psychology) as well as matching appropriate pedagogies to learning outcomes (education), and assessment requires knowledge of research methods. The skill base of the reference archivist is expanding, and educational programs need to adapt to meet these new competencies. We begin this section with a brief discussion of the three major types of users that have been studied: genealogists, historians, and students, and we add one emerging group of users: those interested in identifying and reusing different types of data. Then we discuss modes of interaction beginning with traditional reference services followed by a discussion of online services.

Archival Researchers

An important aspect of any archival interaction is the archival user. Shadrack Katuu (2015) suggests that until the twenty-first century, archivists did not have a comprehensive understanding of the most predominant user types, though they began conducting user studies in the 1980s. He argues that the traditional paradigm of these studies views researchers as passive receivers of information, while a new paradigm frames them as active contributors to the process. Hea Lim Rhee (2015) provides a comprehensive general literature review on user studies published over the past 30 years. Space does not allow for a full review of this literature, but we highlight major literature reviews focusing on key constituencies: genealogists, historians, and students. Although we highlight three audiences, we acknowledge that many other categories of researchers exist; increased technological access has attracted new groups of users—ones who have never visited a physical archive and who might require different modes of access (Sundqvist 2015). Polona Vilar and Elenka Šauperl (2015, 553) note that online archives access is no longer a domain "primarily or exclusively of researchers, but [is] increasingly containing non-researchers (typically inexperienced lay users) who search, browse, or simply look around according to their personal or everyday-life information needs."

Much of the archival research on genealogists has focused on genealogists' social or interactive research processes with archivists, other genealogists, and family members. In this vein, Duff and Johnson (2003) considered genealogists' use (or work-around) of archival finding aids and their face-to-face interactions with archivists and librarians, while Yakel and Torres (2007) examined interactions within the genealogical community and concluded that information sharing fosters a sense of community around the records as well as the people. Paul Darby and Paul Clough (2013) developed a model of the genealogist's research process, linking the stages of the research process with different types of interactions (with family, genealogists, archivists, records, and databases). In a 2014 study of the use of Ancestry.com and Findagrave.com, Heather Willevar-Farr and Andrea Forte (2014) directly addressed the limits of cooperation and control among genealogists. They concluded that genealogists were highly skeptical of participatory sites that did not provide quality control and that these users wanted control over the presentation of information about their families. Comprehensive summaries of the interactions between genealogists and records can be found in dissertations by Scott Lucas (2008) and Susan Tucker (2009).

Studies of historians have focused on interaction with systems and to a lesser extent with the archivist as they search for, locate, and use relevant records in a physical archive (Elena et al. 2010; Sinn and Soares 2014). Duff and Johnson (2002) and Rhee (2012) developed models of historians' information-seeking behaviors. Historians' interactions with systems can be complex. For example, Alexandra Chassanoff (2013) found that respondents used an average of eight different methods to access materials, and Torou Elena et al. (2010) suggested that historians break down their research topic into smaller discrete questions and then search for materials using keywords such as name, place name, occupation, time, and institution to answer these questions. On the other hand, Donghee Sinn and Nicholas Soares's (2014) survey of historians who used digital collections reported that a large number of respondents used Google and Web searches to find information rather than directly accessing repository Web sites. Together, the literature reviews in Chassanoff (2013) and Sinn and Soares (2014) provide a good overview of historians' interactions with archivists and physical and digital archives.

The research on students' use of archives includes traditional user studies (Cole 2000) as well as studies of student learning (Duff, Monks-Leeson, and Galey 2012), historical and critical thinking (Monte-Sano 2011; Wineburg 2001), and the impact of the archives on students (Daniels and Yakel 2013). The research on student researchers in the archives has concentrated primarily on interaction with the archives and the challenges, barriers, and levels of understanding students have about archival research and the archives themselves. Louise Clough's 2014 dissertation provides a good overview of the recent research on student use of archives.

One category of archival user that has recently emerged includes those who reuse data originally collected by other researchers. Archival researchers have remained fairly silent on data reuse and these data reusers. Although there has been a body of literature on faculty papers (e.g., Fournier 1992; Laver 2003; McCarthy and Sherratt 1996), these studies focus primarily on selection and not on the use of research data within faculty fonds. In fact, Frances Fournier (1992, 61) noted that "research files can also be important because they contain unexploited data that can be used by other scholars" even though "professors generally had little sense of the possible use of their research files by others." In the 25 years since Fournier's statement, governmental and professional open data mandates and improved data sharing have advanced the availability of data in some fields, and the number of researchers seeking existing data has grown. Data are curated in a variety of archives, including social science data archives, disciplinary archives, and institutional repositories as well as college and university and governmental archives. Yet, data reuse in archives remains problematic, because it is hidden and archives have often failed to contextualize it properly. Researchers have begun to study the reusers of archival data. However, the data reuse research remains divorced from research on users published in the archival literature. This divide is all the more interesting, because researchers studying data reusers and archival users have identified some of the same issues and behaviors. For example, both bodies of literature highlight the importance of collection/data documentation (Birnholtz and Bietz 2003; Blodgett 2003; Duff, Craig, and Cherry 2004; Niu and Hedstrom 2008). Likewise, researchers' use of peer-reviewed publications to locate data pervades both bodies of literature (Anderson 2004; Chassanoff 2013; Faniel and Jacobsen 2010; Tibbo 2003). However, disciplinary differences in the reason for using publications emerge when reading across the research streams. For example, Tibbo described the historian's use of publications as a means of identifying collections, while Ixchel Faniel and Trond Jacobsen (2010) found that earthquake engineers used peer-reviewed articles to assess the relevance and quality of data for their subsequent use. The data reuse and archival user studies literatures have much to learn from each other.

The Reference Interview

Reference services are complex and multifaceted; James Cross (1997) divides the process into six steps: registration, identification, orientation, the reference interview, continuing interaction, and finally the exit interview. Among these steps, the reference interview is "the centerpiece of reference procedures" (O'Toole 1986, 153).

"Reference interviews are conducted to ascertain the identity of the researcher, as a security measure; to determine the researcher's information needs and purpose; to guide the researcher to appropriate access tools and relevant sources; and to instruct and inform the researcher of basic procedures and limitations on access, handling of documents, and reproduction; and after research has been completed, to evaluate the success of the visit and the effectiveness of the reference service offered" (Pearce-Moses 2005). According to Bonnie Nardi and Vicki O'Day (1996), the reference interview also aims to:

1) Clarify the search request.
2) Adjust the focus of the search.
3) Characterize the expected results of the search.
4) Stretch the boundaries of the search space. (65)

On the surface, conducting reference interviews seems like a simple task. Users tell an archivist what they need, and the reference archivist teaches them ways to navigate the archival systems or helps them locate relevant information or records. The task, however, is far from simple. In a brief interaction, the archivist must solicit information from users who might not know exactly what they want and might be confused, anxious, and afraid of seeming ignorant (Long 1989). Other users are more sophisticated and have learned how to manage the reference interview themselves (Yakel and Torres 2003). Archivists must also help users develop search strategies that are likely to identify relevant sources and information that match the users' needs, capabilities, and time constraints (Dearstyne 2000). This is no simple task. According to Robert Taylor (1968, 180), "Without a doubt, the negotiation of reference questions is one of the most complex acts of human communication."

The Reference Interaction. In the first step in the interview process, archivists attempt to put users at ease (Long 1989; Wilsted 1986) and set the tone (Tibbo 1995) through verbal and nonverbal communication. This helps to build a relationship. The better the relationship between the archivist and the user, the easier it becomes to gather information about a request without making users feel uncomfortable or that their privacy is being violated (Thomsen 1999). There is also a power differential between the user and the archivist. As Linda Long (1989) argues, archivists can provide or deny access to records. Furthermore, some users lack archival experience; therefore, they might not even know where to begin. Nonverbal communication cues such as head nods, facial expressions, posture, and other body movements present a welcoming environment that can reduce users' anxiety levels, facilitate the gathering of information, and increase the users' level of satisfaction (Long 1989). With a welcoming, nonthreatening atmosphere established, archivists can begin an interview by asking users to elaborate on their research topic. The archivists solicit information about the subject matter being studied, the kinds of information being sought, and the purpose of the research. Archivists also probe to gather information about what users already know about their topic and what records or which repositories users have already consulted or plan to consult (O'Toole 1986).

Finally, archivists inquire whether the users are gathering information for a third party or for their own research (Pugh 2005). Knowing the context of a reference request and understanding the user's approach can assist archivists as they search for relevant materials (Trace 2006). This phase of the reference interview is called question negotiation (Long 1989). Mary Jo Pugh (2005) identifies three components of the question negotiation process: query abstraction, resolution, and refinement. Query abstraction involves clarifying and determining the full scope of a topic and translating a question from natural language into the language of an archival system. Query resolution consists of analyzing reference requests in terms of potential sources and helping users develop a search strategy to locate information and records. During query abstraction, archivists ask open-ended questions, inviting users to describe their research. They exploit paralinguistic elements such as pitch, inflection, and loudness of voice to indicate interest in the topic; they also employ techniques related to active listening, such as summarizing and paraphrasing the user's words to encourage the user to elaborate on his or her question (Long 1989). Archivists frame and focus the research by asking neutral questions; by eliciting names of people, organizations, places, and events; and by establishing any boundaries of time and space. Query resolution takes place in a later phase of the reference negotiation process in which archivists either answer the users' questions or help them form a search strategy.

The process of question negotiation facilitates users' ability to articulate and refine their reference questions and archivists' ability to discover *the wanted* (the term that identifies desired information) and *the givens* (the term that describes what users already know). According to Gerald Jahoda and Judith Braunagel (1980, 11), "By categorizing the givens and wanteds from query statements into general descriptors, we can group similar queries together, and often approach their answer searches in similar ways." For example, if the user knows the name, place, and date of birth of an ancestor (the givens) and wants information about the ancestor's parents (the wanted), the archivist might direct the user to the birth records for the appropriate place and date.

Types of Questions. A number of research projects have analyzed reference questions to determine the types of information archival users want, the type of assistance they request (Pugh and Power 2015), and the terms they use in their questions (Bearman 1989–1990; Collins 1998; Duff and Johnson 2001; Gagnon-Arguin 1998; Martin 2001). These studies gathered questions asked on-site at North American archives (Bearman 1989–1990; Collins 1998; Gagnon-Arguin 1998) and remotely (Duff and Johnson 2001; Gagnon-Arguin 1998; Martin 2001) as well as remote requests sent to The National Archives of Great Britain (TNA) (Pugh and Power 2015). David Bearman (1989–1990), Duff and Johnson (2001), Kristin Martin (2001), and Joseph Pugh and Christopher Power (2015) categorized the types of questions asked. These studies found that the percentage of substantial, as opposed to directional, questions ranged from 45 percent to 66 percent.

Duff and Johnson's (2001) study of e-mail reference questions found that only 49 percent were substantial, relating to resource discovery, fact finding, or requested advice. They categorized the remaining questions as service requests, administration or directional questions, or questions that were ill-defined and indicated a need for instruction. Pugh and Power (2015) used Duff and Johnson's coding scheme to analyze inquiries sent to the TNA through four channels: e-mail, telephone, live electronic chat, and Twitter. While Pugh and Power (2015) reported some similarities between their data and that of Duff and Johnson (2001) (e.g., Duff and Johnson classified 10% of the inquiries as fact finding, while Pugh and Power categorized 12% this way), Pugh and Power noted a marked increase in the number of questions asking for known items (27.5% for their TNA study compared to 4% for the 2001 Duff and Johnson study) and a decrease in administrative and service inquiries. Pugh and Power (2015, 113) also posited that to support the increasing number of archival collections being put online, "interactive designers must proactively seek solutions to solve this problem of knowing where to look."

Research has also investigated the type of given information in a question. Louise Gagnon-Arguin (1998) concluded that standard elements are associated with different types of questions, and Karen Collins (1998) found that questions asked at two institutions with historical photograph collections contained common elements such as general subject, specific subject, place, date, genre, visual features, physical format, and creator/provenance. Duff and Johnson (2001) identified similar givens in their questions, including proper names, dates, places, subjects, forms, and occasionally events, but unlike Collins (1998), very few questions included information about the visual features or the physical format of the records. These findings suggest that the elements in questions posed to photographic archives are not present in those posed to other types of archives. This supports Gagnon-Arguin's (1998) assertion that different types of questions contain different elements. These studies also indicate that in many cases, remote archival users require mediation to refine their reference questions and to probe for more information. They suggest that some users need instruction on how to use archives and finding aids systems or help in knowing where to look. Finally, the studies show that about half of the reference questions are substantial, including questions concerning records and facts or indicating a need for consultation with an archivist, while the other half relate to service requests or policy and administrative issues, though Pugh and Power (2015) suggest this could change as more material is put online.

Once archivists have a solid understanding of the users' research questions, they move to the second phase of the reference negotiation process, query resolution, in which archivists answer the users' questions or help them form a search strategy. Pugh (2005) suggests that reference services provide both information about the archival holdings and information from the records. She differentiates the two tasks: 1) When providing information about holdings, the archivist helps users identify likely sources and users do their own research identifying, evaluating, and synthesizing relevant information from documents; and 2) When providing information from holdings, archivists supply information from their own knowledge, from finding aids, or from reference tools, or in some cases, they conduct research in their holdings to answer questions (Pugh 2005, 104).

Sandra Kiemele's (1989) model of the archival reference process placed query resolution between the translation of a query into archival terms and user instruction. It would appear from Duff and Allyson Fox's (2006) research that instruction takes place both before and after translating queries into archival terms. Regardless of whether this step happens prior to or after an orientation, reference archivists often help users develop search strategies.

Interaction Online

Reference services have faced several watershed moments in the past 50 years. Pugh (2005) contends that from 1992 to 2004, archivists experienced a revolution in archives, resulting from increased access and opening of the doors to all types of people. This revolution is also noted by Richard Cox and The Archives Students (2007, 3), who say that "traditional reference activities are in a state of change, greater than many archivists realize." This is very true; the digital environment has expanded and diversified, which has in turn affected all archival functions including reference. Sigrid McCausland (2011) argues that the reference function in particular has changed as a result of digital collections and Web 2.0 technologies. In 2011, she cautioned against abandoning on-site physical reference, but a year earlier Paul Macpherson (2010) had urged archives to close physical reading rooms and move to online services. Although archivists have always provided remote reference services—answering users' questions via mail, phone, and fax—developments in information and communication technologies have created both challenges and opportunities. E-mail reference services have resulted in a dramatic increase in requests; digital collections have attracted new groups of users, many of whom have never visited a physical archive; and collaborative technologies have transformed traditional finding aids. Yakel (2000) posits that reference services on the Web focus on serving targeted audiences rather than individuals and that archivists are no longer limiting their services to records physically held in their archives. In a digital environment, archives can expand their services beyond their physical walls, and users can access collections and pose reference questions 24 hours a day, seven days a week. Cox and The Archives Students (2007) warn that archivists must go further and "learn to shift their concentration from solely being at the reference desk, where they patiently await a researcher's question, to actively formulating new ways to provide those same researchers online access." Virtual services attract a much more diverse group of users; however, new users might not have a useful mental model of archival descriptive systems.

E-mail Reference

Many archives have embraced the changes of the past 30 years and are exploiting the Web to reach out to new users and to better serve their traditional users. In 1994, New York State Archives made its finding aids available via the Internet, encouraging users to submit queries via e-mail. By October 1995, the Archives was receiving 150 questions a month. While Ruller (1997) contends that e-mail reference is more efficient and that archivists find it easier to respond to e-mail than to letters, Tibbo (1995) suggests that getting an answer to a remote reference question takes much longer than getting an answer to a question asked at the reference desk because there is more back-and-forth information seeking in smaller chunks online and there are fewer physical cues, such as nods or furrowed brows, to signal understanding or confusion. Furthermore, many remote users expect rapid answers or have unrealistic goals because of the speed of e-mail communication.

The volume of remote reference questions' archives appears to have dramatically increased over the past few years, with many reference archivists struggling to keep up with this new demand. Some archives have set standard time limits for replying to a request, but to meet these standards while dealing with the increasing demand, archivists must limit the amount of time spent researching and answering each question. Pugh and Power (2015) report that TNA's Research Centre receives 1,000 to 2,000 e-mail inquiries a week. To manage this load, reference staff members reply on standard templates. In 2012, TNA Research Centre staff answered nearly one in six requests using a standard response that included a link to a Web site deemed relevant to the question. Archivists initially had mixed views on the value and efficacy of e-mail inquiries. Cross (1997) suggests that providing reference remotely is less satisfying for reference archivists. Since that time, other writers have noted that archivists have more time to reflect on and answer remote research questions than they do when serving on-site users (Duff and Fox 2006; Tibbo 1995).

Social Media

The use of social media applications by archives has increased significantly over the past five years. In 2008, Mary Samouelian (2009) found that only 38 of 213 (17.8%) archives' Web sites used at least one type of Web 2.0 technology. Five years later, Duff, Johnson, and Joan Cherry (2013) found that one-third (217 of 648) of Canadian archives used at least one social media application. The most common social media applications are Facebook and Twitter (Duff, Johnson, and Cherry 2013; Heyliger, McLoone, and Thomas 2013), though many also use blogs (Heyliger et al. 2013). Today, archives report that they use social media applications to raise their public profile (Hager 2015) and to attract new users, particularly younger ones (Bak and Hill 2015; Hager 2015; Heyliger et al. 2013; Lalonde, Sanagan, and Smith 2014). They also use these applications to share content from collections and to highlight materials (Bak and Hill 2015; Heyliger et al. 2013; Lalonde et al. 2014). In an examination of archives' social media use, Adam Kriesberg (2014) analyzed the content of the Twitterfeeds of 34 archives and found that more than 50 percent of the tweets were related to marketing the archives, including administrative updates, links to institutional site content, and event promotion. Only a small percentage of the archives used Twitter for reference. Although Greg Bak and Amanda Hill (2015) point out that the use of social media applications is not cost-free, most studies indicate that archivists believe their usage of social media is successful (Heyliger et al. 2013; Smith-Yoshimura 2012).

While archives are using social media to raise their profiles or to reach out to new groups of users, many researchers have suggested that archives should use social media to do more than promote archival material (Theimer 2011). Research suggests that archivists could democratize the archives through the use of these technologies, decentering the archivist and empowering archival users to add their voice to the archival discourse (Duff et al. 2013; Theimer

2011). For example, the Koorie Archiving System was designed to support knowledge sharing, land claims, and regeneration of culture and communities with a goal to "set the official record straight" (McKemmish et al. 2011). Furthermore, Gregory Rolan (2015, 43) argues that Web 2.0 interoperability techniques could be used to "overcome organizational and cultural divides and achieve integrated discovery of, and access to, records as well as facilitating memory narratives from a plurality of perspectives." However, other research indicates that archives continue to use the technology to push content to archival users (Duff et al. 2013; Kriesberg 2014). Duff and Jessica Haskell (2015) argue that most archival reference and outreach projects continue to foster a traditional approach in which archivists maintain control over content and access. They have called on archivists to take on a more radical, participatory, and rhizomatic approach to access (for a more in-depth discussion on participatory archives, see Chapter 12).

Interaction with Systems

One of the most underdeveloped research areas in archival reference is search and retrieval or interaction with archival systems. This is unfortunate because searching for information, even with the help and expertise of reference archivists, is a very complex endeavor requiring greater study. The challenge for the user is "to describe for another person not something he knows, but rather something he does not know" (Taylor 1968, 180). Not only may users not know what they want or need, but they also may not know how to translate this knowledge into the language of an archival system. Taylor (1968) posits that an information need involves four steps: a *visceral* need that may be conscious or unconscious but is probably inexpressible in linguistic terms; a *conscious* need in which users recognize their need for information, but their requests are ill-defined and their statements are rambling and ambiguous; a *formalized* need that results in users forming concrete statements of their needs, which may or may not consider the constraints of the system; and a *compromised* need, in which users modify questions according to their expectations of the sources of information.

To answer reference queries, archivists must form search strategies to locate sources, unless they know the answer to the question or can draw on their direct knowledge of the archives' holdings. Archivists usually use one of two main search strategies or methods for locating information: the content indexing method (CI method) and the provenance method (P method) (Lytle 1980a, 1980b). The CI method involves linking subject queries with index or catalog terms or searching finding aids using key words or subject terms. In other words, when using the CI method, archivists or users identify key terms, or givens, in their compromised questions and use these terms—for example, subject, personal name, dates—to search the archival system. The success of the CI method depends upon a match between terms in the descriptions and the words in a user's query. On the other hand, the P method, the traditional method of retrieval in archives, involves translating "a user's subject query into the terms of organizational activity" (Bearman and Lytle 1985, 14). When using the P method, archivists link subject queries with provenance information contained in administrative histories or biographies, thereby producing leads to files. Information in the pure or theoretically defined P method derives only from what is known about the file, the activities of the creating person or organization, and the structure or organizing principles of the file itself (Lytle 1980a, 64–65). The P method depends upon inferential thinking, knowledge of record-creating processes and functions and activities of organizations and individuals who have created records as well as information about the arrangement of the archival units. Archivists search for materials using both P and CI methods, but some archivists have questioned the wisdom of developing provenance-based systems for users. Advocates of the CI method, predominantly from the United States, claim that the traditional P method depends upon "the immortal, omniscient, indispensable reference archivist" and "relies too heavily on the subject knowledge and memory of the individual archivist, and is too dependent on the personalities of the researcher and the archivist" (Pugh 1982, 38). Elsie Freeman (1984) warns that if archives do not become "client-centered" and design access systems that match users' preferred ways of searching, they risk becoming irrelevant to most users. The CI method addresses these concerns by emphasizing a client-centered approach and the design of user-friendly finding aids. This approach aims to have users working as independently as possible (Malbin 1997).

The CI method, however, requires that archivists create subject indexes and describe records using topical terms. Advocates of the P method, or a material-centered approach (Malbin 1997), argue that records are not about subjects. Terence Eastwood (1997) contends that "because by their very nature archival documents are not about things but are rather the byproducts of human activities of all kinds, they are often virtually unsearchable directly in the terms with which users wish to approach them to extract information from them relevant to their purpose." Susan Malbin (1997) questions whether users can work independently even with user-friendly finding aids, as the CI supporters claim. She argues that users still need reference archivists to refine their searches and to help find materials. She states, "In the desire to make archives more 'accessible' to non-specialists, there is a tendency to slight the importance of the personally negotiated element in each user's research" (Malbin 1997, 75). Terry Cook (1990) has gone further. He argues that archivists should give users information needed to access and use records rather than what users may want: fast and easily accessible information. Furthermore, he claims that archivists must continue their materials-centered approach, focusing on contextual information, record-creating processes, diplomatics, record forms, and provenance. In Cook's approach, reference archivists focus on educating users in addition to helping them locate information. He states:

> Every user from the genealogist looking for a single fact or a copy of a single document through the most sophisticated researcher using "discourse" methodology would benefit from this materials-centred approach to archives. The genealogist should not just be handed the land patent or the record of entry relating to his or her ancestor, even if such service can be a quick one-minute "strike." Rather, the user should also be led to information about the contextual significance of that document. What is a land patent; what was the process by which it was issued; what were the requirements that the settler had to meet in order to obtain this document; what is revealed by a diplomatic analysis of the patent form itself; what were the relevant provisions of the Dominion Homestead Act under which it was created; what was the nature of the Department of the Interior, and its local land agents who actually produced it; what other surviving relevant documentation exists to show this broader context? (Cook 1990, 131)

A materials-centered or provenance approach to reference provides users with a better understanding of important contextual information needed to use and interpret records and helps them locate materials. Unfortunately, most users lack the knowledge needed to translate a query into the terms of an organization's functions and activities, and no systems support an automatic translation of a subject query into provenance-relevant terms. Some historians (Anderson 2004; Beattie 1997; Duff and Johnson 2002; Rhee 2012; Tibbo 2003) use contextual knowledge to locate and interpret records, and the P method seems to support their preferred method for finding information. A study of social historians, however, found that these historians search for subjects across many collections and have difficulty using the P method of retrieval (Beattie 1997). Moreover, studies of genealogists (Duff and Johnson 2003; Yakel and Torres 2007) indicate that the P method of description does not match these users' information-seeking behavior. Many users have experience using the CI method of retrieval, which is prevalent in libraries, but few have prior experience with the provenance approach. Reference archivists, however, use the P method effectively. Duff and Fox (2006, 142) found that archivists often use this method instinctively and noted that in the eyes of many experienced reference archivists, translating a request for information into terms of an organization's functions and activities is common sense. Interestingly, few archivists gave examples of using the P method to locate personal papers. This method depends upon having either a sophisticated retrieval system that links subject queries with information about functions, activities, and occupations or archivists who know the activities, functions, and occupations of record creators. Although reference archivists at large archives might remember the functions and activities of major organizations or government departments and the activities, interests, and occupations of personal creators of very important fonds, they are less likely to remember the occupations and activities of all personal record creators. Whether the archival systems of the future will support and facilitate this type of searching for fonds created by corporate bodies, persons, and families remains unknown. Richard Lytle's (1980a, 1980b) dissertation research on the effectiveness of the two retrieval methods using systems developed in the 1970s points to limitations of both methods, although he favors systems built on the P method, arguing that they are more cost-effective. Bearman and Lytle (1985) suggest that systems which support provenance retrieval need to emphasize retrieval by forms of the materials and the functions that created them and have well-developed provenance authority systems that are separate but linked to record descriptions.

Over the past decade, archivists have begun to develop authority files to improve access to provenance information, a prerequisite for an improved version of the P method, according to Bearman and Lytle (1985). The International Council of Archives has developed standards for describing corporate bodies, persons, and families as well as functions that create records. Furthermore, the Encoded Archives Context (EAC) standard aids in the sharing and retrieval of this information. These standards should lay the foundation for the development of systems that support enhanced provenance searching. To date, however, no research has tested Lytle's assertion that the P method is more cost-effective, and, without research, the value and effectiveness of these two search approaches remain unknown.

Nonetheless, the P method is commonly used, even preferred, among expert archivists. Research on the search strategies of novice and expert searchers has provided interesting insights into how archivists search for information. Denise Anthony (2006) found that when searching for information, novice reference archivists began by performing a metasearch using the terms from a reference question. They indicated satisfaction with their search if the documents they retrieved contained terms that matched the terms in the reference question. They did not evaluate their list of retrieved documents, and they did not ask to interview the users who had asked the questions. On the other hand, expert reference archivists did not need to conduct a metasearch to identify sources. Not only did they immediately choose a source that might provide relevant information, but they also had other potentially relevant sources in mind. Expert reference archivists examined the list of citations retrieved and considered the quality of the sources such as the accuracy and the comprehensiveness of the content and whether the form or format of the material facilitated skimming. They also considered who had processed the collection and created the finding aids. In other words, the expert archivists included an evaluation phase as part of their search. Evaluating the results of a search and modifying a search strategy until it identifies accurate, relevant documents are key elements of a successful search.

Anthony (2006) concluded that expert archivists have extensive contextual knowledge, including the history of organizations, their functions, how the functions have changed over time, and the individuals connected with these functions. Archivists also know the resources associated with these people. Anthony (2006) contended that this knowledge facilitates the retrieval of information in archives. In some cases, archivists draw on knowledge gained from processing collections to locate relevant information efficiently and effectively. It would appear from Anthony's research that expert reference archivists use the P method to retrieve information, relying on their knowledge of an organization's history and functions and the names of people connected with the organization. Moreover, experts rarely search for information using the CI method, unlike novice archivists, who often begin with a metasearch using topical terms (Anthony 2006, 100).

In spite of archival advocacy of the P method, and although archivists know that subject searching is fraught with issues from bias to cultural and historical associations that do not translate to broader populations of archival researchers (Beattie 1997; Collins 1998), users still might want to search by subject (Pugh 1982). Fernanda Ribeiro's (1996) retrieval study, comparing the use of controlled and uncontrolled vocabulary, indicates that controlled vocabulary effectively bridges the gap between finding aids and the collections they represent. Rita Czeck (1998) confirmed this finding, though she found little overlap between online finding aids and MARC records. Although she argues for the importance of full text searching in all sections of the finding aid, Tim Hutchinson's (1997) study should make us question whether more is always better.

A number of studies have tested how well archival researchers interact with a variety of systems. Hutchinson (1997) compared four methods of search: searching entire finding aids, searching introductory material to finding aids, searching introductory material plus controlled vocabulary terms, and searching collection-level MARC catalog records. He found that recall increased and precision decreased as the length of the description increased. But the decline in precision was steeper than the gain in recall as description quantity increased. This finding calls into question whether more and not necessarily better description alone is worth providing. Archivists have long wondered whether researchers want recall (retrieval of everything) or precision (retrieval of the most relevant record). Traditionally, studies of historians have found that these scholars want high recall; however, as the diversity of archival researchers grows, this may no longer be the case. In another retrieval study, focused specifically on online finding aids, Morgan Daniels and Yakel (2010) sought to identify successful search strategies. They found that more successful searchers use a broader range of search strategies and query reformulation techniques. Just like in face-to-face reference, the researchers who have more familiarity with system functions and plan their interactions reap better results.

In addition to the issues of controlled vocabulary and different types of representations of archival collections, a number of usability studies have tested how well users navigate the interfaces of online finding aids systems. Each of these studies has pointed to the different ways that interactions between researchers and archival systems fail: major issues with online finding aids include unfamiliarity with archival hierarchies (Prom 2004; Scheir 2005; Yakel 2004) and a lack of knowledge of archival terminology (Altman and Nemmers 2001; Prom 2004; Scheir 2005; Yakel 2004). Interestingly, Wendy Scheir's (2005) novices experienced a learning curve during the experiment and exhibited greater facility with the system as the study progressed.

Issues of search, retrieval, and selection are even more complicated when searching for archival records, either text or images, online. In a study by Jodi Allison-Bunnell, Yakel, and Janet Hauck (2011), participants highlighted the need for better search functions across different representations of records as well as more content and context metadata (to support some combination of the CI and P methods). Participants preferred key word search over browsing categories, because they indicated key words generated more comprehensive results (more recall) and allowed them to then sort or narrow results. Participants agreed, however, that none of the sites featured in the study supplied sufficient descriptive information to confidently select items. Interestingly, participants wanted access to a reference archivist in the online environment and as a whole preferred that online archives match an on-site in-person research experience (e.g., information available, visual cues, and reference services). This is supported by findings of Duff et al. (2013) that study participants valued having access to an archivist in an online environment. Whether using actual images of archival records or representations of records, interacting with archival systems poses difficulties for researchers. In addition to the lack of understanding about archives, system features and user interfaces can create barriers and prevent researchers from locating the archival records they desire.

While archivists remain a crucial component of the research process, the "use of digitized finding aids, digitized collections, and digital cameras [has] altered the way historians interact with primary sources," according to Jennifer Rutner and Roger C. Schonfeld (2012, 8). They continued that "while the centrality of archives to the research process remains, the nature of interactions with archival materials has changed dramatically over time; for many researchers, activities in the archives have become more photographic and less analytical." This finding was reiterated by Sinn (2012), whose study of citations in the *American Historical Review* from 2001 to 2010 found a marked increase in the number of citations to digital archives. In a complementary study of citations to newspapers in Canadian dissertations, Ian Milligan (2013) noted that the use of digitized newspapers had exponentially increased. Sinn and Soares (2014) also reported that historians consulted digital resources at all stages of their research, but they assessed the authority of the institution providing the digital copies when selecting digital sources. These scholars also considered the content, scope, format, and quality of the images in determining whether to use them.

Instruction

In the past several years, the importance of instruction has increased at the reference desk, in classroom sessions, through tutorials, and beyond. Along with the larger focus on instruction, archivists have become more aware of the need to add teaching skills to their portfolio of competencies and to better understand how to assess student learning as well as satisfactory outcomes of the educational programs they offer.

Instruction at the Reference Desk

The reference archivists in Duff and Fox's (2006) study indicated that they spend 50 percent of their time on the reference desk providing a general orientation to the archives, which includes explaining the rules and procedures for ordering materials and photocopies plus providing a general overview to the archival systems. These archivists spend the remaining 50 percent of their time on the desk helping people in other ways. Instruction provided at the reference desk is normally tailored to a specific researcher. Archivists might provide an in-depth orientation to a new doctoral student but a short overview to a casual user. The goal of archival instruction is to provide enough information for the researcher to get started without being overwhelmed. Therefore, archivists often provide a quick orientation but tell new users to come back for more help when they need it (Duff and Fox 2006). Teaching users how to find information in archives and to navigate archival systems is a key role of the reference archivist. A number of studies have investigated the components of formal archival orientation sessions (Allen 1999; Allison 2005; Duff and Cherry 2008), but only Robert Tissing Jr. (1984) studied the orientation interview and developed a guide that identifies the elements an orientation interview should contain.

Not knowing how archives work makes locating materials much more difficult. Furthermore, virtual users are less likely to have used secondary sources prior to seeking archival materials, and some do not know how to use and interpret the materials they find (Tibbo 1995). Although these new users have less experience using archives and an even greater need for instruction (Malbin 1997), few reference archivists attempt to educate remote users. Duff and Fox (2006) note that while archivists spend about half of their time on the reference desk teaching users how to use archival systems, remote reference services rarely involve instruction. Few archives provide live electronic chat or synchronous remote reference, yet these services could potentially educate users who use archival finding aids and systems remotely.

Tutorials

Online Web-based tutorials can assist some users. Although they do not eliminate the need for personalized one-on-one instruction (Malbin 1997), they can help educate remote users who do not have the opportunity to visit the archives. Colleges and universities have created most of the tutorials that are available. The academic library-generated tutorials focus on the distinction between primary and secondary sources and the use of primary sources as evidence; the archives-generated tutorials concentrate on using an archive as well as defining primary sources. Many of these tutorials, however, are static Web pages with minimal interactivity. Archivists need to focus more attention on designing instructional tools that scaffold and reinforce basic concepts.

In addition to Web-based tutorials, a number of archives have posted instructional and promotional videos on YouTube (in addition to posting actual archival materials). These tutorials focus largely on the distinction between primary and secondary sources. Other videos promote collections and provide an online introduction to collections, not unlike the instruction the reference archivist might provide at the reference desk. For example, the University of Manitoba Archives and Special Collections has created a video titled "How to Access Research Materials from the Archives" (University of Manitoba 2008), while Northwestern University has a short film introducing the preservation of the audio and moving image records of its football games (Northwestern University 2008). The range of archival information on YouTube is growing daily.

Classroom Instruction

Reference services outside the reference desk also include instruction. Although Magia Krause (2010a) found that archivists are reluctant to identify as teachers, there has been an increase in the past several years in the number of instructional archivist positions. The number of books (e.g., Bahde, Smedberg, and Taormina 2014; Cotton and Sharron 2011; Mitchell, Seiden, and Taraba 2012) and articles (e.g., Clough 2014; Hensley, Murphy, and Swain 2014; Rockenbach 2011; Weiner, Morris, and Mykytiuk 2015) discussing archival instruction has also increased dramatically. These sources provide lesson ideas, exercises to use in class, and, to a lesser extent, assessment rubrics to help evaluate learning. Furthermore, archivists are focusing more attention on the content of the archival orientation, which has moved from a tour of the archives to a more in-depth instructional experience focused on increasing primary sources literacy and critical thinking skills.

Much of the recent literature on primary sources literacy moves beyond simply detailing what content should be addressed. Archivists draw on pedagogy and learning theory as key components of instruction and best practice when teaching researchers to use the archives and records (e.g., Bahde 2013; Garcia 2015; Krause 2010a; Mazella and Grob 2011; Swain 2015). Archivists are beginning to focus more time and effort on pedagogy and are increasingly identifying as educators. They are now thinking more about learning objectives, designing exercises to meet those objectives, and assessing when they fail to meet those objectives. Archivists are also joining researchers from other disciplines who have focused on the topic of historical thinking, leveraging active pedagogies to teach this concept (e.g., Dutt-Doner, Cook-Cottone, and Allen 2007; Monte-Sano 2008, 2011; Wineburg 2001).

Not only should archivists decide what to teach and the pedagogical approach to take when teaching, but they should also assess the success of the instruction. Partly as a need to demonstrate the contributions of archives to the broader curriculum in colleges and universities and partly as a need to improve teaching about primary sources, a strand of the primary sources literacy research has turned to assessment (e.g., Bahde and Smedberg 2012; Daniels and Yakel 2013; Duff and Cherry 2008; Krause 2010b). For example, Krause (2010b) conducted a field experiment using a pre- and posttest methodology, where half of students in a large American history survey course were given archival instruction and the other half were not. Her findings indicated that instruction significantly improved the students' ability to work with primary sources and enhanced their research skills (sourcing and weighing evidence). Using a posttest survey methodology, Daniels and Yakel (2013) found that using the archives in the classroom increased students' confidence in their research skills and helped them develop life skills such as time management and good study habits. These findings are encouraging. Regarding assessment, Anne Bahde and Heather Smedberg (2012) discussed different assessment techniques within the context of the class (assignments, presentations) as well as assessment rubrics and surveys. These discussions of the options and the growing examples of different types of evaluations in the literature (e.g., Bahde et al. 2014; Cotton and Sharron 2011; Mitchell et al. 2012) and online (e.g., TeachArchives.org [Brooklyn Historical Society 2016]) make for a very dynamic research area.

The Future

Even as archives rush to make their materials available digitally, users require assistance to navigate archival systems, identify records, and interpret them. It appears that the need for reference services might expand rather than contract, but this need extends beyond the reading room and the reference archivist. It seems unlikely that archives will follow Macpherson's (2010) suggestion to close their physical reading rooms any time soon. However, as Gillian Oliver (2012) notes, current workflows that assume a small and homogeneous user population will not be able to meet new expectations of a heterogeneous global population that wants to consult archival material. "It is essential that these workflows are reconfigured to be appropriate for today's digital expectations" (Oliver 2012, 58).

Although research conducted since the 1980s has provided archivists with a much better understanding of some of their most prominent user groups (e.g., historians, genealogists), we know little about other user groups and nonusers. To advance research, we need to compare and contrast the findings from the growing number of research studies focused on archival users and the few studies on different types of archival use. Furthermore, we need to incorporate the findings from such areas as data reuse and information retrieval into our knowledge base and our frameworks.

In the past decade, our understanding of archival interactions has grown more sophisticated. We have a better understanding of user behavior for some types of users. We have models that explicate the knowledge needed to use archives (Yakel and Torres 2003) and that required by reference archivists (Duff et al. 2013), but we still lack a strong theoretical foundation to explain the individual behaviors and social conventions surrounding reference services and interactions. Isto Huvila (2008, 17) argues that "theoretical reasoning is needed as a basis for discussing whether the present patterns of use reflect the actual needs or desires of the users, or whether they make good use of the potential of archival materials." Huvila (2008), Katuu (2015), and others have also urged archivists to move away from their notion of a passive user and embrace researchers as active, participatory partners.

As we embrace and expand our use of systems to provide archival information as well as archival materials and as we invite researchers to cocreate the archives with us, we need to develop a more engaged access model with the public. The demand for current and older records is not just taking place in the archives or on archival Web sites and services. Many users are accessing records through government agencies and other third-party sources, such as Ancestry.com. As Barbara Reed (2014, 126) points out, "We need to engage actively with multiple communities to work through alternatives. For example, are we simply managing access to our archival holdings or are we responsible for implementing a more engaged access model suited to all environments?"

Finally, archivists need more research on all facets of archival interaction. Although the definition of archival reference is straightforward—"a service to aid patrons in locating materials relevant to their interests" (Pearce-Moses 2005)—realizing this definition is not. We need to know more about how archival processes can respond to the myriad needs of both sophisticated and novice users. We need systems (human and computer) that exploit both the P and CI methods of retrieval. We need to work within our profession, together with industry, active researchers, system designers, and others, to rethink how to aid patrons in locating the materials, the evidence, or the information relevant to their interests in a form that is meaningful and actionable. This requires a reexamination of all types of interactions among archivists, researchers, systems, and archival records. This is a lofty goal but one that is vital for the next generation of reference archivists and for the transformation of reference services into the twenty-first century.

REFERENCES

Adkins, Elizabeth W., and Karen Benedict. 2011. "Archival Advocacy: Institutional Archives in Corporations." In *Many Happy Returns: Advocacy and the Development of Archives*, edited by Larry J. Hackman, 45–66. Chicago, IL: Society of American Archivists.

Allen, Susan M. 1999. "Rare Books and the College Library: Current Practices in Marrying Undergraduates to Special Collections." *Rare Books and Manuscripts Librarianship* 13 (2): 110–19.

Allison, Anna Elise. 2005. "Connecting Undergraduates with Primary Sources: A Study of Undergraduate Instruction in Archives, Manuscripts, and Special Collections." Master's Thesis. University of North Carolina. http://ils.unc.edu/MSpapers/3026.pdf (accessed February 20, 2016).

Allison-Bunnell, Jodi, Elizabeth Yakel, and Janet Hauck. 2011. "Researchers at Work: Assessing Needs for Content and Presentation of Archival Materials." *Journal of Archival Organization* 9 (2): 67–104. doi:10.1080/15332748.2011.598400.

Altman, Burt, and John Nemmers. 2001. "The Usability of On-Line Archival Resources: The Polaris Project Finding Aid." *The American Archivist* 64 (1): 121–31. doi:10.17723/aarc.64.1.80300272655rqu74.

Anderson, Ian G. 2004. "Are You Being Served? Historians and the Search for Primary Sources." *Archivaria* 58: 81–129.

Anthony, Denise. 2006. "Beyond Description: An Exploration of Experienced Archivists' Knowledge and Searching Skills." PhD Dissertation. University of Michigan.

Bahde, Anne. 2013. "The History Labs: Integrating Primary Source Literacy Skills into a History Survey Course." *Journal of Archival Organization* 11 (3–4): 175–204.

Bahde, Anne, and Heather Smedberg. 2012. "Measuring the Magic: Assessment in the Special Collections and Archives Classroom." *RBM: A Journal of Rare Books, Manuscripts and Cultural Heritage* 13 (2): 152–74.

Bahde, Anne, Heather Smedberg, and Mattie Taormina, eds. 2014. *Using Primary Sources: Hands-on Instructional Exercises*. Santa Barbara, CA: Libraries Unlimited, an imprint of ABC-CLIO, LLC.

Bak, Greg, and Amanda Hill. 2015. "Deseronto Dreams: Archives, Social Networking Services, and Place." *Archivaria* 79: 1–26.

Bearman, David A. 1989–1990. "User Presentation Language in Archives." *Archives and Museum Informatics* 3 (4): 3–7.

Bearman, David A., and Richard H. Lytle. 1985. "The Power of the Principle of Provenance." *Archivaria* 1 (21): 14–27.

Beattie, Diane. 1997. "Retrieving the Irretrievable: Providing Access to 'Hidden Groups' in Archives." *The Reference Librarian* 26 (56): 83–94.

Birnholtz, Jeremy P., and Matthew Bietz. 2003. "Data at Work: Supporting Sharing in Science and Engineering." In *GROUP '03 Proceedings of the 2003 International ACM SIGGROUP Conference on Supporting Group Work*, 339–48. Sanibel Island, FL: ACM. doi:10.1145/958160.958215.

Blodgett, Peter J. 2003. "Using Our Faculties: Collecting the Papers of Western Historians at the Huntington." *The Western Historical Quarterly* 34 (4): 491–99.

Brooklyn Historical Society. 2016. "TeachAchives.org." http://www.teacharchives.org/ (accessed February 20, 2016).

Chassanoff, Alexandra. 2013. "Historians and the Use of Primary Source Materials in the Digital Age." *American Archivist* 76 (2): 458–80.

Clough, Louise. 2014. "Undergraduate Use of University Archives and Special Collections: Motivations, Barriers and Best Practice." Master's Thesis. Aberystwyth University. http://cadair.aber.ac.uk/dspace/handle/2160/30065 (accessed February 20, 2016).

Cole, Charles. 2000. "Name Collection by Ph.D. History Students: Inducing Expertise." *Journal of the American Society for Information Science* 51 (5): 444–55. doi:10.1002/(SICI)1097-4571(2000)51:5<444::AID-ASI5>3.0.CO;2-Y.

Collins, Karen. 1998. "Providing Subject Access to Images: A Study of User Queries." *The American Archivist* 61 (1): 36–55. doi:10.17723/aarc.61.1.b531vt5q0q620642.

Cook, Terry. 1990. "Viewing the World Upside Down: Reflections on the Theoretical Underpinnings of Archival Public Programming." *Archivaria* 31: 123–34.

Cooper, Alan, Robert Reimann, Dave Cronin, and Alan Cooper. 2007. *About Face 3: The Essentials of Interaction Design*, 3rd ed. Indianapolis, IN: Wiley Publishing.

Cotton, Justine, and David Mark Sharron. 2011. *Engaging Students with Archival and Digital Resources*. Oxford, England: Chandos Publishing.

Cox, Richard J., and The Archives Students. 2007. "Machines in the Archives: Technology and the Coming Transformation of Archival Reference." *First Monday* 12 (11). doi:10.5210/fm.v12i11.2029.

Cross, James Edward. 1997. "Archival Reference: State of the Art." *The Reference Librarian* 26 (56): 5–25. doi:10.1300/J120v26n56_02.

Czeck, Rita. 1998. "Archival MARC Records and Finding Aids in the Context of End-User Subject Access to Archival Collections." *The American Archivist* 61 (2): 426–40. doi:10.17723/aarc.61.2.3764m56l67h827p5.

Daniels, Morgan, and Elizabeth Yakel. 2010. "Seek and You May Find: Successful Search in Online Finding Aid Systems." *The American Archivist* 73 (2): 535–68. doi:10.17723/aarc.73.2.p578900680650357.

Daniels, Morgan, and Elizabeth Yakel. 2013. "Uncovering Impact: The Influence of Archives on Student Learning." *The Journal of Academic Librarianship* 39 (5): 414–22. doi:10.1016/j.acalib.2013.03.017.

Darby, Paul, and Paul Clough. 2013. "Investigating the Information-Seeking Behaviour of Genealogists and Family Historians." *Journal of Information Science* 39 (1): 73–84.

Dearstyne, Bruce W. 2000. *Managing Historical Records Programs: A Guide for Historical Agencies*. Walnut Creek, CA: AltaMira Press.

Duff, Wendy, and Allyson Fox. 2006. " 'You're a Guide Rather than an Expert': Archival Reference from an Archivist's Point of View." *Journal of the Society of Archivists* 27 (2): 129–53. doi:10.1080/00379810601075943.

Duff, Wendy M, Barbara Craig, and Joan Cherry. 2004. "Historians' Use of Archival Sources: Promises and Pitfalls of the Digital Age." *The Public Historian* 26 (2): 7–22.

Duff, Wendy, and Catherine A. Johnson. 2001. "A Virtual Expression of Need: An Analysis of E-Mail Reference Questions." *American Archivist* 21 (1): 43–60.

Duff, Wendy, and Catherine A. Johnson. 2002. "Accidentally Found on Purpose: Information-Seeking Behavior of Historians in Archives." *The Library Quarterly* 72 (4): 472–96.

Duff, Wendy, and Catherine A. Johnson. 2003. "Where Is the List with All the Names? Information-Seeking Behavior of Genealogists." *American Archivist* 66 (1): 79–95.

Duff, Wendy M., Catherine A. Johnson, and Joan M. Cherry. 2013. "Reaching Out, Reaching In: A Preliminary Investigation into Archives' Use of Social Media in Canada." *Archivaria* 75: 77–97.

Duff, Wendy, Elizabeth Yakel, and Helen Tibbo. 2013. "Archival Reference Knowledge." *The American Archivist* 76 (1): 68–94. doi:10.17723/aarc.76.1.x9792xp27140285g.

Duff, Wendy M., Emily Monks-Leeson, and Alan Galey. 2012. "Contexts Built and Found: A Pilot Study on the Process of Archival Meaning-Making." *Archival Science* 12 (1): 69–92.

Duff, Wendy M., and Jessica Haskell. 2015. "New Uses for Old Records: A Rhizomatic Approach to Archival Access." *The American Archivist* 78 (1): 38–58. doi:10.17723/0360-9081.78.1.38.

Duff, Wendy M., and Joan M. Cherry. 2008. "Archival Orientation for Undergraduate Students: An Exploratory Study of Impact." *American Archivist* 71 (2): 499–59.

Dutt-Doner, Karen M., Catherine Cook-Cottone, and Susan Allen. 2007. "Improving Classroom Instruction: Understanding the Developmental Nature of Analyzing Primary Sources." *RMLE Online* 30 (6): 1–20. doi:10.1080/19404476.2007.11462039.

Eastwood, Terence. 1997. "Public Services Education for Archivists." *The Reference Librarian* 26 (56): 27–38.

Elena, Torou, Akrivi Katifori, Costas Vassilakis, George Lepouras, and Constantin Halatsis. 2010. "Historical Research in Archives: User Methodology and Supporting Tools." *International Journal on Digital Libraries* 11 (1): 25–36. doi:10.1007/s00799-010-0062-4.

Faniel, Ixchel M., and Trond E. Jacobsen. 2010. "Reusing Scientific Data: How Earthquake Engineering Researchers Assess the Reusability of Colleagues'

Data." *Computer Supported Cooperative Work* 19 (3–4): 355–75. doi:10.1007/s10606-010-9117-8.

Fournier, Frances. 1992. "'For They Would Gladly Learn and Gladly Teach'—University Faculty and their Papers: A Challenge for Archivists." *Archivaria* 34 (Summer): 58–74.

Freeman, Elsie. 1984. "In the Eye of the Beholder: Archives Administration from the User's Point of View." *The American Archivist* 47 (2): 111–23. doi:10.17723/aarc.47.2.a373340078502136.

Gagnon-Arguin, Louise. 1998. "Les Questions de Recherche Comme Matériau D'études Des Usagers En Vue Du Traitement Des Archives." *Archivaria* 1 (46): 86–102.

Garcia, Patricia. 2015. "Accessing Archives: Primary Sources and Inquiry-Based Learning in K-12 Classrooms." PhD Dissertation. University of California. http://escholarship.org/uc/item/31v4n498 (accessed February 20, 2016).

Gartrell, Ellen G. 1997. " "Some Things We Have Learned ...": Managing Advertising Archives for Business and Non-Business Users." *American Archivist* 60 (1): 56–70.

Hager, Joshua D. 2015. "To Like or Not to Like: Understanding and Maximizing the Utility of Archival Outreach on Facebook." *The American Archivist* 78 (1): 18–37. doi:10.17723/0360-9081.78.1.18.

Hensley, Merinda Kaye, Benjamin Murphy, and Ellen D. Swain. 2014. "Analyzing Archival Intelligence: A Collaboration between Library Instruction and Archives." *Communications in Information Literacy* 8 (1): 96–114.

Heyliger, Sean, Juli McLoone, and Nikki Thomas. 2013. "Making Connections: A Survey of Special Collections' Social Media Outreach." *The American Archivist* 76 (2): 374–414. doi:10.17723/aarc.76.2.t820u33100443q55.

Hutchinson, Tim. 1997. "Strategies for Searching Online Finding Aids: A Retrieval Experiment." *Archivaria* 1 (44): 72–101.

Huvila, Isto. 2008. "Participatory Archive: Towards Decentralised Curation, Radical User Orientation, and Broader Contextualisation of Records Management." *Archival Science* 8: 15–36.

Jahoda, Gerald, and Judith Schiek Braunagel. 1980. *The Librarian and Reference Queries: A Systematic Approach*. New York: Academic Press.

Katuu, Shadrack. 2015. "User Studies and User Education Programmes in Archival Institutions." *Aslib Journal of Information Management* 67 (4): 442–57.

Kiemele, Sandra. 1989. "A Study of Archivists' Perceptions of Reference Service." Master's Thesis. University of British Columbia. https://circle.ubc.ca/bitstream/handle/2429/28707/UBC_1990_A3%20K53.pdf?sequence=1 (accessed February 20, 2016).

Krause, Magia G. 2010a. " 'It Makes History Alive for Them': The Role of Archivists and Special Collections Librarians in Instructing Undergraduates." *Journal of Academic Librarianship* 36 (5): 401–11. doi:10.1016/j.acalib.2010.06.004.

Krause, Magia G. 2010b. "Undergraduates in the Archives: Using an Assessment Rubric to Measure Learning." *American Archivist* 73 (2): 507–34.

Kriesberg, Adam. 2014. "Increasing Access in 140 Characters or Less: Or, What Are Archival Institutions Doing on Twitter?" *The American Archivist* 77 (2): 534–57. doi:10.17723/aarc.77.2.7661l201544xv5qr.

Lalonde, Katy, Chris Sanagan, and Sean Smith. 2014. "The War of 1812 in 140 Characters or Less: 'SuperCool or Super Un-Tweet Worthy?' " *The American Archivist* 77 (2): 558–68. doi:10.17723/aarc.77.2.7016748180782733.

Laver, Tara. 2003. "In a Class by Themselves: Faculty Papers at Research University Archives and Manuscript Repositories." *The American Archivist* 66 (1): 159–96.

Long, Linda. 1989. "Question Negotiation in the Archival Setting: The Use of Interpersonal Communication Techniques in the Reference Interview." *The American Archivist* 52 (1): 40–51. doi:10.17723/aarc.52.1.m021336077782624.

Lucas, Scott Anthony. 2008. "The Information Seeking Processes of Genealogist." PhD Dissertation. Emporia State University. https://esirc.emporia.edu/handle/123456789/3354 (accessed February 21, 2016).

Lytle, Richard. 1980a. "Intellectual Access to Archives: I. Provenance and Content Indexing Methods of Subject Retrieval." *The American Archivist* 43 (1): 64–75. doi:10.17723/aarc.43.1.31031523737j16n7.

Lytle, Richard. 1980b. "Intellectual Access to Archives: II. Report of an Experiment Comparing Provenance and Content Indexing Methods of Subject Retrieval." *The American Archivist* 43 (2): 191–207. doi:10.17723/aarc.43.2.c4777576733114rp.

Macpherson, Paul. 2010. "Building a Better Horse and Buggy: The Privileging of Access in Reading Rooms over Online Access." *Archives and Manuscripts* 38 (2): 61–78.

Malbin, S. L. 1997. "The Reference Interview in Archival Literature." *College and Research Libraries* 58 (1): 69–80. doi:10.5860/crl.58.1.69.

Martin, Kristin. 2001. "Analysis of Remote Reference Correspondence at a Large Academic Manuscripts Collection." *The American Archivist* 64 (1): 17–42. doi:10.17723/aarc.64.1.g224234uv117734p.

Mazella, David, and Julie Grob. 2011. "Collaborations between Faculty and Special Collections Librarians in Inquiry-Driven Classes." *Portal: Libraries and the Academy* 11 (1): 467–87.

McCarthy, Gavan, and Tim Sherratt. 1996. "Mapping Scientific Memory: Understanding the Role of Recordkeeping in Scientific Practice." *Archives and Manuscripts* 24 (1): 78–85.

McCausland, Sigrid. 2011. "A Future without Mediation? Online Access, Archivists, and the Future of Archival Research." *Australian Academic and Research Libraries* 42 (4): 309–19.

McKemmish, Sue, Livia Iacovino, Eric Ketelaar, Melissa Castan, and Lynette Russell. 2011. "Resetting Relationships: Archives and Indigenous Human Rights in Australia." *Archives and Manuscripts* 39 (1): 107.

Milligan, Ian. 2013. "Illusionary Order: Online Databases, Optical Character Recognition, and Canadian History, 1997–2010." *Canadian Historical Review* 94 (4): 540–69.

Mitchell, Eleanor, Peggy Seiden, and Suzy Taraba, eds. 2012. *Past or Portal? Enhancing Undergraduate Learning through Special Collections and Archives*. Chicago, IL: Association of College and Research Libraries, a division of the American Library Association.

Monte-Sano, Chauncey. 2008. "Qualities of Historical Writing Instruction: A Comparative Case Study of Two Teachers' Practices." *American Educational Research Journal* 45 (4): 1045–79. doi:10.3102/0002831208319733.

Monte-Sano, Chauncey. 2011. "Beyond Reading Comprehension and Summary: Learning to Read and Write in History by Focusing on Evidence, Perspective, and Interpretation: EVIDENCE, PERSPECTIVE, AND INTERPRETATION." *Curriculum Inquiry* 41 (2): 212–49. doi:10.1111/j.1467-873X.2011.00547.x.

Nardi, Bonnie A., and Vicki O'Day. 1996. "Intelligent Agents: What We Learned at the Library." *Libri* 46: 59–88.

Niu, Jinfang, and Margaret Hedstrom. 2008. "Documentation Evaluation Model for Social Science Data." *Proceedings of the American Society for Information Science and Technology* 45 (1): 11. doi:10.1002/meet.2008.1450450223.

Northwestern University. 2008. "University Archives to Preserve Football History." YouTube. https://www.youtube.com/watch?v=o1np5sxCmfs (accessed February 20, 2016).

Oliver, Gillian. 2012. "The Digital Archive." In *Evaluating and Measuring the Value, Use and Impact of Digital Collections*, edited by Lorna Hughes, 49–60. London: Facet Publishing.

O'Toole, James M. 1986. "Reference Services in Catholic Diocesan Archives." *The Reference Librarian* 5 (13): 149–58.

Patricio, L., R. P. Fisk, J. Falcao e Cunha, and L. Constantine. 2011. "Multilevel Service Design: From Customer Value Constellation to Service Experience Blueprinting." *Journal of Service Research* 14 (2): 180–200. doi:10.1177/1094670511401901.

Pearce-Moses, Richard. 2005. *A Glossary of Archival and Records Terminology*. Chicago, IL: Society of American Archivists. http://www2.archivists.org/glossary (accessed February 21, 2016).

Prom, Christopher. 2004. "User Interactions with Electronic Finding Aids in a Controlled Setting." *The American Archivist* 67 (2): 234–68. doi:10.17723/aarc.67.2.7317671548328620.

Pugh, Joseph, and Christopher Power. 2015. "Swimming the Channels: An Analysis of Online Archival Reference Enquiries." In *Human-Computer Interaction–INTERACT 2015*, edited by Julio Abascal, Simone Barbosa, Mirko Fetter, Tom Gross, Philippe Palanque, and Marco Winckler, 9298: 99–115. Cham, Switzerland: Springer International Publishing.

Pugh, Mary Jo. 1982. "The Illusion of Omniscience: Subject Access and the Reference Archivist." *The American Archivist* 45 (1): 33–44.

Pugh, Mary Jo. 2005. *Providing Reference Services for Archives and Manuscripts*. Chicago, IL: Society of American Archivists.

Reed, Barbara. 2014. "Re-Inventing Archives." *Archives and Manuscripts* 42 (2): 123–32. doi:10.1080/01576895.2014.926823.

Rhee, Hea Lim. 2012. "Modelling Historians' Information-Seeking Behaviour with an Interdisciplinary and Comparative Approach." *Information Research* 17 (4). http://informationr.net/ir/17-4/paper544.html (accessed October 4, 2016).

Rhee, Hea Lim. 2015. "Reflections on Archival User Studies." *Reference and User Services Quarterly* 54 (4): 29–42.

Ribeiro, Fernanda. 1996. "Subject Indexing and Authority Control in Archives: The Need for Subject Indexing in Archives and for an Indexing Policy Using Controlled Language." *Journal of the Society of Archivists* 17 (1): 27–54. doi:10.1080/00379819609511787.

Rockenbach, Barbara. 2011. "Archives, Undergraduates, and Inquiry-Based Learning: Case Studies from Yale University Library." *American Archivist* 74 (Spring/Summer): 297–311.

Rolan, Gregory. 2015. "Towards Archive 2.0: Issues in Archival Systems Interoperability." *Archives and Manuscripts* 43 (1): 42–60. doi:10.1080/01576895.2014.959535.

Ruller, Thomas J. 1997. "Open All Night: Using the Internet to Improve Access to Archives: A Case Study of the New York State Archives and Records Administration." *The Reference Librarian* 26 (56): 161–70. doi:10.1300/J120v26n56_12.

Rutner, Jennifer, and Roger C. Schonfeld. 2012. *Supporting the Changing Research Practices of Historians*. Ithaka S+R. http://www.sr.ithaka.org/wp-content/mig/reports/supporting-the-changing-research-practices-of-historians.pdf (accessed February 20, 2016).

Samouelian, Mary. 2009. "Embracing Web 2.0: Archives and the Newest Generation of Web Application." *American Archivist* 72 (1): 42–71.

Scheir, Wendy. 2005. "First Entry: Report on a Qualitative Exploratory Study of Novice User Experience with Online Finding Aids." *Journal of Archival Organization* 3 (4): 49–85. doi:10.1300/J201v03n04_04.

School of Information. University of Michigan. 2016. "Citizen Interaction Design." https://www.si.umich.edu/academics/project-i-citizen-interaction-design (accessed February 20, 2016).

Sinn, Donghee. 2012. "Impact of Digital Archival Collections on Historical Research." *Journal of the American Society for Information Science and Technology* 63 (8): 1521–37.

Sinn, Donghee, and Nicholas Soares. 2014. "Historians' Use of Digital Archival Collections: The Web, Historical Scholarship, and Archival Research." *Journal of the Association for Information Science and Technology* 65 (9): 1794–1809. doi:10.1002/asi.23091.

Smith-Yoshimura, Karen. 2012. *Social Metadata for Libraries, Archives and Museums*. Dublin, OH: OCLC Research.

Society of American Archivists. n.d. "Core Archival Knowledge." http://www2.archivists.org/category/book-page-types/gpas-component/core-archival-knowledge (accessed February 20, 2016).

Sundqvist, Anneli. 2015. "Conceptualisations of the Use of Records." *Tidsskriftet Arkiv* 6: 1–15.

Swain, Ellen D. 2015. "Best Practices for Teaching with Primary Sources." In *The New Information Literacy Instruction: Best Practices*, edited by Patrick Ragains and Sandra Wood, 189–204. Lanham, MD: Rowman & Littlefield.

Taylor, R. S. 1968. "Question-Negotiation and Information Seeking in Libraries." *College and Research Libraries* 29 (3): 178–94. doi:10.5860/crl_29_03_178.

Theimer, Kate. 2011. "What Is the Meaning of Archives 2.0?" *The American Archivist* 74 (1): 58–68. doi:10.17723/aarc.74.1.h7tn4m4027407666.

Thomsen, Elizabeth. 1999. *Rethinking Reference: The Reference Librarian's Practical Guide for Surviving Constant Change*. New York: Neal-Schuman Publishers. http://eric.ed.gov/?id=ED441522.

Tibbo, Helen. 1995. "Interviewing Techniques for Remote Reference: Electronic versus Traditional Environments." *The American Archivist* 58 (3): 294–310. doi:10.17723/aarc.58.3.61625250t016287r.

Tibbo, Helen R. 2003. "Primarily History in America: How US Historians Search for Primary Materials at the Dawn of the Digital Age." *American Archivist* 66 (1): 9–50.

Tissing, Robert, Jr. 1984. "The Orientation Interview in Archival Research." *The American Archivist* 47 (2): 173–78.

Trace, Ciaran B. 2006. "For Love of the Game: An Ethnographic Analysis of Archival Reference Work." *Archives and Manuscripts* 34 (1): 124.

Trace, Ciaran B., and Carlos J. Ovalle. 2012. "Archival Reference and Access: Syllabi and a Snapshot of the Archival Canon." *The Reference Librarian* 53 (1): 76–94. doi:10.1080/02763877.2011.596364.

Tucker, Susan N. 2009. "The Most Public of All History: Family History and Heritage Albums in the Transmission of Records." PhD Thesis. University of Amsterdam. http://dare.uva.nl/record/1/319580 (accessed February 20, 2016).

University of Manitoba Archives and Special Collections. 2008. "How to Access Research Material from the University of Manitoba Archives." YouTube. https://www.youtube.com/watch?v=cwLYryOhK18 (accessed February 20, 2016).

Vilar, Polona, and Alenka Šauperl. 2015. "Archives, Quo Vadis et Cum Quibus? Archivists' Self-Perceptions and Perceptions of Users of Contemporary Archives." *International Journal of Information Management* 35 (5): 551–60.

Weiner, Sharon A., Sammie Morris, and Lawrence J. Mykytiuk. 2015. "Archival Literacy Competencies for Undergraduate History Majors." *The American Archivist* 78 (1): 154–80. doi:10.17723/0360-9081.78.1.154.

Willever-Farr, Heather, and Andrea Forte. 2014. "Family Matters: Control and Conflict in Online Family History Production." In *Proceedings of the 17th ACM Conference on Computer Supported Cooperative Work & Social Computing*, 475–86. New York: ACM.

Wilsted, Thomas. 1986. "Establishing an Image: The Role of Reference Service in a New Archival Program." *The Reference Librarian* 5 (13): 159–72. doi:10.1300/J120v05n13_14.

Wineburg, Samuel S. 2001. *Historical Thinking and Other Unnatural Acts: Charting the Future of Teaching the Past*. In *Critical Perspectives on the Past*, edited by Susan Porter Benson, Stephen Brier, and Roy Rosenzweig. Philadelphia, PA: Temple University Press.

Yakel, Elizabeth. 2000. "Thinking Inside and Outside the Boxes: Archival Reference Services at the Turn of the Century." *Archivaria* 48: 140–60.

Yakel, Elizabeth. 2004. "Encoded Archival Description: Are Finding Aids Boundary Spanners or Barriers for Users?" *Journal of Archival Organization* 2 (1–2): 63–77. doi:10.1300/J201v02n01_06.

Yakel, Elizabeth, and Deborah Torres. 2003. "AI: Archival Intelligence and User Expertise." *The American Archivist* 66 (1): 51–78. doi:10.17723/aarc.66.1.q022h85pn51n5800.

Yakel, Elizabeth, and Deborah A. Torres. 2007. "Genealogists as a 'Community of Records.' " *American Archivist* 70 (1): 93–113.

9

Archival Public Programming

Sigrid McCausland

Public programs are not frills, but an integral part of the institutional mission.
(Pugh 2005, 145)

Archival public programming is recognized today as a core function in archival institutions whose mandate includes providing services to the public. It plays a critical role in communicating what archives and archivists do to the wider world. Put simply, archival public programming is the means by which archives present themselves, their collections, and their services to their audiences. This formulation is easily understood today, and there are many sources explaining how and why archives should be in the public eye. However, fostering the relationship between archives and their audiences was not always a priority for archival practitioners or theorists. Archival public programming (or outreach) developed as an area of archival practice after the cornerstones of description, preservation, and appraisal had been embedded in archival programs in the third quarter of the twentieth century. Although embraced quickly by some archivists and their professional associations, others took longer to recognize its potential and to be convinced about its status as an archival function. This essay considers the origins and development of archival public programming and its theoretical and philosophical underpinnings. It then considers the role played by technology in shaping and delivering public programs and concludes with an exploration of trends and speculations on the future of the function of archival public programming.

Archival public programming emerged at a time when archival institutions were rethinking their relationships with their users. Government archives, like other institutional archives, had traditionally focused first on providing services to the parent institution and to internal users who needed information to carry out their responsibilities and, second, to external users undertaking academic or other specialized research. Research manuscript repositories tended to provide services only to scholars. Neither archives nor manuscript repositories had an orientation to the general public. Both were just beginning to acknowledge the existence of other users and audiences whose needs were different from those of the traditional academic researcher.

WHAT IS ARCHIVAL PUBLIC PROGRAMMING?

Discussions about the nature and role of archival public programming began in the 1970s. Since then, several different terms have been used to describe the function, notably *public programs*, *outreach*, and *archival public programming*, and archivists have developed a range of definitions for the activities that comprise the function. In 1978, the pioneer of the field, Elsie Freeman, wrote, "So new is the concept of outreach that as yet we have no generally accepted term for it." She noted that "archival education is used interchangeably with outreach, outreach programs and education programs" (1978, 147). In the United States, *public programs* was initially adopted, for example, in the Society of American Archivists' (SAA) basic manual *Archives & and Manuscripts: Public Programs* (Pederson and Casterline 1982) and in the *Modern Archives Reader* (Daniels and Walch 1984). The first comprehensive definition was offered by Ann Pederson and Gail Casterline:

> Public programs are tools that support and enhance other archival functions, including research, reference, preservation, and collecting. They can be highly educational, both for planners and participants; they can foster a greater appreciation for history and historical records; and they help ensure firm and continuing support for archival endeavours. (1982, 8)

This definition is aspirational, stressing the value of public programs to the archival institution as well as the public and reflecting the need to promote a function that was then still emerging. Interestingly, it does not refer specifically to the relationship between archivists and users, considered central by Freeman (1978) and many other later writers, including Tim Ericson (1990–1991), Verne Harris (1993), and Kate Theimer (2014). We will return to the question of the importance of users, actual and potential, to archival public programming later in this essay. In Canada, *public programming* was adopted as the name for the function by the early 1990s. Gabrielle Blais and David Enns offered another high-level definition, describing public programming as "... those activities that result in direct interaction with the public to guarantee the participation and support necessary to achieve an archival repository's mission and fulfil its mandate" (1990–1991, 103). The inclusion of "mission" and "mandate" here is instructive, suggesting that archival public programming as a function is intended both to engage with the public and to provide support for the overall mission of the archival repository.

Outreach, Public Programming, or Public Programs?

By 1992, *outreach* was the SAA's preferred term, as stated in *A Glossary for Archivists, Manuscript Curators, and Records Managers*: "Outreach program: Organized activities of archives or manuscript repositories intended to acquaint potential users with their holdings and their research and reference value" (Bellardo and Bellardo 1992, 24). *Public programming* appears as a nonpreferred term. In 1994, Elsie Freeman Finch reflected that the advocates for the function had used the terms *outreach*, *public programs*, and *educational programs* interchangeably as descriptors over the years (1994, 1). Later, American definitions of *outreach* emphasize the role of providing services and informing external audiences about the repository's purpose and collections. The SAA's online *Glossary of Archives and Related Terminology* defines *outreach* as "the process of identifying and providing services to constituencies with needs relevant to the repository's mission, especially underserved groups, and tailoring services to meet those needs" (Pearce-Moses 2005). In 2014, Theimer wrote that to her *outreach* means "carrying out activities designed to inform potential users about a repository's collections and attract their interest in learning more about those collections" (2014, vii).

There was (and is) no consensus on the name for the archival public programming function across the main Anglophone countries. For example, Gabrielle Hyslop explained why *public programs* prevailed over *outreach* at the National Archives of Australia (NAA):

> In writing and talking about programs for the public, archivists often use the term *outreach*. At the National Archives we prefer the term *public programs*. This is not only because it is the term used by other national cultural institutions but also because it focuses explicitly on the public. (Hyslop 2002, 49)

Australia, despite its contributions in other areas of archival theory and practice, was a latecomer to public programs. There was little writing about the field before Helen Nosworthy's account of the establishment of the public programs branch of the NAA (then known as Australian Archives) in 1993 (Nosworthy 1994). *Public programs* is still used by the NAA (National Archives of Australia 2015). Similarly, "Archives Inspire," the U.K. National Archives plan for the period 2015–2019, includes among its goals for inspiring the public "develop new and exciting public programmes and services which rival those of other pre-eminent institutions" (The National Archives 2015, 4). In the United Kingdom, the term *public services* is also used, for example, in the name of the Public Services Quality Group, which among other activities conducts surveys of users of archives. Chris Cooper's discussion of efforts to establish new audiences for archives at The National Archives (United Kingdom) also uses the term *public services* (Cooper 2008).

Outreach and Advocacy: How Do They Differ?

One persisting conundrum for archivists, in North America at least, has been to define *outreach* and to decide whether it is essentially the same thing as advocacy or not. Studies of archivists in the United States have found that they have difficulty in identifying outreach as opposed to basic services (Chute 2002) and in separating outreach from advocacy as an archival function (Brett and Jones 2013). Here, Daniel Elves makes a useful distinction between archival public programming and advocacy: "Advocacy as a political- and policy-focused activity to convince a targeted audience to act is distinguished from archival public programming that is centered around outreach, publicity, exhibitions, and reference services" (2012). Jeremy Brett and Jasmine Jones quote Richard Cox who categorizes outreach as public relations and advocacy as political (2013, 52). Mary Jo Pugh acknowledges the importance of the link between outreach and advocacy and reference services (2005, 29). Likewise, in her entry on "public service" in the *Encyclopedia of Archival Science*, Victoria Lemieux nominates archival outreach and public programming as one of two interrelated archival functions that concern accessibility and communication relating to archives, the other function being reference services (2015). In its "Guidelines for a Graduate Program in Archival Studies (GPAS)" curriculum statement, SAA treats outreach and advocacy as inseparable, describing them together as comprising "[t]he theories and practices used to identify archival constituencies and their needs and to develop programs to promote increased use, understanding of archival materials and methods, resources, visibility, and support" (Society of American Archivists , n.d.). This description is helpful because it confirms that outreach (and advocacy) involves theory as well as practice. It also acknowledges earlier definitions that incorporate the two key elements: first, identifying the targets for outreach activities and, second, developing programs that enact the goals of increased use and understanding of archival materials and methods (Pederson and Casterline 1982, 8).

Some writers emphasize the difference between outreach and advocacy. James O'Toole and Cox note that the purpose of public programs is to "raise public awareness of archival programs and work," while advocacy is intended to achieve change, such as new legislation or improved financial support (2006, 131). Brett and Jones report on a survey for the SAA's Issues and Advocacy Roundtable where they concluded that outreach and advocacy have different meanings for archivists despite some continuing confusion. Outreach is understood as being an awareness-raising and educational activity, directed primarily at those who might use collections and services, while advocacy is directed at stakeholders who have power or authority to make decisions that help the institution (2013, 65–66). Larry Hackman's characterization of advocacy as "activities consciously aimed to persuade individuals or organizations to act on behalf of a program or institution" (2011, vii) does not describe or explain outreach which is something that archivists are required to do themselves as part of their professional responsibilities. I would like to speculate that one practical reason for the continuing confusion might be that outreach and advocacy activities are similar. For example, the case studies in Hackman's volume on advocacy illustrate clearly that successful archival advocacy often employs public programming techniques and tools (Hackman 2011).

Use and the Impact of New Users

The initial focus of archival public programming was on finding ways to attract new users to archives (Freeman 1978). Blais and Enns describe the model of service that favored individual support to academic historians as a long-standing feature of the approach by archivists to the use of archives (1990–1991). This model was under challenge by the 1970s with the emergence of new fields of historical research, including social history with its interest in everyday life rather than government policy. Women's history was one field where archivists participated with users in developing new archival programs that supported the demand for new sources (Zanish-Belcher and Voss 2013). This change was accompanied by the appearance of a more diverse user population. Prominent among the "new" users of archives were genealogists. In most countries, the boom in demand for access to archives by genealogists was linked to the anniversary of a significant historical national event: in Canada, to the centenary of Confederation in 1967 and in the United States, to the bicentenary of the American Revolution in 1976 and to the television miniseries *Roots* in 1977. In Australia, it was linked to the bicentenary of the first voyage of Captain James Cook to the South Pacific in 1970. Finding ways to satisfy the demand from genealogical users occupied the energy of reference archivists well before the bicentenary of European settlement in Australia in 1988 (Berzins 2007).

PUBLIC PROGRAMS AND THE INSTITUTIONAL MISSION

So far, this essay has considered the reaching-out aspects of public programming. Yet, to serve their publics adequately, archivists involved in public programming need to know their collections and how their organization works. In other words, they need to reach in to the organization, especially if they wish to meet the goal of serving the institutional mandate that appears in some of the definitions discussed earlier. As early as 1978, Freeman identified multiple roles as well as multiple audiences for public programs. She noted that the type of activity required to influence resource allocators was different from the exhibitions or other multipliers directed at public audiences (Freeman 1978, 148–50). Decades later, O'Toole and Cox gave public programs a central, normalized role in the work of archivists, arguing that "developing public programs is a natural extension of other archival tasks. In all the activities archivists engage in, they have always had one eye on the people who want to use their records" (2006, 130). Thus, public programming as the activity that connects the user to the audience (or multiple publics) can be seen as supporting the institutional mission of the archives, whichever context it may belong to. For example, public program activities in a government archives enable the archives to meet its legislative obligations to make records available to the public and to support the work of its current employees (here, it is worth recalling that the taxpayer helps fund government archives). In the case of university archives, the university funds the archives on the expectation that it will be used by scholars, students, and employees. In the case of corporate archives, the company expects the archives to serve its goals, for example, to provide an efficient service to support decision making or to assist in providing material that promotes the company's public image. In the case of archival collections that are acquired and maintained by a university library, state historical society, or government-funded major library, the host organization expects the collections to be used and its employees to provide services that engage public interest, in person and online.

Some of the leading writers on public programs (or outreach) have argued that, as a function, it means much more than providing efficient and appropriate services to external and internal audiences. They consider that public programming is a central archival function, linked closely to the mission of the institution (Ericson 1990–1991, 114–15; Pearce-Moses 2005; Pederson and Casterline 1982, 8; Pugh 2005, 145). Over the decades, this position has not always been accepted. There have been disputes over the role of public programming and whether it deserved to be welcomed and funded as a function, arriving as it did after other functions.

A Core Function for Archives?

At their broadest, public programs have been viewed as vehicles for bringing the archives to the attention of the public, for example, "... a public program is any activity that contributes to a greater awareness of archives and what they do" (Pederson and Casterline 1982, 7). However, this has not always meant that public programs themselves have been accepted as important within archival institutions. Pederson wrote that they were perceived as "a drain" on other functions, including preservation and arrangement and description (1978, 159). Public programming was not a particularly visible archival function in the professional literature. Authors writing about archival reference have commented on the paucity of the treatment of archival reference in the literature (e.g., Duff 2010; Pugh 2005). The literature on archival public programming was even more scant. For many years, Pederson and Casterline's *Archives and Manuscripts: Public Programs* (1982) and Finch's *Advocating Archives: An Introduction to Public Relations for Archivists* (1994) were the only full-length works by archivists devoted to archival public programming. Some general texts identified the potential of outreach to contribute to a full archives program but urged caution about implementing outreach before the basics of archival work were bedded down (Taylor 1984, 85; Yakel 1994, 53–56). Journal articles and book chapters on public programs and outreach noted that the function was considered as something to be added once the more important work of appraisal and arrangement and description was completed or always placed last in the trinity of selection, preservation, and use (Bradley 2006; Ericson 1990–1991; Harris 1993; Nosworthy 1994). Likewise, it has been viewed either as a luxury or as a poor cousin to other archival functions (Condé 2007; Nicholls 2001).

Early on, Freeman had called for outreach to be accepted as a core program (Freeman 1978). Blais and Enns pressed for a new understanding which would recognize public programs as core archival functions. Intrinsic to this new understanding of public programs was a need for archivists to acknowledge that they should change their orientation to their various publics and embrace new approaches to interacting with them (Blais and Enns 1990–1991). Cox considered that public programming had become an accepted archival function by 1993, as indicated by its inclusion in basic texts and its role in archival discourse (1993, 123–24). Hyslop (2002, 59) argued that public programs were increasingly recognized as core functions of archives around the world. Caroline Williams's British text lists advocacy and outreach as core functions of archives (2006, 19). Today, there appears to be no dispute on this point in the United States, when outreach and advocacy are curriculum elements in the SAA's GPAS (SAA, n.d.) and the Academy of Certified Archivists includes outreach, advocacy, and promotion as one of the seven domains of professional competencies for archivists (Academy of Certified Archivists 2014).

INFLUENCES ON PUBLIC PROGRAMMING THINKING

So what were the ideas and influences behind archival public programming and how did they shape its development? The 1970s were a time of questioning and change in many fields, including the humanities and social sciences. Long-accepted practices in academic history were challenged by the ideas of history from below which articulated a broader, more inclusive vision of the past. This included a critique of archives as being closely allied to the dominance of history from above where the voices of the powerful were heard and the voices of the marginalized were absent from the archives (Zinn 1977). Many archivists were encouraged by the growing emphasis on social history. They began to think about and then implement ways of redressing the gaps in their collections, for example, through oral history projects (Pederson and Casterline 1982). However, the influence of history as a discipline on archival public programming should not be overestimated, as the paths of history and archives were beginning to diverge (Blouin and Rosenberg 2011).

The early years of public programs were largely driven from within the archival profession by archivists who recognized the need to provide different kinds of programs to meet the needs of new types of users for whom the traditional archival reference service designed for the academic historian was no longer adequate (Cox 1993; Freeman 1978). The SAA's 1976 survey of outreach found that archivists in universities, government archives, and state historical societies were providing a range of programs, including exhibits, publications, lectures, site visits, teachers' kits, and internships. These programs were oriented to three different audience types, namely professionals, educators, and the general public. Many of the activities comprising outreach reported in this survey were aimed at increasing awareness of archives rather than direct use (Pederson 1978, 158).

To characterize the challenges facing archivists working with users, some writers on public programming highlighted the differences between primary or direct use (including traditional scholarly use in reading rooms) and secondary or indirect use (including "use" such as reading books or viewing documentaries based on research using archives) (Nosworthy 1994, 71; Pugh 2005, 34–40). We have seen that from the 1970s, archivists had to acknowledge the reality of more diverse and less scholarly user populations. Further, archivists were now beginning to think about how to reach nonusers, sometimes using market research techniques to try to discover more about why some audiences were yet to be reached (Williams 2006, 148–49).

While use and users were always front of mind for the pioneer exponents of public programming such as Freeman and Pederson, the relationship between the archival profession and the wider world was investigated in the 1980s through such initiatives as the SAA's Task Force on Archives and Society. From this, it was reasonable to conclude that archivists were responsible for their low profile and that the way to address this problem was to adopt marketing approaches and in doing so to become more user-friendly (Jimerson 1989). Lawrence Dowler (1988) proposed that use should become the basis of archival theory and practice.

Use is in fact central to thinking about archival public programming. This is the critical factor distinguishing it from most other archival theory which is centered on the record (Cook 1990–1991; Craig 1990–1991). The use versus record dichotomy was of particular concern to Terry Cook (1990–1991). Cook, while sympathetic to the advocates of public programming, foresaw long-term problems if use were to come to dominate archival theory and practice. In particular, he was concerned that appraisal based on predicted research use would distort practice and result in a compromised record being retained for the future. However, macro-appraisal theory, developed by Cook and others in the 1990s, has proved durable and has not been replaced by use-driven appraisal criteria. Writing not long after Cook and profoundly influenced by regime change in South Africa, Harris emphasized the importance of according a proper place to use in archival theory (Harris 1993). He argued that use had to be not only democratized from its traditional academic base, but also that it had to be accepted by archival theorists. Harris, too, saw a role for archival public programming in supporting other archival functions and linked public programming to the success of all archival operations where a new archives was necessary for a new national government (1993). In Australia, use and user perspectives were still on the way to recognition. On the one hand, they were covered in several chapters of *Keeping Archives*, first published in 1987 (Pederson 1987). On the other hand, the compilation of Australian archival writing *Debates and Discourses: Selected Australian Writings on Archival Theory 1951–1990* (Biskup et al. 1995) contained no pieces concerning users or reference, reflecting the dominance in that country of theory and practice that focused on records and their context. Blais and Enns proposed a public programming framework based on four concepts: image, awareness, education, and use (1990–1991, 101–02). Nosworthy (1994, 70–71) considered this model applicable in the Australian context.

Public programming in the 1990s was connected to contemporary trends in historical and philosophical thought. Writing in 1993, Cox argued that the concept of public memory had much to contribute to archival work, and he saw that in particular it was important for public programming. If archivists were to improve their profile, they needed to endorse public programming as the means to conveying the message about the role of archives in society. At the same time, they needed to be aware of how the wider public viewed the past (Cox 1993). Cook and other archival thinkers who were influenced by postmodern ideas were interested in the role of public programming as mediation, in the connection between public programming and other archival functions, and in how archives could be made more inclusive of previously silent voices (Bradley 2006).

The Role of Professional Associations

Professional associations have been significant in the development of archival public programming in various ways. Their publications have provided avenues for the dissemination of ideas, and their structures have provided opportunities for public programming archivists to join together. Their conferences have provided space for presentations and debates. The SAA sponsored the first survey of outreach in 1976 (Pederson 1978) and published significant writing on public programs by Finch (1994), Freeman (1978), and Pederson and Casterline (1982). In the mid-1980s, members of the Australian Society of Archivists worked as volunteers to write *Keeping Archives* (Pederson 1987). The book was partly intended to provide the material to support proposed workshops for amateurs keen to learn about archival practice (McCausland 1989). The 1990 Association of Canadian Archivists conference can be seen as critical to understandings of public programming. It sparked a debate that advanced the professional discussion and exposed the essential differences between the advocates of public programming and their critics. In helping to spread public programming ideas and in reaching new audiences, professional associations have at times led and at times followed the efforts of formal programs in archival institutions. Today, professional associations provide workshops and online training programs as well as online resources on outreach for archivists (e.g., the SAA's ArchivesAware blog).

ELEMENTS OF PUBLIC PROGRAMS

Having considered definitions and the ideas behind public programming, we now turn to the content of public programs. The type of activity will be influenced by the institutional context of the archives, its knowledge of its community/communities, and funds available (Millar 2010, 194–95). Over the years, there has been remarkable stability in the scope of activities classified as public programs that are directed at users or the general public. They include:

- publications: *print* or *digital*, including guides, monographs, brochures, souvenir books, information leaflets, subject guides, newsletters, postcards, greeting cards and bookmarks, and reproductions of collection items (Millar 2010, 198; O'Toole and Cox 2006, 129; Williams 2006, 152–53);
- exhibitions (on-site or travelling; *digitized virtual exhibits*, artifacts versus documents (Williams 2006, 156–57);

- publicity (newspaper or magazine articles or regular columns; local television or radio advertisements or programs; placing stories; competitions for captioning or recognizing photographs from the collection; radio talks (O'Toole and Cox 2006, 129; Williams 2006, 158);
- educational programs (for school students or for specific user groups such as genealogists) (Millar 2010, 198);
- seminars and workshops;
- talks and lectures (including author talks);
- tours (including tours of the archives itself or local walking tours) (Pugh 2005, 97; Williams 2006, 159); and
- festivals (including local archives or heritage open days) (Pugh 2005, 97, 147)

As late as 2010, some writers still enunciated cautionary notes about the need for archival public program activities to include particular communities and potential audiences that do not have guaranteed Internet access (Millar 2010, 195; Williams 2006, 153). O'Toole and Cox identified the elderly as one group who may benefit from structured viewing of exhibition content that can confirm their own experiences (2006, 129–30).

Whose Work Is It?

In the early days of public programming, public program activities were carried out almost exclusively in-house (Pederson 1978). However, as time progressed and public programs became more closely tied to institutional missions (a pointer to their acceptance as mainstream functions), more resources were available for public programs. This sometimes meant hiring experts from other fields such as marketing, design, journalism, and exhibition curation to do specialized work or to be members of multidisciplinary teams for major activities such as traveling exhibitions (Hyslop 2002, 51). Public program archivists were thus often quite open to working with other professionals, reflecting the outward orientation of the whole endeavor of engaging with new audiences. Sometimes archives engage with popular audiences in indirect ways. For several years now, archives and archivists have benefited from their exposure to mass audiences via reality television in the form of celebrity family history programs such as *Who Do You Think You Are?* and *Faces of America*. This is an example of the collaboration between commercial enterprises with a brief for popularizing personal histories and archives and other cultural institutions.

Exhibitions

Exhibitions are a traditional public program activity. Exhibitions go to the heart of archival public programming both in attempting to reach new audiences and to educate the public about archives. While exhibitions may seem to be a relatively recent phenomenon in archives, Gail Farr notes that the British Records Association set up a subcommittee in 1949 to investigate the use of exhibitions as a way of encouraging local interest in archives. She elaborates that while there was interest from archivists in North America, it was not until the 1970s and the Bicentennial of the American Revolution that exhibitions became a major interest of American archivists (Farr 1980, 7).

Exhibiting archives has traditionally been viewed as more difficult than exhibiting objects, because the viewer is not as interested in reading texts as opposed to engaging with unusual or beautiful objects chosen carefully for their visual appeal in museums (Farr 1980, 9–10; Nicholls 2003, 36). However, the power of the document in communicating meaning to the viewer can be the key to successful exhibition practice, as Anne-Marie Condé (2007) argues in her study of the experience of the exhibition of documents by the Australian War Memorial between 1925 and 1964.[1] Condé describes how viewing original documents from World War I, such as short battlefield messages, resonated with the Australian public in the 1920s and into the 1930s, because Australians were still mourning an experience that had changed their lives immeasurably (Condé 2007, 33–35). Both context and audience were critical here, as they were with the first major exhibition presented by the long-running *Between Two Worlds* exhibition presented by NAA. This exhibition, which traveled around the country for over six years from 1993, evoked strong sympathy from the public toward Aboriginal and Torres Strait Islander people, whose stories of separation and loss were generally not well known among the wider Australian community at the time (Hyslop 2002; Nicholls 2001, 2003). *Between Two Worlds* told the story through archival documents held by NAA; it succeeded in raising awareness of the Stolen Generations and in making the NAA's role as custodian of significant records documenting the lives of Indigenous Australians better known (Nicholls 2003). Hyslop (2002) and Nosworthy (1994) argued strongly for the role of exhibitions at NAA in interpreting archives to new audiences.

In 1980, Farr identified many benefits of exhibitions in communicating and educating the public and in serving other archival functions. Exhibitions could encourage the study of the past, teach people about the nature of archival and historical work, encourage donations, announce new acquisitions, commemorate important events, and make contributions to scholarship. Added to these benefits were "a greater and more imaginative use of archival materials by a wider clientele and the reinforcement of a favourable image that reflects the archivist's interest and involvement in the larger community" (Farr 1980, 8). In the digital age, exhibitions offer more possibilities to achieve the goals of using archival materials more imaginatively to reach untapped audiences and of promoting archives and the work of archivists (Lemieux 2015).

Publications

Publications are another traditional public programming activity. A public programming approach enables archives to plan comprehensive strategies, including both print and online publications. Previously, archives tended to have sporadic programs of publishing guides and exhibition-related materials. Last century, archivists pronounced the imperative for publishing guides to holdings and for publishing documentary sources (Schellenberg 1959). In the twenty-first century, however, archives can participate in national and international online databases to describe collection-level and series-level finding aids and to create online publications of significant records. Now archival institutions such as The National Archives (United Kingdom) offer a wide range of publications that respond to user demand, such as genealogical literature, or that fit in with other public program activities, such as the extensive and varied World War I commemorative events. Public programs also support the work of other functions of the archives by producing and marketing books on specialized archival work, thus taking local expertise to a broader audience. One example of this was the publication by NAA of *Solid, Safe and Secure: Building Archives Repositories in Australia* (Ling 1998), a book based on scholarship and practical experience that filled a gap in the professional literature.

ARCHIVAL PUBLIC PROGRAMMING IN THE TWENTY-FIRST CENTURY

Today, the online visitor to the home page of an archives Web site expects to find there the familiar row of icons of their social media favorites—Facebook, Twitter, Flickr, Tumblr, YouTube, WordPress, and so on. The public expects archivists to have a vibrant social media presence if they are to succeed in the online world. Archivists are also expected to participate in online projects, including those that share information about collections and services at national and international levels. Staff with public programming responsibilities are usually involved in creating and maintaining the organization's social media presence. Social media techniques enhance the potential for reaching new audiences and for sustaining relationships with established audiences (Theimer 2011). They extend the possibilities of public programming as a core archival function rather than redefining it entirely (Liew et al. 2015). For example, online guides and online exhibitions share or complement their analog equivalents, and, in many cases, they coexist. The path toward the integration of online public programming has been gradual. In the early days of the Web, archives typically relied on static Web sites, e-mail, and Listservs as their key online tools. The Web site typically included basic information about services and procedures, supplemented by descriptive information about holdings directed at intending on-site researchers (Millar 2010, 194). Information about events and online versions of print newsletters linked to the Web site could tell users and potential users much more about programs and services. This, however, was largely still one-way communication, from archives to audience.

Web 2.0 offers much more to the archivist involved in public programming, with the availability of tools such as blogs, Facebook, Twitter, podcasts, YouTube, and crowdsourcing. These tools can enhance the richness of content communicated to the reader or viewer of an online publication or an online exhibition (Liew et al. 2015). Podcasts and webinars offer new opportunities for education programs for students and other groups (Millar 2010, 196; Theimer 2014). Web sites are still important, but they need to be updated frequently to provide current information to existing and potential users (Purcell 2012, 234–35). The opportunity to contribute content via social media promises another level of interaction among the institution, the archivist, and the audience. Activities here include user participation in description (e.g., through tagging and other social media applications) and contributing to knowledge bases through wikis. Many benefits accrue when archives open up to the public in ways not imagined so very long ago. However, depending on the level of control the institution is willing to cede to the public, archives may limit public participation in such applications (Duff and Haskell 2015).

Archivists in government archives are using social media to connect with different audiences (e.g., State Records, New South Wales). Their Web sites often offer different suites of online services to the public and to the government agencies they serve. They use public programming techniques (as well as Web 2.0 tools) to improve relationships with agencies and thus hope to improve compliance with archival legislative regimes. This replaces reliance on purely pre-Internet agency training methods such as face-to-face training sessions. Is this today's realization of the expectation that public programming would be effective in supporting other archival functions? While there is more than can be done to deliver public programs in the digital world and how access is provided is changing (Lemieux 2015), successful archival public programming depends on collaboration among archivists as well as on their ability to interact with their audiences in creative ways, and it also depends on adequate resourcing.

The variety of activities under the umbrella of public programs is continuing to expand (Millar 2010, 195–98; Theimer 2014). Theimer suggests that the importance of the outreach function has increased recently. The possibilities of reaching new audiences that the Web offers is one reason for this; another is "greater competition for more limited funding and resources." In Theimer's view, greater awareness leads to "greater potential public support" for archives. Theimer adds that another reason for new approaches is the desire by archivists to open up to new kinds of users who may not feel welcome in an archives or special library (2014, vii).

Today the U.S. National Archives and Records Administration distinguishes between public programs (exhibits and events) and education programs (for schools). For the latter, distance learning programs and major events such National History Day aim to make archives more visible. A museum within the National Archives building is responsible for presenting its major, permanent exhibitions as well as temporary thematic exhibitions. History-engaged Americans are invited to spend the night in the hallowed space housing the Declaration of Independence in Washington (National Archives Foundation, n.d.). Such programs and events are indeed a long way from the traditional academic historian in a quiet research room.

However, this is not the only direction for public programming. Exhibitions such as *Records of Rights* at the National Archives remind the public of the importance of archives to democracy and relate directly to the mission of the organization. Other public program activities such as those exposing the wrongs of past policies toward indigenous people (Nicholls 2003) help educate the public through the record and thus go some way toward Tom Nesmith's goal of public programming in the service of public affairs (Nesmith 2010). We are also reminded from time to time about the power of the record and of our knowledge of it; for example, Joanna Sassoon exhorts archivists to remember that we are custodians of records concerning climate change and suggests that we should be more assiduous in participating in public debates on such important issues of our time (2007).

CONTINUITY AND CONTESTATION

As noted, archival public programming emerged later than other functions such as description, appraisal, and preservation in the mid- to late twentieth century. Initially, it was not recognized as a function. Indeed, Cox described Freeman as a "voice in the wilderness" for quite some time (1993, 123). Advocates for public programs repeatedly claimed that public programs were indeed core functions and should be recognized as such, especially since they were aligned to organizational missions and they were directed at improving the relationship between archives and their publics (Ericson 1990–1991; Freeman 1978). Ericson argued that introspective, custodial thinking where use always came last in the list of archival functions was a factor in the poor status of outreach within the profession. He further argued that use should come first because it was the goal, while other functions such as acquisition and description were means by which the goal would be reached (Ericson 1990–91, 116–17). In the post-custodial era, the boundaries between functions are less pronounced, and there is more understanding of the interdependence of different functions in assuring the survival of the archival record. Cook's critique that the focus on use detracted from the record and his warning that this could skew appraisal practice was a significant contribution to the debate (Cook 1990–1991; Harris 1993). However, both appraisal and public programming flourished in the 1990s, and the two functions have managed to work alongside each other since then.

Some archivists expressed concern that public programs, in particular, exhibitions, threatened the impartiality and authoritative qualities of archives because they involved interpreting archives (Millar 2010, 198) in direct conflict with Jenkinsonian principles on the role of the archivist where interpretation was antithetical to proper professional practice (Williams 2006, 38–39). On the other hand, Hyslop (2002) considered that interpretation was necessary if archives were to be understood by the nonusers in their audiences.

A more general problem was that archival public programming emerged at the same time as the philosophies of neoliberalism (also known as economic rationalism) took hold in public sector management. This meant that government priorities were viewed almost exclusively through the lens of economic worth (Pusey 1991). In practice for archives this often meant a reduction in funding and concomitant cuts to long-standing programs and the axing of new initiatives. I would argue that, in the long term, public programming has often brought new sources of income as well as more recognition to archives, including more understanding and appreciation of their worth by resource allocators.

A fairly recent analysis of the problems of public programming comes from Nesmith. He outlines a new direction for public programming, one which would see the record and use reconciled in support of the goal of an enhanced public presence for archives:

> … "new public programming" would have two interrelated dimensions: greater commitment to the history of records and archives and more active pursuit of a wider role for archives in public affairs. The two come together as archivists employ their knowledge of records and archiving to help identify and contextualize records for public affairs purposes. (Nesmith 2010, 171)

Despite the debate about the orientation of public programming and the difficulty of achieving it in the circumstance of limited resources, there is a general agreement that archives need to reach out to the wider world both as a matter of principle and as practical strategy to make their way in the contemporary world.

CONCLUSION

Over time, archival public programming has developed from being a fringe function to a mainstream one. Although different terms are used for naming public programming, its role is better understood now both within the archival world and in wider society than it was in the last quarter of the twentieth century. There is evidence that popular understanding of archives has increased, and archives are using public programming techniques and tools to reach diverse audiences. The digital era has brought more possibilities rather than an entirely new direction for public programming. The future of the function appears to be assured as long as archivists need to communicate about their work and their collections.

ENDNOTE

1. The Australian War Memorial combines the roles of museum, library, and archives.

REFERENCES

Academy of Certified Archivists. 2014. "Role Delineation Statement for Professional Archivists." http://www.certifiedarchivists.org/get-certified/role-delineation-statement/ (accessed October 23, 2015).

Bellardo, L. J., and L. L. Bellardo. 1992. *A Glossary for Archivists, Manuscript Curators, and Records Managers*. Chicago, IL: Society of American Archivists.

Berzins, B. 2007. "The Mitchell Library Reading Room: A Personal Memoir about the 1960s to the 1980s." *Australian Library Journal* 56 (November, 3–4): 312–21.

Biskup, P., K. Dan, C. McEwen, G. O'Shea, and G. Powell, eds. 1995. *Debates and Discourses: Selected Australian Writings on Archival Theory 1951–1990*. Canberra: Australian Society of Archivists Inc.

Blais, G., and D. Enns. 1990–1991. "From Paper Archives to People Archives: Public Programming in the Management of Archives." *Archivaria* 31: 101–13.

Blouin, F. X., and W. G. Rosenberg. 2011. *Processing the Past: Contesting Authority in History and the Archives*. New York: Oxford University Press.

Bradley, C. 2006. "Meditate, Mediate, Celebrate: Public Programming in a Postmodern World." *Archives and Manuscripts* 34 (2): 172–86.

Brett, J., and J. Jones. 2013. "Persuasion, Promotion, Perception: Untangling Archivists' Understanding of Advocacy and Outreach." *Provenance: The Journal of the Society of Georgia Archivists* 31 (1): 51–74.

Chute, T. G. 2002. "What's in a Name? Outreach vs. Basic Services: A Survey of College and University Archivists." *Journal of Archival Organization* 1 (2): 5–40. doi:10.1300/J201v01n02_02.

Condé, A.-M. 2007. " 'War History on Scraps of Paper': Exhibitions of Documents at the Australian War Memorial, 1925–1954." *Public History Review* 14: 25–43.

Cook, T. 1990–1991. "Viewing the World Upside Down: Reflections on the Theoretical Underpinnings of Archival Public Programming." *Archivaria* 31: 123–34.

Cooper, C. 2008. "Online On-Site: Transforming Public Services at The National Archives." *Journal of the Society of Archivists* 29 (October, 2): 193–206.

Cox, R. 1993. "The Concept of Public Memory and Its Impact on Archival Public Programming." *Archivaria* 36: 122–35.

Craig, B. L. 1990–1991. "What Are the Clients? Who Are the Products? The Future of Archival Public Services in Perspective." *Archivaria* 31: 135–41.

Daniels, M. F., and T. Walch, eds. 1984. *A Modern Archives Reader: Basic Readings on Archival Theory and Practice*. Washington, D.C.: National Archives and Records Service.

Dowler, L. 1988. "The Role of Use in Defining Archival Practice and Principles: A Research Agenda for the Availability and Use of Records." *American Archivist* 51 (Winter/Spring): 74–86.

Duff, W. 2010. "Archival Mediation." In *Currents of Archival Thinking*, edited by T. Eastwood and H. MacNeil, 115–36. Santa Barbara, CA: Libraries Unlimited.

Duff, W., and J. Haskell. 2015. "New Uses for Old Records: A Rhizomatic Approach to Archival Access." *American Archivist* 78 (1): 38–58.

Elves, D. 2012. "Advocating Electronic Records: Archival and Records Management Promotion of New Approaches to Long-Term Digital Preservation." Master of Arts Thesis. University of Manitoba, Winnipeg. http://hdl.handle.net/1993/14234; http://mspace.lib.umanitoba.ca/bitstream/1993/14234/1/Elves_Daniel.pdf (accessed April 30, 2015).

Ericson, T. 1990–1991. " 'Preoccupied with Our Own Gardens': Outreach and Archivists." *Archivaria* 31: 114–22.

Farr, G. 1980. *Archives and Manuscripts: Exhibits*. Chicago, IL: Society of American Archivists.

Finch, E. F., ed. 1994. *Advocating Archives: An Introduction to Public Relations for Archivists*. Metuchen, NJ: Society of American Archivists and Scarecrow Press.

Freeman, E. 1978. "Education Programs: Outreach as an Administrative Function." *American Archivist* 41 (2): 147–53.

Hackman, L. J., ed. 2011. *Many Happy Returns: Advocacy and the Development of Archives*. Chicago, IL: Society of American Archivists.

Harris, V. 1993. "Community Resource or Scholars' Domain? Archival Public Programming and the User as a Factor in Shaping Archival Theory and Practice." *South African Archives Journal* 35: 4–13.

Hyslop, G. 2002. "For Many Audiences: Developing Public Programs at the National Archives of Australia. *Archives and Manuscripts* 30 (1): 48–59.

Jimerson, R. C. 1989. "Redefining Archival Identity: Meeting User Needs in the Information Society." *American Archivist* 52: 332–40.

Lemieux, V. 2015. "Public Services." In *Encyclopedia of Archival Science*, edited by L. Duranti and P. Franks, 300–03. Lanham, MD: Rowman & Littlefield.

Liew, C. L., S. Wellington, G. Oliver, and R. Perkins. 2015. "Social Media in Libraries and Archives: Applied with Caution." *The Canadian Journal of Information and Library Science* 39 (3/4): 377–96.

Ling, T. 1998. *Solid, Safe and Secure: Building Archives Repositories in Australia*. Canberra: National Archives of Australia.

McCausland, S. 1989. "The Keeping Archives Workshop Program." *Archives and Manuscripts* 17 (2): 151–63.

Millar, L. 2010. *Archives: Principles and Practices*. London: Facet.

The National Archives. 2015. "Archives Inspire: The National Archives Plans and Priorities 2015–19." http://www.nationalarchives.gov.uk/documents/archives-inspire-2015-19.pdf (accessed October 8, 2015).

National Archives of Australia. 2015. "National Archives of Australia Corporate Plan 2015–16 to 2018–19." http://www.naa.gov.au/about-us/organisation/accountability/corporate-plan/index.aspx (accessed October 11, 2015).

National Archives Foundation. n.d. "National Archives Sleepover." http://www.archivesfoundation.org/sleepover/.

Nesmith, T. 2010. "Archivists and Public Affairs: Towards a New Archival Public Programming." In *Better Off Forgetting: Essays on Archives, Public Policy, and Collective Memory*, edited by C. Avery, and M. Holmlund, 169–91. Toronto: University of Toronto Press.

Nicholls, C. 2001. "The Role of Outreach in Australian Archive Programs." *Archives and Manuscripts* 29 (1): 62–70.

Nicholls, C. 2003. "Exhibiting Evidence: A Case Study." *Archivaria* 55 (Spring): 27–42.

Nosworthy, H. 1994. "Reaching Out: A Core Program for Australian Archives." In *The Records Continuum: Ian Maclean and Australian Archives First Fifty Years*, edited by Sue McKemmish and Michael Piggott, 64–77. Clayton, Victoria: Ancora Press in association with Australian Archives.

O'Toole, J. M., and R. J. Cox. 2006. *Understanding Archives and Manuscripts.* Chicago, IL: Society of American Archivists.

Pearce-Moses, R. 2005. *A Glossary of Archival and Records Terminology*. Chicago, IL: Society of American Archivists.

Pederson, A. 1978. "Archival Outreach: SAA's 1976 Survey." *The American Archivist* 41 (2): 155–62. doi:10.17723/aarc.41.2.l2070166pt18j487.

Pederson, A. 1987. *Keeping Archives*. Sydney: Australian Society of Archivists.

Pederson, A., and G. F. Casterline. 1982. *Archives and Manuscripts: Public Programs*. Chicago, IL: Society of American Archivists.

Pugh, M. J. 2005. *Providing Reference Services for Archives and Manuscripts*, 3rd ed. Chicago, IL: Society of American Archivists.

Purcell, A. D. 2012. *Academic Archives: Managing the Next Generation of University Archives, Records, and Special Collections.* Chicago, IL: Neal-Schuman.

Pusey, M. (1991). *Economic Rationalism in Canberra: A Nation-Building State Changes Its Mind*. Cambridge, England: Cambridge University Press.

Sassoon, J. 2007. "Sharing our Story: An Archaeology of Archival Thought." *Archives and Manuscripts* 35 (2): 40–54.

Schellenberg, T. R. 1959. "The Future of the Archival Profession." *American Archivist* 22 (1): 49–58.

Society of American Archivists. n.d. "Guidelines for a Graduate Program in Archival Studies (GPAS). Curriculum. Outreach and Advocacy." http://www2.archivists.org/gpas/curriculum/outreach-advocacy (accessed September 24, 2015).

Taylor, H. 1984. *Archival Services and the Concept of the User*. Paris: UNESCO.

Theimer, K., ed. 2011. *A Different Kind of Web: New Connections between Archives and Our Users*. Chicago, IL: Society of American Archivists.

Theimer, K., ed. 2014. *Outreach: Innovative Practices for Archives and Special Collections*. Lanham, MD: Rowman & Littlefield.

Williams, C. 2006. *Managing Archives: Foundations, Principles and Practice*. Oxford, England: Chandos Publishing.

Yakel, E. 1994. *Starting an Archives*. Lanham, MD: Society of American Archivists and Scarecrow Press.

Zanish-Belcher, T., and A. Voss, eds. 2013. *Perspectives on Women's Archives*. Chicago, IL: Society of American Archivists.

Zinn, H. 1977. "Secrecy, Archives, and the Public Interest." *Midwestern Archivist* 2 (2): 14–26.

PART III

Frameworks

10

Right to Information

Elizabeth Shepherd

"Right to information" (RTI), "access to information" (ATI), or "freedom of information" (FOI) has been adopted by countries around the world to enable the rights of citizens to freedom of opinion and expression, which is a prerequisite for human rights. In 1948, the UN Universal Declaration of Human Rights Article 19 stated the fundamental "right to freedom of opinion and expression; this right includes freedom to hold opinions without interference and to seek, receive and impart information and ideas through any media and regardless of frontiers" (United Nations 1948, sec. 19). In 1966, the International Covenant on Civil and Political Rights also declared that the right to freedom of expression "shall include freedom to seek, receive and impart information and ideas of all kinds" (United Nations 1966, sec. 19). The RTI has frequently been linked to trust in public discourse and to enabling accountable and open government. ATI establishes a right for individuals to seek information held by public authorities, often in a manner defined by the law and generally subject to exemptions for such things as national security, defense, international relations, police investigations, and privacy (Shepherd 2015, 717).

Recordkeeping professionals in corporate and public organizations provide access to records for internal business use to support current activities as well as ensure access to records needed over the longer term for the study of cultural heritage and the history of communities and families. In addition, in the accountability domain, records can be used to hold individuals, officials, and corporations to account, both internally and externally. Providing access to reliable records is commonly cited as a necessary prerequisite for accountability, transparency, and good governance. Transparency International (Pope 2003, 19) asserted that "when we campaign for greater access to information we must at the same time campaign for improved records management. There seems little point in having access to information that is chaotic and unreliable." Archives have been called "arsenals of democratic accountability" (Eastwood 1993; Iacovino 2010), and this chapter will examine the recordkeeping role in providing access to records so that individuals can exercise their "right to information." It will consider four different aspects of ATI: national archives and records legislation; secrecy and privacy; responsive release of information by governments under FOI; and proactive release of information under open government policies. It will reflect upon whether these aspects together provide citizens with "a right to information" and therefore whether such a right can be said to exist in practice. Unofficial routes to information access, such as whistle-blowing or unauthorized disclosure by activists, will not be covered in this chapter.

ACCOUNTABILITY, TRANSPARENCY, GOOD GOVERNANCE, AND RECORDKEEPING

Three terms are commonly associated with the RTI: *accountability*, *transparency*, and *good governance*. As Alvaro Herrero asserts (2015, 4), "Access to Information is not only a fundamental human right but also a key instrument contributing towards transparency and accountability to build more open institutions." We can think about accountability as the "requirement to perform duties, including financial and operational responsibilities, in a manner that complies with legislation, policies, objectives and expected standards of conduct" (International Records Management Trust 2009, 5). Albert Meijer (2001) identifies three phases in the process of accountability: the information phase, the discussion phase, and the sanction phase. He sets out the accountability processes which follow from a "trigger" event, which encompass identifying an accountable person, outlining the situation or action for which the public authority needs to account, specifying the accountability forum or setting within which the process of accountability takes place, identifying the relevant criteria for making a judgment, and setting out and implementing sanctions. Records can document the accountability events and causes and allow sanctions to be implemented and audited, although Chris Hurley (2005) cautions that "effective recordkeeping is a necessary, but not a sufficient, condition for accountability." Hurley identifies some recordkeeping roles required for accountability, including regulatory and enforcement functions and service and enabling functions. For Onora O'Neill (2002), reductive accountability leads to an audit culture, whereas intelligent accountability leads to good governance.

Transparency is a wider concept that includes making public affairs open to public scrutiny so as to enable citizens to understand the actions of their governments. Ann Florini tells us that transparency is a continuum, "at one extreme, nothing is hidden. All government files are open to inspection by anyone wanting to see them, and meetings are always public. At the other, secrecy reigns supreme" (2002, 4). Transparency is therefore a prerequisite for, but not the same as, accountability (Florini 2007). Richard Chapman and Michael Hunt express the relationship thus: "A commitment to transparency forms an essential part of the process of accountability" (2006). Transparency represents a policy and culture of openness that allows parties equal ATI, thus improving information asymmetries between the state and its citizens, although the practical implementation varies considerably from democratic to more authoritarian states.

FOI is often considered a necessary part of transparency, given that such scrutiny cannot be easily conducted without access to the official records of policymaking and its execution. However, O'Neill presents a more nuanced argument given the growth of public distrust in politicians and the state, despite greater openness and transparency, leading her to suggest that transparency and openness are not unconditional goods, as they are so often presented, and saying "transparency certainly destroys secrecy: but it may not limit the deception and deliberate misinformation that undermine relations of trust" (2002, lecture 4, sec. 1). As O'Neill points out, digital technologies spread information and misinformation equally efficiently. In other words, access to trusted information may be more important than transparency, and trusted information derives from records which are authentic, reliable, accessible, and useable.

Transparency has been described as "the key to better governance" (Hood and Heald 2006), which is often seen as a benefit of open government policies. The World Bank (2007, i) defines governance as "the manner in which public officials and institutions acquire and exercise the authority to shape public policy and provide public goods and services." Anticorruption measures, including "reforms to strengthen the accountability and transparency of state institutions," promote good governance (World Bank 2007, v). Open government takes this idea a step further by asserting a participatory democratic approach "in which the influence of the people could be brought to bear at all stages of the decision making" (Robertson 1999, 21). Openness "goes beyond access to documents to cover such items as opening up of processes and meetings of public bodies . . . concentrating on processes that allow us to see the operations and activities of government at work" (Birkinshaw 2010, 29).

Recordkeeping throughout the continuum plays a significant part in providing accountability, transparency, and good (or more open) governance. In Meijer's phase model of the accountability process (2001), records allow for the production of information and evidence that support the investigatory phase of the accountability process; records are created to document the discussion phase, and they capture the decisions made about sanctions, which in turn allow citizens to check that sanctions are properly enforced. Without reliable recordkeeping, accountability would not be a trusted process, and it would not be auditable. Historical accountability can be provided through key recordkeeping activities, in particular archival appraisal, that is, the selection of records for permanent preservation. There are various analyses in the archival science literature (including Avery and Holmlund 2010; Hurley 2002, 2005) of the recordkeeping role in accountability, following statutory obligations for the selective preservation of records, even sometimes in cases when the record creators sought to destroy records. When the accounting firm, Arthur Andersen, unlawfully destroyed records relating to the firm's relationship with the collapsed energy giant, Enron, in 2002, apparently with no recordkeeping intervention, accountability was impeded. The so-called Heiner Affair in Australia in 1990 developed when the newly elected Queensland Government shredded the records accumulated by a retired magistrate, Noel Heiner, who had been investigating alleged abuse at a youth center, a scandal which the government believed (rightly) would damage its reputation and which it sought to conceal. Since the records were subject to public archives law, they could not be destroyed without the permission of the state archivist, which was sought and given, leading to a crisis in the Council of Australasian Archives and Records Authorities and the Australian Society of Archivists over ethics and professional accountability. Should the archivist only be concerned with historical value when undertaking appraisal or also with the value of records for accountability and transparency in the present? Should the archivist follow the interests of his or her employer or pursue some greater idea of professional and public accountability?

Transparency and accountability by making public affairs more open to scrutiny rely on the systematic creation and capture of records, their proper organization so that they provide evidence of transactions, their selection and preservation for an appropriate length of time in a trustworthy recordkeeping system, and their retrievability when needed. Good governance is encouraged by more open systems. Trust in government and openness are enhanced by responsive release of records under legislative regimes such as FOI and proactive release by government of open information about the conduct of public business. If information released is to be trusted, it must originate in a trustworthy recordkeeping system. The rest of this chapter will explore the legal and policy frameworks and the recordkeeping role in the creation, preservation, and provision of access to records and data, which together constitute an essential underpinning of the RTI.

ACCESS TO PUBLIC RECORDS: NATIONAL ARCHIVES AND RECORDS LEGISLATION AND SERVICES

Following the upheaval of law, administration, and governments in nineteenth-century Europe, came the emergence of national identity, sovereign nation-states, and national archives. Citizens were given the right to access public archives for the first time: as Michel Duchein (1992) said, "The notion that research in archives was a civic right was increasingly recognised." *L'archives nationales* was established in France by state decree in 1794. *Archivo Historico Nacional* was founded in Spain in 1866. In the United Kingdom, for the first time in law, the Public Record Office (PRO) Act of 1838 established public access to central legal and court records, extended to executive records from government administrative departments under an Order in Council in 1852 (Shepherd 2009). Centralized provision for public access to public records ("created by a government or a department of government in the course of the business of government") was made in the new search rooms built in Chancery Lane, London, from 1851 onward. The Public Record Office Act of 1877 established a system for the transfer of records from government departments to the PRO and allowed records dated after 1715 and "not of sufficient public value to justify their preservation" to be destroyed (U.K. Committee on Departmental Records 1954, 17). Schedules of records for destruction were drawn up by a Committee of Inspecting Officers. A further act of 1898 extended the destruction date back to 1660. National archives legislation in many countries in nineteenth-century Europe established a public right of access to records of governments for the first time.

By 1950, the record-generating activities of the two world wars, the extension of the state machinery, and "the invention of such devices as the typewriter and the duplicating machine" exposed weaknesses in the public records systems established in the United Kingdom and in other countries (U.K. Committee on Departmental Records 1954, 5). For example, 120 miles of records in U.K. government departments awaited transfer to the PRO. A committee was established, chaired by Sir James Grigg (U.K. Committee on Departmental Records 1954, 2, 6), "to review the arrangements for the preservation of the records of government Departments," on the premise that "the making of adequate arrangements for the preservation of its records is an inescapable duty of the Government of a civilized state." Its main recommendations were enacted in the Public Records Act of 1958. The 1958 act took a big step toward ensuring public access, as it required public records selected for permanent preservation to be transferred to the

PRO when they were no more than 30 years old and to be made publicly accessible there, usually when they were 50 years old (reduced to 30 years under the Public Records Act of 1967). The standard closure period is gradually being reduced to 20 years, following a review in the light of the U.K. Freedom of Information Act of 2000.

Philip Coppel (2014, 246), however, reminds us that "there is an important legislative distinction between the obligations in relation to the preservation of public records and those in relation to the access to such records. Generally, the framework given by the public records legislation has been retained for the preservation of records, whilst the Freedom of Information Act 2000 controls the ability to access such records." Most countries with national archives and records legislation include provisions for a public right of access to government records after a specified closure period, typically 20 or 30 years. However, in some countries, the right of access under archives legislation is being replaced by FOI legislation, which enables requests for information of any age. Nevertheless, without systematic archival preservation, public access will be impossible. If no additional resources are provided for recordkeeping activities under FOI, then the routine archival work of selection for permanent preservation, which will underpin access after a stated period, maybe abandoned in favor of responding to FOI requests for specific records or information. Records provided in response to an FOI request may or may not be selected for permanent preservation. Archival preservation and public access under FOI do not result in identical rights to information.

Other parts of the Anglophone world established different access traditions through archives services. In North America, a "public archives tradition" developed alongside a "historical manuscripts tradition" (O'Toole and Cox 2006, 53, 55). The historical manuscripts tradition emerged from state historical societies, beginning with Massachusetts in 1791. State archives departments were established in the wake of the Public Archives Commission in 1899, starting in 1901 with Alabama: the state archives network was eventually completed in 1978 with New York (Shepherd 2009, 9–10). According to James O'Toole and Richard Cox (2006, 53), the public archives tradition in the United States "assumed that government authorities at both the local and the colony-wide levels, as representatives of the whole community, would be creators and maintainers of records," to ensure legal rights for all citizens. In 1934, legislation was passed that established the U.S. National Archives as an independent federal agency. The first archivist of the United States, Robert Connor, was appointed, and construction began on a building to house federal records and provide access to them. The National Archives began to accept record transfers from federal agencies in 1935. In 1949, the service was renamed National Archives and Records Service (NARS), as it took on responsibility for current records of government, which was reflected in updated legislation in the Federal Records Act of 1950.

In 1984, the National Archives Act established the National Archives and Records Administration (NARA) as an independent agency. The legislation established a closure period of 30 years for federal records.

The Canadian archival tradition evolved differently from those in Europe and the United States (Shepherd 2009, 13–14). In Canada, government archives preserved not only the official records of the state but also private and other records, creating "total archives" which were embraced within the official mandate of many publicly funded cultural agencies (Wilson 1982). The acquisition of copies of archives relating to Canada but held elsewhere was an important part of the early nineteenth-century archival endeavor, initially in the provinces of Quebec and Nova Scotia (Millar 1998). In 1872, Douglas Brymner was appointed to preserve the archives of the Dominion of Canada. The Public Archives Act of 1912 allowed the Public Archives to acquire "public records, documents and other historical material of every kind," that is, records relating to the Dominion, provinces, and municipalities of Canada, both government records and historical archives, all of which were important in documenting the historical identity of Canada (Millar 1998). By 1968, archive services were established in all Canadian provinces, and archives were also started in the Northwest Territories and the Yukon in the 1970s, although only Ontario had a full-scale records management program (Swift 1982–1983). In 1987, the Public Archives was renamed the National Archives of Canada. The creation of a unified Library and Archives Canada in 2004 (under the Library and Archives of Canada Act) provided a new model of public access to information, seldom seen at national level, where the user need for information regardless of source overrode the traditional distinction between records created by government (held in national archives) and collections of published materials (held in national libraries).

In Australia, soon after federation in 1901, there were proposals to establish a Commonwealth Archives (Shepherd 2009, 15–17). The first official archive was the Australian War Records Section established in 1917, which was incorporated into the Australian War Memorial in 1925. National archival developments began again in the 1940s, with the establishment of the War Archives Committee in 1942 and the appointment of government archivists in half of the Australian states (McKemmish and Piggott 1994). These were gradually enshrined in law, beginning with Tasmania's Public Records Act of 1943, followed in 1960 by the Archives Act in New South Wales. In 1944, the appointment of an archives officer in the Commonwealth National Library was the precursor to the Commonwealth Archives Office, eventually founded in 1961. The Commonwealth Archives Office became Australian Archives in 1974. The Commonwealth Archives Act of 1983 established, among other things, a public right of access to Commonwealth government records after 30 years. Following amendments to the act in 2010, the access period for Commonwealth records is being reduced to 20 years.

Many countries enacted national records and archives legislation in the second half of the twentieth century, ensuring the preservation of and public access to archives. UNESCO drafted a "Model Law on Archives" in 1972 and published guidance (Ketelaar 1985), which stated that "freedom and liberty of access to archives constitutes a right of every citizen." This right was often enacted through national archives legislation. The International Records Management Trust published a Model Records and Archives Law in 1999, which made a clear link between proper management of current government records and reliable and trustworthy archives (International Records Management Trust 1999). A further wave of archival legislation in the early 2000s focused on updating legislative provisions, not only in the light of changes in government services such as privatization but also responding to the new demands of digital records. Many acts, such as the National Archives of South Africa Act of 1996 and the National Archives Act of Malaysia of 2003, sought to provide for the preservation and use of the national archival heritage through public access and also for the proper management of current records. Increasingly, national archive services were mandated to take a role in the current records and information management of government as well as the preservation of access to its archival heritage. Some, such as the Public Records Act of New Zealand of 2005, went as far as to state the larger principles that lie behind national archives: enabling government to be held accountable, enhancing public confidence and trust in the public record and enhancing cultural heritage and national identity as well as providing for a public right of access to records.

SECRECY AND PRIVACY: KEEPING INFORMATION CLOSED

On the contrary, other legislation emerged during the twentieth century, which sought to keep information closed. From the end of the nineteenth century, legislation was enacted that prohibited public access to some types of government information, designated official secrets. In the later twentieth century, laws preventing access to personal information about individuals, so-called data protection or privacy legislation, were passed. Secrecy and privacy legislation is designed to prevent public access to records and information on the grounds of harm to the state or to the individual. Recordkeepers are an important operational part of the secrecy and privacy processes, that is, of preventing ATI.

Secrecy

Patrick Birkinshaw (2010, 76–77) reminds us that while the U.K. Parliament exercised its RTI in a variety of ways from the late eighteenth century, including by means of government publication of reports and evidence from Royal Commissions and annual reports to Parliament by different state agencies, government controlled what information came into the public domain. As government grew, keeping information confidential became more difficult. The United Kingdom, for the first time, "provided for the prosecution and punishment of unauthorised disclosure of official information" in the Official Secrets Act, 1889 (Birkinshaw 2010, 82). The act was considered somewhat ineffective, and a new statute, in 1911, dealt more firmly with leaks and disclosure in a period of foreign threat, espionage, and suspicious activities. The broad scope of the Official Secrets Act of 1911 endured until the global availability of information and its easy access in the 1980s, together with some high-profile publication of secret government information, led to the breakdown of traditional approaches to government controls of information and the repeal of the act. Jeremy Pope (2003) suggests that a "preoccupation with secrecy" is common in many countries with a history of colonial rule and an inheritance of "administrative systems and officials obsessed with secrecy," as well as in developing and emerging democracies, such as in Eastern Europe.

Many British Commonwealth countries adopted the U.K. Official Secrets Acts or their provisions from 1889 onward, including Canada, for example. India adopted an Official Secrets Act in 1923. Malaysia also adopted U.K. provisions in its Official Secrets Act of 1972. Birkinshaw (2015, 381) considers the U.K. Official Secrets Act of 1989 "the first significant concession by central government towards relaxation of official secrets laws," since only a few specified classes of information were protected from unauthorized disclosure (relating to security and intelligence, defense, international relations, prevention of crime, and information entrusted in confidence). Some countries have replaced official secrets with legislation aimed at increasing national security and information control in the face of terrorism and security threats, such as Canada's Security of Information Act of 1985. The introduction of such legislation has been criticized for reducing government transparency and seems to run counter to more general moves toward openness. By the twenty-first century, official secrets were generally limited to a fairly small number of specific instances, and the emphasis moved from keeping official information closed to a widespread presumption of openness and encouragement of information reuse.

Privacy

There is, however, one type of information which is still considered closed, that is, personal data about individuals. Privacy legislation gives data subjects (usually limited) rights over the processing of their own personal data and regulates the creation, processing, and retention of personal data and records. There are significant national and cultural differences over privacy and protection of personal data. The greater availability of data about individuals held in a form that could be computer processed in data banks and data centers led to concerns over the proper protection of personal data in the 1960s and 1970s. The United States enacted a Privacy Act in 1974 to control the collection, use, and sharing of information in order to protect the privacy of individuals identified in federal information systems. In Canada, the Privacy Act of 1985 provided Canadian citizens with a right to request access to and correct their personal information held by a federal government institution, subject to some exceptions. Australia, likewise, introduced a Privacy Act in 1988 that set out Information Privacy Principles to regulate the handling of personal information by federal agencies and some private organizations and to allow individuals to correct information about themselves.

The first U.K. Data Protection Act of 1984, which came into force in 1986, brought the United Kingdom in line with the requirements of a European directive on data protection, which had to be enacted in each European member state. In the European Union (EU), privacy laws are generally entitled data protection and apply only to living people. The U.K. Data Protection Act of 1998 extended the data protection regime, which had applied only to records in electronic form to all record formats. The Data Protection Act set out eight data protection principles, including fair and lawful processing of personal data for a specified and lawful purpose, data controllers having to be registered, and some protections for the rights of data subjects. The U.K. act imposed a duty on those holding personal data about living people to comply with the eight data protection principles, to register with the data protection registrar (now the information commissioner), and to allow data subjects access to the data and, if necessary, to correct it.

Different countries have different cultural attitudes to personal information: Nordic countries regard personal tax and salary data as open, but most other countries regard personal financial data as intensely private.

The privacy principles raise some ethical dilemmas for recordkeepers, for example, access to data about third parties for research or the accessibility and use of personal records in cases of historic child abuse, regime change, and human rights abuses, which are not easy to resolve. Archives have been challenged to protect sensitive personal data about individuals involved in cases of historic abuse in institutional settings, including children's homes, residential schools, church institutions, and adoption agencies. Many countries have now set up historical reviews of institutional settings where children and young people were subject to abuse, to investigate the accusations of survivors and their families. For example, in Australia, between 1910 and 1970, many indigenous children were forcibly removed from their families, "taught to reject their Indigenous heritage, and made to adopt white culture. Their names were changed, and they were forbidden to speak their traditional language. Some were adopted by white families, and many were placed in institutions, where abuse and neglect were common" (Australians Together 2015). A government report on what had happened, "Bringing Them Home," gives voice to many of the survivors in a very personal way, albeit anonymized. The inquiry took public evidence "from Indigenous organisations and individuals, State and Territory Government representatives, church representatives, other nongovernment agencies, former mission and government employees and individual members of the community. Confidential evidence was taken in private from Indigenous people affected by forcible removal and from adoptive and foster parents. Many people and organisations made written submissions to the Inquiry, including many who also gave oral evidence" (Commonwealth of Australia 1997, 16). There are now questions for recordkeepers about the continuing preservation and access to all these records, in particular where family members want access to records about themselves and their siblings or parents, whom they may be trying to trace. Often their requests are turned down on the grounds of the privacy of the other individuals involved, thus preventing some survivors accessing their own records (and thus their stolen lives) in full.

In Scotland, the Shaw Report (Scottish Government 2007, 3) considered "the systems of laws, rules and regulations (the regulatory framework) that governed residential schools and children's homes," "against the background of abuse suffered by children in residential schools and children's homes in Scotland between 1950 and 1995." The review reported that a significant obstacle in finding out what had happened was poor recordkeeping in the past and present difficulties in identifying and accessing records which did exist. For instance, "some potentially significant records in archives were closed," and "there was no legal requirement for local authorities and organisations to help by giving access to information. Some were helpful; some were less so" (Scottish Government 2007, 5). The review identified "an urgent need to take action to preserve historical records, to ensure that residents can get access to records and information," including a review of public authority recordkeeping under the section 61 Code of Practice on Records Management under the Freedom of Information Scotland Act of 2002 and the "permanent preservation of significant records held by private, non-statutory agencies that provide publicly funded services to children" (Scottish Government 2007, 7). It recommended that "voluntary organisations, religious organisations and local authorities, working in partnership, should commission guidance to ensure that their children's residential services records are adequately catalogued to make records readily accessible" (Scottish Government 2007, 7). Recordkeeping issues are critical to such historic inquiries, and recordkeepers find themselves in difficult situations in trying to preserve confidentiality and privacy of different data subjects and yet ensure access to the records needed for the public good.

Increasingly, researchers and policymakers want to use individual-level data produced by government bodies for a variety of public policy, education, and health improvement research projects. Access to personal data by accredited researchers under controlled conditions such as safe havens and secure sites may be negotiated, for instance, under national schemes such as the U.K. Administrative Data Research Network (2015). Linking data together can provide richer sources for analysis than a single data set created by one government agency. Data must first be deidentified using good practice guidelines, which seek to guarantee and secure individual rights to privacy and confidentiality of the data, such as the U.K. Information Commissioner Office's Code of Practice on Anonymisation (UK ICO 2012). Anonymized data can then be aggregated and linked in different ways, such as different cohorts in a single set of data or different data sets about the same individuals (e.g., on educational outcomes and health). However, the possibility of deanonymization and reidentification through linked data raises privacy concerns.

The recent "right to be forgotten" introduces another twist in the story. As a result of a court case in 2014, Google Spain's search engines and access to third-party data were made subject to the EU Data Protection Directive on personal data processing. A consequence is that data subjects are now allowed to require the removal of their names and of personal data from Google searches and links, a so-called right to be forgotten (Birkinshaw 2015). This "censorship" of personal data has been controversial.

RESPONSIVE RELEASE OF GOVERNMENT INFORMATION: ACCESS TO AND FREEDOM OF INFORMATION

FOI concepts date back as far as Sweden's Freedom of the Press Act of 1766, but FOI legislation has only been widely adopted in the early twenty-first century. In some countries, RTI is enshrined in the constitution or a Bill of Rights, although in many countries RTI is brought about through primary legislation to give citizens FOI. Several phases or "waves" of adoption of FOI have been identified, beginning with the United States (1966). The second wave in the 1980s included Canada (1983), Australia (1982), and New Zealand (1982). The United Kingdom (2000) was part of a third wave, including Ireland (1997), South Africa (2000), and much of Eastern Europe (Shepherd 2015, 716). More than half the number of existing FOI laws have been adopted since 2000, while other countries have drafted or discussed FOI but not yet fully enacted the legislation (e.g., in Kenya, Botswana, Ghana). By 2006, 70 countries had ATI legislation, and a further 50 had made some moves toward it. By 2014, over 100 countries had FOI legislation (50 in Europe, a dozen in Africa, 20 in the Americas and the Caribbean, more than 15 in Asia and the Pacific, 2 in the Middle East), and the number is still growing (Banisar 2016).

Often FOI is a part of complex web of laws regulating information access, adopted for a variety of reasons. FOI is rarely established by a single piece of comprehensive legislation: often it interacts with, contradicts, or is complemented by other legislation concerning privacy, data protection, human rights, health and safety, and the environment. It is not a single universal concept and has some very different characteristics in different cultural contexts and legal jurisdictions. Sometimes, as in the United Kingdom, it was part of a cultural and societal shift from a more secretive, closed society where access to government records and official secrets was restricted and controlled to a more open one in which ATI is seen as a civic right. FOI is often the focus of campaigns by the media and civil society groups, such as the Campaign for Freedom of Information in the United Kingdom. FOI is sometimes linked to modernizing government, new public management, and good governance. FOI is sometimes envisaged as a constitutional right in new democracies or as a part of public sector reform in developing countries required by funding bodies (such as the World Bank or the International Monetary Fund). FOI is also seen as a strategy for deepening democracy and increasing government accountability to its citizens and as a tool of anticorruption. Once enacted, FOI has rarely, if ever, been repealed, although a few governments have attempted to limit its use by, for instance, the introduction of charges.

Although FOI establishes a statutory right to access government information, it does not in itself guarantee free and unlimited information access. The legislative rights and the mechanisms by which these rights are implemented differ. In some countries, legislation may be enacted but never used or written so as to prevent access, for instance, through excessive exemptions. FOI may be contradicted or limited by other pieces of legislation, such as data protection or privacy laws, which prevent the release of personal data, as discussed earlier. In case of threats to national security, information access maybe restricted and FOI maybe suspended, weakened, or overruled. Even when FOI legislation has been fully enacted, a number of operational requirements are needed to make it usable. These differ in detail from jurisdiction to jurisdiction but include appeals tribunals, regulatory authorities, reporting mechanisms, publication schemes, access protocols and request systems, time limits for responses and appeals, improved recordkeeping systems, and training for government staff in request handling. Government and organizational culture may obstruct access: culture change in government is often needed to ensure sufficient awareness of the legislation and regulations by public officials. Bureaucratic system failures, more than secrecy, can often inhibit public information access. Advocacy is needed to ensure that citizens understand how to exercise their new rights. In some jurisdictions, access is effectively restricted by excessive delays, for example, if there is no statutory time limit for responses or by excessive fees for making applications or receiving information. Some governments favor providing free access to government data for commercial exploitation rather than seeking to recover access costs from business.

Birkinshaw (2010) points out that information is not neutral, its "control, use and regulation" are exercises in power. Examples of information asymmetry between governments and their citizens abound, such as police "stop and search" powers or investigations into historic abuse in institutional settings. Governments control the FOI system even in the most open regime by creating and holding the information that might be made accessible. Politicians and officials can resist disclosure or introduce delays in releasing information, although media coverage, appeals systems, and sanctions discourage this. Governments are frequently viewed as secretive and untrustworthy. Poor recordkeeping systems can contribute to a lack of trust, by making information deliberately inaccessible or inadvertently hard to find, resulting in failures of searches to retrieve information and in records that are incomplete, unreliable, or missing.

There has been debate over the chilling effect of FOI on record creation. FOI is said to encourage public officers to make decisions without making an official record, by oral agreements and the use of nonofficial channels of communication, such as private e-mail accounts. Archivists and historians have debated whether FOI leaves behind "empty archives" (Flinn and Jones 2009). Governments may be creating fewer and less reliable official, written records as a result of the degradation of centralized registry systems and cultural moves to more informal structures of policymaking rather than as a result of FOI. Fewer government records may be captured and preserved because of the failure to manage digital records systems efficiently, resulting in uncontrolled recordkeeping. Arguably, the ease of digital records creation and storage is leading to more records being created and preserved in multiple versions. Public and private organizations with poorly managed digital records systems often fail to destroy records that are no longer needed and potentially expose themselves to legal requirements for recovery or the risk of unauthorized disclosure. U.K. research has suggested little evidence of the chilling effect on "the thoroughness and frankness of official advice" or on the quality of U.K. government records in spite of the "powerful myth . . . which is hard to eradicate despite the lack of evidence" (Hazell, Worthy, and Glover 2010, 13, 256). Officials were "confident that the quality and thoroughness of submissions had not changed" and that recordkeeping had not been adversely affected by FOI (Hazell, Worthy, and Glover 2010, 263).

The U.K. Freedom of Information Act of 2000 exemplifies the important link between records management and the ability of citizens to retrieve reliable and trustworthy information under FOI. U.K. public authorities need to know what information they hold and to manage and retrieve information effectively in order to respond to FOI requests within the statutory time limit of 20 days. Records management practices were therefore explicitly promoted as essential to a public authority's ability to comply with the act, formally recognized by Parliament in a Code of Practice on Records Management. The code stated that "freedom of information legislation is only as good as the quality of the records and other information to which it provides access. Access rights are of limited value if information cannot be found when requested or, when found, cannot be relied upon as authoritative" (U.K. National Archives 2009, 4). The code has enabled the regulator, the Information Commissioner, to intervene where public authorities were found to be failing to meet expected standards of good practice in records management.

FOI in most jurisdictions has limited effects on the private sector, since it generally only applies to government or public institutions (unlike data protection or privacy laws that tend to apply to personal data regardless of where or by whom it is held). As governments privatize services, enter into public-private partnerships, or co-opt third sector bodies to provide services to citizens, nongovernmental institutions are increasingly responsible for public services. And, yet, these institutions often fall outside of FOI boundaries. FOI requires resources to operate efficiently and is vulnerable to resource reductions and cuts in an austerity era. Some politicians have even argued that the legislative force of FOI would no longer be needed if more government information were published proactively and made open.

OPEN GOVERNMENT AND OPEN GOVERNMENT DATA: PROACTIVE RELEASE OF DATA

Good governance, open government, and open government data are closely related concepts. Although there is no single agreed definition of open government data, it has been described as "data that meets the following criteria; accessible (ideally via the Internet, . . . without limitations based on user identity or intent), in a digital machine readable format for interoperation with other data and free of restriction on use or redistribution in its licensing conditions" (U.K. Cabinet Office 2012, 8). Among its significant characteristics, government's "open data and content can be freely used, modified, and shared by anyone for any purpose" (Open Knowledge Foundation 2012) and is not restricted by privacy concerns. It can be reused for research, civic or personal interest, and commercial purposes. However, open government data are not the same as FOI, since proactive data release relies on the government to decide which data can be released. Under FOI, requesters make the choice of which information to ask for. Given that it is difficult to fully anticipate what requestors want, since many are pursuing specific interests or are single issue activists or journalists following a particular story, FOI reduces the information asymmetry (by placing control with the requester) in a way that open data may not.

Antti Halonen (2012) notes that "the open-data movement did not originate in a vacuum" but has grown from a long tradition of access to and reuse of public information, some of which is set out in the preceding sections of this chapter. The Public Sector Information (PSI) European Directive (2003) introduced a new era of reuse of government information by researchers (Cerrillo-I-Martínez 2012), based "on principles of accountability and transparency on the one hand and innovation and economic growth on the other hand" by "creating jobs and stimulating innovation and at the same time increase transparency and accountability of the government" (Janssen 2011, 451).

The U.K. government has been prominent in the open data movement. In 2010, data.gov.uk was launched, "a web portal that provides a single access point to thousands of data sets held by different public bodies, freely available for any type of use" (Janssen 2011, 451). Public Data Transparency Principles were published in 2012 (U.K. Open Government Data 2015), the Open Data Institute was set up, and an Open Data White Paper was published (U.K. Cabinet Office 2012). U.K. government has published open data, including data on the environment, towns and cities, health, the economy, transport, and government spending, such as requiring local public authorities to publish monthly all spending over £500. In 2015, data.gov.uk held around 25,000 data sets from a large number of mainly public sector organizations.

The U.K. government was one of the eight founding countries of the Open Government Partnership (OGP) in 2011, along with Brazil, Indonesia, Mexico, Norway, the Philippines, South Africa, and the United States. All of them endorsed the Open Government Declaration that commits countries to "foster a global culture of open government that empowers and delivers for citizens, and advances the ideals of open and participatory 21st century government" (Open Government Partnership 2015). OGP has since grown to 69 governments. ATI is one of four eligibility criteria for participation in OGP, alongside citizen engagement, fiscal transparency, and income and asset disclosure. Signatories pledge to "increase the availability of information about governmental activities." This objective states that "governments collect and hold information on behalf of people, and citizens have a right to seek information about governmental activities" (Open Government Partnership 2015). In support of this RTI, countries will increase ATI about governmental activities and "systematically collect and publish data on government spending and performance." There is a focus on "high-value information, including raw data, in a timely manner, in formats that the public can easily locate, understand and use, and in formats that facilitate reuse" (Open Government Partnership 2015). Herrero (2015, 4) suggests that "the emergence of access to information as one of the central tenets of the Open Government Partnership (OGP) has become a major driving force in the promotion of ATI reforms worldwide."

Each country appoints an Independent Reporting Mechanism (IRM) and conducts annual self-assessments of progress.

Countries signed up to OGP must develop action plans in conjunction with civil society organizations, which contain "commitments that advance transparency, accountability, participation and/or technological innovation" (Open Government Partnership 2015). The United Kingdom's Second National Action Plan commitments include developing an inventory of all government data sets, published and unpublished, and identifying those with the most significant economic and social impact that will form a "National Information Infrastructure" (Open Government Partnership 2015). In the United States, President Barack Obama made open government a high priority, symbolized by his first executive action to sign the Memorandum on Transparency and Open Government. The United States is one of few countries to have issued a third OGP Action Plan, in 2015, which includes commitments to redesign the government portal, USA.gov, and improve the range and accessibility of government information online. Other commitments relate to better management of federal records and e-mails and to improvements in the implementation of FOI, such as a pilot to test the feasibility of posting all FOI-released records online. The U.S. National Archives is developing tools to teach students about how best to use FOI. Commitments by other countries in their action plans vary depending on the state of open government development but include specific improvements to access legislation, in-country infrastructure developments to support ATI, implementation of e-commerce systems, Internet portals and request systems, research into public attitudes, and capacity building and training (Open Government Partnership 2015).

Many governments assert the relationship between more open government processes and the proactive publication of government data. However, opening up government data is not a "matter of simply publishing public data" (Janssen 2011). Data release requires additional data processing in order to produce reusable and releasable data (e.g., to remove personal data about individuals). Publishing raw data without context in heterogeneous formats and with risks of the identification of individuals will not enhance the cause of open government data. Data redundancy and inconsistency, poor data integrity and quality, and a lack of interoperability can be mitigated partly through the development of standards and implementation of policies. For example, the United Kingdom has promoted the use of a Five Star Scheme (http://5stardata.info/), which classifies data from that published in proprietary formats (1 star) to data which can be fully accessed online and is linked to other data (5 star) (U.K. Cabinet Office 2012). An alternative emerging approach is the creation of Open Data Certificates (Open Data Institute 2015), which seek to improve the quality of data publication for reuse by providing information, including descriptive metadata, about the attributes of each data set. As Halonen

(2012, 83) asserts, "The value of transparency increases when data is given a proper context and thus people can truly understand and use it."

Opening up government data will, however, tend to increase information asymmetries, unless citizens are actually able to use open data. Even within a single country, not everyone has equal access to open data. As Michael Gurstein (2011, sec. 2) points out, users need "digital infrastructure [...], hardware or software, financial or educational resources/skills which would allow for the effective use of data." Gurstein (2011, sec. 4) identified seven elements necessary in this process, including access to the Internet, up-to-date computers and software, mastering the ICT skills needed, having the data available, having the skills to interpret the data, and having sufficient resources to enable the reuse of the data. The digital infrastructure in many countries and regions does not easily allow citizens to access and reuse government open data.

Implementing an open data policy incurs costs to public authorities and requires systems, protocols, and specialist skills. Recordkeepers in public organizations need to work in partnership with ICT system designers and data creators to ensure that data are managed and released appropriately. Data which are made open ought to be managed as part of the records and information systems in the creating organization. Open government data should originate from authentic recordkeeping systems so that the data can be trusted. The data which are released should then have characteristics that will make them trustworthy: authenticity, integrity, reliability, and usability. As with other records, open data should be genuine and trustworthy, reliable and accurate, and they should have been maintained over time in a way which guarantees their integrity.

Open data use and reuse can raise complex issues from the data producer's perspective. Open data should never include identifiable personal data, yet managing data anonymization is challenging, both technically and procedurally. The risks of deanonymization and reidentification of data subjects need to be considered. Data creators and publishers often worry about data misuse or its misinterpretation. Researchers and policymakers are reluctant to publish data while they are still using them in development, as they worry that their ideas may be copied or misunderstood. Even after the publication of research results, many researchers regard data as private rather than public intellectual assets, even if they are producing using public money, for example, in a university.

Many governments assert that open data will drive economic development. Some businesses rely on open data to produce commercial products, such as transport apps which give you bus or train timetables, or apps which tell you about the hygiene of restaurant kitchens (so-called scores on the doors). In this way, government views the commercial data user as a partner in developing public information services without direct cost to the public authority. Civil society organizations sometimes accuse government of wasting valuable public assets by giving the data away freely to businesses which are then able to add value and profit from using open data.

Recordkeepers play a major part in ensuring that open data are accessible and usable over time and are contextualized through good metadata. Too often, open data are regarded as ephemeral, and the recordkeeper's role is bypassed when data are released directly by the creator, the Web site manager, or by the public relations department. Once published, open data are then no longer seen as the creating body's responsibility. Standardized metadata, contextual descriptions, data documentation and codebooks, and searchable tagging are needed if data are to be more easily accessible and interpretable over time. If open data are to have long-term public value or are to form the basis of accountable public policy and decision making, they need to be managed over time in a systematic and properly documented way. As with organizational records, administrative data which are made open should be subject to appraisal so that data can be selected for permanent preservation in an archive or subject to systematic deletion periodically. Maintaining all open data on a public Web site in a usable form (the approach taken at present by many public organizations) is likely to prove costly and over time will prove impossible. Open data portals and Web sites are already difficult to search, and relevant data is often difficult to find and use.

If open data are not well managed over time, the result will be less transparency and openness and a loss of trust. In a quest for more openness to provide citizens with a practical "right to information," poor data management may result in citizens failing to find what they need and want.

CONCLUSION

This chapter has considered the concept of RTI, ATI, or FOI, which has been adopted by many countries around the world, often linked to the rights of citizens to information for public accountability, transparency, and good governance and for their own freedom of opinion and expression and the exercise of their human rights. The chapter has addressed the question, "does a right to information exist?" by consideration of four different aspects of ATI: national archives and records legislation; secrecy and privacy including official secrets and personal data; the responsive release of information by governments under FOI laws; and the proactive release of information under open government data policies. In each section, there has been consideration of the legislative and historical context, drawing on examples from different countries, and an examination of themes from relevant literature, drawn from recordkeeping, law, and politics literatures.

The chapter has considered at each stage what the recordkeeping role could or should be in the various legislative and government policy contexts. The professional archival role that began to develop in the late nineteenth and early twentieth centuries, underpinning national archives and records legislation and services, focused on the selection and preservation of records deemed to have permanent value as archives so that these archives could be systematically transferred to national archive services, where they could be made available to the public after a specified closure period. In this role, recordkeepers needed to be able to undertake appraisal and selection of administrative and policy records of government and ensure their proper description and accessibility once the physical records were transferred to the archive service. Recordkeepers seldom played a role in the operation of secrecy laws, which developed separately from archival legislation and were applied to records considered to need security classifications in the national interest. Often these records were not transferred to the national archives, and records of secret and intelligence services were not historically subject to routine appraisal and selection under national archives legislation. Recordkeepers have, however, been active in operating information laws and policies, including privacy, FOI, and open government data. Although recordkeepers often need to advocate for the important role they can play in these spheres, increasingly, their expertise in managing administrative data and records is crucial to the proper protection of personal and official data while ensuring the release of information into the public domain. Recordkeepers need knowledge and skills in the complex legal framework and administrative processes that deliver the RTI if they are to provide expert advice to ensure that secrecy and privacy are respected and yet information is released for the benefit of society. This analysis demonstrates the essential role played by archives and records as "arsenals of democratic accountability" and by archivists and recordkeepers as essential actors in ensuring a citizen's RTI.

REFERENCES

Avery, C., and M. Holmlund, eds. 2010. *Better Off Forgetting: Essays on Archives, Public Policy, and Collective Memory.* Toronto: University of Toronto Press.

Australians Together. 2015. "The Stolen Generations." http://www.australians together.org.au/stories/detail/the-stolen-generations(accessed January 2, 2016).

Banisar, D. 2016. "National Comprehensive Data Protection/Privacy Laws and Bills 2016 Map." http://dx.doi.org/10.2139/ssrn.1951416.

Birkinshaw, P. 2010. *Freedom of Information: The Law, the Practice and the Ideal,* 4th ed. Cambridge, England: Cambridge University Press.

Birkinshaw, P. 2015. "Regulating Information." In *The Changing Constitution*, 8th ed., edited by J. Jowell and D. Oliver, 378–409. Oxford, England: Oxford University Press.

Cerrillo-I-Martínez, A. 2012. "The Reuse of Public Sector Information in Europe and Its Impact on Transparency." *European Law Journal* 18 (6): 770–92.

Chapman, R. A., and M. Hunt. 2006. *Open Government in a Theoretical and Practical Context.* Aldershot, England: Ashgate.

Commonwealth of Australia. 1997. "Bringing Them Home: Report of the National Inquiry into the Separation of Aboriginal and Torres Strait Islander Children from Their Families." Sydney: Commonwealth of Australia.

Coppel, P. 2014. *Information Rights: Law and Practice*, 4th ed. Oxford, England: Hart Publishers.

Duchein, M. 1992. "The History of European Archives and the Development of the Archival Profession in Europe." *American Archivist* 55 (1): 14–25.

Eastwood, T. 1993. "Reflections on the Development of Archives in Canada and Australia." In *Archival Documents: Providing Accountability through Recordkeeping*, edited by S. McKemmish and F Upward, 27–39. Melbourne, Australia: Ancora Press.

Flinn, A., and H. Jones, eds. 2009. *Freedom of Information: Open Access, Empty Archives?* London: Routledge.

Florini, A. 2002, September 1. "Increasing Transparency in Government." *International Journal on World Peace* 19 (3): 3–37.

Florini, A. 2007. *The Right to Know: Transparency for an Open World.* New York: Columbia University Press.

Gurstein, M. B. 2011. "Open Data: Empowering the Empowered or Effective Data Use for Everyone?" *First Monday* 16 (2).

Halonen, A. 2012. *Being Open about Data. Analysis of the UK Open Data Policies and Applicability of Open Data.* London: Finnish Institute.

Hazell, R., B. Worthy, and M. Glover. 2010. *The Impact of the Freedom of Information Act on Central Government in the UK: Does FOI Work?* Basingstoke, England: Palgrave Macmillan.

Herrero, A. 2015. "Access to Information Commitments in OGP Action Plans: A Report on the Progress of Reforms Worldwide." World Bank Governance Global Practice and Red de Transparencia y Acceso a la Información Pública (RTA). http://redrta.org/ (accessed January 2, 2016).

Hood, C., and D. Heald. 2006. *Transparency: The Key to Better Governance?* Oxford, England: Oxford University Press.

Hurley, C. 2002. "Records and the Public Interest." In *Archives and the Public Good: Accountability and Records in Modern Society*, edited by R. J. Cox and D. A. Wallace, 293–318. London: Quorum Books.

Hurley, C. 2005. "Recordkeeping and Accountability." In *Archives: Recordkeeping in Society*, edited by S. McKemmish, M. Piggott, B. Reed, and F. Upward, 223–53. Wagga Wagga, New South Wales: Charles Sturt University.

Iacovino, L. 2010. "Archives as Arsenals of Accountability." In *Currents of Archival Thinking*, edited by T. Eastwood and H. MacNeil, 181–212. Santa Barbara, CA; Oxford, England: Libraries Unlimited.

International Records Management Trust. 1999. *A Model Records and Archives Law.* http://www.irmt.org/documents/educ_training/public_sector_rec/IRMT_archive_law.pdf (accessed January 2, 2016).

International Records Management Trust. 2009. *Training in Electronic Records Management. Glossary of Terms.* http://www.irmt.org/.

Janssen, K. 2011. "The Influence of the PSI Directive on Open Government Data: An Overview of Recent Developments." *Government Information Quarterly* 28 (4): 446–56.

Ketelaar, E. 1985. *Archival and Records Management Legislation and Regulations: A Ramp Study with Guidelines*. Paris: UNESCO.

McKemmish, S., and M. Piggott, eds. 1994. *The Records Continuum: Ian Maclean and Australian Archives First Fifty Years*. Clayton, Victoria: Ancora Press and Australian Archives.

Meijer, A. 2001. "Accountability in an Information Age: Opportunities and Risks." *Archival Science* 1 (4): 361–72.

Millar, L. 1998. "Discharging Our Debt: The Evolution of the Total Archives Concept in English Canada." *Archivaria* 46: 103–46.

O"Neill, O. 2002. "The Reith Lectures: A Question of Trust." *BBC Radio 4*. http://www.bbc.co.uk/programmes/p00ghvd8 (accessed January 2, 2016).

Open Data Institute. 2015. https://theodi.org/ (accessed January 2, 2016).

Open Government Partnership. 2015. http://www.opengovpartnership.org/ (accessed January 2, 2016).

Open Knowledge Foundation. 2012. "The Open Definition." http://opendefinition.org (accessed January 2, 2016).

O'Toole, J., and R. Cox. 2006. *Understanding Archives and Manuscripts*. Chicago, IL: Society of American Archivists.

Pope, J. 2003. "Access to Information: Whose Right and Whose Information?" In *Transparency International. Global Corruption Report 2003*, edited by R. Hodess, 8–23. London: Profile Books.

Robertson, K. G. 1999. *Secrecy and Open Government: Why Governments Want You to Know*. Basingstoke, England: Macmillan.

Scottish Government. 2007. "Historical Abuse Systemic Review: Residential Schools and Children's Homes in Scotland 1950 to 1995 (The Shaw Report)." Edinburgh: The Scottish Government.

Shepherd, E. 2009. *Archives and Archivists in 20th century England*. Aldershot, England: Ashgate.

Shepherd, E. 2015. "Freedom of Information, Right to Access Information, Open Data: Who Is at the Table?" *The Round Table* 104 (6): 715–26.

Swift, M. D. 1982–1983. "The Canadian Archival Scene in the 1970s: Current Developments and Trends." *Archivaria* 15 (Winter): 47–57.

U.K. Administrative Data Research Network. 2015. http://adrn.ac.uk/ (accessed January 2, 2016).

U.K. Cabinet Office. 2012. *Open Data White Paper: Unleashing the Potential*. (Cm 8353). London: Stationery Office.

U.K. Committee on Departmental Records. 1954. "The Grigg Report." (Cmd 9163). London: HMSO.

U.K. Information Commissioner's Office (ICO). 2012. https://ico.org.uk/ (accessed January 2, 2016).

U.K. National Archives. 2009. *Lord Chancellor's Code of Practice on the Management of Records, Issued under Section 46 of the Freedom of Information Act 2000*. http://www.nationalarchives.gov.uk/documents/foi-section-46-code-of-practice.pdf (accessed January 2, 2016).

U.K. Open Government Data. 2015. https://data.gov.uk/ (accessed January 2, 2016).

United Nations. 1948. *Universal Declaration of Human Rights*. http://www.un.org/en/universal-declaration-human-rights (accessed January 2, 2016).

United Nations. 1966. *International Covenant on Civil and Political Rights.* http://www.ohchr.org/en/professionalinterest/pages/ccpr.aspx (accessed January 2, 2016).

Wilson, I. E. 1982. "A Noble Dream: The Origins of the Public Archives of Canada." *Archivaria* 15: 16–35.

World Bank. 2007. "Strengthening World Bank Group Engagement on Governance and Anticorruption: Main Report." Washington, D.C.: World Bank Group. http://documents.worldbank.org/curated/en/2007/03/7478369/strengthening-world-bank-group-engagement-governance-anticorruption-vol-1-2-main-report (accessed January 2, 2016).

11

Archives and Social Justice

David A. Wallace

The ambit of social justice rings diversely across archival scholarship and praxis. Its relevance and applicability have found both support and repudiation. This range of response stems in part from the wide diversity of archives, their histories, mandates, and collecting and accessing strategies. It also stems from disputes over professional identity and responsibility and the often-contradictory edicts and guidance offered by professional ethics. Though working toward social justice has been endorsed and condemned in the professional literature, the actual intended meaning of "social justice" too frequently goes undefined and conceptually unarticulated. Most archival writings take its meaning as assumed and use it as a marker that connects to a vast range of issues under social contestation. Despite this imprecision, archival approaches to and the calling forth of social justice have grown substantially since 2000 and even more dramatically so since 2010. This trend has resulted in a variety of substantial analyses that reflect a deepening and growing commitment by many archivists worldwide who see social justice as an identity-framing and mobilizing concept.

Struggles for social justice exist within contexts that manifest structural and institutionalized oppression and domination. Such struggles have been and remain "controversial, contrarian, subversive, unpopular, and frequently subjected to state violence and broader social antagonisms." Both historically and in more contemporary settings, they have highlighted and challenged issues such as "slavery; exploitive labor conditions; racism; colonialism; [indigenous rights]; militarism and war; gender and ethnic inequities; violations of civil liberties; immigrant rights; environmental health; and . . . crushing poverty" (Wallace 2010, 185–86). Efforts against these injustices have included civil disobedience, protest, mass movements, public education, legislative campaigns, and armed struggle. They have also incorporated information collection, production, and dissemination initiatives to enact social change. Striving for social justice in an archival context requires a nuanced and multifaceted understanding of both justice and injustice and how they can be furthered and combatted respectively through overt political activism and promotion of professional standards and norms. In such settings, archival effects are not restricted to binaries of good-bad, positive-negative, partial-substantial but rather sit along continua that lead to different kinds of outcomes for different actors (individuals, institutions, communities, society) at different points in time (Duff et al. 2013).

Advocacy and rejection of social justice as an appropriate frame for archival theory and praxis dates back to the early 1970s and was stimulated by broader contemporaneous struggles for justice and the pushback against them. In these initial discussions, "social justice" was *implicit* and reflected in the nature of the topics debated. Four decades later, the dramatic rise of the *explicit* use of social justice in the archival literature has been matched by a second round of debate over the appropriateness of social justice as an ethical and operational frame for archival work. These parallel discussions and the debates they engendered identify key unresolved themes—primarily the legitimacy of the politically active archivist who pivots on the union and disunion between the personal (mis/characterized as "political," "emotional," "subjective," and "irrational") and the professional (also mis/characterized as "nonpolitical," "nonemotional," "objective," and "rational"). Disputes over neutrality and nonpartisanship sit at the center of both eras of debate and are especially charged given that they continue to be promoted as benchmarks for professional codes and disciplinary acculturation.

This chapter first develops a framework for understanding social justice by drawing upon key texts that incorporate perspectives from philosophy, history, political economy, culture, criticism, postmodernism, and cross-cultural views. This framework promotes a structural and institutional understanding of justice and injustice. It then links this framework to recent archival efforts that explicitly define and elaborate relationships between archives and social justice. It then turns to a broader historical analysis and range of more recent monographs to uncover the multiple relationships of archives and records to social control and injustice. It highlights how archival connections to historical production and consciousness reflect politicized efforts to shape narratives and ideological belief systems through intentional processes of forgetting and unforgetting and raises substantial questions about the obligations and responsibilities of memory professionals such as archivists. A review of archival discourses on social justice and injustice charts how archivists have framed, debated, discussed, and deployed the social justice concept. This segues into an analysis of professional codes' ethics to examine lingering beliefs about objectivity and professional responsibilities before turning to the conclusion.

FRAMING SOCIAL JUSTICE AND INJUSTICE

Examinations of social justice tend to leave the term conceptually and pragmatically undefined or opaque. This is a feature of the depth, complexity, and reach of social justice as well as its often-assumed obvious nature. It has been described as an "activity, a philosophical stance, a value system . . . a process . . . an analytical research lens, an objective, a call to activism, . . . [and] an unwanted attempt at social engineering" (Duff et al. 2013). Attempts to name social justice traditionally pivot on a reductionist philosophical approach that restricts it to the economic distributive paradigm of material goods and resources: assessing need; rewarding benefits based on effort; and struggles for greater equality. More recently, and well reflected in archival treatments, notions of social justice have become more broadly constituted and incorporate features of the globalized political economy, labor, health, education, environmental and ecological issues, indigeneity, postcolonialism, and restitution and reparations for historical injustices. Critical approaches to law, corrections policy, class, race, gender, sexuality, ethnicity, identity, and historical construction and reconstruction as well as the charged issues of relativism and pluralism are also included within the orbit of social justice. Postmodernist approaches move beyond strictly legal and distributive remedies to ask more probing questions about the scope and application of social justice beyond a grand narrative and toward numerous petite and often conflicting narratives to uncover a multiplicity of social justices and injustices that defy ready calculation. These approaches demand diverse interpretive frameworks that enable counter-narratives beyond the perspectives of dominant groups that seek to universalize their experiences (Capeheart and Milovanovic 2007).[1] This multi-domain and multi-perspective approach to social justice imbues it with qualities of dynamism and indefiniteness. As such, it will "always be in flux, always subject to reflection, augmentation, qualification, deletion, and even replacement . . . [as there] is no one justice that will incorporate all the dimensions of struggle, becoming, and the coming of a good society" (Capeheart and Milovanovic 2007, 177).

Despite the challenges of grappling with the contours, boundaries, and contingencies of social justice, it is equally important to recognize that it strongly inheres in ethical frameworks and that it can be meaningfully sketched out and given concrete substance. Social justice is made politically and socially relevant and meaningful through efforts to apply values and standards associated with calls for justice within specific situations (Miller 1999, ix–x). It factors in social structure and institutional contexts where decision-making power and procedures, the division of labor, and culture are activated. Social justice therefore is not an abstract philosophical ideal oriented solely toward realizing the just distribution of material goods and burdens, but rather is a socially assembled context-specific praxis that can be promoted and advocated in concrete settings of struggle characterized by unequal power within social and political relationships that manifest *injustice* (Capeheart and Milovanovic 2007; Young 1990, 2013). Injustice is characterized by two structural conditions: oppression and domination (Young 1990, 38):[2]

> *Oppression:* systematic institutional processes [exploitation, marginalization, powerlessness, social division of labor, cultural imperialism, and violence] which prevent some people from learning and using satisfying and expansive skills in socially recognized settings, or institutionalized social processes which inhibit people's ability to play and communicate with others or to express their feelings and perspectives on social life in contexts where others can listen.
> *Domination:* institutional conditions which inhibit or prevent people from participating in determining their actions or the conditions of their actions. Persons live within structures of domination if other persons or groups can determine without reciprocation the conditions of their action, either directly or by virtue of the structural consequences of their actions.

Through these lenses, social justice assumes "equal moral worth of all persons" and seeks to eliminate institutionalized oppression and domination. However, elimination of oppression and domination is complex and challenging since a society's operational normalities are often sublimated and unrecognized as instruments of injustice. Oppression and domination in this sense are not tied to an easily identified coercive tyrannical power but rather to the "everyday practices" unconsciously rooted within a "well-intentioned liberal society" through its "unquestioned norms, habits, and symbols [and] institutional rules." As a result, some societal groups and actors experience substantial social injustice through the "unconscious assumptions and reactions of well-meaning people in ordinary interactions, media, cultural stereotypes, and structural features of bureaucratic hierarchies and market mechanisms—in short, the normal processes of everyday life [where] oppressions are systematically reproduced by major economic, political, and cultural institutions." Through this frame, social justice in a society can be assessed as the degree to which it provides and upholds the "institutional conditions necessary for ... developing and exercising one's capacities and expressing one's experiences, [as well as participation] in determining one's action and the conditions of one's action" (Young 1990, 33–41, 65).

In reference to archival science, despite an impressive surge of interest in social justice since 2000, very few writings offer an explicit definition or description of social justice. The meaning of social justice is either assumed or left unstated or narrowly casted to the author's primary case or topic. Hence, pathways to understand archival social justice are normally opaque, though they touch upon a broad range of relevant subject matter. Three archival treatments of social justice, however, do make an explicit effort in terms that aligns with the preceding discussion. Anthony Dunbar (2006), Amanda Strauss (2015), and Wendy Duff et al. (2013) deploy critical race theory, liberation theology, and multidisciplinarity, respectively, to characterize social justice in order to illustrate how archival institutions, content, and practices can both replicate and challenge institutional and structural features of injustice.

Dunbar uses *critical race theory*, an approach to understanding society through examination of how relationships framed by race manifest social injustice. He emphasizes how "oppression," its structural societal pervasiveness, the ways in which it restricts self-development and self-determination, how it presents a naturalized view of social hierarchy, and how it "others" dominated groups, operates in and through archives both as a place and as a professional practice. Drawing from the field of education, he provides a goal-oriented approach to understand archival social justice as a praxis that enables individuals and groups to "express their own agency, reality or representation," foster open communication among groups with divergent cultural viewpoints, and create space where oppression can be recognized and scrutinized across "individual, cultural, and institutional" lenses (citing Bell 1997, 3–4). Strauss (2015) proposes a definition of social justice deriving from *liberation theology*,[3] a leftist Christian religious and moral philosophy and practice emanating from Latin America in the latter part of the twentieth century that sought to challenge and overcome the region's extremes of poverty, inequality, and oppression. She defines *social justice* as a "tangible commitment to actively engaging in 'service to others, especially the neediest' " and places it under "the premise that all individuals have fundamental human rights," as enshrined in the 1948 Universal Declaration of Human Rights (United Nations 1948), such as "the right to 'recognition everywhere as a person before the law,' the right to not be 'subjected to torture or to cruel, inhuman or degrading treatment or punishment,' and the right 'to freedom of thought, conscience and religion.' " She promotes these rights in reference to proactive archival practices seeking to expose the human rights violations of Augusto Pinochet's dictatorship in Chile (1973–1990) in order to secure legal and historical accountability. Finally, Duff et al. (2013, 324–25) use a *multidisciplinary* orientation to develop a robust and comprehensive social justice approach to archives and an archival approach to social justice that argues that archives are always situated in contexts shaped by power (political, economic, organizational, and individual). Their analysis yields a series of concepts to frame social justice by identifying what it *strives toward* (recognition; fair and just redistribution; full and equal participation; and acknowledgment and remedy of historical inequalities with specific measures) and *strives against* (dominance and systemic inequities; disrespect; marginalization; exclusion; and nonrecognition). They define *social justice* as the equal worth of all individuals and groups who are "entitled to shared standards of freedom, equality, and respect" and where violations of these standards demand confrontation. They further acknowledge systemic disparities of power that result in varying outcomes for different groups in society. Their archivally aware approach to social justice recognizes that "contestations over recordmaking (including what gets recorded and how it gets recorded) and recordkeeping (including how records and other information objects are managed, selected, controlled, accessed, and preserved) implicates social justice endeavors" (329).

These three archival writings locate archival social justice through the lenses of institutional and structural injustice. They advocate acting on behalf of those who have been marginalized and silenced through structures of oppression and domination that are enacted, in part, through normative, yet biased, recordmaking, recordkeeping, and archiving. They acknowledge that archives play contributive roles in shaping which versions of the "past" get constituted and legitimized as a consequence of which documents archives value, collect, and make accessible through widely accepted methodologies and practices. These writings also demonstrate how archives can become politically and socially relevant in the service of contemporary struggles for justice through their mobilization and harnessing for self-representation, narrative plurality, and rights seeking and promotion. All three also explicitly support archival activism and non-neutrality as a means to serve the social justice objectives they identify.

CONNECTING RECORDS AND ARCHIVES TO SOCIAL JUSTICE AND INJUSTICE

Following these lines of analysis we can see that the adoption and integration of writing as a communication system and tool for organizing complex social aggregations strongly attach to systems and structures of justice and injustice. Of significance to archivists is the reality that oppression and domination emanate from concrete historical circumstances that are frequently reflected in and operationalized through documentary processes. These connections demonstrate how contributive records and archives are to human communication and action and that, as a consequence, it is virtually impossible for archivists to avoid considering issues of social justice and injustice irrespective of whether they emanate from discussions on the origin and spread of literacy and recordkeeping, the role of writing systems for social control, or archival relationships to historical consciousness. Historical production regularly features politicized efforts to shape archives, narratives, and ideological belief systems through processes of forgetting and unforgetting. Scholars and writers from many disciplines actively mine and engage records and archives to uncover complex mechanisms of domination, oppression, and struggles for justice. Their work provides context with which to reassess archival professional and social responsibilities to the past and to the present.

The relationship among literacy, recordkeeping, social organization, and systems of justice and injustice dates back to the dawn of writing systems thousands of years ago. Integrating findings from behavioral economics, evolutionary psychology, and anthropology, Daniel A. Mullins, Harvey Whitehouse, and Quentin D. Atkinson (2013) demonstrated that the advent of writing and recordkeeping helped to "solve the problem of cooperation in large groups by transcending the severe limitations of our evolved psychology." They did so by enabling reciprocity (through tracking, verification, recall, and persistence of multiple heterogeneous interactions), reputation formation and maintenance (through identification, validation, and relationship building), social norms standardization and their enforcement, and the promotion of group identity and empathy through the sharing of others' life experiences. Records and archives as instruments of power for control can be ascribed to their pervasiveness and ability to establish and delegate authority by "fixing" communications to ensure their stability and repeatability. Such processes can exert social influence by permitting and forbidding classes of action and behavior (Levy 2001, 21–38). While recordmaking and recordkeeping in these veins can clearly cut toward both justice and injustice, some observers are more circumspect on their positive social aspects, focusing instead on their effects toward domination and social control in economic, political, legal, and religious arenas (Goody 1986). Control over access and distribution can place limits over what is publicly knowable or acknowledged, which can reinforce domination and limit accountability. Claude Lévi-Strauss (1961, 292), one of the founders of structural anthropology, theorized that "the primary function of writing, as a means of communication, is to facilitate the enslavement of other human beings." He argued that the debut and integration of writing systems into increasingly complex social, economic, and political structures manifested foremost as an instrument of "exploitation" and only secondarily as one for "enlightenment" and only then in a supportive subservient role in "reinforcing, justifying, or dissimulating" its exploitive properties.

The reality is that the social consequences of recordmaking, recordkeeping, and archiving can be located across the entire spectrum of justice and injustice. The potential slant of records and archives toward injustice and their mobilization in struggles for justice are evident in texts largely unconsidered by archival scholarship. These cases stretch across time and space and touch profoundly on the production, control, use, and dissemination of information, records, and archives.

We see it in state-based efforts to institute and sustain injustice through records-driven bureaucratic processes that ensure racist domination (Crais 2002; Foster, Haupt, and De Beer 2005), in how law enforcement records are consciously and maliciously misformed to cover up criminal actions such as evidence planting, assaults, and even homicide (Carroll 2015; Drake 2014; Van Maanen and Pentland 1994), and in regard to how abuses of secrecy conceal controversial and even criminal actions that evade democratic governance and criminal justice structures (Callinan 2016; Danner 1994, 2006; Harris 2002; Medsger 2014; Welsome 1999). They are evident in intense class-based contestations over land records (Hetherington 2011; Hull 2012) and in how recordkeeping manifests as "structural violence" against the illiterate poor (Gupta 2012). They are witnessed in colonial-era projects of classification that recorded and operationalized imagined identities and sexualities of subaltern populations for domination and control purposes (Arondekar 2009; Stoler 2009). They also surface in efforts to recover and promote suppressed and invisibleized memories (Hochschild 1999; Papailias 2005) and in works to repurpose records designed for political repression as instruments of historical clarification and justice (Bruce 2012; Dinges 2004; Garton Ash 1997; Kornbluh 2003; Weld 2014). They are discernable through creative uses of new and emergent forms of documentation for human rights campaigns (American Association for the Advancement of Science, n.d.; Center for Research Libraries 2012; Hochschild 2005). Finally, they also demonstrate exclusionary practices of archival institutions as public historical spaces that slant and obscure past injustices (Brundage 2005; Elkins 2005) and dampen efforts to open up uncomfortable institutional pasts (Platt and O'Leary 2006; Wright 2005).

A key association between recordkeeping and archives along these spectra of social justice and injustice involves the nature of historical production and narration in terms of how we understand the past and its contemporary relevance. As noted by historian Geoffrey Cubitt (2007), the past fundamentally shapes the present, while the present and the past create the past. History and the reconstruction of the past serve as a powerful political instrument, whereby the ideological reconstruction of the past through acts of selection, promotion, obliteration, and suppression enacts forgetting as much as remembering, shaping not only what societies choose to remember but also what they choose to omit and forget (Bloxham 2005; Cubitt 2007;

Stern 2006; Wallace 2006, 2011). The recent turn toward memory as a feature of social justice places new emphases on "unforgetting" and positioning history as a moral obligation to ensure that the oppressed and dominated are not written out of history and that narratives regarding them are not shrouded in distortions and partial representation (Akçam 2006; Chang 1997; Turse 2013). Such unforgetting is obviously not recovering that which has been completely forgotten but rather is more about opening a space for those who remember but are limited in their legitimacy and cultural capital to have their version of the past validated and safely expressed. The construction of the past in these settings is therefore associated with the "politics of memory" framed within relationships of power (Confino 1997) that implicate professional responsibilities. As Jacques Le Goff (1996, 99; see also Blustein 2008) pointedly writes, it is "incumbent upon professional specialists in memory ... to make of the struggle for the democratization of social memory one of [their] primary imperatives." This duty is reinforced by Iris Marion Young (2013, 182):

> [T]he mere unchangeability of historic injustice ... generates a present responsibility to *deal with* it as a memory. We are responsible in the present for how we narrate the past. How individuals and groups in the society decide to tell the story of past injustice and its connection to or break with the present says much about how members of the society relate to one another now and whether and how they can fashion a more just future. In a plural and divided society ... the politics of historical narrative should make room for plural stories .... A society aiming to transform its present structures of injustice requires a reconstitution of its historical imaginary, and the process of such reconstitution involves political contest, debate, and the acknowledgment of diverse perspectives on the stories and the stakes.

Contestation over the nature and direction of contemporary society, the construction and reconstruction of the past and how it is relayed, and the troubled myriad relationships among recordmaking, recordkeeping, and archiving to social justice and injustice are the exact contact zones that have given birth to archival social justice advocacy. This advocacy, however, has not gone unchallenged as many of its philosophical and tactical underpinnings represent direct assaults on long-standing assumptions, practices, and values that have guided professional identity and assimilation of new members. Despite these controversies, the overwhelming professional publishing and scholarship trend embraces and advocates archival social justice.

PROFESSIONAL ARCHIVAL DISCOURSES ON SOCIAL JUSTICE AND INJUSTICE

Initially, it was an outsider, radical historian Howard Zinn, who, in a speech at the 1970 conference of the Society of American Archivists (SAA), first called upon the archival profession to examine and reassess its standard operating procedures and relationships to power, domination, and injustice. While specifically calling for broadening collecting and challenging national security information classification, his biting critique and the debate which ensued were framed around the notion of the "activist archivist" who proactively and explicitly engages politicized spaces in a non-neutral manner toward the goal of enacting social change. Much of Zinn's criticism assails professionalism, whose operating ideology and practicing norms of neutrality and technical proficiency he saw not as markers of disinterested integrity but rather as "powerful form[s] of social control." He charged that professionals, such as archivists, were cultivated through social reward mechanisms (remuneration, prestige, and legitimation) to obscure or not acknowledge broader social responsibilities to consider whether their labors were a benefit or hindrance to a more just society. By not acknowledging the broader political and social implications of their work, archivists in effect denied that it had any connection with structures of domination and oppression. Normative professional values of impartiality and neutrality reinforced these structures (Zinn 1977, 15–17):

> The archivist, in subtle ways, tends to perpetuate the political and economic status quo simply by going about [their] ordinary business. [This] supposed neutrality is . . . fake . . . . Scholarship in society is inescapably political. Our choice is not between being political or not. Our choice is to follow the politics of the going order, that is, to do our job within the priorities and directions set by the dominant forces of society, or else to promote those human values of peace, equality, and justice, which our present society denies. (20)

Zinn's indictment, which is very much in tune with Young's (1990, 41) argument that social justice thrives in the unconscious "everyday practices . . . [of] . . . unquestioned norms, habits . . . symbols [and] institutional rules," led to the quick establishment in 1971 of Archivists for Change(ACT)[4]—a small cohort of primarily younger archivists who had internalized the anti-systemic values of radical social and economic change. ACT moved "out from behind the protective shield of professionalism" (Brothman 2011, 420). ACT concentrated on democratizing SAA's decision making and enhancing diversity within the profession. This push was not always well received. In at least one instance, a senior member of the SAA was reported to have questioned whether the society was "getting too large" and "wondered aloud about the credentials of the new members who had recently joined" (Quinn 1977). Certainly, a generational dynamic *was in fact in play* and driving social justice activism. This younger generation of archivists had come of age during the battles over civil rights and the Vietnam War, increasing awareness of economic inequality and its consequences and the emergence of a broad range of social liberation movements along gradients of race, gender, sexuality, and ethnicity (Hinding 1975). By 1972, the SAA's Committee for the 1970s promoted language on "social relevance," approved by the society's membership, that included commitments to "racial justice, equal employment, and reasonable access to research materials," countering secrecy and overblown confidentiality claims and curtailing over-collecting of records documenting social, political, and economic elites. The society accepted that it had a "moral obligation to take official positions on those contemporary public issues, however controversial, which affect the archival profession" (Mason 1981, 203–04).

An early rebuke of the activist archivist was published by then assistant state archivist at the Maryland Hall of Records, Gregory Stiverson (1977). Although his article has been almost ignored in comparison to repeated citations to Zinn in the literature, Stiverson lays out in greatest depth the early counter position to the call for archival social justice. Stiverson (1977, 4–6) argued that since archival work results in little of social consequence, it compels the activist archivist, operating from a status of insecurity and inferiority, to unnecessarily politicize and expand the archival endeavor by taking on work better left to historians. He saw the activist archivist as a sulking professional who "blame[ed] the establishment" for his or her lack of recognition and thus felt compelled to "strike back" against traditionalists. The activist archivist went too far by challenging "sound" practices that served the profession well and threatened to undermine its role as a trusted "guardian." The activist archivist, misguided by "whimsy, fad, or serendipity," effaced and compromised archival "integrity and impartiality." Stiverson was distressed by the call for "redress" of perceived "inequities" of prior archival work. He saw such moves as imprudent as they ignored "the basics" and sabotaged "projects of lasting utility." Specialized guides from reassessed holdings that sought to locate and document "*women, blacks, and other special interest groups*" were particularly criticized as largely feel-good but wasteful efforts that ended up "robbing the *general public* who need[ed] those comprehensive guides" (italics added).

Stiverson saw danger in utilizing oral history to represent the naturally less documented "less fortunate." Because society was "dominated by the rich and powerful," they were consequently and logically better documented. It made perfect sense for archivists to attend more to them as the "mass of humanity" actually had "little influence or power" and hence were of little historical importance. To act otherwise would "politicize" archival work and "pervert [and] not improve upon the record . . . ." (8–9). As if to ensure no room for misunderstanding, he stated that "[n]o amount of vocalizing by women, blacks, or other *allegedly oppressed, ignored, or misunderstood segments* of American society will change the fact that until the last few years our culture was indisputably dominated by white Protestant males, and in most respects it still is" (italics added). To be "forced to judge that particular groups have been wrongfully ignored in the past" would "compromise [archival] principles" by artificially improving the "status of recently activated groups who demand that . . . archivists provide them with historical legitimacy" (9–14).

Stiverson's language and attitudes duly reflect the pushback against the social movements of the 1960s and foreshadow the "culture wars" that were to emerge in subsequent decades, which saw heated contestations over the meaning and constitution of the past, the values of multiculturalism, and the merit of critical analyses that sought to overturn received norms and widely held conventions. They are also reflective of some of the tensions that dominate more current debates over archival social justice. From this distance, it seems clear that Stiverson did not see how documentation practices of a society reflect cultural norms tied to systems of oppression and domination, or how recordkeeping practices distort our perception of those who are less fortunate in our society.

Despite Stiverson's confident claims of extant "sound" practices and traditionalist "projects of lasting utility," change was in the air, especially in the core functions of appraisal and collection building. At the time of his writing, in the mid-1970s, we see the seeds of efforts to consciously broaden the historical record beyond elites and socially dominant groups as well as greater self-reflection over how archival agency shaped and validated the historical record and the absences and oversights created by such practices. The widely touted call by F. Gerald Ham (1975) for early life cycle intervention on vulnerable records, such as of the 1960s social justice movement on civil rights, student activism, and the anti-Vietnam War protests, well reflected the activist message to the profession. Ham called upon the profession to recognize that its mandate had been "permanently altered" in light of the challenge of preserving contemporary documentation that could easily disappear before archivists got around to collecting it. What was instead needed was systematic review of existing collections to detect collecting biases, especially in regard to the already "well documented."

Despite a willingness at this time to democratize documentary collection practices, archivists as a whole were still reluctant to challenge their professional ideology of neutrality and impartiality. By the 1980s, SAA's membership soured on activist social endeavors (Mason 1981), no doubt reflecting the broader conservative social and political changes ushered in at that time. It instead embraced a deeper focus on methods, techniques, and professional development that by and large sidestepped the difficult issues raised by Zinn in regard to archival social justice activism. Despite this broader professional retreat into technique and method and the enduring belief that archival work stood apart from the social and political controversies raging in the outside world, the belief that archiving was inherently political and connected to structures of power and injustice failed to dissipate completely. It is important to note that from the 1960s through the 1980s and onward, pockets of activist archival work, largely unheralded and underpublicized, continued to occur both within and outside of professionalized institutional settings and academic publishing and conference circles. These ongoing efforts dedicated themselves to mobilizing archives and archival work to confront injustice along contours of politics, race, class, gender, and sexuality (Flinn and Alexander 2015; Pell 2015; Wakimoto, Bruce, and Partridge 2013).

New voices emerged in the new millennium recontending that archives and professional practices were more complex and troubled than the pacifying notions of professional objectivity and neutrality continued to imply. The advent of the new century witnessed a dramatic surge in archival social justice through conferences and publications. These developments would motivate a renewed rebuttal to archival social justice that mirrored the contours of the debate from the 1970s, specifically on issues of activism, political advocacy, willingness to choose a side versus neutrality-impartiality, normative ethics, and separating the personal from the professional.

The collected writings of Verne Harris (2007) and Rand Jimerson (2009b) have strongly influenced a new generation of archival social justice advocates. Despite their differences, both forcefully argue beyond professional ethics and toward a broader moral dimension to archiving, as similarly expressed by O'Toole (2004). Harris (2007, especially 244–49, and recalled throughout the volume), the most cited archivist on the subject, frames social justice primarily as the "call of justice" and connects it to issues of appraisal, description, professional ethics, indigeneity and orality, freedom of information, whistle-blowing, social memory, and apartheid and postapartheid South Africa. In each of these arenas, he calls upon archivists to think anew and recognize how their actions either service or block broader moral responsibilities. Mobilizing postmodern writers such as Jacques Derrida, Emmanuel Levinas, and Gayatri Chakravorty Spivak, he locates the call of justice well beyond, but not alien to, archives and archivists. While final justice is ultimately unreachable, it features centrally as a site of continuous struggle framed by relationships with and hospitalities to "the other." For Harris, the archive *is political*, period, and recordmaking and recordkeeping, a "messy business" that fundamentally discomforts and ruptures professional norms and assumptions, especially those enshrined in codes of ethics and narrowly focused techniques and methods that encourage archivists to see themselves as separate from politics, as individuals who belong on the sidelines. Harris instead argues that structures of oppression and social control manifest everywhere and are enacted and supported in large part through systems and processes of information creation, dissemination, and use. He calls upon archivists everywhere to recognize that they reside within such systems whether they believe so or not and that presumptions of a safe, separate, and neutral professional impartiality that can and does sit outside such structures are a dangerous reactionary mirage.

Jimerson (2007, see also 2009b, 260–67, 290–95), seeking a more broadly inclusive and conventionally "optimistic" mandate, positions social justice as an objective that could be embraced and promoted within the totality of the profession. Whereas Harris provides a more challenging and less coalescing view that calls out splintering interests, motivations, and objectives within the profession, Jimerson situates archival social justice as a personal choice that can promote a broader professional "social conscience" in areas of social memory, accountability, open government, and diversity. He argues that archivists can promote social justice without sacrificing professional values of "fairness, honesty, detachment, and transparency." He is careful, though, to distinguish objectivity from neutrality. We should strive for the former but be clear that the latter does not require abandonment of facts and truthfulness under the ruse of securing a presumed balance where differences of opinion are given equal weight in order to avoid charges of partisanship. Jimerson specifically frames archival social justice around contemporary efforts and responsibilities associated with the duty to remember versus intentional forgetting to overcome past injustices. He promotes archival social justice with calls for internal professional dialogue and through direct connection to broader societal actors, such as human rights organizations and those struggling to preserve at-risk heritage.

Contemporaneous to these writings of Harris and Jimerson and right up through the present, we see a dramatic rise in social justice-focused archives literature. While most references to social justice leave the concept formally undefined, they do link it to a diverse range of issues that promote the view that the choices and actions archives pursue have social justice consequences. We see this in new pedagogical approaches that foreground the politics behind the construction of the past and promotion of a social justice consciousness within graduate archival education (Caswell et al. 2012; Gilliland 2011; Gilliland et al. 2008). It is evident in advocacy for new relationships with indigenous individuals and communities to surface and acknowledge how recordkeeping has historically enacted injustice and where archivists develop new methodologies that better respect and support indigenous "self-determination, non-discrimination, and the exercise of cultural rights as human rights" (Upward, McKemmish, and Reed 2011). Joanne Evans et al. (2015) review a series of Australian cases that had detrimental effects on children, as a platform to advocate "archival autonomy," an approach promoting an expanded set of user rights in records and archival processes, whereby communities are able to engage with records to locate their own archival traces for purposes of "memory, accountability, redress and recovery." Specific attention is given to how normative archival processes blunt recovery efforts and can generate harm. In a related vein, "affect" theory and studies, which examine the relationships between corporeal and external environments and their effect on social relations and physical and psychological states, ask archivists to more formally consider concepts of pain and healing and advocate "emotional justice" in collection building (Cifor 2016). Archival activism continues to be a particularly strong theme in the emerging archival social justice literature. Andrew Flinn and Ben Alexander (2015) promote an activist social justice agenda from the political left that recognizes that the field is equally open to other ideological persuasions that would deploy archiving for political objectives that engage the present and seek to "influence the future." Susan Pell (2015) reviews the United Kingdom's 56a Archive's resistance to local gentrification through mobilizing the archive as an overt political strategy that develops historical and contemporary materials to support local activism. Sonia Yaco et al.'s (2015) oral history project documents "passive participants" (the Birmingham kids) in the 1963 civil rights struggles in Birmingham, Alabama, and mobilizes these accounts to inspire today's young people "to join the cause for social justice." The project promotes a model that other communities can replicate through Web-based, educational, and media platforms to fill gaps in historical source materials and create linkages between historical and contemporary social justice movements. Strauss (2015) identifies three ways archivists in post-Pinochet Chile have promoted social justice activism: documenting the dictatorship's human rights violations; aggressively capturing and generating new materials bearing on these crimes; and enabling and promoting access to these materials.

These writings and projects are emblematic of a larger outpouring of archival social justice scholarship and advocacy (see Duff et al. 2013 for a summary of this literature). These developments, however, have not been greeted as a uniformly positive development. They have, in fact, aroused deep skepticism and reservations that such efforts represent a polarizing threat to collegiality and to long-cherished and promoted values of neutrality, nonpoliticalness, and separating the personal from the professional. The primary voice championing this pushback belongs to Mark Greene, whose initial unease (2009) developed into a fully developed rebuttal in 2013. Reacting primarily to the works of Harris (2007) and Jimerson (2006, 2007, 2009a, 2009b), he also takes issue with Michelle Caswell (2010a, 2010b) and Yaco and Beatriz Hardy (2013) and to a lesser extent with Chris Hurley (2001), David Wallace (2008), and Richard Cox (2005). Greene (2013) rejects calls for an archival social justice approach as an all-profession encompassing value, seeing it as "overly politicizing and ultimately damaging" to archivists and their "ethical standing" (303). He critiques Harris's claim that no archivist can be an impartial actor as too one-dimensional and takes strong exception with Harris's assertion that archivists have a moral duty to work against complicity with and reproduction of unjust systems of power. This is seen as opening the door of irresolution, because interpretations of what justice is and on whose behalf it can be claimed are ultimately ambiguous and easily muddled. For Greene, promoting social justice as an "ethical mandate" crosses the clear line he sees between "documenting social issues and actively participating in them" (316). He is therefore discomforted by projects such as the Desegregation of Virginia Education (DOVE), which encourages archivists to engage in political activism. Greene defends the concept of archival neutrality by relating his own personal experiences of how a demeanor of political nonpartisanship with prospective donors had led him to "winning donations from across the political spectrum" (312–13). In contrast, the archival embracement of partial social justice activism would likely "result in the acquisition and preservation *only* of records with a clear social justice agenda" and further "certainly destroy any chance of acquiring documentation from the other side" (317). This last point is openly admitted to by DOVE archivists Yaco and Hardy (2013, 254) who recognize that their advocacy in "speaking out about racism in education lessens the likelihood that segregationists will allow [DOVE] volunteers to survey or collect their records." Greene fundamentally disagrees on the need expressed by Yaco and Hardy to choose a side (antiracism) and become an activist in support of it. This is fine as a private citizen but not when acting in a professional capacity. But, as pointed out by Jimerson, the extant archival record in Virginia was already replete with proracist memorialization. DOVE's effort was looking to achieve some notion of equilibrium to an already lopsided documentary heritage that bred legitimate distrust by African Americans and civil rights activists (Jimerson 2013, 339–40). In this regard, the profession's vaunted neutrality had historically muted antiracist collecting by reflecting then dominant social prompts. The rich heterogeneous archival institutional landscape of today means that different archives can focus on different aspects of the documentary universe and as such do not require individual institutions to take on the mandate to create a "balanced" comprehensive record for which they are ill-equipped. Greene's (2013) impassioned rejection of archival social justice called the profession to band together and rally to:

> dissuade our colleagues actively from a social justice course [for] as long as one person's social justice is another's injustice; as long as nothing in our ethics demands serving society as a whole (unless such service is within one's institutional mandate) or playing the role of an internal whistle-blower; as long as we wish both the political left and the right to view at least some of our repositories as neutral ground, where one set of records (and ideas) is not consciously privileged over others; and as long as such perceived neutrality is essential to earning the voluntary commitment of private donors to make their records publicly accessible; then for just as long must we reject social justice as the end of all archival effort. (323)

Greene's main concern stems from a belief that archival social justice advocates threaten a totalizing dominion over archival practice through a decidedly politically leftist social justice orientation that would attempt to squeeze out other perspectives as unjust and therefore illegitimate. The archival landscape, however, remains too diverse to continue to function under a solitary animating ideology. The push for archival social justice represents a pushback against the presumptions of an extant totalizing philosophy that promotes contested markers of professionalism. What archival social justice advocates most readily find wanting and overtly or implicitly critique are key assumptions that are seen as increasingly untenable and misrepresentative: neutrality-impartiality, edicts from professional ethics, and claims of nonpoliticalness. For, as noted by Young (1990), assumptions of, or advocacy for, impartiality are deeply problematic once closely examined. The moral universality implied by impartiality and objectivity places it outside of concrete, nonabstract, real-world situations. It instead offers an awkward "transcendental 'view from nowhere' " (100). This "idealist fiction" unrealistically seeks analysis and understanding disconnected from difficult social realities with all of their conflict, complexity, and power and resource differentials that manifest injustice (104). In reality, there is no "nowhere" to retreat to or from which to view the world. The hard fact is that social and political context and situational circumstances impact archival work and therefore have to be considered by archivists. Recent research on objectivity (Uhlman and Cohen 2007, 221), albeit from hiring discrimination practices, found that "[w]hen people feel that they are objective, rational actors, they act on their group-based biases more rather than less . . . . Feeling objective appears to [make] people more likely to act on their stereotypic thoughts that, though they may arise from incidental environmental cues, subjectively feel like objective reflections of reality." This finding is easily relatable to reflexively accepted archival assumptions of neutrality, assumptions that are crumbling under recent scholarship historicizing archival practices (Brundage 2005; Elkins 2005; Platt and O'Leary 2006; Poole 2014). Further research incorporated by Duff et al. (2013, 326) indicates that the increasing corrosion of boundaries between objectivity and subjectivity has compelled professionals from many fields to "more explicitly understand and challenge their traditional embeddedness within contemporary structures of power and social stratification that produces and reproduces social injustice." Hence, the archival disciplinary struggles over the merit of social justice as impugning professional values are not unique to the field. The challenging cognitive and praxis pathways offered by archival social justice advocates reflect wider societal-professional trends that are seeking to bring deeper, if controversial, self-awareness to how professions constitute and understand themselves and the effects of their labors.

Archival professional ethics have long represented one of the ways for the profession to understand and promote itself. However, they continue to largely mask and evade how societal processes of oppression and domination affect archival work and its outcomes. The "box" of professional ethics denies upstream and downstream societal processes and power dynamics impacting archives, either by locating them as "outside" of our professional concerns or avoiding them completely, thus rendering them invisible. More commonly, concepts of balance, neutrality, impartiality, and law abidingness have been and remain constitutive of professional ethical codes. But interestingly, a close reading of archival codes of ethics demonstrates that they do so incompletely and with ample ambiguity, in effect trying to serve potentially incongruous ends by promoting impartiality as well as pursuit of some abstract notion of the social good, as if the former automatically results in the latter. They also, oddly, replicate each other, sometimes word for word, evidencing a concretized mentality over undertaking the hard effort at deeper analysis and consideration of fresh approaches. Objectivity and impartiality as a measure of professionalism are reflected in identical and nearly identical language in the codes of the Archives Association of Catalonia (n.d.), the Archives and Records Association U.K. and Ireland (2016), and the International Council on Archives (ICA) (1996). These last two also make identical statements on archivists' need to protect "national security," certainly a concept in dire need of critical analysis as opposed to unexamined assent.

However, these and similar instruments can also be read as internally contradictory on essential values and objectives and thus also offer us multiple and confusing ways of understanding our professional responsibilities vis-a-vis social justice. This is evident in the Archives Association of Catalonia's Code of Ethics, which states that "archivists contribute to the development of society on the basis of respect for human dignity and equality and action at all times in accordance with justice, upholding the basic rights and freedoms related to archives, records and information" despite next maintaining that archivists "shall act in accordance with current applicable law and ensure observance of that law." The Association of Canadian Archivists (1999) code promotes the belief that "archivists use their specialized knowledge and experience for the benefit of society as a whole," a clause begging for clarification and amplification. The most significant contribution in this line of thought is the SAA "Core Values Statement" (2011), which is affirmatively linked to the society's Code of Ethics. It seeks to offer guidance to be applied in those instances when archivists are "subjected to competing claims and imperatives" and in circumstances when they find themselves "in certain situations [where] particular values may pull in opposite directions." Its clauses on accountability, advocacy, diversity, history and memory, selection, and social responsibility, which while carefully crafted to be broadly inclusive of diverse archival institutions, nevertheless can be read to accommodate a more permissive and even supporting view of archival social justice objectives without stating so outright.

Growing evidence shows that archivists are increasingly being pulled into and shaped by larger social forces that both impinge on ethical presumptions and fracture notions of a unified field that shares a common identity and orientation. An ICA 2008 questionnaire survey yielding 150 responses found that half of respondents "faced an ethical dilemma in the course of their career" with access issues being the most common. Interestingly, the most substantive tool noted for addressing these dilemmas was "existing law." Respondents further noted that their "primary loyalty" as archivists/records managers was to the law. Less well-represented loyalties included "citizens and the truth" (ICA. Section of Records Management and Archives Associations 2008). A more recent survey (Yaco and Hardy 2013) of 78 self-identified activist archivists, three-quarters of whom worked in universities and governments, found that the positive effects of archival activism (workplace recognition, employer support, promotion) overwhelmingly surpassed negative effects (stalled advancement, minor and major punishment, firing). The internal tensions and alternative approaches offered by these surveys suggest an intractable problem for which there is no definitive or needed resolution. A discipline as heterogeneous and diverse as archives can equally serve nonoverlapping and even contradictory objectives and render futile efforts to provide overarching common ground orientations on archivists' social roles and responsibilities. Such realities undermine the confident assertions and claims of objectivity and impartiality. Previously, the profession largely sublimated these tensions as a sort of unspoken arrangement where politics were personal and separate from professional obligations. As ennobling as that sounds, it is clear that there are politics in recordkeeping and archiving and that "the past" and its construction and reconstruction are sites of active contestation.

For example, when we give donors, even institutionally based ones, the power to decide what to give and what to hold back and even what they create as a feature of institutional logic and administration, we are already allowing the shaping of the record despite whatever agency we can provide to the process. And historically and even contemporarily, granting such power to creators has been a vehicle that submerges or ignores the partiality we claim to work against. Even given our best efforts at promoting access, we are still legitimating and lending our professional endorsement as "history" the decisions made by others, who are usually more powerful actors we are beholden to for our collection building efforts. As a result, we thus find ourselves irreversibly embedded in political and non-neutral contexts. The social justice ethic, for whatever criticisms can be laid at its door, seeks in part to decloak these assumptions and state them more overtly and explicitly and even to resist them. This is a pressing issue since society appears to place great value and significance on archival collecting efforts as providing the raw materials of legitimate historical narrative, even if it remains deeply uninformed about archival processes.

Ironically, much of what can be called social justice archiving can actually be seen as an effort to "balance" the already skewed "organic" record we have long accessioned in service to the status quo, which has long had its own agenda on the uses of the past. Social justice archiving can be seen as an effort to confront and play some small part in rectifying the injustices of the past, whether through new collecting priorities, creating documentation to overcome gaps and silences of "organic" documentation processes, giving voice and supporting rights or restitution or redress to those who experienced domination and injustice by more powerful social actors, or even to mobilize archiving to counter contemporary injustices of which there is no shortage. While it is apparent that social justice has become a significant research and praxis topic in the field, it remains to be seen if it has staying power, or if, as witnessed in the 1980s–1990s, its intensity fades.

CONCLUSION

Contestation over the nature and direction of contemporary society, the construction and reconstruction of the past and how it is relayed, and the troubled myriad relationships between recordmaking, recordkeeping, and archiving, on the one hand, and injustice, on the other, are the contact zones that fuel archival social justice advocacy. It recognizes that archiving serves as a powerful political instrument, whereby the ideological reconstruction of the past through acts of selection, promotion, obliteration, and suppression enacts forgetting as much as remembering, shaping not only what societies choose to remember but also what they choose to omit and forget. Often these dynamics serve the biased interests of some, usually more powerful and better-resourced societal actors, at the expense of others. The turn toward memory as a feature of social justice positions archival work as a moral obligation to ensure that the oppressed and dominated are not written out of history and that narratives regarding them are not shrouded in distortions and misrepresentations. Archives are also becoming politically and socially relevant in the service of contemporary social justice struggles through their mobilization for self-representation, narrative plurality, and rights seeking and promotion.

Promoting an archival social justice agenda means acknowledging and defending its inherently political character and not, as tradition would have it, uncritically mimicking a version of archiving that promotes an idealized abstraction that believes its roles and efforts to sit above and beyond politics and concrete human relations and struggles. The long-promoted "two-sides" framework that seeks to blunt partisanship advocacy in actuality elides more complex social realities that have multiple sides and begs for more nuanced approaches that acknowledge multifaceted affinities and conflicts that are not easily documented through binary assumptions about societal contestations. Such efforts also require archivists to rethink and implement new approaches that acknowledge rights and interests in archives that go beyond traditional notions about principles such as provenance and practices such as description, reference, and public programming.

It is also important to understand that archival social justice advocacy has always been and remains controversial because many of its philosophical and tactical underpinnings represent direct assaults on long-standing assumptions, practices, and values that have guided professional identity. To various critics it is positioned and seen as a battle over the soul and legitimacy of the profession. Disputes over neutrality and nonpartisanship sit at the center of these debates and remain the most combative and controversial. This is especially salient today given the profession's drive to seek legitimacy as a "science" in its own right. These normative values have proven resilient and continue to be seen as benchmarks for professional codes and disciplinary acculturation. As a result, professional ethics continue to largely mask and evade that societal processes of oppression and domination affect archival work and its outcomes. Ironically, though, these instruments are often contradictory on archival responsibilities and can be easily read as promoting a social justice ethic as much as they can be seen as touting impartial professionalism.

Overwhelmingly, recent professional publishing trends embrace and advocate archival social justice. We see it clearly through linkages to a diverse and substantive range of theories, professional practices and wider societal issues that promote the view that archival work contributes and is fundamental to the shaping of knowledge that has the prospect for altering consciousness and social outcomes and that, indeed, the choices and actions archives pursue have social justice consequences. These efforts attach to issues such as diversity within the profession and activism for social change in regard to human rights, government secrecy, racism, gender, sexuality, identity, indigeneity, colonialism, and postcolonialism. They foreground emotional and psychological impacts concerning how the past is actually constructed and its potency for supporting and informing renewed claims of respect and autonomy. They also engage with contemporary struggles for justice and seek to offer political support through efforts such as community archiving and developing documentation to overcome the silences and gaps in "organically produced" documentation. Finally, they speak forcefully to the ongoing promise of archives and archival work to overcome injustices associated with oppression and domination.

ENDNOTES

1. Though the authors are based in "justice studies" academic programs that focus on criminal justice, Loretta Capeheart and Dragan Milovanovic's text provides

a more expansive understanding of social justice and brings in perspectives from philosophy, history, political economy, culture, criticism, postmodernism, and cross-cultural views.

2. Young was an academic political scientist and political theorist.

3. See: Cleary (1985); Engler (2003); Gutiérrez (1983).

4. A spotty and partially redacted collection of ACT newsletters is available at http://www.libr.org/progarchs/pdf/ACT.pdf.

REFERENCES

Akçam, T. 2006. *A Shameful Act: The Armenian Genocide and the Question of Turkish Responsibility*. New York: Metropolitan Books.

American Association for the Advancement of Science. n.d. "Geospatial Technologies Project: Human Rights Documentation." http://www.aaas.org/geotech/humanrights (accessed March 10, 2016).

Archives Association of Catalonia. n.d. "Code of Ethics of Catalan Archivists." http://www.concernedhistorians.org/content_files/file/et/143.pdf (accessed March 10, 2016).

Archives and Records Association U.K. and Ireland. 2016. "Code of Ethics." http://www.archives.org.uk/images/ARA_Board/ARA_Code_of_Ethics_final_2016.pdf (accessed September 19, 2016).

Arondekar, A. 2009. *For the Record: On Sexuality and the Colonial Archive in India*. Durham, NC: Duke University Press.

Association of Canadian Archivists. 1999. "Archivist's Code of Ethics." http://archivists.ca/sites/default/files/Attachments/About_Us_attachments/Code-of-Ethics.pdf (accessed March 10, 2016).

Bell L. A.1997. "Theoretical Foundations and Frameworks." In *Teaching for Diversity and Social Justice: A Sourcebook*, edited by M. Adams, L. A. Bell, and P. Griffin, 3–15. New York: Routledge.

Bloxham, D. 2005. *The Great Game of Genocide: Imperialism, Nationalism, and the Destruction of the Ottoman Armenians*. New York: Oxford University Press.

Blustein, J. 2008. *The Moral Demands of Memory*. New York: Cambridge University Press.

Brothman, B. 2011. "The Society of American Archivists at Seventy-Five: Contexts of Continuity and Crisis, a Personal Reflection." *American Archivist* 74 (Fall/Winter, 2): 387–427.

Bruce, G. 2012. *The Firm: The Inside Story of the Stasi*. Oxford, England: Oxford University Press.

Brundage, W. F. 2005. *The Southern Past: A Clash of Race and Memory*. Cambridge, MA: Belknap Press of Harvard University Press.

Callinan, R. 2016. "Secret Archive of Paedophile Crime Kept by Catholic Church's Insurers." *The Age*, March 27. http://www.theage.com.au/national/secret-archive-of-paedophile-crime-kept-by-catholic-churchs-insurers-20160317-gnlc6k.html (accessed March 27, 2016).

Capeheart, L., and D. Milovanovic. 2007. *Social Justice: Theories, Issues, and Movements*. New Brunswick, Canada: Rutgers University Press.

Carroll, J. B. 2015. "Leaked Documents Reveal Dothan Police Department Planted Drugs on Young Black Men for Years, District Attorney Doug Valeska Complicit." *Henry County Report*, December 1. https://web.archive.org/web/20160203073418/http://henrycountyreport.com/blog/2015/12/01/leaked-documents-reveal-dothan-police-department-planted-drugs-on-young-black-men-for-years-district-attorney-doug-valeska-complicit/ (accessed September 20, 2016).

Caswell, M. 2010a. "Hannah Arendt's World: Bureaucracy, Documentation, and Banal Evil." *Archivaria* 70 (Fall): 1–25.

Caswell, M. 2010b. "Khmer Rouge Archives: Accountability, Truth, and Memory in Cambodia." *Archival Science* 10 (March, 1): 25–44.

Caswell, M., G. Broman, J. Kirmer, L. Martin, and N. Sowry. 2012. "Implementing a Social Justice Framework in an Introduction to Archives Course: Lessons from Both Sides of the Classroom." *Interactions: UCLA Journal of Education and Information Studies* 8 (2). http://eprints.cdlib.org/uc/item/2jx083hr (accessed March10, 2016).

Center for Research Libraries. 2012, February. *Human Rights Electronic Evidence Study: Final Report*. http://www.crl.edu/sites/default/files/attachments/pages/HREES_Final_Report_Public.pdf (accessed March 10, 2016).

Chang, I. 1997. *The Rape of Nanking: The Forgotten Holocaust of World War II*. New York: Basic Books.

Cifor, M. 2016. "Affecting Relations: Introducing Affect Theory to Archival Discourse." *Archival Science* 16 (March, 1): 7–31. Published online November 2.

Cleary. E. L. 1985. *Crisis and Change: The Church in Latin America Today*. New York: Orbis Books. http://opcentral.org/resources/2014/09/05/crisis-and-change/ (accessed March 10, 2016).

Confino, A. 1997. "Collective Memory and Cultural History: Problems of Method." *American Historical Review* 102 (December, 5): 1386–1403.

Cox, R. J. 2005. "Letter to the Editor." *American Archivist* 68 (Spring/Summer, 1): 8–11.

Crais, C. 2002. *The Politics of Evil: Magic, State Power and the Political Imagination of South Africa*. Cambridge, England: Cambridge University Press.

Cubitt, G. 2007. *History and Memory*. Manchester, England: Manchester University Press.

Danner, M. 1994. *The Massacre at El Mozote: A Parable of the Cold War*. New York: Vintage Books.

Danner. M. 2006. *The Secret Way to War: The Downing Street Memo and the Iraq War's Buried History*. New York: New York Review of Books.

Dinges, J. 2004. *The Condor Years: How Pinochet and His Allies Brought Terrorism to Three Continents*. New York: The New Press.

Drake, J. M. 2014. "Insurgent Citizens: The Manufacture of Police Records in Post-Katrina New Orleans and Its Implications for Human Rights." *Archival Science* 14 (October, 3–4): 365–80.

Duff, W. M., A. Flinn, K. E. Suurtamm, and D. A. Wallace. 2013. "Social Justice Impact of Archives: A Preliminary Investigation." *Archival Science* 13 (December, 4): 317–48.

Dunbar, A. 2006. "Introducing Critical Race Theory to Archival Discourse: Getting the Conversation Started." *Archival Science* 6 (March, 1): 109–29.

Elkins, C. 2005. *Imperial Reckoning: The Untold Story of Britain's Gulag in Kenya.* New York: Henry Holt and Company.

Engler, M. 2003. "Toward the 'Rights of the Poor': Human Rights in Liberation Theology." In *Liberating Faith: Religious Voices for Justice, Peace, and Ecological Wisdom*, edited by R. S. Gottlieb, 203–21.. Lanham, MD: Rowman & Littlefield.

Evans, J., S. McKemmish, E. Daniels, and G. McCarthy. 2015. "Self-Determination and Archival Autonomy: Advocating Activism." *Archival Science* 15 (December, 4): 337–68.

Flinn, A., and B. Alexander. 2015. " 'Humanizing an Inevitability Political Craft': Introduction to the Special Issue on Archiving Activism and Activist Archiving." *Archval Science* 15 (December, 4): 329–35.

Foster, D., P. Haupt, and M. De Beer. 2005. *The Theatre of Violence: Narratives of Protagonists in the South African Conflict.* Oxford, England: James Currey.

Garton Ash, T. 1997. *The File: A Personal History.* New York: Random House.

Gilliland, A. 2011. "Neutrality, Social Justice, and the Obligations of Archival Education and Educators in the Twenty-First Century." *Archival Science* 11 (November, 3): 193–209.

Gilliland, A., S. McKemmish, K. White, Y. Lu, and A. Lau. 2008. "Pluralizing the Archival Paradigm: Can Archival Education in Pacific Rim Communities Address the Challenge?" *American Archivist* 71 (Spring/Summer, 1): 87–117.

Goody, J. 1986. *The Logic of Writing and the Organization of Society.* New York: Cambridge University Press.

Greene, M. 2009. "The Power of Archives: Archivists' Values and Value in the Postmodern Age." *American Archivist* 72 (Spring/Summer, 1): 17–41.

Greene, M. 2013. "A Critique of Social Justice as an Archival Imperative: What Is It We're Doing That's All That Important?" *American Archivist* 76 (Fall/Winter, 2): 302–34.

Gupta, A. 2012. *Red Tape: Bureaucracy, Structural Violence, and Poverty in India.* Durham, NC: Duke University Press.

Gutiérrez, G. 1983. *The Power of the Poor in History.* Translated by Robert R. Barr. New York: Orbis Books.

Ham, F. G. 1975. "The Archival Edge." *American Archivist* 38 (January, 1): 5–13.

Harris, S. S. 2002. *Factories of Death: Japanese Biological Warfare, 1932–45, and the American Cover-Up*, 2nd ed. London: Routledge.

Harris, V. S. 2007. *Archives and Justice: A South African Perspective.* Chicago, IL: Society of American Archivists.

Hetherington, K. 2011. *Guerilla Auditors: The Politics of Transparency in Neoliberal Paraguay.* Durham, NC: Duke University Press.

Hinding, A. 1975. "The Third Generation: War, Choice and Chance." *American Archivist* 38 (April, 2): 155–58.

Hochschild, A. 1999. *King Leopold's Ghost: A Story of Greed, Terror, and Heroism in Colonial Africa.* New York: Houghton Mifflin.

Hochschild, A. 2005. *Bury the Chains: Prophets and Rebels in the Fight to Free and Empire's Slaves.* New York: Houghton Mifflin.

Hull, M. S. 2012. *Government of Paper: The Materiality of Bureaucracy in Urban Pakistan.* Berkeley: University of California Press.

Hurley, C. 2001. "The Evolving Role of Government Archives in Democratic Societies." Paper presented at the Association of Canadian Archivists annual conference, Winnipeg, Manitoba, June.

International Council on Archives. 1996. "ICA Code of Ethics." http://www.ica.org/en/ica-code-ethics (accessed March 10, 2016).

International Council on Archives. Section of Records Management and Archives Associations. 2008, June. "Questionnaire on the ICA Code of Ethics: Results and Recommendations." http://www.ica.org/en/questionnaire-ica-code-ethics-results-and-recommendations-0 (accessed March10, 2016).

Jimerson, R. C. 2006. "Embracing the Power of Archives." *American Archivist* 69 (Spring/Summer, 1): 19–32.

Jimerson, R. C. 2007. "Archives for All: Professional Responsibility and Social Justice." *American Archivist* 70 (Fall/Winter, 2): 252–81.

Jimerson, R. C. 2009a. "Archivists and the Call of Justice." Paper presented at Society of Archivists conference, Bristol, England, September 1. http://faculty.wwu.edu/jimerson/ArchivistsandJustice.htm (accessed March10, 2016).

Jimerson, R. C. 2009b. *Archives Power: Memory, Accountability, and Social Justice*. Chicago, IL: Society of American Archivists.

Jimerson, R. C. 2013. "Archivists and Social Responsibility: A Response to Mark Greene." *American Archivist* 76 (Fall/Winter, 2): 335–45.

Kornbluh, P. 2003. *The Pinochet File: A Declassified Dossier on Atrocity and Accountability*. New York: The New Press.

Le Goff, J. 1996. *History and Memory*. New York: Columbia University Press.

Lévi-Strauss, C. 1961. *Tristes Tropiques*. New York: Criterion Books. English translation by John Russell.

Levy, D. 2001. *Scrolling Forward: Making Sense of Documents in the Digital Age*. New York: Arcade Publishing.

Mason, P. P. 1981. "Archives in the Seventies: Promises and Fulfillment." *American Archivist* 44 (Summer, 3): 199–206.

Medsger, B. 2014. *The Burglary: The Discovery of J. Edgar Hoover's Secret FBI*. New York: Alfred A. Knopf.

Miller, D. 1999. *Principles of Social Justice*. Cambridge, MA: Harvard University Press.

Mullins, D. A., H. Whitehouse, and Q. D. Atkinson. 2013. "The Role of Writing and Recordkeeping in the Cultural Evolution of Human Cooperation." *Journal of Economic Behavior and Organization* 90S: S141–S151.

O'Toole, J. 2004. "Archives and Historical Accountability: Toward a Moral Theology of Archives." *Archivaria* 58 (Fall): 3–19.

Papailias, P. 2005. *Genres of Recollection: Archival Poetics and Modern Greece*. New York: Palgrave Macmillan.

Pell, S. 2015. "Radicalizing the Politics of the Archive: An Ethnographic Reading of an Activist Archive." *Archivaria* 80 (Fall): 33–57.

Platt, A. M., and C. E. O'Leary. 2006. *Bloodlines: Recovering Hitler's Nuremburg Laws from Patton's Trophy to Public Memorial*. Boulder, CO: Paradigm Publishers.

Poole, A. 2014. "The Strange Career of Jim Crow Archives: Race, Space, and History in the Mid-Twentieth-Century American South." *American Archivist* 77 (Spring/Summer, 1): 23–63.

Quinn, P. M. 1977. "Archivists and Historians: The Times They Are a-Changin'." *Midwestern Archivist* 2 (2): 5–13. http://www.libr.org/progarchs/documents/Quinn_Article_MwA_1977.html (accessed March10, 2016).

Society of American Archivists. 2011, May. "SAA Core Values Statement and Code of Ethics." http://www2.archivists.org/statements/saa-core-values-statement-and-code-of-ethics (accessed March 10, 2016).

Stern, S. 2006. *Remembering Pinochet's Chile: On the Eve of London 1998*. Book one of the trilogy *The Memory Box of Pinochet's Chile*. Durham, NC: Duke University Press.

Stiverson, G. 1977. "The Activist Archivist: A Conservative View." *Georgia Archives* 5 (January, 1): 4–14.

Stoler, A. L. 2009. *Along the Archival Grain: Epistemic Anxieties and Colonial Common Sense*. Princeton, NJ: Princeton University Press.

Strauss, A. 2015. "Treading the Ground of Contested Memory: Archivists and the Human Rights Movement in Chile." *Archival Science* 15 (December, 4): 369–97.

Turse, N. 2013. *Kill Anything that Moves: The Real American war in Vietnam*. New York: Picador.

Uhlman, E. L., and G. L. Cohen. 2007. " 'I Think It, Therefore It's True': Effects of Self-Perceived Objectivity on Hiring Discrimination." *Organizational Behavior and Human Decision Processes* 104 (February, 2): 207–23.

United Nations. 1948. *The Universal Declaration of Human Rights*. http://www.un.org/en/universal-declaration-human-rights/index.html (accessed March 10, 2016).

Upward, F., S. McKemmish, and B. Reed. 2011. "Archivists and Changing Social and Information Spaces: A Continuum Approach to Recordkeeping and Archiving in Online Cultures." *Archivaria* 72 (Fall): 197–237.

Van Maanen, J., and B. Pentland. 1994. "Cops and Auditors: The Rhetoric of Records." In *The Legalistic Organization*, edited by S. B. Sitkin and R. J. Bies, 53–90. Thousand Oaks, CA: Sage Publications.

Wakimoto, D., C. Bruce, and H. Partridge. 2013. "Archivist as Activist: Lessons from Three Queer Community Archives in California." *Archival Science* 13 (December, 4): 293–316.

Wallace, D. A. 2006. "Historical and Contemporary Justice and the Role of the Archivist." In *Arkiv, Demokrati Og Rettferd* (*Archives, Justice, Democracy*), 14–27. Oslo: ABM-Utvikling. http://www.kulturradet.no/documents/10157/2a26a331-d3e3-4a10-b8e4-d120e021a40e (accessed March 10, 2016).

Wallace, D. A. 2008. "Locating Agency: Interdisciplinary Perspectives on Professional Ethics and Archival Morality." Background document to paper presented at the Society of American Archivists annual conference, San Francisco, California, August 28. http://www.archivists.org/conference/sanfrancisco2008/docs/sessionGlobalIssuesForum-wallace.pdf (accessed September 20, 2016).

Wallace, D. A. 2010. "Locating Agency: Interdisciplinary Perspectives on Professional Ethics and Archival Morality." *Journal of Information Ethics* 19 (Spring, 1): 172–89.

Wallace, D. A. 2011. "Introduction: Memory Ethics—or the Presence of the Past in the Present." *Archival Science* 11 (March, 1–2): 1–12.

Weld, K. 2014. *Paper Cadavers: The Archives of Dictatorship in Guatemala*. Durham, NC: Duke University Press.

Welsome. E. 1999. *The Plutonium Files: America's Secret Medical Experiments in the Cold War*. New York: The Dial Press.

Wright, W. 2005. *Harvard's Secret Court: The Savage 1920 Purge of Campus Homosexuals*. New York: St. Martin's Press.

Yaco, S., A. Jimerson, L. Cadlwell Anderson, and C. Temple. 2015. "A Web-Based Community-Building Archives Project: A Case Study of *Kids in Birmingham*." *1963 Archival Science* 15 (December, 4): 399–427.

Yaco, S., and B. Betancourt Hardy. 2013. "Historians, Archivists, and Social Activism: Benefits and Costs." *Archival Science* 13 (June, 2–3): 253–72.

Young, I. M. 1990. *Justice and the Politics of Difference*. Princeton, NJ: Princeton University Press.

Young, I. M. 2013. *Responsibility for Justice*. Oxford, England: Oxford University Press.

Zinn, H. 1977. "Secrecy, Archives, and the Public Interest." *Midwestern Archivist* 2 (2): 14–26. https://minds.wisconsin.edu/handle/1793/44118 (accessed March 10, 2016).

12

Participatory Archives[1]

Alexandra Eveleigh

"Participatory archives" is one of a number of shorthand phrases used in the archival literature in reference to contemporary initiatives, which seek to engage non-archivists—generally through the medium of social Web technology—either to contribute to archives or to comment on archival practice. The term has achieved a certain currency in the professional literature despite little consensus having yet been reached on a precise definition (Duranti and Franks 2015; Huvila 2011). Other expressions which loosely overlap with participatory archives (or, as in Huvila's formative article on the subject, "the participatory archive" in the singular) include crowdsourcing, citizen archivists (Ferriero 2011), Archives 2.0 (Palmer 2009; Theimer 2011c), user participation (Yeo 2010), the Archival Commons (Anderson and Allen 2009), and citizen-led (crowd)sourcing (Grant et al. 2013). All of these terms are inventions of the first decade and a half of the twenty-first century, and accordingly, the concept of participatory archives is usually portrayed as a new and still evolving model of archival practice (Duranti and Franks 2015). Indeed, in coining a range of archive-specific terms for participatory practice, professional archivists have deliberately sought to capitalize on broader societal and popular culture trends toward the active engagement of the public in creating knowledge (e.g., Shirky

2010) and specifically to tap into the rich potential offered by online technology to produce and share historical information as the key asset of archives within the new global knowledge economy (Benkler 2002; Evans 2007, 400).

Thus, a professional desire to be (or to be seen to be) pioneering and involved at the cutting edge of the online world drives much practical experimentation with participatory archives: the hope of emulating the broad success of certain collaborative online communities (particularly Wikipedia) and the chance to exploit the ready availability of social media and other so-called Web 2.0 tools and platforms for annotation and interaction (for examples in archives, see Theimer 2011a). But many participatory archives' developments are also inspired by the postmodernist turn in archival theory,[2] whereby technology is heralded as an opportunity to "democratize" the archive to reveal a multiplicity of different perspectives, meanings, and contexts around the archival record, including traditionally excluded voices and minority communities (Flinn 2010; Yakel 2011b). Joy Palmer (2009) describes this as the "triumphal rhetoric" of Archives 2.0: a perceived shift toward a new generation of archival practice centered around a reconceptualization of archives' "users" as active participants in the coproduction of historical understanding.

This said, whilst a few participatory archives initiatives have been explicitly change-oriented in seeking to address issues of power or social (in) justice (notably in the context of indigenous human rights and in postcolonial societies, e.g., Iacovino 2015; see also McKemmish et al. 2012), perhaps the majority are founded on a simpler, more pragmatic encounter of the "other" with archives and archives professionals:

> An organization, site or collection in which people other than the archives professionals contribute knowledge or resources resulting in increased understanding about archival materials, usually in an online environment. (Theimer quoted in Duranti and Franks 2015, 262)

Even if such interactions can be claimed to belong to, and contribute toward, trends in the archive profession toward greater openness and transparency of practice, then it is asserted that this is still to a large degree a transformation led and shaped by archivists, an endeavor in which members of the public are permitted or encouraged to contribute rather than stimulated by activism from the "bottom-up." Many early developments in the use of social media in archives in particular can be seen in retrospect as clustering around the periphery of the professionalized curation functions of the archives service. Blogs and Twitter have proved a popular method of permitting an archivist-choreographed insight and limited feedback into the processing process; generic Web platforms such as Flickr allow for user tagging and commenting but upon carefully curated digitized collections.

Additionally, not all participatory archives initiatives are necessarily purposeful: indeed, it seems that many are experiments evoked simply by the ready availability of social Web resources such as Flickr, examples of an emergent "strategy in action" (Moncrieff 1999) which are only later rationalized as part of a strategic shift toward participatory practice.

This is not to deny the existence and significance of online communities of interest who create and share digitized images, descriptions, and memories about a particular place or topic among themselves and without any professional mediation. Doubtless, many contributors feel more comfortable, or are better motivated to participate, in community settings, and consequently such independent heritage groups form an important part of the wider context for participatory archives where they have similar aims to harvest contributors' resources, skills, or knowledge or to provide alternative access routes to archival materials. But insofar as these grassroots initiatives are more typically focused upon the collation of thematic collections of archival content and the dissemination of these materials to a self-defined and potentially private community of shared identity or interests (Flinn 2007), rather than concerned with the description or interpretation of that content *per se* and for the benefit of the public at large, a distinction is drawn in this chapter between participatory and community-led archives (for which see Chapter 14).

PARTICIPATORY TRADITIONS

Magia Krause and Elizabeth Yakel (2007, 288) observe in their evaluation of one early example of participatory archives, the Polar Bear Expedition Finding Aid, that "this idea that users can contribute to descriptive products is not new." Operational projects have often drawn heavily on established traditions of volunteering (Bateson and Leonard 1999), antiquarian collecting, and "serious leisure" (Stebbins 2007) interests in archives (which over a protracted period helped to shape description itself "before the advent of archives as a profession" [Bateson and Leonard 1999, 83]). A more recent example of an analog form of participatory archives is the United Kingdom's "Revisiting Archives" methodology, which uses a focus group approach to facilitate the creation of new interpretations and personal opinions about archive documents, with the objective of incorporating this "user-generated" content into professionally structured finding aids (Newman 2012). Indeed, one understanding of participatory archives (those projects focused on transcription or description in particular) regards the concept as simply extending an acknowledged tradition of user involvement in calendaring, document editing, and publication ("It will be apparent, therefore, that whilst the preparation of Lists or inventories of Archives is ostensibly the business of archivists, the compilation of

Indexes, like the preparation of Calendars or the transcription of texts, is a matter which chiefly concerns the historical student" [Hall 1908, 80]).

A precedent for involving nonprofessionals in archives work can even be traced back to one of the establishment figures of the archives profession, Hilary Jenkinson, who in 1947 inaugurated the new course in Archive Administration at University College London saying:

> I hope there always will be, room for the Amateur, and in large numbers . . . that our School will always find a place for the part-time student—the Local Official or other enthusiast whose Archives do not need and cannot claim the whole of his time; but who can find enough to undertake their listing or repair or photographing and wishes to acquire, within those limits, something of a professional technique. (Jenkinson 1948, 29)

The juxtaposition of "amateur" and "professional" in this quote is noteworthy; as Brabham (2012, 402) observes, "there is power in professionalization, and so long as individuals are seen as outside of the boundaries of a profession, they will be seen as not having access to that power." Similarly the language of (virtual) volunteering perhaps serves to distinguish "amateur" engagement in participatory archives from professional practice, helping to maintain the traditional position of the authoritative archivist and countering fears about the accuracy and reliability of public contributions as potentially creating a "chimera of false democracy" that "detract[s] from scholarship" (Kennedy 2009). The association of volunteering with the virtual world also does little to temper a professional defensiveness (or insecurity) concerning an archivist's specialist knowledge, skills, and employability (e.g., see Archives and Records Association 2011) but merely moves the front line beyond the doors to the archives institution.

That said, there is scant evidence in the literature on participatory archives for the term *amateur* being applied in a derogatory manner or shrouding condescension in "a veneer of praise" (Brabham 2012, 404) (although the gulf between amateur and professional may perhaps be wider amongst historians [see Mortimer 2002]). Where the term *amateur* is encountered in archives and related domains, it generally has more positive connotations: Marta Nogueira (2010) speaks of "quite unexpected but well-informed sources" providing a contrasting, not competing, perspective to the professional or, as in the Jenkinson extract above, where the amateur's capacity is limited by time only, not skill. Trevor Owens (2013, 122) further argues that professionals should seek to embrace the involvement of these "lovers of" cultural heritage as peer participants in a new ethical form of crowdsourcing without the crowds, while from an academic perspective, Ruth Finnegan (2005, 9) suggests that amateur participants may even have the advantage over professionals in exploring innovative technologies or new areas of study, having the freedom to "take risks and venture beyond disciplinary regimes and regurgitations."

THE PARTICIPATION CONTINUUM

However, as the continuum model of recordkeeping makes clear (Hurley 1994), there are no real hard or fixed boundaries to the archive or the archival process, and so the potential to benefit from the knowledge or skills of people who are not professional archivists arises at most, if not all, stages of the archives' life cycle. Livia Iacovino (2015, 30, 37) is concerned with challenging the "conventional understanding of the relationship between record subjects as third parties and record creators as the principal parties to the record transaction," and introduces a category of "recordkeeping participants who took part in the record's formation" alongside the idea that such subjects of the record have an ongoing right to "add their narratives to records held in public and private archival institutions, and to participate as co-creators in decision-making about appraisal, access and control." However, she concedes that most projects to date have focused on annotations to records already in archival custody, since participatory creation poses major challenges to institutional ownership and control (38). Katie Shilton and Ramesh Srinivasan (2007) propose the "Participatory Archiving Model" as a community-oriented rearticulation of traditional archival concepts of appraisal, provenance, and ordering (arrangement and description) but acknowledge that their methodology is "particularly labour-intensive" and therefore "outside the scope of most archival institutions." Isto Huvila's (2008) comprehensive "radical participatory archive" meanwhile centers around the collaborative management of the entire archival process without privilege as to either structure or professional status:

> Otherwise than from the technical point of view, information managers are equal to other users of the archive. Their role is not to direct the process of how an archive emerges, how something is described or appraised or what provenances relate to the materials. (Huvila 2008, 26)

Each of the above models of participatory archives chooses to focus on the record's contemporaneous internal stakeholders (i.e., the record cocreator(s) and authors and later users within the record's immediate chain of custody), whereas other participation frameworks largely involve *post hoc* commentators. Practical initiatives across the information and cultural heritage sectors have long been directed at the potential for stakeholders external to the creation and curation cycle (historians or museum visitors, for instance) to help address acknowledged problems in the description and representation of collections (Duff and Harris 2002; Karp and Lavine 1991). But although the argument for a more flexible theory and practice of archival description predates, and is independent of, theorizing around participatory archives (Cook 1997), "inviting users into the virtual spaces of the archive in a more active way" is proposed as a means of facilitating this shift in the archives domain (MacNeil 2011, 187): rethinking archival processing as a dynamic, creative process that constructs a narrative rather than seeing arrangement and description as a one-time collation of factual data into a static product. Wendy Duff and Verne Harris (2002, 272) explain that "the power to describe is the power to make and remake records and to determine how they will be used and remade in the future." Geoffrey Yeo (2010, 102) picks up this point in relation to participatory archives, arguing that "opening description to user participation gives a voice to minority groups and marginalized communities, enables users to supply additional perspectives and differing opinions, and recognizes that final or definitive descriptions are never possible. Descriptions are, or should be, 'always beta', always responsive to new understandings and further development."

Consequently, a wide spectrum of participatory archives initiatives is designed specifically around improving the quality of metadata or descriptions of records and seeks to benefit from the skills or knowledge of diverse user groups: from mass participation transcription and indexing initiatives, which rely on automated techniques for data verification via double-keying, to the building of user communities with the aim of enriching traditional catalogs with "thick" description and creating multiple narrative access points to archives (Eveleigh 2014). Caroline Haythornthwaite (2009a; 2009b) distinguishes between "crowds" and "communities" as the opposite ends of this spectrum. "Crowd" here does not necessarily refer to large numbers of people but instead relates to the relative strength of social ties between participants, being strong within a community but weaker among the participants in a crowd. Commentators in the archival literature can struggle to disentangle the inherent contradictions between web scale and community focus (Evans 2007) but have generally preferred the notion of online community over the crowd as the conceptual template for participatory archives. Huvila (2008, 27), for example, explicitly conceives of his concept of a radical participatory archive as something which goes *beyond* crowdsourcing: "Even though a participatory archive is about crowdsourcing, it focuses on deeper involvement and more complex semantics rather than on larger crowds and simple annotations." Whereas participants in a community might be entrusted with a significant degree of self-regulation and agency and may well be experts in their own particular field (Flinn 2010; Yakel 2011b), typically the predefined tasks in a "crowd" project offer limited choice to contributors and require limited expertise.

Archive organizations' early practical experiments with participatory archives also tended to assume a level of prior expertise more characteristic of community-oriented endeavors. Significant archival domain knowledge (and familiarity with the markup language) would be required to contribute an article to an archives wiki, (e.g., Grannum 2011). But examples of participatory archives shaped more to a "crowd" model are increasing: those characterized by low barriers to entry where contributors are not obliged to make a long-term commitment or need necessarily take part in community discussions. These crowdsourcing projects are knowledge aggregators, designed to appeal to the widest possible range of people. The net result may be merely to transfer some of the more tedious or repetitive parts of the archival processing workflow to unpaid volunteers, with only limited impact on professional practice. This style of participatory archives may still however be considered appropriate where an initiative is planned as a short-term, project-based scheme, since fostering a community takes time and effort and is also difficult to bring to an end without adversely affecting the relationship with the participants.

Again though, whether modelled on the crowd or the community, description-centered participatory archives mostly assume a custodial model of the archival process and involve retrospective description, that is, taking place after records have been transferred to a formal archives repository. Given that most archive institutions struggle with significant processing backlogs, the idea that members of the public might write, or enhance, descriptions has a strong pragmatic appeal: "Crowdsourcing may help institutions in the process of contributing metadata ... If the experience engages participants and they value it, the 'labor' involved in the exchange can be considered a voluntary, in-kind contribution" (Flanagan and Carini 2012, 536). Participatory archives promise a solution to these multiple problems, enabling a richer description—even transcription—of content at a detailed level across a broad range of subjects and collections. Participatory archives can even offer the opportunity to embrace a different style of description, capturing users' visceral or affective responses to archives and perhaps also helping to bridge the semantic gap between professional description and the terms that users might employ in searching for information from archives (Noordegraaf 2011).

This is not to say that stakeholder participation in the descriptive process or the resulting descriptive outputs are necessarily seen as constrained by the traditional boundaries of the archive. Rather than expecting participants and users to engage with bespoke archival description tools, there may often be a perceived benefit to harnessing existing online resources in order to deliver digitized archival content proactively into user networks (Flickr groups, for instance) or onto established participation platforms (as illustrated perhaps by the growing number of archives-related projects hosted by the citizen science consortium, Zooniverse). Enabling the participation of external stakeholders in description has also been found to induce a feedback loop into collection building and appraisal:

> Several of the commentators offered archival materials [to the archive] or digital copies of items that they wanted to see incorporated into the Polar Bear Expedition website ... Although we did not intend that our descriptive system would be transformed into a collection development system, this is a logical extension. (Krause and Yakel 2007, 299)

As archives and archival theory shift from a centralized, gateway model of information provision toward more dispersed frameworks for both custody and use (Bastian 2002), there is scope too for participatory methods to be applied not only toward descriptive input but also to promote descriptive output or access. Jennifer Schaffner (2009, 5), for example, suggests that users may "want to be autonomous and discover information about primary sources at the network level, not the institutional level" and that consequently the archivist's role may now lie in "making the collections more visible and staying out of the way." Similarly, Chris Hurley (2011, 8) identifies "a fundamental shift in the balance of power between the user and the provider of information . . . away from the provider and into the hands of the user" in the context of Web 2.0 technologies where "we can no longer construct pathways along which users will approach archival resources we describe, or control the way they will be used." This puts a strain on professional conventions of arrangement and description such as *respect des fonds* and original order through the very diversity of users' connections to the records. For instance, the "radical user orientation" of Huvila's participatory archive "assumes no consensus on order, no first order of order, just the necessity of keeping information findable" (2008, 26).

RECASTING THE PROFESSIONAL IDENTITY

Certainly a significant part of the debate on participatory archives—particularly discussions around technology-mediated participation—grapples with the implications of a participatory paradigm for archival theory and practice, including issues of professional function, power, and identity (Lehane 2006; Theimer 2011b, 2011c; Yakel 2011a). According to Heather MacNeil (2011, 175), the archivist's "professional identity is constructed around the twin notions of archivists as trusted custodians and of archival institutions as trusted repositories," and the image of the archivist as the impartial gatekeeper of cultural memory figures strongly in the traditional canon of archival science. Participatory archives do not necessarily fit comfortably within this custodial paradigm, with its emphasis on establishing control over not only the material traces of the past (the archives and the information contained within them) but also over the representation or representations of those traces through arrangement and description (and in the modern era, perhaps, through digitization)—that is, Jenkinson's (1922) primary professional duties of the physical and moral defense of archives. Regardless of repeated postmodernist critiques of the singular contextual perspective of archival finding aids (Light and Hyry 2002; Moss 2007) and a recognition of the power of the archivist to shape the user's understanding (Harris 2009; Hedstrom 2002), an illusion of neutrality in respect of arrangement and description remains an influential notion in archival practice. A belief in the archivist as an impartial and systematic analyst of records' provenance is also closely connected to archival conceptions of authenticity, as MacNeil (2009, 91) has also demonstrated. Participatory archives opening up to a multiplicity of user perspectives—"to create holes that allow in the voices of our users" (Duff and Harris 2002, 279)—is controversial, even threatening, in this professional context, as a risk to the function of archives as a trusted place of custody and a threat to the archivist's role in both description and access:

- These types of systems undermine the archives' control over their records and could perhaps threaten the traditional role of an archives as a trusted third party that protects the authenticity of records. (Duff 2010, 131)
- By opening up descriptive tools for comment, criticism, and review, not only from other archivists but also from researchers, annotations could threaten archival professionalism. (Light and Hyry 2002, 228)
- Allowing visitors to implicitly or explicitly recommend collections and finding aids to each other challenges the hegemony of the reference archivist. (Yakel 2006, 162)

Even Angelika Menne-Haritz's (2001) appeal for a reformulation of professional principles toward access is grounded upon ("enlarges") the traditional custodial paradigm, and thus, despite being user-oriented, leaves much of Jenkinson's moral defense framework intact:

> Access does not mean that the description and presentation of archives are user driven. They cannot try to replace the interpretation by the user because only the researchers really know what is needed for their questions. Access puts emphasis on an enabling approach. It opens information potentials in their context of creation, that guarantees them their plausibility. (Menne-Haritz 2001, 63)

As Huvila (2008, 18) observes in his article on the participatory archive, "Menne-Haritz sees access more as a concept and an attitude, rather than as an actual use of archives." For Menne-Haritz, archives must be fixed or "finished before they can be interpreted" by users. Participatory archives would be seen as compromising objectivity in this interpretative activity. Archivists themselves are painted as somewhat paternalistic, neutral enablers who "[open] the records for insight by third parties, who gain all the possibilities of questioning and investigation and protect them [users] at the same time from becoming part of and being involved with the activities" (Menne-Haritz 2001, 61).

If participatory archives then involve a radical user (re)orientation that moves the guiding professional paradigm even beyond access, shifting the responsibilities for custody and curation beyond the traditional custodians (archivists) and recontextualizing not only the archive records but also the entire archival process (Huvila 2008), what might this mean for the future role of the archivist? Duff and Harris (2002, 279) are explicit: "Making space for the voice of the other means that we must relinquish some of our power to the other—power of voice, construction and definition." For Paul Clarke and Julian Warren (2009), as for Yakel (2011b, 258), concepts of cocreation and corepresentation necessitate a shift in the professional mind-set away from the functional linearity of archival processes (and "static repositories") as the locale for participation, making participation itself the starting point for housing "living" memories "so that we might all play archon, produce our own collections that may be appraised and added to as we wish, classified according to our own taxonomic commands and rearranged in many ways" (Clarke and Warren 2009, 61). In the words of Elisabeth Kaplan (2002, 219), archivists in the postmodern world "must learn to live with uncertainty." MacNeil (2011, 187) too suggests that participatory archives can be construed as a means to acknowledge the partiality of professional representations and "to accommodate uncertainty, contingency and difference" in archival description. Living with uncertainty might also involve embracing "data of varying levels of currency and quality" although perhaps only for limited durations (Lankes et al. 2007, 26). These implicit uncertainties in participatory archives also involve accepting new and shifting patterns of influence between archivists and their stakeholders and establishing a more transparent but accountable descriptive practice, including a recognition of the rights of others to control how they themselves are represented (Kaplan 2002; Sassoon 2007).

Conversely, claims to archival authority tend to be taken as a provocation by those who would promote participatory archives in the professional literature. To assert this authority is (according to the rhetoric) to make a claim to superiority and to demand power and to privilege the position of the archivist (and of the archives as an institution). Jennifer Trant (2008, 290), writing in a museums' context, counsels cultural institutions to change their stance about the nature of their role: "It is possible to contribute authenticity without demanding authority. Authenticity is a value: its maintenance an imperative in collections of lasting value. But demanding authority is an act, often of arrogance, that denies the contributions of others to the development of knowledge." Archival authority has also, as Yakel (2011a, 2011b) observes, been portrayed as a fixed, limited commodity so that "participating in the social web means that archives either give up authority or their authority is called into question by competing and erroneous information about their collections" (Yakel 2011a, 91). She insists instead that authority should be considered a non-rival good, which can be shared with users, and in similar vein, Kate Theimer (in Duranti and Franks 2015, 261) identifies the "the sharing of authority and control/curation" as the "critical element" of several different models of participatory archives.

For even if participatory archives imply a destabilizing of traditional hierarchies, this need not imply that the expert voice of the archivist will become irrelevant, merely that any such claim to authority must be justified and earned as a relationship of mutual respect and trust (Yeo 2013). The archivist is still recognized by some users as being "critically important" (Rutner and Sconfeld 2012, 10) in guiding research, and even Huvila (2008, 27) is concerned that the participatory archive "does not attempt to trivialise the role of archivists or the importance of archival work." From the participant's perspective, accepting the invitation to take part or even making use of others' contributions need not preclude an appreciation of the expertise of the professional archivist. In an article arguing for the establishment of a new theory of digital historiography, Sternfeld (2011, 548) comments that "the trust bond between archivists and archival users over time has been well established." Users then might still be enthusiastic about the potential benefits of a participatory approach without necessarily understanding this in the democratizing terms in which participatory archives are frequently promoted in the archival literature, although this is difficult to judge thoroughly given the dearth of users' and participants' perspectives given in the debates (in cultural heritage contexts generally, not just in the archival literature). The jargon terms adopted by professionals (even crowdsourcing) have seemingly not translated well into the user domain, and genuinely analytical comment by users is hard to trace. But searching informal (mostly genealogical) forum and blog threads surfaces some discussion whose themes are remarkably consistent with issues raised in the professional domain: around the accuracy and reliability (or otherwise) of contributions, with opinions divided between those who find corrections and alternative interpretations generally helpful, and those who question the value of increasing quantities of user-contributed information that might be inaccurate or unchecked.

An updating of the "boundary spanner" (Nardi and O'Day 2000; Yakel 2000) professional role, the "knowledge intermediary" or "broker between users and sources" (Duff, Craig, and Cherry 2004), therefore gives the archivist in the participatory context an additional responsibility for shepherding and checking (Causer, Tonra, and Wallace 2012; Fleurbaay and Eveleigh 2012) contributions from participants (and deterring abuse or deliberate misuse [Looseley and Roberto 2009]) and then for ensuring the usability of the resulting "crowdsourced descriptions" (Anderson 2004).

An alternative view of the archivist's role in participatory archives takes a more enterprising approach to the cultivation of relationships with would-be participants and research users. There is a common thread between this understanding and traditional outreach and advocacy activities, whereby "archivists create as much as respond to needs" and actively encourage user involvement. The professional role here is not just to collect contributions, but instead the archivist is "imagined as a facilitator, removing barriers to participation and developing new avenues for engagement" (Sherratt 2009, 27). A degree of professional humility might also be required in asking users to submit information about previously unidentified material (for examples, see Theimer 2010, 89, 99). We might envisage the archivist here in more of a directing role, with a remit for providing the frameworks (practical and conceptual) through which users are encouraged to participate and are supported to create new knowledge. For instance, this might involve establishing certain permitted standards for participation (Grannum 2011), or the opposite, intentionally lowering cognitive or administrative barriers in order to induce more participation (Ridge 2011). Richard Lehane (2006, 5, 13) also suggests that, in the context of use, "user contribution [might] free archivists to take on a new role as contextualisers and educators, who assist users in viewing records and descriptions critically" and provide guidance "in ways of evaluating the reliability of online material." Akin to the "gardener" role of the reference archivist then (Yakel 2000), the professional mission in this conception of participatory archives is to assist users "in learning how to accomplish tasks themselves," whether those tasks be research or leisure use related, or "to empower users to share their ... story" (Alain and Foggett 2007).

But for all the language of empowerment, much of this activity can be parsed as a process of the attempted conversion of users into an archival perspective, encouraging "authoritative annotation" (Meissner and Greene 2010, 197) or participation in the service of the archivist's objectives. Max Evans (2007, 398), for example, states that "the archivist's job is to make sure that [this] tagging supports archival access systems." Indeed, it is possible that, far from the cacophony of the crowd drowning out the authoritative, expert voice of the archivist, some of the more attenuated forms of participatory archives may enable the professional to exert stronger control over contributions and the methods of participation. Here the implied shift in the professional role is if anything *extending* control over input standards down to a micro level. Although tight professional control appears initially incongruous against the deep involvement and community interaction envisaged for, say, the Archival Commons (Anderson and Allen 2009; Evans 2007), professional oversight is widely accepted and expected in transcription projects, for example, where there is a need to control for accuracy either by specifying the types and format of acceptable contributions in advance or through stringent mechanisms of post-participation review or revision (Brumfield 2012). Micromanagement is even made a design feature in the trend toward the competitive "gamification" of crowdsourcing (Flanagan and Carini 2012).

Yet, another reading of participatory archives plays up the archivist's contextualizing role but now as a single participant among many equals in the shaping of collective memory (Ketelaar 2001; Meehan 2009). Participants' contributions here are fostered as a means to "supplement archivists as mediators in the source finding process" (Lehane 2006, 7), but more than this, to transcend the institutional archive by "embrac[ing] multiple simultaneous views of provenance, description and interpretation" (Reed 2005, 182). For Huvila (2008, 27), "a participatory archive is not a complementary layer, but a primary knowledge repository about records and their contexts." Barbara Reed (2005, 189) observes that archivists themselves are often reluctant to take on an active (or perhaps activist), interpretative mantle but contends that "such thinking would not displace or supersede a perfectly legitimate organisational interpretation of role, but begin to enable alternative readings of processes to coexist" (183). The notion of archival description as a neutral, objective professional function, devastated anyway at the hands of postmodernist critics, is superseded too in the literature on online practice, where it is argued that new audiences create new demands for interpretation and narrative around records beyond mere description (Hill 2004, 142). The collaborative, or at least collective, dimension to user participation extends this argument by "alert[ing] all recordkeepers to the inherently contested and political nature of description processes [which reflect] the time and place of description, a realisation which is not restricted to archivists alone" (Reed 2005, 184). The role of the archivist in this perspective upon participatory practice must be negotiated with users, where responsibilities are shared and the relationship(s) are dynamic across time.

SUSTAINABILITY

The quiet disappearance from the Internet of several early, wiki-based experiments in participatory archives (including those discussed in Grannum 2011; Looseley and Roberto 2009; Shilton and Srinivasan 2007) draws attention to issues of the resilience of online participation and of the sustainability of participatory archives projects outside of previously established communities. Other examples prominent in the archival literature, including the University of Michigan's pioneering Polar Bear Expedition prototype (Krause and Yakel 2007; Yakel, Shaw, and Reynolds 2007), remain available but as read-only resources or like the Saari Manor Digital Archive (Huvila 2008) or the Plateau Peoples' Web Portal (Christen 2011) show little evidence of recent interaction or else appear heavily curated by professional hands.

Much of the early discussion about participatory archives rather expected contribution inevitably to follow once provision for participation had been made available. For Huvila (2008, 30), for instance, "the radical user orientation assumes that the moment when an archive is built is the starting point for participation." Rosenzweig (2006, 137) promotes participation by academic historians almost as a moral duty: "If historians believe that what is available on the Web is low quality, then we have a responsibility to make better information sources available online." Huvila's (2008, 28) attitude is similar: "All individual members of this participatory community have a responsibility to provide enough contextual information on records and their descriptions so that the content is independently understandable to their peers and not only for themselves." In both these cases, the participants are anticipated to be subject matter experts in the field in which they will contribute and as such are likely already to be users of archives. Their motivation is also assumed to be primarily altruistic in that their participation is expected to benefit others as well as (or rather than) themselves.

The archetypal community behind the usual conception of participatory archives in the archival literature is that of genealogy, where expert participants are not only willing to share their knowledge (Duff and Johnson 2003; Yakel and Torres 2007) but may even feel under some reciprocal obligation to do so (Lambert 1996; Yakel 2004). The outcome of this investment in participation is an "extensive social network of fellow researchers [which] facilitates the work of genealogists" (Duff and Johnson 2003, 90), both reactively (in response to other genealogists' questions) and proactively, by way of specialized information retrieval systems designed by genealogists for other genealogists (Duff and Johnson 2003). But this is a model of participation that not only requires community commitment but also assumes significant archival domain knowledge. Where participation appeals only to volunteers who are prepared or able to commit substantial amounts of time, energy, and expertise to the contribution task, this jeopardizes not only project sustainability but also the scalability of online participatory archives: as the range of initiatives on offer continues to grow, projects cannot afford to rely on core groups of participants with a preexisting intrinsic enthusiasm for a particular topic, who additionally are willing to devote considerable personal effort to achieving project goals.

Empirical research into online participation in other domains such as citizen science has also largely proceeded under the assumption that "sustained contribution by individual volunteers is critical for the viability of such communities" (Nov, Arazy, and Anderson 2011, 250). Attrition rates also tend to be high as contributors slow down or drop out of projects after an initial flurry of activity. However, Andrea Wiggins and Kevin Crowston (2010) suggest that in the "crowd" model circumstances in citizen science, project sustainability results not so much from persistent and committed individual effort as from a ready supply of fresh participants. Participatory archives no doubt conform loosely to the 90-9-1 principle of participation inequality common to all Internet communities (which posits that 90% of users are lurkers who may read contributions but do not interact, 9% make occasional contributions, and the remaining 1% account for almost all activity on the site [Nielsen 2006]); there is likely to be significant variation too in the depth of participation ranging from committed "super-volunteers" (Causer and Wallace 2012; Holley 2009) to more casual visitors. Hence Geoffrey Rockwell (2012) advises that projects should plan to support imbalance and diversity, recognizing the cumulative importance of small-scale contributions and the invisible value of nonactive participation to advertising the project and recruiting new contributors (Eveleigh et al. 2014).

MOTIVATION

Understanding participants' motivations for taking part in participatory archives has become increasingly important, since the results of practical initiatives have been so mixed. While some (particularly transcription) projects have reported apparently runaway success, others have struggled to attract and maintain contributors at a level that warrants ongoing organizational support.

Motivation as a theoretical construct in psychology divides broadly into two categories: *intrinsic* (those motivations that stem from the task itself) and *extrinsic* (the outcomes of an activity) (Amabile et al. 1994). In the context of participatory archives, examples of intrinsic factors might include subject interest and curiosity, competence in the participation task, and an enjoyment derived from taking part. Intrinsic motivational factors are increasingly identified as being important in a variety of online settings (Benkler 2006). Examples of participatory archives that replicate traditional communities of practice in an online setting would be expected to rely upon intrinsic, social systems of recognition and reputation to motivate contributions. Extrinsic rewards are, however, attracting increasing attention, particularly in the context of gamification and the search for motivational features, which can be easily operationalized through competition and target setting (Flanagan and Carini 2012; Ridge 2011) or by providing a forum to encourage discussion and interaction around project tasks. Even so, the focus remains more on sustaining rather than attracting new participants.

Rewards for participation need not be tangible. Stuart Dunn and Mark Hedges (2013, 153) note the importance of a feedback loop as a motivating factor in online participation, not only as a means of improving contributors' quality of work (Causer et al. 2012) but also for building a sense of community ownership or to provide personal benefits, such as learning (von Hippel and von Krogh 2003). Ronald Lambert (1995, 153) describes a reputational reward for participation in genealogical research—a social prestige and recognition within the family as an authority and keeper of records. These culturally contingent social capital aspects of motivation offer an avenue to analyze why some traditional groupings of archive users (academics, say) may be more reluctant to share their expertise online than others (such as local or family historians [Duff and Johnson 2003]). They are also testimony to the kinds of social barriers that may not only act to preclude poor quality contributions but also prevent contribution altogether where the participant—although motivated to contribute—is intimidated by the perceived superior cognitive expertise of other contributors (Wasko and

Faraj 2005) or by the perceived authority of an institution (Looseley and Roberto 2009).

Tim Causer et al. (2012) observe that mutual respect and trust are vital if projects are to avoid exploiting participants who give freely of their skills or knowledge and time. In some instances, this respect for participants' culture or point of view may perhaps, somewhat counterintuitively, involve enabling contributions to be made in a closed space private to the community in question (Christen 2011; Ridolfo, Hart-Davidson, and McLeod 2010). Potential participants may fear being unable to control how their contributions are used, or their willingness to share may fluctuate anyway according to the type of information and who might have access to it (Olson, Grudin, and Horvitz 2005). Accepting participants as moderators is another conceivable step toward ceding control of archival spaces, giving participants the "freedom to 'describe the world in which they see it' " (Samouelian 2009, 48, citing Krystyna Matusiak), and developing the potential for digital technologies to "enable the coexistence of different perspectives in shared, networked spaces in which all parties are considered co-creators of records" (McKemmish 2011, 133).

PARTICIPATORY INNOVATION AND MEANING MAKING

Social and personal motivations to contribute converge in the context of user innovation, as users begin to customize resources or develop new ones to suit their own requirements or for the wider benefit of their community of practice. Eric Raymond's first lesson of collaborative software development "starts by scratching a developer's personal itch" (1998). Wendy Duff and Catherine Johnson (2003, 92), similarly, highlight the significance of specialist finding aids designed by and for the use of other family historians as "a parallel system to help them retrieve records because the archival information system fails them." Innovation is something which is regularly anticipated to emerge from participatory practice (Flanagan and Carini 2012; Rockwell 2012) but has rarely been defined in the archival literature; therefore, it is necessary to look outside of the discipline in order to evaluate the promises and claims of new knowledge creation arising from participatory archives.

Susanne Justesen's (2004) model of "innoversity" draws on social network concepts to distinguish between learning (where the host sphere of practice ["competence regime"] remains strong, absorbing new knowledge into the established domain rather than being challenged by it) and innovation (which is not merely about generating new ideas but equally about the successful diffusion of that knowledge). Similarly, the Japanese management theorists Ikujiro Nonaka and Hirotaka Takeuchi (1995, 69) model learning (or internalization, converting explicit knowledge to tacit) as one of the four phases of a "knowledge spiral" that feeds innovation. On the few occasions where "new types of knowledge" are referred to in the existing literature on participatory archives, these seem better classed as examples of learning than of innovation: for instance, Mary Flanagan and Peter Carini (2012, 514) promise that "mass participation ... opens the door for archivists, researchers, and the public to unearth new knowledge that could radically enhance scholarship across the disciplines," but the examples they provide ("new classifications, observations, descriptions, narratives, and practices" [520]) seem mostly (with the possible exception of "practices") to be about gathering "diverse bits of data and information" or "learning from others or acquiring knowledge from the outside" (Nonaka and Takeuchi 1995, 10) rather than the iterative, creative process of innovation modeled by either Justesen or Nonaka and Takeuchi. Similarly, we might posit that at present most participatory archives realize at best the "limited form[s] of knowledge creation" (Nonaka and Takeuchi 1995, 70) associated with individual phases of the knowledge spiral. For example, practice in palaeographical transcription might match the definition of socialization or knowledge transfer of technical skills acquired through experience, "observation, imitation and practice"; reflection and dialogue (externalization) might be triggered by the comment threads associated with historical images on platforms such as Flickr or on the discussion pages of archives' wikis or Wikipedia history articles; many participatory indexing projects fit the description of the combination phase—"reconfiguration of existing information through sorting, adding, combining, and categorising of explicit knowledge" that "can lead to new knowledge," while the compilation of Frequently Asked Questions guidance by project participants is an illustration of individuals internalizing their experience and knowledge. But for the most part, these examples of learning or knowledge conversion occur in isolation—both from each other and with participants' experiences having little impact upon the general practices and cultures of using archives.

More radical innovations can be said to occur when a complete new knowledge domain is created (Justesen 2004, 84), combining together the different modes of knowledge conversion (Nonaka and Takeuchi 1995, 70). Such outcomes are often the aspiration of participatory archives established with an adaptive, organic orientation, aiming to achieve much more than simply extending conventional research and knowledge-exchange practices (Huvila 2008). Several authors hint too at the possibility of user-led innovations in the display and navigation of archival records, such as data mashups and visualization techniques (Duff 2010; Landis 2002; Sherratt 2009; Whitelaw 2009). Hurley (2011, 8) predicts that "archival resources, once they are released in cyberspace, will be used in ways that we cannot anticipate and cannot determine. Our materials can be combined with other resources to produce quite unforeseen results." "Archives thus become a part not only of the information economy, but of the knowledge and creative economy" (Evans 2007, 400). Sue Breakell (2011, 26) views this as a personalization of use in antithesis to professional standardization: "The pull of the general user is in the opposite direction entirely, towards creating customised structures and meanings, through which archives are continually becoming different things to different people." Use in the participatory environment is then not merely about seeking and (hopefully) finding but also about being able to "conceptualize, mediate and tailor the information provided" (Anderson 2004, 114).

Wendy Duff, Emily Monks-Leeson, and Alan Galey (2012, 77) also discuss how "meaning is mediated by a person's mental model or knowledge structures—the filters of individual experience" in which archival finding aids (and by extension, other users' contributions) may or may not feature. Eric Ketelaar (2005, 48) invokes Jeannette Bastian's notion of a "community of records" in support of the idea that records are as much constructive as they are reflective of the past, mediating "tacit narratives [which] are constantly reactivated and reshaped." The implicit interpretative contexts here are both collective and contested: "Memory texts do not speak for themselves but only in communication with other agents; networked or distributed remembering," for "there is no single collective memory. Even if members of a group have experienced what they remember, they do not remember the same or in the same way" (Ketelaar 2005, 47).

CONCLUSION: REACHING THE LIMITS OF PARTICIPATORY ARCHIVES

Accepting that the meaning(s) of archival texts are not constant, emanating from the text, but instead are implicit within the social context through which an interpretation is made (Duguid 2005, 113; Ketelaar 2001) has important consequences for understanding the limits of participatory paradigms of knowledge diffusion or knowledge creation. The same archival source may be interpreted or used in multiple ways by different interpretative communities, but these different interpretations may not all be equally acceptable, or even intelligible, to users approaching the archive from another disciplinary angle or community context. Furthermore, users' information needs and expectations may change over time and space (Duff 2001). It cannot therefore be assumed that the expertise of individuals "on different aspects of the documents and their contexts" (Huvila 2008, 20), expressed through participatory practice, will inevitably prove either accessible or acceptable to other users.

These interpretative barriers are particularly problematic in the case of newcomers, who lack experience of the archives discipline or an established community of archives users—all the more so in the apparently attenuated social environment of Web-mediated interaction (Hildrum 2009), since "transferring knowledge, particularly to newcomers, involves more than transferring codified knowledge" (Duguid 2005, 112). This is already recognized in the archival literature on description and use although primarily in respect of a binary distinction between a "professional" (insider) perspective—those already inducted into an archival understanding of the world—and outsiders, who are not (Craig 2003; Ketelaar 2001; MacNeil 2012; Yeo 2008). Ketelaar (2001, 135), for instance, writes of "numerous tacit narratives ... hidden in categorization, codification and labeling," although he carries on to explicate multiple "social, cultural, political, economic and religious contexts [which] determine the tacit narratives of an archive" (137), contexts extending much wider than the professional purview of the archivist. Barbara Craig (2003, 99) urges the "critical importance of knowing the nature of community borders" and calls for improved "border management" from archivists, but it is Heather MacNeil (2012, 497) who overtly shifts the theoretical discussion toward a consideration of the "multiple, disparate, and overlapping" genre systems emergent with the rise of Web-based participatory archives and how "conflict and consensus" might be negotiated within (and presumably also between) these groups.

For it is these same social conventions that enable members of one community to communicate efficiently among themselves, which also serve to limit the exchange of knowledge beyond that group (Brown and Duguid 2000; Craig 2003). Paul Duguid (2005, 113) points out that information may "appear to have global reach" but only where different communities already share common ground and can therefore attempt to parse each other's articulations. The options then are either to try to convert tacit disciplinary knowledge to an explicit form in order to make it understandable for outsiders, or would-be users must themselves learn the appropriate interpretative conventions from the perspective of the community they wish to join: here participation functions as an apprenticeship for use, and we have simultaneously reached the logical limits of the notion of participatory archives, led and shaped by professional archivists.

ENDNOTES

1. This chapter is based on the author's PhD thesis (Eveleigh 2015).

2. Postmodernist critics challenge traditional understandings of archives as the passively accumulated by-products of actions or administrations and of archivists as neutral commentators on, and custodians of, a documented past reality. For more detail on the postmodernist turn in archives, see Terry Cook's "What Is Past Is Prologue" and two further articles also by Cook, "Fashionable Nonsense or Professional Rebirth: Postmodernism and the Practice of Archives," *Archivaria* 51 (Spring 2001): 14–35 and "Archival Science and Postmodernism: New Formulations for Old Concepts" *Archival Science* 1, no. 1 (2001): 3–24.

REFERENCES

Alain, A., and M. Foggett. 2007. "Towards Community Contribution: Empowering Community Voices on-Line." In *Museums and the Web 2007: Proceedings*, edited by J. Trant and D. Bearman. Toronto: Archives and Museum Informatics. http://www.museumsandtheweb.com/mw2007/papers/alain/alain.html (accessed October 26, 2015).

Amabile, T. M, K. G. Hill, B. A. Hennessey, and E. M. Tighe. 1994. "The Work Preference Inventory: Assessing Intrinsic and Extrinsic Motivational Orientations." *Journal of Personality and Social Psychology* 66 (5): 950–67. doi:10.1037/0022-3514.66.5.950.

Anderson, I. G. 2004. "Are You Being Served? Historians and the Search for Primary Sources." *Archivaria* 58: 81–129.

Anderson, S. R, and R. B. Allen. 2009. "Envisioning the Archival Commons." *American Archivist* 72 (2): 383–400.

Archives and Records Association. 2011. "Policy on Volunteering in Archives." http://www.archives.org.uk/careers/volunteering.html (accessed October 26, 2015).

Bastian, J. A. 2002. "Taking Custody, Giving Access: A Postcustodial Role for a New Century." *Archivaria* 53: 76–93.

Bateson, M., and R. Leonard. 1999. "Social Club or Compulsory Experience: Reflections on the Proper Role of Volunteers in Record Offices." *Journal of the Society of Archivists* 20 (1): 75–84. doi:10.1080/003798199103749.

Benkler, Y. 2002. "Coase's Penguin, or, Linux and the Nature of the Firm." *Yale Law Journal* 112 (3): 369–446. doi:10.2307/1562247.

Benkler, Y. 2006. *The Wealth of Networks: How Social Production Transforms Markets and Freedom*. New Haven, CT; London: Yale University Press.

Brabham, D. C. 2012. "The Myth of Amateur Crowds: A Critical Discourse Analysis of Crowdsourcing Coverage." *Information, Communication and Society* 15 (3): 394–410. doi:10.1080/1369118X.2011.641991.

Breakell, S. 2011. "Encounters with the Self: Archives and Research." In *The Future of Archives and Recordkeeping: A Reader*, edited by J. Hill, 23–36. London: Facet.

Brown, J. S., and P. Duguid. 2000. *The Social Life of Information*. Boston, MA: Harvard Business School Press.

Brumfield, B. W. 2012. "Quality Control for Crowdsourced Transcription." *Collaborative Manuscript Transcription*, March 5. http://manuscripttranscription.blogspot.co.uk/2012/03/quality-control-for-crowdsourced.html (accessed October 26, 2015).

Causer, T., J. Tonra, and V. Wallace. 2012. "Transcription Maximized; Expense Minimized? Crowdsourcing and Editing the Collected Works of Jeremy Bentham." *Literary and Linguistic Computing* 27 (2): 119–37. doi:10.1093/llc/fqs004.

Causer, T., and V. Wallace. 2012. "Building a Volunteer Community: Results and Findings from Transcribe Bentham." *Digital Humanities Quarterly* 6 (2). http://www.digitalhumanities.org/dhq/vol/6/2/000125/000125.html (accessed October 26, 2015).

Christen, K. 2011. "Opening Archives: Respectful Repatriation." *American Archivist* 74 (1): 185–210.

Clarke, P., and J. Warren. 2009. "Ephemera: Between Archival Objects and Events." *Journal of the Society of Archivists* 30 (1): 45–66. doi:10.1080/00379810903264617.

Cook, T. 1997. "What Is Past Is Prologue: A History of Archival Ideas since 1898, and the Future Paradigm Shift." *Archivaria* 43: 17–63.

Craig, Barbara L. 2003. "Perimeters with Fences? Or Thresholds with Doors? Two Views of a Border." American Archivist 66 (1): 96–101.

Duff, W. M. 2001. "Evaluating Metadata on a Metalevel." *Archival Science* 1 (3): 285–94. doi:10.1007/BF02437692.

Duff, W. M. 2010. "Archival Mediation." In *Currents of Archival Thinking*, edited by T. Eastwood and H. MacNeil, 115–36. Santa Barbara, CA; Oxford: Libraries Unlimited.

Duff, W. M., B. Craig, and J. Cherry. 2004. "Finding and Using Archival Resources: A Cross-Canada Survey of Historians Studying Canadian History." *Archivaria* 58: 51–80.

Duff, W. M., and C. A. Johnson. 2003. "Where Is the List with All the Names? Information-Seeking Behavior of Genealogists." *American Archivist* 66 (1): 79–95.

Duff, W. M., E. Monks-Leeson, and A. Galey. 2012. "Contexts Built and Found: A Pilot Study on the Process of Archival Meaning-Making." *Archival Science* 12 (1), 69–92. doi:10.1007/s10502-011-9145-2.

Duff, W. M., and V. Harris. 2002. "Stories and Names: Archival Description as Narrating Records and Constructing Meanings." *Archival Science* 2 (3): 263–85. doi:10.1007/BF02435625.

Duguid, P. 2005. " 'The Art of Knowing': Social and Tacit Dimensions of Knowledge and the Limits of the Community of Practice." *The Information Society* 21 (2): 109–18. doi:10.1080/01972240590925311.

Dunn, S., and M. Hedges. 2013. "Crowd-Sourcing as a Component of Humanities Research Infrastructures." *International Journal of Humanities and Arts Computing* 7 (1–2): 147–69. doi:10.3366/ijhac.2013.0086.

Duranti, L., and P. C. Franks. 2015. "Participatory Archives." In *Encyclopedia of Archival Science*. Lanham, MD: Rowman and Littlefield.

Evans, M. J. 2007. "Archives of the People, by the People, for the People." *American Archivist* 70 (2): 387–400.

Eveleigh, A. 2014. "Crowding out the Archivist? Locating Crowdsourcing within the Broader Landscape of Participatory Archives." In *Crowdsourcing Our Cultural Heritage*, edited by M. Ridge, 211–29. Farnham, U.K.: Ashgate Publishing.

Eveleigh, A. 2015. "Crowding out the Archivist? Implications of Online User Participation for Archival Theory and Practice." Doctoral thesis. University College London. http://discovery.ucl.ac.uk/1464116/ (accessed May 25, 2016).

Eveleigh, A., C. Jennett, A. Blandford, P. Brohan, and A. L. Cox. 2014. "Designing for Dabblers and Deterring Drop-Outs in Citizen Science." In *Proceedings of the SIGCHI Conference on Human Factors in Computing Systems*, 2985–94. New York: ACM. doi:10.1145/2556288.2557262.

Ferriero, D. S. 2011. "Crowdsourcing and Citizen Archivist Program." Blog. *AOTUS: Collector in Chief*, May 19. http://aotus.blogs.archives.gov/2011/05/19/crowdsourcing-and-citizen-archivist-program/ (accessed October 26, 2015).

Finnegan, R. 2005. "Introduction: Looking beyond the Walls." In *Participating in the Knowledge Society: Research beyond University Walls*, edited by R Finnegan, 1–20. Basingstoke, England: Palgrave Macmillan.

Flanagan, M., and P. Carini. 2012. "How Games Can Help Us Access and Understand Archival Images." *American Archivist* 75 (2): 514–37.

Fleurbaay, E., and A. Eveleigh. 2012. "Crowdsourcing: Prone to Error?" Paper presented at International Council on Archives Conference, Brisbane, Australia. http://ica2012.ica.org/files/pdf/Full%20papers%20upload/ica12Final00271.pdf (accessed October 26, 2015).

Flinn, A. 2007. "Community Histories, Community Archives: Some Opportunities and Challenges." *Journal of the Society of Archivists* 28 (2): 151–76. doi:10.1080/00379810701611936.

Flinn, A. 2010. " 'An Attack on Professionalism and Scholarship'? Democratising Archives and the Production of Knowledge." *Ariadne* 62 (January). http://www.ariadne.ac.uk/issue62/flinn/ (accessed October 26, 2015).

Grannum, G. 2011. "Harnessing User Knowledge: The National Archives' 'Your Archives' Wiki." In *A Different Kind of Web: New Connections between Archives and Our Users*, edited by K. Theimer, 116–27. Chicago, IL: Society of American Archivists.

Grant, S., R. Marciano, P. Ndiaye, K. E. Shawgo, and J. Heard. 2013. "The Human Face of Crowdsourcing: A Citizen-Led Crowdsourcing Case Study." In *2013 IEEE International Conference on Big Data*, 21–24. doi:10.1109/BigData.2013.6691679.

Hall, H. 1908. *Studies in English Official Historical Documents*. Cambridge, England: Cambridge University Press.

Harris, V. 2009. "Against the Grain: Psychologies and Politics of Secrecy." *Archival Science* 9 (3): 133–42. doi:10.1007/s10502-009-9096-z.

Haythornthwaite, C. 2009a. "Crowds and Communities: Light and Heavyweight Models of Peer Production." In *Proceedings of the 42nd Hawaii International Conference on System Sciences*, 1–10. Los Alamitos, CA: IEEE. doi:10.1109/HICSS.2009.137.

Haythornthwaite, C. 2009b. "Online Knowledge Crowds and Communities." Reno, NV: Center for Basque Studies. doi:2142/14198.

Hedstrom, M. 2002. "Archives, Memory, and Interfaces with the Past." *Archival Science* 2 (1): 21–43. doi:10.1023/A:1020800828257.

Hildrum, J. M. 2009. "Sharing Tacit Knowledge Online: A Case Study of E-Learning in Cisco's Network of System Integrator Partner Firms." *Industry and Innovation* 16 (2): 197–218. doi:10.1080/13662710902764360.

Hill, A. 2004. "Serving the Invisible Researcher: Meeting the Needs of Online Researchers." *Journal of the Society of Archivists* 25 (2): 139–48. doi:10.1080/0037981042000271466.

Holley, R. 2009. *Many Hands Make Light Work : Public Collaborative Text Correction in Australian Historic Newspapers*. Canberra: National Library of

Australia. http://www.nla.gov.au/ndp/project_details/documents/ANDP_ManyHands.pdf (accessed October 26, 2015).

Hurley, C. 1994. "The Australian ("Series") System: An Exposition." In *The Records Continuum: Ian MacLean and Australian Archives First Fifty Years*, edited by S. McKemmish and M. Piggot, 150–72. Clayton, Victoria: Ancora Press in association with Australian Archives.

Hurley, C. 2011. "Strength below and Grace Above: The Structuration of Records." Rio de Janeiro, Brazil. http://infotech.monash.edu/research/groups/rcrg/publications/strength-below.pdf (accessed October 26, 2015).

Huvila, I. 2008. "Participatory Archive: Towards Decentralised Curation, Radical User Orientation, and Broader Contextualisation of Records Management." *Archival Science* 8 (1): 15–36. doi:10.1007/s10502-008-9071-0.

Huvila, I. 2011. "What Is a Participatory Archive? For Real(?)." Blog post. *Isto Huvila's Blog*, August 31. http://www.istohuvila.se/what-participatory-archive-real (accessed October 26, 2015).

Iacovino, L. 2015. "Shaping and Reshaping Cultural Identity and Memory: Maximising Human Rights through a Participatory Archive." *Archives and Manuscripts* 43 (1): 29–41. doi:10.1080/01576895.2014.961491.

Jenkinson, H. 1922. *A Manual of Archive Administration Including the Problems of War Archives and Archive Making*. Oxford, England: The Clarendon Press.

Jenkinson, H. 1948. *The English Archivist: A New Profession, Being an Inaugural Lecture for a New Course in Archive Administration Delivered at University College, London, 14 October, 1947*. London: HK Lewis.

Justesen, S. 2004. "Innoversity in Communities of Practice." In *Knowledge Networks: Innovation through Communities of Practice*, edited by P. M. Hildreth and C. Kimble, 79–95. Hershey, PA; London: Idea Group Publishing.

Kaplan, E. 2002. " 'Many Paths to Partial Truths': Archives, Anthropology, and the Power of Representation." *Archival Science* 2 (3): 209–20. doi:10.1007/BF02435622.

Karp, I., and S. Lavine, eds. 1991. *Exhibiting Cultures: The Poetics and Politics of Museum Display*. Washington, D.C.: Smithsonian Institution Press.

Kennedy, M. 2009. "Cautionary Tales: Archives 2.0 and the Diplomatic Historian." *Ariadne* 61 (October). http://www.ariadne.ac.uk/issue61/kennedy/ (accessed October 26, 2015).

Ketelaar, E. 2001. "Tacit Narratives: The Meanings of Archives." *Archival Science* 1 (2): 131–41. doi:10.1007/BF02435644.

Ketelaar, E. 2005. "Sharing: Collected Memories in Communities of Records." *Archives and Manuscripts* 33 (1): 44–61.

Krause, M. G, and E. Yakel. 2007. "Interaction in Virtual Archives: The Polar Bear Expedition Digital Collections Next Generation Finding Aid." *American Archivist* 70 (2): 282–314.

Lambert, R. D. 1995. "Looking for Genealogical Motivation." *Families—Journal of the Ontario Genealogical Society* 34 (3): 149–60.

Lambert, R. D. 1996. "Doing Family History." *Families—Journal of the Ontario Genealogical Society* 35 (1): 11–25.

Landis, W. E. 2002. "Nuts and Bolts: Implementing Descriptive Standards to Enable Virtual Collections." *Journal of Archival Organization* 1 (1): 81–92. doi:10.1300/J201v01n01_07.

Lankes, R. D., J. Silverstein, S. Nicholson, and T. Marshall. 2007. "Participatory Networks: The Library as Conversation." *Information Technology and Libraries* 26 (4): 17–33. doi:10.6017/ital.v26i4.3267.

Lehane, R. 2006. "Allowing Talking in Virtual Reading Rooms: User-Contributed Content and Online Archive Finding Aids." Sydney, Australia. https://deffeblog.files.wordpress.com/2007/11/social-archives.pdf (accessed October 26, 2015).

Light, M., and T. Hyry. 2002. "Colophons and Annotations: New Directions for the Finding Aid." *American Archivist* 65 (2): 216–30.

Looseley, R., and F. Roberto. 2009. "Museums and Wikis: Two Case Studies." In *Museums and the Web 2009: Proceedings*, edited by J. Trant and D. Bearman. Toronto: Archives and Museum Informatics. http://www.archimuse.com/mw2009/papers/looseley/looseley.html (accesed October 26, 2015).

MacNeil, H. 2009. "Trusting Description: Authenticity, Accountability, and Archival Description Standards." *Journal of Archival Organization* 7 (3): 89–107. doi:10.1080/15332740903117693.

MacNeil, H. 2011. "Trust and Professional Identity: Narratives, Counter-Narratives and Lingering Ambiguities." *Archival Science* 11 (3–4): 175–92. doi:10.1007/s10502-011-9150-5.

MacNeil, H. 2012. "What Finding Aids Do: Archival Description as Rhetorical Genre in Traditional and Web-Based Environments." Archival Science 12 (4): 485–500. doi:10.1007/s10502-012-9175-4.

McKemmish, S. 2011. "Evidence of Me ... in a Digital World." In *I, Digital: Personal Collections in the Digital Era*, edited by C. A. Lee, 115–48. Chicago, IL: Society of American Archivists.

McKemmish, S., L. Iacovino, L. Russell, and M. Castan. 2012. "Editors' Introduction to Keeping Cultures Alive: Archives and Indigenous Human Rights." *Archival Science* 12 (2): 93–111.

Meehan, J. 2009. "The Archival Nexus: Rethinking the Interplay of Archival Ideas about the Nature, Value, and Use of Records." *Archival Science* 9 (3–4): 157–64. doi:10.1007/s10502-009-9107-0.

Meissner, D., and M. A. Greene. 2010. "More Application while Less Appreciation: The Adopters and Antagonists of MPLP." *Journal of Archival Organization* 8 (3): 174–226. doi:10.1080/15332748.2010.554069.

Menne-Haritz, A. 2001. "Access—The Reformulation of an Archival Paradigm." *Archival Science* 1 (1): 57–82. doi:10.1007/BF02435639.

Moncrieff, J. 1999. "Is Strategy Making a Difference?" *Long Range Planning* 32: 273–76. doi:10.1016/S0024-6301(99)00033-3.

Mortimer, I. 2002. "Discriminating between Readers: The Case for a Policy of Flexibility." *Journal of the Society of Archivists* 23 (1): 59–67.

Moss, M. 2007. "Choreographed Encounter—The Archive and Public History." *Archives* 32 (116): 41–57.

Nardi, B. A., and V. O'Day. 2000. *Information Ecologies: Using Technology with Heart*. Cambridge, MA: MIT Press.

Newman, J. 2012. "Revisiting Archive Collections: Developing Models for Participatory Cataloguing." *Journal of the Society of Archivists* 33 (1): 57–73. doi:10.1080/00379816.2012.666404.

Nielsen, J. 2006. "Participation Inequality: Encouraging More Users to Participate." Webpage. *Jakob Nielsen's Alertbox*, October 9. http://www.nngroup.com/articles/participation-inequality/ (accessed October 26, 2015).

Nogueira, M. 2010. "Archives in Web 2.0: New Opportunities." *Ariadne* 63 (April). http://www.ariadne.ac.uk/issue63/nogueira/ (accessed October 26, 2015).

Nonaka, I., and H. Takeuchi. 1995. *The Knowledge-Creating Company: How Japanese Companies Create the Dynamics of Innovation.* New York; Oxford, England: Oxford University Press.

Noordegraaf, J. 2011. "Crowdsourcing Television's Past: The State of Knowledge in Digital Archives." *Tijdschrift Voor Mediageschiedenis* 14 (2).

Nov, O., O. Arazy, and D. Anderson. 2011. "Technology-Mediated Citizen Science Participation: A Motivational Model." In *Proceedings of the Fifth International AAAI Conference on Weblogs and Social Media.* AAAI, Barcelona, Spain. Palo Alto, CA: *Association for the Advancement of Artificial Intelligence.* http://www.aaai.org/ocs/index.php/ICWSM/ICWSM11/paper/viewFile/2802/3288 (accessed October 26, 2015).

Olson, J. S., J. Grudin, and E. Horvitz. 2005. "A Study of Preferences for Sharing and Privacy." In *CHI '05 Extended Abstracts on Human Factors in Computing Systems*, 1985–88. New York: ACM. doi:10.1145/1056808.1057073.

Owens, T. 2013. "Digital Cultural Heritage and the Crowd." *Curator: The Museum Journal* 56 (1): 121–30. doi:10.1111/cura.12012.

Palmer, J. 2009. "Archives 2.0: If We Build It, Will They Come." *Ariadne* 60. http://www.ariadne.ac.uk/issue60/palmer (accessed October 26, 2015).

Raymond, E. S. 1998. "The Cathedral and the Bazaar." *First Monday* 3 (3). http://firstmonday.org/ojs/index.php/fm/article/view/578/499 (accessed October 26, 2015).

Reed, B. 2005. "Beyond Perceived Boundaries: Imagining the Potential of Pluralised Recordkeeping." *Archives and Manuscripts* 33 (1): 176–98.

Ridge, M. 2011. "Playing with Difficult Objects—Game Designs to Improve Museum Collections." In *Museums and the Web 2011: Proceedings*, edited by J. Trant and D. Bearman. Toronto: Archives and Museum Informatics. http://www.museumsandtheweb.com/mw2011/papers/playing_with_difficult_objects_game_designs_to (accessed October 26, 2015).

Ridolfo, J., W. Hart-Davidson, and M. McLeod. 2010. "Balancing Stakeholder Needs: Archive 2.0 as Community-Centred Design."*Ariadne* 63 (April). http://www.ariadne.ac.uk/issue63/ridolfo-et-al/ (accessed October 26, 2015).

Rockwell, G. 2012. "Crowdsourcing the Humanities: Social Research and Collaboration'." In *Collaborative Research in the Digital Humanities: A Volume in Honour of Harold Short, on the Occasion of His 65th Birthday and His Retirement, September 2010*, edited by M. Deegan and W. McCarty, 135–54. Farnham, U.K.: Ashgate Publishing Ltd.

Rosenzweig, R. 2006. "Can History Be Open Source? Wikipedia and the Future of the Past." *Journal of American History* 93 (1): 117–46. doi:10.2307/4486062.

Rutner, J., and R. C. Sconfeld. 2012. "Supporting the Changing Research Practices of Historians." Ithaka: Ithaka S&R. http://www.sr.ithaka.org/wp-content/uploads/2015/08/supporting-the-changing-research-practices-of-historians.pdf (accessed October 26, 2015).

Samouelian, M. 2009. "Embracing Web 2.0: Archives and the Newest Generation of Web Applications." *American Archivist* 72 (1): 42–71.

Sassoon, J. 2007. "Sharing Our Story: An Archaeology of Archival Thought." *Archives and Manuscripts* 35 (2): 40–54.

Schaffner, J. 2009. "The Metadata Is the Interface: Better Description for Better Discovery of Archives and Special Collections." Dublin, Ohio: OCLC Research. http://www.oclc.org/research/publications/library/2009/2009-06.pdf (accessed October 26, 2015).

Sherratt, T. 2009. "Emerging Technologies for the Provision of Access to Archives: Issues, Challenges and Ideas." http://www.scribd.com/doc/24402148/Emerging-technologies-for-the-provision-of-access-to-archives-issues-challenges-and-ideas (accessed October 26, 2015).

Shilton, K., and R. Srinivasan. 2007. "Participatory Appraisal and Arrangement for Multicultural Archival Collections." *Archivaria* 63: 87–101.

Shirky, C. 2010. *Cognitive Surplus: Creativity and Generosity in a Connected Age*. London: Allen Lane.

Stebbins, R. A. 2007. *Serious Leisure: A Perspective for Our Time*. New Brunswick, NJ: Transaction Publishers.

Sternfeld, J. 2011. "Archival Theory and Digital Historiography: Selection, Search, and Metadata as Archival Processes for Assessing Historical Contextualization." *American Archivist* 74 (2): 544–75.

Theimer, K. 2010. *Web 2.0 Tools and Strategies for Archives and Local History Collections*. London: Facet.

Theimer, K., ed. 2011a. *A Different Kind of Web—New Connections between Archives and Our Users*. Chicago, IL: Society of American Archivists.

Theimer, K. 2011b. "Archivists and Audiences: New Connections and Changing Roles in Archives 2.0." In *A Different Kind of Web: New Connections between Archives and Our Users*, edited by K. Theimer, 334–46. Chicago, IL: Society of American Archivists.

Theimer, K. 2011c. "What Is the Meaning of Archives 2.0?" *American Archivist* 74 (1): 58–68.

Trant, J. 2008. "Curating Collections Knowledge: Museums on the Cyberinfrastructure." In *Museum Informatics: People, Information and Technology in Museums*, edited by P. F. Marty and K. B. Jones, 275–91. New York; London: Routledge.

von Hippel, E., and G. von Krogh. 2003. "Open Source Software and the" 'Private-Collective' "Innovation Model: Issues for Organization Science." *Organization Science* 14 (2): 209–23. doi:10.1287/orsc.14.2.209.14992.

Wasko, M. M. L., and S. Faraj. 2005. "Why Should I Share? Examining Social Capital and Knowledge Contribution in Electronic Networks of Practice." *MIS Quarterly* 29 (1): 35–57.

Whitelaw, M. 2009. "Visualizing Archival Collections: The Visible Archives Project." *Archives and Manuscripts* 37 (2): 22–41.

Wiggins, A., and K. Crowston. 2010. "Developing a Conceptual Model of Virtual Organisations for Citizen Science." *International Journal of Organisational Design and Engineering* 1 (1–2): 148–62. doi:10.1504/IJODE.2010.035191.

Yakel, E. 2000. "Thinking inside and outside the Boxes: Archival Reference Services at the Turn of the Century." *Archivaria* 49: 140–60.

Yakel, E. 2004. "Seeking Information, Seeking Connections, Seeking Meaning: Genealogists and Family Historians." *Information Research* 10 (1). http://www.informationr.net/ir/10-1/paper205.html (accessed October 26, 2015).

Yakel, E. 2006. "Inviting the User into the Virtual Archives." *OCLC Systems and Services: International Digital Library Perspectives* 22 (3): 159–63. doi:10.1108/10650750610686207.

Yakel, E. 2011a. "Balancing Archival Authority with Encouraging Authentic Voices to Engage with Records." In *A Different Kind of Web: New Connections between Archives and Our Users*, edited by K. Theimer, 75–101. Chicago, IL: Society of American Archivists.

Yakel, E. 2011b. "Who Represents the Past? Archives, Records, and the Social Web." In *Controlling the Past: Documenting Society and Institutions (Essays in Honor of Helen Willa Samuels)*, edited by T. Cook, 257–78. Chicago, IL: Society of American Archivists.

Yakel, E., and D. A. Torres. 2007. "Genealogists as a 'Community of Records.'" *American Archivist* 70 (1): 93–113.

Yakel, E., S. Shaw, and P. Reynolds. 2007. "Creating the Next Generation of Archival Finding Aids." *D-Lib Magazine* 13 (5/6). doi:10.1045/may2007-yakel.

Yeo, G. 2008. "Concepts of Record (2): Prototypes and Boundary Objects." *American Archivist 71 (1): 118–43.*

Yeo, G. 2010. "Debates about Description." In *Currents of Archival Thinking*, edited by T. Eastwood and H. MacNeil, 89–114. Santa Barbara, CA; Oxford: Libraries Unlimited.

Yeo, G. 2013. "Trust and Context in Cyberspace." *Archives and Records* 34 (2): 214–34. doi:10.1080/23257962.2013.825207.

13

GLAMs, LAMs, and Archival Perspectives

Jeannette A. Bastian

> *Archives, libraries and museums are memory institutions: they organise the . . . cultural and intellectual record. Their collections contain the memory of peoples, communities, institutions and individuals, the scientific and cultural heritage, and the products throughout time of our imagination, craft and learning. They join us to our ancestors and are our legacy to future generations. They are used by the child, the scholar, and the citizen, by the business person, the tourist and the learner. These in turn are creating the heritage of the future. Memory institutions contribute directly and indirectly to prosperity through support for learning, commerce, tourism, and personal fulfillment. (Dempsey 1999)*

In a 1982 *Archivaria* article, Canadian archivist Hugh Taylor reflected on archives and libraries together as stewards of cultural heritage and repositories of the nation's collective memory, writing that "there is a balance, a complementary symmetry between archives and libraries which if at times uneasy has great potential for a co-operative future based on a rich and varied heritage jointly achieved" (Taylor 1982–83, 130). In an address several years later to the Association of Canadian Archivists, Taylor pushed that partnership a little further by introducing the concept of the "integrated professional," noting, "there is a sense in which the dichotomy between library and archives is an illusion fostered by the dominance of print" (Taylor 2003, 152). Pondering the implications of nascent automation on media in all formats, Taylor urged archivists to broaden their thinking and, adding museums to the mix, concluded with this challenge: "Is it not time archivists, librarians, museum curators, and conservators sat around the table and did a little joint planning about the knowledge of the past that remains to us ... Should we have not only an integrated profession, but also an integrated concern which spans several professions? I rather think so" (2003, 158).

In his call for a more holistic configuration of cultural heritage institutions, Taylor's challenge was both a prescient harbinger of the technological future and reminiscent of past practices. The great library at Alexandria in the third century BC housed a dynamic mixture of texts, manuscripts, and objects and saw itself as a single repository of universal knowledge, a concept that much later undergirded the founding of major cultural institutions such as the British Museum and the Smithsonian Institution. Beginning around the seventeenth century, however, evolving differences in theories, purpose, interpretation, audience, organization and, most importantly, the developing technologies of print encouraged separation of "universal knowledge" into the specific component parts and purpose-built cultural institutions of today.

The similarities, differences, and overlaps among libraries, archives, and museums (LAMs, and more recently with the addition of galleries, GLAMs),[1] their relationships to one another, and the theoretical structures that have developed around the cultural heritage they maintain have encouraged rigid distinctions and well-defined borders. At the same time, these differences and affinities have also facilitated the blurring of those borders, both internally and externally. And while professionals in these areas have been generally committed to maintaining distinctions among these institutions, their collections, and the disciplines that undergird them, these distinctions have not always been easy for the public to understand.

Today, in a complex economic climate as well as an increasingly global one, the LAMs, both individually and together, are undergoing renewed scrutiny as well as dramatic changes. In some respects, these institutions seem to be taking a 360-degree turn back to the concepts of integrated knowledge, as technology offers vibrant and compelling paths to bridging differences, enhancing similarities, and taking advantage of overlaps.

For archivists, as for all cultural heritage professionals in the twenty-first century, the potential convergences of the LAMs are major issues as it becomes abundantly clear that users not only demand coherence, speed, completeness, and transparency of access, but that technology also increasingly offers the ability to deliver all of those things. Adding to these pressures, funders and governments, alert to the financial advantages of the digital environment, have been quick to encourage economies of scale. In this complex environment with many different stakeholders, archivists not only need a clear understanding of their own mission and a vision of where they fit in this cultural mix but also a recognition of the need to protect as well as project core archival values. As Robert Martin, former director of the Institute for Museum and Library Services, notes, "In spite of their similarities and in spite of the apparent momentum toward convergence, libraries are not archives and museums are not libraries. There are very real differences between these cultural heritage agencies" (Martin 2007, 83).

While physically like or complementary materials might reside in separate institutions, in separate parts of the same institution, or in multiple formats within an institution, the potentials of technology bringing these materials together intellectually are not only enticing but also have become imperatives and in some cases, mandates. These imperatives in turn raise many questions and concerns for cultural heritage institutions and cultural heritage materials, including those of viability, sustainability, and values.

Convergence of libraries, archives, and museums can be intrainstitutional or interinstitutional; it can merge materials within institutions, and it can merge institutions.[2] At an intrainstitutional level, a converging cultural heritage institution is one that combines library, archival, and museum material and is working toward implementing a set of standards and best practices that unite traditional theory and operations within these three disciplines (Bastian and Harvey 2014, 31). At an interinstitutional level, converging cultural heritage institutions can cooperate on many different levels, including federated searching, sharing resources, and linking related resources, essentially offering a wider array of content to a broader community of users than one institution could alone.

This essay examines the development of the LAMs with particular attention to the place and function of archives in the LAM environment. It will briefly review the history of convergence reflecting on the efforts toward convergence while pondering their efficacy, review case studies testing LAM concepts, and examine the lessons learned. As an essay in a book devoted to current archival trends and concerns, written by an essayist who advocates for strong archival voices, particular attention will be paid here to the potential role of archives as well as archivists in a convergence environment. We will also consider how archives fit into various convergence models and whether, viewed from the perspectives of both materials and discipline, archives stand to gain or lose in the LAM environment. And for all types of cultural institutions, is LAM success just a question of time, timing, and resources? Or is this still *only* a good idea?

Combinations of galleries, libraries, archives, and museums in a wide variety of hybrid institutions such as historical societies and cultural centers have existed over the centuries, with different ways of organizing, maintaining and providing access to information and cultural heritage often coexisting side by side. Many museums include libraries and archives, libraries often house artworks, and archives generally contain artifacts. But even hybrid institutions that mingle books, manuscripts, and artifacts generally maintain organizational distinctions. Historical societies, for example, presenting the history and heritage of a town or a region are often hybrid institutions that may physically exhibit materials in a wide variety of formats but will generally keep their intellectual arrangement separated or may choose to focus all their materials on one particular type of arrangement. For example, they may describe artworks and other artifacts as components of archival collections or catalog books and furniture equally as single items.

Convergence of cultural heritage institutions poses both organizational and more personal questions for the professions and professionals involved. As their institutions converge, so, likewise, do the professions converge? Do these institutions share the same missions? Do they have the same purposes, uses, and values? Are the public and the materials themselves best served by convergence? Does a cultural heritage umbrella resolve all differences by eliminating them and is that in the best interests of the materials or the users? And what about the education of these new professionals? Can and should archivists, librarians, and museum curators merge into Taylor's "integrated professional"?

Since the 1990s, as the affordances of technology began to become more apparent and the chimera of convergence a plausible reality, discussions around the issues posed by convergence have greatly accelerated, experimentation with different models has proliferated, governments, seeing opportunities to consolidate resources, have created mandates, and above all, the virtual environment has opened the door to solutions. That there is a natural affinity between archives, libraries, and museums seems beyond doubt as evidenced by the many institutions that combine two or all of these components. Whether that affinity naturally results in convergence, reconvergence, or close cooperation remains an open question.

For despite all the combinations, endeavors, studies, cases, and good intentions and notwithstanding acronyms and labels, convergence to a great extent remains a goal that seems logical to strive for but somehow continues to thwart the best intentions and often seems unattainable. The fact that both the means and the will toward convergence have now existed for decades, yet convergence is still an unrealized struggle in all but a few large institutions, primarily universities and government entities, raises important questions about its overall viability, particularly for small institutions in a severely resource-driven cultural climate. With so much effort for so little results, is convergence on a broad scale even achievable? Various experiments as well as advances and trends in digitization continually suggest that successes may be on the horizon, but the situation is further complicated because a consensus around convergence has not yet developed. While interest in convergence seems global, particularly on the part of national governments seeking to consolidate resources as well as provide more public access to heritage, there is not necessarily agreement on what it should actually look like. Each institution—and nation—interprets convergence in ways that best suit its own culture, political climate, and resources.

Concerns about standards, best practices, audience, and even terminology also play major parts in this discussion. But at the center of the debate lies a concern with the distinctiveness and integrity of each profession. Each of the LAMs has strong and specific theoretical frameworks that have been carefully honed and shaped to address all aspects of their relationship with the materials that they collect, preserve, maintain, and make accessible and the various publics that they serve. And it is these critical theoretical centers that are difficult to reconcile in ways that are equitable, both to the materials themselves and to the stewards and the users of the materials. How these professions can converge while maintaining their own identities is a key challenge to their success. As Paul Marty, a leading scholar of convergence, observes, "How can (or should) information professionals in libraries, archives and museums, and other cultural heritage organizations maintain the traditional distinctions between their collecting institutions while simultaneously providing access to information in ways that increasingly blur those distinctions for the users of their resources" (Marty 2014, 614).

More specifically, since we speak primarily from an archival perspective here, how do concepts of convergence impact archival values and core concepts? How should archivists think about convergence? What are the benefits, what are the concerns, what are the opportunities, and what are the hazards? In a recent study of three cultural heritage institutions in New Zealand, the author, Shannon Wellington, concludes that "more than any of the other entities studied, the Archives in all three institutions struggled to carve out real estate in the liminal organisational structures" (Wellington 2013, 295). For archivists, promoting cooperation and parity in a parallel environment rather than settling for second place in an unequal convergence might be the major challenge in this new cultural arena.

A BRIEF HISTORY OF THE LAMS

From the unity of the Mouseion/Library of Alexandria in the ancient world (third. century BC to thirtieth. century BC) to the fractured LAMs of the twenty-first century, cultural heritage institutions have pursued parallel paths that have, on the one hand, often intersected and intermingled and, on the other, built strong individual identities. Archeologist Beverly Butler writes that "the ancient Alexandrina brought together texts, learned men, and artefacts in an attempt to fuse 'Greek' heritage with aspirations of acquiring 'universal knowledge.' Writ larger, the archive and wider mythologisations of the city merge powerfully to cast the city as 'centre-point' as 'microcosm of the world' and as 'memory of the world" (Butler 2007, 17).

The early mission of "universal knowledge" has refracted into multiple missions that foster specific knowledge, particular theoretical perspectives, and distinct organizational structures. Understanding the source and history of this refraction can illuminate the development of libraries, archives, and museums individually as cultural institutions and also suggest some of the obstacles to as well as the promise of convergence. The genealogies of these three disciplines have been well recounted throughout the extensive literatures surrounding them. It is not the purpose of this chapter to recount that history again, but some background is useful in order to better understand the values and perspectives of each institution and the convergence pressures they face.

Background

Although the Library of Alexandria may be one of the oldest examples of a collection of diverse and varied knowledge, archives and records hold pride of place in terms of earliest recorded information. The dates are in millennia rather than centuries, recalling the earliest need to record transactions and where, as archival historian Ernst Posner has noted, "writing was invented to serve the administrator rather than the man of learning" (Posner 1972, 23). Examples of these administrative records have been discovered as far back as the eighth millennium BC in the form of *bulla*, inscribed pieces of clay used by the Sumerians for agricultural transactions as forms of identification and proof of authenticity. Bulla served as receipts, and they encapsulated clay tokens that represented the quantity and types of goods involved in the transaction.

Governments have created and maintained records throughout the ages. Modern archival thinking is rooted in the French Revolution, when public demand for access to their records necessitated methods of organization to meet those demands. The principle of provenance or *respect des fonds*, or organization by the context of creation, was born to meet that need and remains the central organizing principle of archival collections at all levels.

As the generally unpublished by-products of the actions and interactions of society, be it through government records, church records, correspondence, corporate accounts, manuscripts, diaries, blogs, e-mails, or electronic records, archives and records continue to serve a multiplicity of purposes. Although their primary purpose is as evidence of these actions and interactions, archives are also information sources for researchers. And as cultural records, they are repositories of societal memory.

Libraries also have an ancient history. Prior to Gutenberg's first printed book in 1439, the earliest libraries consisted of archives, collections of clay tablets in cuneiform script discovered in temple rooms in Sumer around

2600 BC and mainly consisting of the records of commercial transactions. Today, these cuneiform tablets can be found in museums.

Library collections have been discovered at all stages of civilization and in all geographic areas. Personal libraries existed in fifth-century Greece; the Chinese scholar, Liu Xiang, invented a cataloging system for the imperial library in the first century BCE. While a library can be simply defined as "a collection or group of collections of books and/or other print or non-print materials organized and maintained for use (reading, consultation, study, research, etc.)" (Reitz 2004), libraries both today and through the ages have not only been much more complex but also, as noted in the *Encyclopedia of Library and Information Science*, are continually changing and adapting to societal needs—an important point when considering convergence. The *Encyclopedia* asserts that "while generally defined as a collection of materials organized so that they may be easily identified and used by an individual or group, libraries have actually taken many forms over time, reflecting the cultures in which they are embedded and propelled by technological innovations and social currents" (Arns 2010, 3281). Nowhere is that flexibility better on display than in the public library movement of the late nineteenth century where collections of books gradually took precedence over "collections of material objects" (Given and McTavish 2010, 13).

Fueled by the building of Carnegie libraries, libraries became publicly available collections, organized and staffed by professional librarians and dedicated to public education, equitable access, and freedom of information. There are a number of distinct types of libraries—national, academic, public, school, and special—each serving targeted audiences and each with their own particular missions and purposes. Although today we think of libraries as primarily containing published materials, there are many significant manuscript collections as well as art and other cultural objects that are important aspects of library collections.

A museum has been defined by the International Council of Museums (ICOM) as "a non-profit, permanent institution in the service of society and its development, open to the public, which acquires, conserves, researches, communicates and exhibits the tangible and intangible heritage of humanity and its environment for the purposes of education, study and enjoyment" (ICOM, n.d.). Although the etymology of museums has been traced to the classical days of Alexandria, the museum as the institution we know today emerged from the "cabinets of curiosities" of the seventeenth century. Also known as "wunderkammer" or "rooms of wonder," cabinets of curiosities were eclectic collections of objects that spanned the world of the individual who collected them. These collections were not restricted to objects alone but could and did include books and manuscripts. Many of these private collections formed the basis of some of the great museums of today such as the British Museum and the Ashmolean.

At the same time, museums have also served a variety of publics and functions. Wellington observes that "fundamental to the mission of the museum and gallery as an institution is the selection, interpretation, preservation and exhibition of objects of cultural heritage that create and maintain culture and identity for their communities and wider society" (2013, 25). Today, museums have important educational as well as research functions. "The museum as we know it today grew out of a form of entertainment that slowly evolved into a deliberate practice of collecting," assert Margaret Hedstrom and John Leslie King (2004, 5), also noting that museums as they evolved from the cabinets of curiosities also served research and scholarly functions and increasingly an education mandate. Importantly, Wellington similarly notes that "a shift in ideology [in the modern museum] can be traced through a change from passive collection development and classification towards an active, open and user centric approach to the interpretation and communication of cultural information" (2013, 26).

Despite the initial conceptual, intellectual, and physical unity of LAMs, changes in production, purpose, organization, and use inevitably led to divisions. As Deanna Marcum points out, "In time, the story continues, cracks in the unified face of collecting began to appear. The development of printing increased the quantity as well as the availability of books. The 'rational bureaucratization of governments' led to the separation of official records from other kinds of documents. Expanding collections outgrew their cabinets and, by the eighteenth century, became more specialized in subjects, objects, places, or times to make them more manageable. Housing for them split off into archives, museums, and libraries, each focusing on a different form of information and on users of different kinds. Slowly, professionalism within these collecting institutions evolved" (Marcum 2014, 82). To this list of distinctiveness, the education of professionals within each of these evolving disciplines should also be added, since it is largely through that distinctive education that separate disciplines have emerged.

Values

While the vision of merging or overlapping cultural heritage institutions is not new, efforts to merge these institutions through the affordances of technology may represent a turning point in these endeavors. But side by side with technology, a primary consideration in reviewing and forecasting the potential of convergence is the question of values. This essay suggests that it is not so much the physical disparities among LAMs that separate them as their conceptual, theoretical, and functional differences. While merging, fusing, and connecting information in the quest toward "universal knowledge" may be an aspiration with ancient roots and one that has taken on new energy with the emergence of digital technologies, the connecting, merging, and possibly fusing of equally relevant values and theories may be the greatest challenge facing professionals trying to bring these areas together. For, while "universal knowledge" may have been the initial impetus driving the eclectic assembling of diverse assortments of manuscripts, books, and objects and the construction of cabinet of curiosities, the division of these assortments also means the rechannelings of mission and purpose into different directions.

This essay suggests that what divide the LAMs are not so much the materials they collect and maintain but the values, theories, and intellectual constructs that drive their efforts, all of which, in turn, profoundly affect the ways in which they acquire, evaluate, organize, preserve, present, and use these materials. Again, Taylor points the way in a 1992 essay coauthored with Cynthia Durance. They write, "The distinction really lies in the way each profession approaches the material in its custody. . . . It is our contention that librarians and archivists (and museologists and art curators . . .) differ professionally only insofar as they approach the documentary heritage from a different point of view" (Durance and Taylor 1992,43).

As an example of these different approaches to materials, Durance and Taylor point to a collection of war paintings commissioned by the Canadian government in World War II and initially housed in the National Archives of Canada but later transferred to the National War Museum. The value of the paintings can be seen from many perspectives: as documentary evidence of the war and the roles of Canadian soldiers; information about how and where the war was fought; as artifacts of the war itself; and as artworks. They ask, "Where does this collection rightfully belong: in the National Library, the National Gallery, the National Archives, or the National Museum?" (Durrance and Taylor 1992, 43). Similarly, museums often exhibit papyri, clay tablets, and other forms of writing as artifacts, but these could also be viewed as archival records that contain information about ancient civilizations. Cave paintings may be artwork or they may be records that document events in the lives of the community or the artists.

Core values articulated by professional associations bring professional similarities and differences into sharper focus and reflect the ways in which each profession views its primary responsibilities. Library associations in both the United States and Canada, for example, support equal access to information, intellectual freedom, and accountability to their users. Archives, while sharing those values, add responsibility both to the materials in their charge and to the creators and donors of those materials. Museums put a premium on public use and education. And while all three disciplines highly value similar missions of preservation and use, their different perspectives are to a great extent reflected in the ways that each organizes its material and makes it accessible.

The fundamental organizing principle for archival records is provenance or *respect des fonds*, and this organization by creator, whether person, corporation, family, or government reflects the primary reasons for keeping archives—as evidence of actions and transactions. Archives are kept and preserved for their enduring value as evidence or information. Cataloging standards are the organizing principles that guide libraries, and these standards, shared internationally, support the library's primary mission of access to information at all different levels and to all publics. Museums organize their materials around exhibits with a primary function of public education. As one field museum states, "The exhibit is the principal avenue of learning. Exhibits are augmented by people-mediated programs and a visitor-oriented museum-wide staff, which reaches out to assist all visitors" (Smithsonian Institution 2002).

Canadian archivist Katherine Timms uses the descriptive practices of LAMs to illustrate both their differences and similarities. While in libraries, "description predominantly entails cataloguing and classification activities," in archives, "description involves research into the context of the records and their creators, including identifying and documenting relationships between records and groups of records." Museums "create preliminary descriptions as part of their accession files for internal administrative purposes. In addition, they catalogue and classify their collections." Timms points out that "descriptive practices may vary between archives, libraries, and museums but they may also be complicated within single institutions themselves" so that institutions with a variety of collections may also follow a variety of standards. As an example of this, she notes that "it is interesting to reflect on what constitutes a publication, record, or artifact. If a map or photo is framed or appears on a cookie tin, does it become an artifact? Is an old commercial film an archival record or publication? Is a rare book just a book or also an artifact or an archival document? Which designation takes precedence and why?" (Timms 2009, 74–75). While description is a practice shared by all three institutions, each has its own standards that may also overlap within the institutions themselves. The particular perspective and values of the institution may be the determiner as to which standard is emphasized.

At the same time, despite the differences in perspectives, the LAMs overall also share many values, including equitable access, diversity of materials, privacy and copyright concerns, strong ethical principles, and a firm belief in their social and public obligations to preserve, maintain, and make accessible the cultural record in all its forms and formats. While the LAMs may differ in purpose, in many respects, they are all cultural heritage and societal memory institutions and therefore share similar missions of social responsibility, not only to the present but also to the past and the future.

A LONG CONVERSATION: LITERATURE, CONVERGENCE, AND THE LAMS

Discussions around information convergence beginning around the mid-1970s focused not on the LAMs but on the potential for connections among information, communications, and technology. The early literature on convergence targeted computers and the developing virtual technology. The convergence addressed was that of the alignment of computers with information work.

Famously, Vannevar Bush in 1945 had already alerted the world to the dawning information era in his prophetic article, "As We May Think," in which he anticipated both the desktop computer and a version of Google in the form of the memex machine. Bush writes, "Consider a future device for individual use, which is a sort of mechanized private file and library. It needs a name, and, to coin one at random, 'memex' will do. A memex is a device in which an individual stores all his books, records, and communications, and which is mechanized so that it may be consulted with exceeding speed and flexibility. . . . Thus science may implement the ways in which man produces, stores, and consults the record of the race" (Bush 1945, 101).

Concerns about convergence revolved around information processing, data storage, telecommunications, and issues associated with digital transmission. By the early 1980s, however, the confluence of electronic transmissions from various sectors began to translate into concern for information policy. Inevitably, considerations of the various dispensers of information focused attention on knowledge institutions such as libraries. Implementing enhancements to knowledge accessibility by bringing automation to libraries rapidly became a central concern for information professionals. A 1986 *Library Journal* article, for example, reported on a meeting of the Seventh International Online Information Conference, sponsored by the British Library in London. Anticipating the iSchool movement by several decades, the author noted trends away from traditional libraries and toward information specialists, even going so far as to wonder whether the American Library Association could continue to require such a library-centered curriculum as part of its accreditation (Koenig 1984, 863–66).

Meanwhile, the many crossovers and similarities between libraries and archives had long encouraged thinking about them as closely related, particularly in the area of cultural heritage. Early articles in international journals in the 1970s such as *International Federation of Library Associations* and *ASLIB*[3] indicated a growing awareness of the importance of seeing libraries, archives, and museums as cultural heritage institutions and of understanding and taking advantage of the relationships among them. As an early advocate of the convergence between libraries and archives, former national archivist of the United States and dean of the University of Michigan School of Information, Robert Warner, observed in the early 1980s that "librarians and archivists, historically dissimilar in their training, outlook, methodology, and philosophy, are today facing very similar problems and challenges" (Warner 1986, 167).

It was through the recognition of those challenges, particularly as technology opened up new ways of organizing and accessing information, that the similarities between the LAMs began to outweigh the differences. The early

1980s, for example, saw the emergence of the MARC AMC format, a standards project jointly designed by a committee of the Society of American Archivists and the Library of Congress. As the then editor of the National Union Catalog of Manuscript Collections (NUCMC) pointed out, "It was not until the1980s that the growing impact of improved automation technology revealed to many members of both groups [librarians and archivists] that they had much in common and could benefit from mutual concern and cooperation" (Ostroff 1986, 1) Driven by automation, the need to provide access to their materials through standardized formats brought librarians and archivists closer together, at least as regards use.

Technology and use demands were also drivers in reconnecting libraries and museums, and connections among cultural education, public demands, and information, through the trilogy of the LAMs, continued to emerge in the 1990s. The formation, in the United States, of the Institute of Museum and Library Services (IMLS) in 1996 (an amalgamation of two government agencies, Library Services and Technology in the U.S. Department of Education and the Institute of Museum Services) not only reinforced the relationship between libraries and museums but also offered funding opportunities for promoting those relationships through cooperative projects. Changing perspectives on the roles of museums as venues for public education rather than as storehouses of objects suggested ways in which libraries and museums could partner to both inform the public and show the interrelationship of knowledge (Dilevko and Gottlieb 2003, 160–98).

In 1999, *Ariadne*, a Web-based journal with an international scope published a research framework for LAMs for the European Commission that focused on the commonalities between the LAMs and their potentials for networking and convergence in shared virtual spaces. The report identified several challenges for these entities that included service delivery, where the "user wants resources bundled in terms of their own interests and needs"; "living with the radically new," where traditional analog understandings of "document," "publication," or "exhibit" no longer applied in a digital environment; and "planning for the radically unpredictable," in times of fluid and rapid change. The report suggested multiple approaches to building "cross-domain collections," redefining archives, libraries, and museums as memory institutions that organized and preserved cultural heritage and made it accessible and emphasizing their need to work together (Dempsey 1999).

By the beginning of the new century, the LAM communities had started to coalesce around the idea of convergence, and a consensus tentatively began to emerge around the benefits of cooperation and sharing in the digital environment. In addition to IMLS, other government initiatives such as the establishment of Library and Archives Canada (LAC) in 2004 (a joining of the National Archives of Canada and the National Library) signaled the official support of convergence. How that convergence was to be achieved, however, remained an open question, one that, since the early 2000s, has fueled an extensive literature falling generally into several categories: historical/descriptive/prescriptive, case studies, and cautionary tales.

The Descriptive Literature of the LAMs

Detailing the genealogy of the LAMs through tracing the history of each discipline—both separately and together—has been the focus of much of the literature in the twenty-first century. The evolution of the LAMs from unified centers of knowledge to separate institutions and then returning toward reunification is a fascinating story of the impact of technology on society and one that in the telling illustrates both the pitfalls and benefits of separation and togetherness. It is a story that demonstrates the efficacy as well as the power and durability of cultural heritage throughout the history of mankind as well as the strength and power of cultural heritage institutions. Driven by the notion that by understanding their history better we will understand how to make them work together, the various histories of the LAMs follow similar trajectories but often reach different conclusions.

A 2004 article by Hedstrom and King, for example, traces the history of each institution in detail, focusing on the philosophical and political shifts toward LAM institutions in government and public perceptions through the centuries. They point to the benefits as well as the challenges of technology, specifically in the economic sphere where commercial services such as Amazon can cause "a subtle but important shift in the political and economic ecology of the LAM" (Hedstrom and King 2004, 23), because the LAM is not only traditionally seen as a public good but has also been supported by not-for-profit entities. Other challenges posed by the Web include information quality control and universal access. While Hedstrom and King acknowledge the "complementary nature of the traditional LAM and the emerging Web," they also affirm the crucial roles that libraries, archives, and museums, individually and together, play in the accumulation and long-term preservation of cultural heritage, universal access, and their critical research and education functions, concluding that "they constitute one of modern society's most vibrant and effective mechanisms for dealing with the extraordinarily challenging and conflicting demands to preserve parochial local perspectives in the service of identity formation and preservation ... LAM must work at the center of epistemological frameworks that are simultaneously coherent and destabilizing, for there is no alternative mechanism for progress in knowledge"(32).

Another study, supported by the European Union from 2003 to 2005, surveyed local LAMs throughout Europe with the purpose of designing models for information sharing across these domains. The objective was to "help ensure that local cultural heritage institutions and their users—ordinary citizens—are able to benefit from the European Commission's information policy" (Brophy and Butters 2007, 3). The study developed a model that included a greater understanding of user requirements, tools enabling users to create and manage content, collaborative systems within a local context, dissemination of information about content and services, and interoperability between systems.

Similar strategies around use as well as concerns about commercial reappropriation, reminiscent of views expressed by Hedstrom and King, were articulated in a 2007 issue of the journal *Rare Books and Manuscript Librarianship*, devoted entirely to the question of the emerging LAMs and reflecting presentations at the 2006 RBMS annual conference. Martin may have best captured the general sentiment observing that "the boundaries between types of cultural heritage institutions that we now accept as common are simply lines that we ourselves have drawn" (Martin 2007, 82).

Case Studies

The string of conferences and articles on convergence over the past decade may be indicators of the consensus building underway. If any consensus has yet been reached, it is that convergence, or at the very least, cooperation between cultural heritage institutions is not only in the best interests of access, use, and the development of collections and content, but it is also critical for the continued relevance of these institutions. Fueled by user demands for seamless access to collections, convergence also offers the potential for users to add value to what they have access to through enhancements and combinations (Bastian and Harvey 2014). It holds out the promise of creating a coherent and broader information society. As Jeannette Bastian and Ross Harvey write, "The driver for convergence is the use of technology for the representation, documentation, archiving, preservation and communication of cultural heritage knowledge. The outcome is the creation of new relationships and new knowledge by bringing digital data sets representing social and cultural activity together in novel ways."

A number of important case studies have tried to point the way toward how that might best be done. A pivotal study sponsored by the Research Libraries Group (RLG) in 2007 explored ways in which LAMs could collaborate particularly in the area of creating research environments for users, essentially to "move beyond the often-mentioned silos of LAM resources which divide content into piecemeal offerings" (Zorich, Waibel, and Erdway 2008, 8). The five institutions participating in a series of self-study workshops were all large and included a mix of the three disciplines within their institution. All were looking to further their own convergence. While recognizing that there were "no hard and fast rules for ensuring success in LAM collaborations," the study outlined a number of "catalysts" that could "help LAM partners find greater collaborative opportunities" (Zorich et al. 2008, 21). These included a vision shared by the partners; a mandate, possibly imposed by a government or by the institutions; incentives for the people involved in the collaboration; a game-changer, or a person or circumstances that would drive innovation, resources, and flexibility.

The critical role of these "catalysts" became clear in a 2012 study of digital convergence in small cultural heritage institutions (Bastian and Harvey 2014). Of the six institutions studied over a three-year period, each of which included a combination of library, archival, and museum collections and each of which wanted to find ways to digitally merge its collections, only one was ultimately successful. Its success was largely due to its access to technical resources, particularly technical expertise. In addition, it had an institutional mandate that actively supported bringing separate information sources, a vision of the final outcome, and, importantly, a cooperative organization structure for realizing that vision. Overall, this study concluded that "although many of the convergence problems seemingly centered on technical issues, the larger, overarching obstacles were not technical. Rather, they stemmed from the organizational culture at the sites, from competing interests between creators and preservers, and differing access and preservation philosophies" (Bastian and Harvey 2014, 38).

Researchers at the University of Toronto iSchool documented and analyzed the different types of convergence and collaboration experiences of five large institutions (two in Canada and three in New Zealand). Their findings supported both the need for vision, mandate, and resources and the importance of organizational culture. They identified motivations for convergence, including "to serve users better; to support scholarly activity; to take advantage of technological developments; to take into account the need for budgetary and administrative efficiencies; to adapt to an evolving understanding of digital surrogates as objects; and to obtain a holistic view of collections" (Duff et al. 2013). Significantly, the Toronto study also identified concern with professional identity as one of the greatest challenges for successful convergence, concluding that "it is a question of adaptation, as historically distinct professional identities and cultures learn the languages, practices, and expertise of their colleagues."

Vision, mission, organizational culture, professional identity—these concerns support and lead directly back to the critical question posed by Marty in the introduction to this essay, one particularly critical for archivists, namely how LAM professionals can maintain the distinctiveness, identity, integrity, and values of their separate collections while also providing access and use to those collections in ways that are seamless and interconnected.

ISSUES, CONCERNS, DISSENTING VOICES

The question of professional identity is only one of several concerns in the struggles toward LAM convergence. Not least is that of the identity and distinctiveness of the material itself. Will the varied many-dimensional contents of cultural heritage institutions work against uniqueness, resulting in sameness as they are digitized? Lisa M. Given and Lianne McTavish suggest that sweeping and indiscriminate digitization is not universally favored with opponents arguing "that the materiality of collections is being lost as information is homogenized and simplified for public consumption" (Given and McTavish 2010, 9). Along with devaluing the identity of the materials is the fear that convergence might also dilute individual areas of expertise and skills. The professional may be devalued as well.

Given and McTavish also suggest a number of additional convergence concerns. Pointing out that current movements toward convergence are really a "re-convergence" rather than a completely new idea, they demonstrate historical interdependency over time through the trajectories of a wide variety of cultural heritage institutions. Suggesting that "the lines between libraries, museums, archives and related organizations have become blurred in the last decade, particularly in the eyes of citizens who may be unfamiliar with the divided territory that has come to shape traditional approaches to gathering and providing access to cultural materials" (22), they echo Taylor in his call for a different kind of professional, one who is able to bridge the divides between these disciplines. They warn that "as long as librarians, archivists and museologists ... continue to be educated in isolation from one another ... real boundaries to collection, management, and access of materials will remain"(23).

Hedstrom and King point out that despite all the benefits of bringing cultural institutions together, each separately serves a particular unique and important societal function that must be maintained. Along similar lines, museum theorist Helena Robinson points to the specificity and contextualization of domain knowledge and the difficulties inherent in translating that knowledge into general policies and practices. She writes, "By considering the way in which information is created and transmitted, we see that libraries, archives and museums should not automatically be regarded as 'knowledge institutions' ... they do not and cannot transmit knowledge. Rather, they offer particular opportunities and settings where users can encounter different forms of *information*, creating knowledge and personal meaning for themselves" (Robinson 2014, 219). In other words, the context of the information is critical to engaging with it, finding and making meaning. The institution itself, the ways in which it keeps and interprets its materials, and even the way in which it provides access are all critical components of that context. Digital convergence risks destroying the context that each institution brings to its own content.

Robinson also questions the wide use of the term *memory institutions* to describe and characterize the LAMs, arguing that "their sweeping classification as 'memory institutions' in the public sector and the academy oversimplifies the concept of memory and marginalizes domain-specific approaches" and finding that these generalizations do not acknowledge the "nuance, diversity and polyphony in the representation of history and cultural memory" (2012, 414). She points out the relationships between the various processes and perspectives toward items and collections in archives, libraries, and museums and how each offers different paths to memory noting that "each collecting domain can be seen as a particular 'category of experience'; a framework for perception, corresponding to the specific ways in which each institution orders and assembles information resources" (2012, 423). Convergence threatens these distinctive interpretations, diminishing "the potential for collections to deliver a variety of important cultural narratives" (424) in favor of one perspective.

While proponents of the LAMs cite vision and mandate as central to success, critics point to those essentially top-down management functions as first steps toward commodification of these institutions and of the cultural heritage that they contain. They note with alarm the economic and corporate factors that both drive convergence and simplify complex structures. This dedifferentiation of the LAMs both threatens their distinctiveness and specialization and privileges consumerism over core principles. In this "corporatization of the cultural sphere," critics claim, "A trip to the mall and a visit to the local library or museum become increasingly difficult to distinguish from each other. While the day that the commercial sector and memory institutions have become completely enmeshed has not arrived (yet), there is an uncomfortable amount of spill-over from the former to the latter" (Cannon 2013, 79).

Although vision and mandate are crucial issues, as discussed earlier, it is perhaps the competencies and skills of the people who are to implement convergence that are not only the key resources but also present the greatest challenge. The importance of individual expertise was raised in the University of Toronto report where one of the professionals, Thomas Hickerson, interviewed for that research, himself leading a major convergence effort, writes that "it's not about worrying about what one knows or what everybody else knows, it's really about bringing knowledge sets together; not to mash them together, but in fact to align them toward a common practical application and then a broader mission" (Duff et al. 2013, n.p.).

Similarly, Timms notes that "this is not necessarily to say that professional theories and their resultant methodologies for each discipline should be neglected when enabling digital access to collections. Rather, the digital realm can act as a meeting point where digital collections from all three types of cultural heritage institutions can intersect and coexist" (2009, 68).

Along related lines, Marty suggests that the unique opportunities offered by convergence can only be realized if the professionals responsible for these materials and institutions are willing to cooperate. Meeting the needs of convergence will require "cultural heritage professionals who can transcend the traditional boundaries between libraries, archives and museums in the information age. They will need the ability to maintain key distinctions between libraries, archives and museums on the back end, while making information access more universal and more transparent on the front end" (2014, 624). And so the education of LAM professionals is a central issue in bringing the LAM disciplines together.

EDUCATING FOR CONVERGENCE

Education is emerging as an important factor in bringing the LAMs closer together, specifically, education in information science and digital technologies. Marty highlights the role of educators in the LAM process, pointing to "the ability of educators to meet the information needs of cultural heritage organizations and to encourage closer relations between education and practice in library and information science, museum studies, and archival studies programs" (Marty 2009) as critical to the success of convergence.

For similar reasons, Given and McTavish endorse the iSchool movement as a potential path to seamless integration basing this belief on their understanding that "what the iSchools do offer at present . . . is a consistent theory of knowledge not based on distinctions between objects but based on their complimentarity, in keeping with nineteenth-century ideals" (2010, 25).

However, interdisciplinarity is also a key. Information theorist Jennifer Trant points out that "current methods of training librarians, archivists and museum professionals emphasize the historic differences between these types of institutions, rather than their emerging similarities" (Trant 2009, 380). Trant offers a laundry list of curricula items from management to cultural policy to digital representation and managing digital collections, all of which emphasize the connectedness and interrelationship of the institutions. Above all, she emphasizes that "any 'shared practice' needs to reflect differences" (387).

Over the past several years, a hybrid discipline is emerging, particularly in iSchools, that treats the LAMs as one cultural entity. Cultural Heritage Informatics is a theoretical framework that "generally refers to the intersection between computer science and cultural heritage; to the application of information technology to the legacies of the past that are found in cultural heritage institutions, such as libraries, archives, and museums. Cultural heritage informatics focuses on the use of technology for the representation, documentation, archiving, preservation, and communication of cultural heritage knowledge" (Bastian and Harvey 2014). One of the goals of Cultural Heritage Informatics is the creation of new or additional cultural value by the bringing of disparate data sets together.

Curriculum in cultural heritage and museum studies is beginning to appear in a number of library and information schools in the United States and Canada, complementing the already robust course offerings in digital preservation, digital stewardship, and digital asset management.[4]

Currently, Cultural Heritage Informatics curricula in schools of information attempt to introduce students to all LAM environments, focusing on the differences and similarities in theory, organization, and access. Ideally these curricula should take full advantage of all the diverse offerings in schools of information, offerings that may range from rare books to archives to the preservation of digital assets. Field studies where students have opportunities for experimentation work with cultural institutions is an essential component in recognizing both the realities as well as the possibilities of convergence. That the information profession has recognized that LAM convergence requires a LAM education is an encouraging portent for the viability of both.

ARCHIVES IN A GLAM ENVIRONMENT—CONVERGENCE FOR ARCHIVISTS

The 2008 study *Beyond the Silo of the LAMs: Collaboration among Libraries, Archives and Museums* includes the comments of one participant who felt it was time "to start focusing energies on making rare and unique materials a valuable part of the information landscape." But, as the study indicated, "While the inclination by campus-based LAM's was to do so by focusing on delivery and access ... current patterns of user access and engagement increasingly take place at a broader level ... This very real requirement may motivate cross-domain collaborations aimed at increased access to cultural heritage collections" (Zorich et al. 2008, 34–35). In this environment, the uniqueness of archival collections are key offerings that bring added value to the information in libraries and museums.

The literature on the LAMs has tended to conflate archives and libraries, but in practice, this ignores critical functions of archives, particularly those related to records and records management. Despite similarities in the preserving of cultural heritage information, archives and libraries are not the same, and convergence should not make them so. Braden Cannon quotes from a presentation to the Archives Society of Alberta by archival theorist Terry Cook who suggested that convergence among memory institutions "does not mean that librarians and archivists are interchangeable, that the archival focus on context and research need be jeopardized, that curating digital objects using shared methods and technologies in libraries and archives means that rich knowledge about such media as maps or photographs, or records classification systems, or rare books, or the history of records and their creators, should disappear into some bland new 'information professional' " (Cannon 2013, 84). In a similar vein, librarian Gerald Beasley, defining the differences among libraries, archives, and museums, suggests that while libraries are all about systems, museums are all about programs and that "it is sheer hubris on the part of librarians to believe that they organize knowledge. They do not. Archivists do that and museum curators do that. Librarians just apply various systems to pre-organized knowledge and then answer questions about what they have done" (Beasley 2007, 24).

Archivists bring a unique and invaluable perspective to the LAMs. The story of the Myron Eells collection is apocryphal. The collection, created in the nineteenth century was, in the collecting tradition of the times, a mixture of records, books, and artifacts. Following the death of the collector in 1907, the collection was dispersed into its component parts—the books were cataloged as items and became part of a library, the objects and artifacts formed the beginnings of a natural history museum, and the manuscript materials and personal papers were described as collections using the principle of provenance. Today, the author of this history speculates, "It might be possible to digitally bring all these items together, while information about and items from the Eells' collection live in different systems and departments, Eells' collection could be reunified in a digital information environment by the creator" (Paulus 2011, 197).

Archivists have been doing just that for a long time. Bringing this collection together digitally as one fonds could satisfy archival requirements of provenance, would unify the collection, and might also offer an example of how a collection could be organized in many different ways at the same time. While the umbrella is the Eells collection, the component parts might still be accommodated with the added value of being united within one context.

If, through the LAMs, the goal of a memory institution is to combine "digital surrogates of the collections of archives, libraries and museums in rich interactive environments and . . . to preserve this content for future generations and support its use and management over time" (Schweibenz 2004, 3), then preserving context is equally, if not more, important in order that this memory can be understood by future generations. Archives may offer unique material to the convergence of the LAMs, but their unique theory of provenance offers an organizing principle that can accommodate this convergence and retain the contextualization that might easily be lost in a digital environment.

CONCLUSION

> *Librarians, archivists, curators, and museum educators, among all people, must know best that collections are not a static heritage but rather comprise countless changing images and ideas; they require reinvention and rethinking, generation by generation. Perhaps we need to remind ourselves every day that we are not living or speaking a text that has already been written for us, but one that might best be described as flowing streams of the possible, generated in the moment-by-moment conversations and questions of users. (Carr 2002, 288)*

Like King Canute on the seashore, information professionals cannot hold back the tides of digitization, but they can surf the waves of cooperation and perhaps, convergence. How that could be done might require some adjustments in current thinking among GLAM professionals that include sharing and accommodation. Understanding and acknowledging each discipline as being equal avenues to information may be one fruitful way to begin working together. Recognizing each of the LAMs as a memory institution in its own right and an equal contributor to society's collective memory may be another.

Each of the LAMs offers paths to a particular type of knowledge, and each needs to be similarly valued. Rather than the convergence of institutions, the convergence of skills or distinct professional competencies of individual archivists or librarians maybe yet another way of thinking about what each profession has to offer.

Librarians and archivist may overlap in their thinking, but their theoretical framework and their practices are not the same. Yet, each has a valuable knowledge perspective, a way of organizing and presenting information that contributes to a wider understanding of the materials in their charge. Archives and libraries should be understood and valued for their differences as well as their similarities. Museums and galleries are not outliers in the information arena but similarly offer ways of thinking about information that adds new dimensions and are, in their visual aspects, particularly relevant in a digital arena.

Employing all theories to figure out what serves the user best maybe the primary role of information professionals in a convergence environment. Overcoming concerns about professional identity and acknowledging the contributions of all identities equally maybe the ultimate way to cooperate. While convergence is undoubtedly about vision, mandate, and resources, ultimately it is about having, then sharing a point of view and recognizing and accepting others. That is where we start.

ENDNOTES

1. LAM will be used throughout this paper rather than GLAM as the more recognized terminology. LAM implicitly includes galleries as part of museums.

2. LAM convergences both within and between institutions abound and are growing rapidly. Some examples include a number of digital convergence initiatives online at http://www.digitalpreservation.gov/, hosted by the Library of Congress; Library and Archives Canada merged its national archives and national library in 2004, and, through digital initiatives, they provide access across their collections at http://www.bac-lac.gc.ca/eng/Pages/home.aspx; the Online Archive of California Web site, http://www.oac.cdlib.org/, serves as a portal for library and archives collections across California; the Harvard University Library offers access to selected digital collections from across Harvard's libraries and archives at http://lib.harvard.edu/digital-collections.

3. For examples, see, Josephine Fang, "Professional Associations at the National Level: A Survey of Their Major Interests," *IFLA Journal* 2 (December 1976): 237–41, and Lord Donaldson, "The Dissemination and Preservation of Information," *Aslib Proceedings* 29 (1977): 272–78.

4. Examples include Catholic University, Kent State University, Simmons College, University of Toronto.

REFERENCES

Arns, J. W. 2010. "Libraries." *Encyclopedia of Library and Information Science*, 3rd ed, 3281–3286. Boca Raton, Florida: CRC Press.

Bastian, J. A., and R. Harvey 2014. "Experiments in Cultural Heritage Informatics: Convergence and Divergence." In *Annual Review of Cultural Heritage Informatics, 2012–2013*, edited by Samantha Hastings, 29–42. London: Facet Books.

Beasley, G. 2007. "Curatorial Crossover: Building Library, Archives and Museum Collections." *RBM: A Journal of Rare Books, Manuscripts and Cultural Heritage* 8: 20–28.

Brophy, P., and G. Butters. 2007. "Creating a Research Agenda for Local Libraries, Archives and Museums across Europe." *New Review of Information Networking* 13 (1): 3–21.

Bush, V. 1945. "As We May Think." Originally published in *The Atlantic* (1932–1971) 176 (1): 101–08. http://www.theatlantic.com/magazine/archive/1945/07/as-we-may-think/303881/ (accessed October 5, 2016).

Butler, B. 2007. *Return to Alexandria: An Ethnography of Cultural Heritage, Revivalism and Museum Memory.* Walnut Creek, CA: Left Coast Press.

Cannon, B. 2013. "The Canadian Disease: The Ethics of Library, Archives and Museum Convergence." *Journal of Information Ethics* 22: 66–89.

Carr, D. 2002. "A Community Mind." *Public Libraries* 41 (5): 284–88.

Dempsey, L. 1999. "Scientific, Industrial and Cultural Heritage: A Shared Approach." *Ariadne, Web Magazine for Information Professionals* 22. http://www.ariadne.ac.uk/issue22/dempsey.

Dilevko, J., and L. Gottlieb. 2003. "Resurrecting a Neglected Idea: The Reintroduction of Library-Museum Hybrids." *Library Quarterly: Information, Community, Policy* 73 (2): 160–98.

Duff, Wendy M., Jennifer Carter, Joan M. Cherry, Heather MacNeil, and Lynne C. Howarth. 2013. "From Coexistence to Convergence: Studying Partnerships and Collaboration among Libraries, Archives and Museums." *Information Research* 18 (3). http://www.informationr.net/ir/18-3/paper585.html#.Usg_WBg1bw4 (accessed October 5, 2016).

Durance, C. J., and H. A. Taylor. 1992. "Wisdom, Knowledge, Information and Data." *Alexandria* 4: 37–61.

Given, L. M., and L. McTavish. 2010. "What's Old Is New Again: The Reconvergence of Libraries, Archives, and Museums in the Digital Age." *The Library Quarterly: Information, Community, Policy* 80 (1): 7–32.

Hedstrom, Margaret, and John Leslie King. 2004. "On the LAM: Library, Archive and Museum Collections in the Creation and Maintenance of Knowledge

Communities." http://www.oecd.org/education/educationeconomyandsociety/32126054.pdf (accessed October 5, 2016).

"ICOM, The World Museum Community." n.d. http://icom.museum/the-vision/museum-definition/ (accessed October 5, 2016).

Koenig, M. E. D. 1984. "The Convergence of Information Politics." *Library Journal* 109(8): 863–66.

Marcum, D. 2014. "Archives Libraries and Museums, Coming Back Together." *Information and Culture: A Journal of History* 49 (1): 74–89.

Martin, R. S. 2007. "Intersecting Missions, Converging Practice." *RBM: A Journal of Rare Books, Manuscripts and Cultural Heritage* 1: 80–88.

Marty, P. F. 2009. "An Introduction to Digital Convergence: Libraries, Archives, and Museums in the Information Age." *Archival Science* 8 (4): 247–326.

Marty, P. F. 2014. "Digital Convergence and the Information Profession in Cultural Heritage Organizations: Reconciling Internal and External Demands." *Library Trends* 62 (3): 613–27.

Ostroff, H. 1986. "From Clay Tablets to MARC AMC: The Past, Present and Future of Cataloging Manuscript and Archival Collections." *Provenance, Journal of the Society of Georgia Archivists* 4 (2): 1–11.

Paulus, M. J., Jr. 2011. "The Converging Histories and Futures of Libraries, Archives and Museums as Seen through the Case of the Curious Collector, Myron Eells." *Libraries and the Cultural Record* 46 (2): 185–205.

Posner, E. 1972. *Archives in the Ancient World.* Cambridge, MA: Harvard University Press.

Reitz, J. 2004. "Libraries." *Online Dictionary for Library and Information Science.* Santa Barbara, California: Libraries Unlimited. http://www.abc-clio.com/ODLIS/odlis_l.aspx (accessed September 21, 2016).

Robinson, H. 2012. "Remembering Things Differently: Museums, Libraries and Archives as Memory Institutions and the Implications for Convergence." *Museum Management and Curatorship* 27 (4): 413–29.

Robinson, H. 2014. "Knowledge Utopias: An Epistemological Perspective on the Convergence of Museums, Libraries and Archives." *Museum and Society* 12 (3): 210–24.

Schweibenz, W. 2004. "The Development of Virtual Museums." *ICOM News* 3. http://icom.museum/pdf/E_news2004/p3_2004-3.pdf (accessed September 21, 2016).

Smithsonian Institution. 2002, October. "The Making of Exhibitions: Purpose, Structures, Roles and Process." http://www.si.edu/Content/opanda/docs/Rpts2002/02.10.MakingExhibitions.Final.pdf (accessed September 21, 2016).

Taylor, H. A. 1982–1983. "The Collective Memory, Library and Archives as Heritage." *Archivaria* 15: 118–30.

Taylor, H. A. 2003. *Imagining Archives, Essays and Reflections.* Edited by T. Cook and G. Dodds. Lanham, MD: Scarecrow Press.

Timms, K. 2009. "New Partnerships for Old Sibling Rivals: The Development of Integrated Access Systems for the Holdings of Archives, Libraries, and Museums." *Archivaria* 68: 67–75.

Trant, J. 2009. "Emerging Convergence? Thoughts on Museums, Archives, Libraries and Professional Training." *Museum Management and Curatorship* 24 (4): 369–86.

Warner, Robert M. 1986. "Librarians and Archivists: Organizational Agenda for the Future." In *Archives and Library Administration: Divergent Traditions and Common Concerns*, edited by Lawrence J. McCrank, 167–176. New York: Haworth.

Wellington, S. 2013. "Building GLAMour: Converging Practice between Gallery, Library, Archive and Museum Entities in New Zealand Memory Institutions." PhD Dissertation. Victoria University of Wellington, New Zealand.

Zorich, D., G. Waibel, and R. Erdway. 2008. *Beyond the Silo of the LAMs, Collaboration among Libraries, Archives and Museums*. Report produced by OCLC Research. Published online at http://www.oclc.org/content/dam/research/publications/library/2008/2008-05.pdf (accessed September 21, 2016).

14

Community Archives[1]

Rebecka Sheffield

Community archives grow out of the desire to collect documentary heritage that reflects our common identities, experiences, and interests. Often used as a shorthand for the myriad community-based archival initiatives that come together outside of formal heritage networks, the term, *community archives*, can describe local history museums, historical societies, ethnocultural collections, religious and spiritual archives, resource centers, and sports and leisure clubs as well as a growing number of activist archives that preserve materials related to social justice struggles for human rights. In 2011, Archives Canada reported nearly 200 community archives in the country, mostly organized around efforts to preserve and promote interest in the history of a region or ethnocultural community, including First Nations and Inuit cultures. This number is likely a conservative estimate and does not include the inestimable number of digitally mediated archival initiatives that have emerged alongside the proliferation of Internet technologies over the past two decades. Nor does this figure include archives that are primarily personal collections with community oversight, such as the B.C. Gay and Lesbian Archives in Vancouver, British Columbia. As Anne Gilliland and Andrew Flinn (2013) note, the number of community archives and interest in these endeavors are increasing on a global scale, creating opportunities for archivists to reinvigorate their profession with new methodological approaches to documenting cultural heritage and making this material accessible to a broader public. At the same time, the upsurge in independent community archives has produced tensions among heritage professionals largely trained in European traditions concerned with the intellectual, legal and, physical control of records in formal archival networks (Flinn 2007, 2010, 2011). Whether community archives identify themselves as cultural or political endeavors, the very act of taking control over the documentation and storytelling about one's own community calls attention to issues of power and politics manifest in our traditional approaches to creating and maintaining archives.

This essay provides a brief history of the community archives movement in the United States, Canada, and the United Kingdom, where community archiving practices have received the most attention from scholars and practitioners. An overview of the literature on community archives examines current approaches to the study of these endeavors and offers several frameworks for understanding how and why communities come together to build collections. In the final section, I outline the four stages in a community archives life cycle and suggest opportunities for future research and learning.

THE COMMUNITY ARCHIVES MOVEMENT

Although local historical and antiquarian societies, churches, and regional museums have been collecting community records for more than a century, the veritable boom in community archives did not occur until the mid-1970s and early 1980s. Gilliland and Flinn (2013) suggest that interest in collecting community records is, in part, a response to the protest cycles that began in the 1960s, which included antiwar, feminist, civil rights, gay, and student activism emerging as expressions of larger postwar antiestablishment movements. Howard Zinn's groundbreaking 1970 speech at the annual meeting of the Society of American Archivists, in which he challenged archival neutrality, is also a probable catalyst for a growing awareness of and attention to community documentary projects. Zinn's insistence that the most powerful and wealthy "have the greatest capacity to find documents, preserve them, and decide what is or is not available to the public" pushed archivists to consider their complicity in reproducing heritage that is more concerned with nation building than adequately or accurately representing a plurality of voices, interests, or experiences (Zinn 1977, 20). As a result, the profession has been more responsive to community histories that have often been neglected by mainstream heritage organizations.

The rise of oral history and public history has also contributed to the growth of community archives. According to Robert Perks and Alistair

Thomson (2006), the discipline of oral history came into its own in the 1960s and 1970s, alongside the introduction of inexpensive and increasingly available portable tape recorders. In Britain, oral history grew out of folklore studies as a desire to create "history from below" and to document the experiences of "so-called ordinary working people" (2). In the United States, oral history remained more closely aligned with academic work until the 1960s, when public historians began to use the technique to make visible hidden narratives of African-American history. Perks and Thomson credit Alex Haley's best-selling book, *Roots: The Saga of an American Family*, with popularizing oral history within and outside of black communities. This encouraged communities not only to record their own "roots" but also to reinvest in local and community documentary heritage as a vital part of community building. Bella Dicks (2003) notes that governments faced with deindustrialization clamored to invest in these kinds of community documentation projects as a way to revitalize economically depressed regions through cultural tourism. Furthermore, John R. English (1983) suggests that community archives also benefited from the dearth of academic work for trained historians graduating in the 1970s, leading many to find jobs in the cultural sector.

In Canada, the Canadian Gay Archives, now the Canadian Lesbian and Gay Archives (CLGA), was likely the first organization to incorporate as a community archives without affiliations. Founded in 1973 with the working files of *The Body Politic*, a gay liberation newsmagazine, the archives took its first steps toward independence in 1978, after a police raid resulted in the removal of several boxes of archival material without explanation or recourse (Barriault 2009). The following year, the archives established its first board of directors and attempted to register as a nonprofit corporation (Sheffield 2015). The request was initially denied when the ministry responsible for approving new applications for corporate names determined that the organization did not meet the definition of an archives and thus could not use the term in its title. Referring to the *Concise Oxford Dictionary*, the ministry representative indicated in a letter to the organization that an *archives* should be narrowly defined as a "place in which public records are kept . . . or preserved by the various levels of government or by organizations funded by government" (quoted by Sheffield 2015, 67). With the help of the Toronto Area Archivists Group (TAAG), the board responded to the ministry and was able to show evidence that archives could not only be extensions of private or service organizations, as was the case with churches and corporations, but that they could also exist as stand-alone organizations, such as neighborhood historical collections. The registration was then accepted in early 1980, paving the way for other independent archives to formalize in the same way.

In the United Kingdom, government funding for job creation and skills exchange programs provided necessary financial support for local history projects throughout the 1970s and 1980s (Gilliland and Flinn 2013). A combination of new technologies, a resurgence of interest in cultural heritage, and the establishment of the Heritage Lottery Fund in 1994 also contributed to the growth of community archives by creating a sustainable infrastructure that allowed these kinds of organizations to flourish. David Mander (2009) and Gilliland and Flinn (2013) recognize the significance of the Community Multimedia Archives Network (Comm@NET), a not-for-profit technology support group that grew out of a community regeneration project in the 1990s. Comm@NET provided technological expertise for community documentation projects as well as the provision of simple preservation tools that could be adopted by groups with little technical ability. Mander describes how Comm@NET inspired the Hemsworth and District Community Archive in West Yorkshire, for example, to set up scanning sessions during which local residents brought in their family photographs and other important documents so that they could be copied and added to the archives. These sessions not only built up the collection but also contributed to community building for the town and surrounding area. Although Mander notes a lull in the growth of community archives in the late 1990s, he suggests that, by this time, policymakers had already started to integrate community collecting into new socioeconomic and cultural strategies designed to prepare society for the knowledge economy and to leverage these practices to provide necessary training in information communication technology (ICT) skills for a rapidly changing job market.

Community archives received another boost when The National Archives (TNA) and the Museums, Libraries and Archives Council (MLA) formalized investment in community archives with two significant projects that looked at the relationships between cultural heritage and social inclusion. In 2003, TNA founded a partnership program, known as Linking Arms, and launched the Community Access to Archives Project (CAAP) to examine community involvement in U.K. archives (CAAP 2004). The following year, TNA issued a press release that quoted Gerry Slater, CAAP project partner, Record Office of Northern Ireland, as stating:

> Community archive projects can contribute greatly to social inclusion, community development, skills development and the preservation of "unofficial" history, and are a means of encouraging non-traditional users to become involved with archives. (CAAP 2004)

The second project was the creation of an Archives Task Force under the auspices of the MLA, a development agency responsible for advising governments of policies related to heritage bodies. A core finding of the Archives Task Force was the need to develop a digitally mediated archives gateway that could link content from community archives across the United Kingdom and make this available to the public. Although the proposal was ultimately abandoned due to lack of funding, MLA's final report on the work of the task force highlighted the importance of investing in community archives as key players in building shared heritage across the United Kingdom's increasingly diverse ethnocultural communities (MLA 2004). The report also underscored the capacity of community archives to strengthen cultural identity and community development, provide opportunities for lifelong learning and intergenerational dialogue, and encourage regeneration through reminiscence and storytelling.

Perhaps the most influential development in the United Kingdom was the establishment of the Community Archives Development Group (CADG) in 2005. With support from TNA and the U.K. National Council on Archives, the CADG endeavored to build capacity for all community archives by coordinating activities at a national level. By 2011, the group had broadened its scope as the Community Archives and Heritage Group (CAHG) and formalized as a special interest group of the Archives and Records Association (U.K. and Ireland). It also developed a constitution, launched a Web site, established an annual conference, and awarded its first Community Archive and Heritage Award to celebrate innovative community practices (CAHG 2011). Today, the CAHG's vision statement outlines its commitment to:

- encouraging growth and increased participation in community archive and heritage initiatives across the UK
- acting as a forum to bring together those involved and interested in community archives to exchange ideas, to offer guidance and advice, and to develop standards and training which support the sustainability and accessibility of community archive and heritage collections
- providing a collective voice for community archives, heritage professionals and other stakeholders; and
- acting as a point of contact between community archive activists and other community development practitioners and cultural heritage professionals (including librarians, archivists and museum curators) to enable, where appropriate, mutually beneficial relationships. (CAHG 2011)

Gilliland and Flinn (2013) acknowledge the importance of the CAHG for strengthening heritage initiatives across the United Kingdom and for underscoring the value of these types of organizations for communities across Britain, Scotland, Wales, Ireland, and Northern Ireland. The CAHG now lists almost 600 community archives and heritage organizations in its directory, which acts similarly to the archives gateway once proposed by the CAAP (CAHG 2016).

Recently, a number of projects have suggested that we are experiencing a new wave of investment in community history documentation that takes advantage of digital technologies to pull in records and make them available to communities in a manner that transcends geographic and temporal boundaries. Michelle Caswell's (2014a, 2014b) work on the South Asian American Digital Archive (SAADA) is of particular note. SAADA was established in 2008 to bring together disparate records of South Asian-American experiences using a digital platform that catalogs, preserves, and makes available descriptive metadata to the community and to researchers interested in this history. The Digital Transgender Archives (DTA), which launched in 2015, serves as both a repository and union catalog by harvesting metadata from various partner organizations to build a database of primary source materials created by, for, and about transgender people around the world (DTA 2015). Similarly, the Archives of Lesbian Oral Testimony (ALOT) works with community documentarians to collect oral history records documenting lesbian experiences and makes these accessible through digitization (Chenier 2009, 2015, 2016). As Elise Chenier (2009) explains in her description of the ALOT project, the use of digital technologies can bring together dispersed collections that were previously rendered inaccessible because they were either recorded in now defunct media formats or housed in apartments or offices among personal collections. The act of bringing together dispersed records online, what Ricardo L Punzalan (2014) has called "virtual reunification," can not only present a more holistic understating of community history but also strengthen ties among community members. This new model for digital community archives does, however, veer slightly from other forms of community archives due to the complexity of the technology. Digital repositories, as in each of the examples provided here, require infrastructure to ensure that platforms are developed and supported over time, which can have implications for communities that cannot support these endeavors on their own and wish to remain autonomous. Community archives could work together to build collaborative platforms, as Grant Hurley (2016) suggests; however, this will require coordination.

SCHOLARLY RESEARCH ON COMMUNITY ARCHIVES

Archival scholars paid little attention to the work of community archives until the early 2000s, when a series of studies were published that examined the relationships among archives, communities, and collective memory. One of the most significant of these, Jeannette Bastian's *Owning Memory: How a Caribbean Community Lost Its Archives and Found Its History*, grew out of the author's dissertation project about the value of records to the people of the U.S. Virgin Islands. A former colony of Denmark, the Virgin Islands were purchased by the United States in 1917, which resulted in the transfer of nearly all governmental records of the colonial rulers back to Europe. Bastian's case study investigates the impact of this loss of documentary heritage and the efforts of Virgin Islanders to rebuild their "house of memory" (Bastian 2003, 13). Although the case itself focuses on state recordkeeping activities and does not look specifically at community archives, Bastian introduces useful concepts for the study of communities and recordkeeping. In particular, her notion of "community of records," which refers to a community as both a "record-creating entity and as a memory frame that contextualizes the records it creates," has been picked up in subsequent work on community archives (3). Eric Ketelaar (2005) uses the concept to discuss how records can shape community identities; Andrew Flinn and Mary Stevens (2009) use community of records to describe the intimate and emotional connections that communities have to their own documentary heritage. Randall Jimerson (2006) responds by suggesting that one of the primary reasons that ethnocultural groups, gays and lesbians, and others have created their own archives is to maintain custody over their own documentary heritage and to manage its access, presentation, and interpretation. Bastian's coedited anthology, *Community Archives: The Shaping of Memories*, brings many of these discussions together in what is likely the first collection of scholarly work concerned specifically with community archives (Bastian and Alexander 2009).

A second major study is the U.K. Arts and Humanities Research Council-funded Community Archives and Identities project, led by University College London (UCL) researchers Mary Stevens, Andrew Flinn, and Elizabeth Shepherd. Launched in 2008, the 20-month project aimed to investigate the potential benefits of community archives and heritage bodies. Flinn, who had helped draft the initial vision statement of the CADG, was interested in learning more about how community archives can contribute to cohesive multicultural society and how these organizations might be better supported by professional archivists. Framed as a collaborative and participatory study, the project involved four community archives with activist roots: Future Histories, rukus!, Moroccan Memories, and Eastside Community Heritage. Researchers looked at the particular political and social contexts that gave rise to these initiatives and how the collections have contributed to the production of public histories, exhibitions, and other interactions. In the final report, Flinn, Shepherd, and Stevens (2009) recognize a growing interest in community archives as a "new and rich source" of heritage material and note a significant number of collaborations between community groups and professionals to preserve, catalog, and make accessible community-based collections (2).

The Community Archives and Identity project has produced more than a dozen articles and scholarly presentations, largely focused on the community archives movement in the United Kingdom and issues related to community collecting practices, autonomy, and professionalism. Flinn, Stevens, and Shepherd (2009) explore the motivations for the founding of grassroots archival projects and report that some custodians and creators of these collections are determined to remain autonomous from formal heritage networks. Direct ownership and physical custodianship are primary reasons for keeping collections in the community for the foreseeable future. Stevens, Flinn, and Shepherd (2010) argue that mainstream publicly funded archives in the United Kingdom need to develop more flexible, sensitive relationships with community archives that not only ensure long-term preservation of material but also allow communities to retain custody and control of their records. Flinn (2010) acknowledges the tension between professional archivists and what he calls the democratizing of archives and the production of knowledge through community-led endeavors. The UCL research team has also contributed to other scholarly projects on community archives, including a chapter in Bastian and Alexander's *Community Archives* (Flinn and Stevens 2009). An edited transcript of an interview with rukus! founders Ajamu X and Topher Campbell appears in *Archivaria*'s 2009 special issue on queer archives (X, Campbell, and Stevens 2009). The unusual format of the article is intended to foreground the voices of community activists in a publication otherwise intended for the professional archivist.

The body of literature produced by the UCL team has stimulated an entire cohort of writing about community archives. If not directly influenced by the UCL study, projects such as Lyz Bly and Kelly Wooten's (2012) *Make Your Own History: Documenting Feminist and Queer Activism in the 21st Century* and Alana Kumbier's (2014) *Ephemeral Material: Queering the Archive* appear to benefit from the increased attention to community archiving practices. My own doctoral research on the emergence, survival, and sustainability of four lesbian and gay archives was aided significantly by the Community Archives and Identities project (Sheffield 2015).

Another wave of scholarly interest in community archives has grown out of the interdisciplinary fields of cultural studies, feminist studies, diaspora studies, and ethnocultural studies. While much of this literature is only tangentially related to archival methodologies or practices, some writing has found its way into archival literature as an avenue to talk about the aspirational and symbolic power of community archives. Stuart Hall (2001) writes about the power of archives to recognize the existence of previously unexplored histories, and he sees the moment of constituting an archives as foundational. This sentiment is echoed in Arjun Appadurai's (2003) claim that an archives is a "deliberate project ... based on the recognition that all documentation is a form of intervention" (24). The work of community archiving is not just about collecting the records of a community but also a political project to both legitimize the experiences of this group and as a creative endeavor that reflects the values of this group. Ann Cvetkovich's (2003) *An Archives of Feelings: Trauma, Sexuality and Lesbian Public Cultures* repositions community archives as potentially reparative spaces, where marginalized people can create shared heritage to resist everyday traumas of sexism and homophobia and to strengthen community and individual identities. Kate Eichhorn (2013) picks up Cvetkovich in her book,

The Archival Turn in Feminism: Outrage in Order, in which she examines the power of community-built collections to inspire new generations of feminists, even when these collections have been institutionalized and no longer reside in the communities that created them. This interdisciplinary work has been taken up by archival scholars such as K. J. Rawson (2009), Mél Hogan (2009), Michelle Caswell (2014a), Jamie A. Lee (2016), and Marika Cifor (2015). Cristine Paschild's (2012) critique of the emphasis of positive identity construction and Caswell's (2014b) response also offer insight into the complexities of engaging with and working to sustain community archives from a professional standpoint.

As scholarly interest in community collecting practice has swelled, community archives have also become an entrenched part of archival education. In Canada, the nature and characteristics of community archives are taught as part of courses on personal archives (University of British Columbia) and specialized archives (University of Toronto). In the United States, archival studies programs at University of California—Los Angeles and Simmons College now offer entire courses on community, recordkeeping, and archival practices. Whether components or features of programs, community archives and the increasing body of literature on community-led archival practices offer emerging heritage workers the opportunity to reflect on the role of these organizations in society and the impact they have on professional practices.

WHAT ARE COMMUNITY ARCHIVES?

Despite growing interest in community archives as both a critical practice and community building exercise, much of the literature continues to evoke *community archives* without drawing a compass around the meaning of this term. One of the challenges in defining *community archives* is that the term itself is a composite of two already deeply contested words. As Flinn, Shepherd, and Stevens (2009) have shown, the term *community* is often little more than a "reductive euphemism for an ethnic or faith community" (3). Emma Waterton and Laurajane Smith (2010) suggest that this rather simplistic understanding of community does not take into account the considerable variability in what creates community, how these social groupings emerge, thrive, and dissolve, and how they are imagined. Community may be self-identified or individuals may be ascribed membership in a particular community by another agency—for example, government or mass media—and members may not even recognize that they are part of a defined community. Because a community-based collection can represent virtually any kind of group that comes together for any period of time, it is difficult to identify locations where these kinds of collections might originate or anticipate which communities will participate in archival practices. Not only this, but the people who constitute collections of documentary heritage might not acknowledge themselves as a community at all, making it inappropriate to apply the term *community archives* in all cases of community archiving practices.

Equally problematic is the use of the term *archives* to describe community-based collections. In the vernacular, *archives* has come to refer to any kind of collection, both tangible and intangible—for example, historical documents, ideas and discourse, or a database of electronic media. Traditional archival literature, however, defines an *archives* as a collection of materials created or received by a person, family, or organization, public or private, in the conduct of their affairs (Pearce-Moses 2005). These materials are preserved because of their enduring evidential and informational value and maintained using the principles of provenance, original order, and collective control. An archives, therefore, collects particular kinds of records and arranges them in ways that highlight the contextual relationships between and among these records. Based on these defining features, archives have not traditionally been interested in collecting ephemera, published material such as books or journals, or records lacking contextual information that ties them to a larger fonds—for example, a photograph missing information about its provenance or custodial history. In general, archives do not collect based on a principle of pertinence, although they may keep subject files to assist with research. In contrast, community-based collections usually bring together materials artificially based on their pertinence to the community and include ephemera, such as pamphlets, postcards, and buttons, and other materials that may not meet the conditions of authenticity and reliability demanded by a traditional archival program. Community archives often collect books, artwork, and other non-archival records that hold special meaning for the community. In fact, a community archives may not even identify itself as an archives but instead use terms such as *library*, *resource center*, or *historical association* to describe the work that it does.

Considering the ambiguity present in the definitions of both *community* and *archives*, attempting to produce a clear-cut and simple definition of *community archives* can be a diverting and sometimes frustrating task. As Gilliland and Flinn (2013) note, the CAHG developed a working definition of *community archives* as distinct from community archiving practices. That is, community archives should include actual collections of material (digital or physical) that are created by, for, and about a community of people. The CAHG's definition allows for the possibility of professional support and intervention; however, the key characteristic is that there is community involvement in the management and development of the collection. The CAHG's 2009 vision statement reads:

> Community archives and heritage initiatives come in many different forms (large or small, semi-professional or entirely voluntary, long-established or

> very recent, in partnership with heritage professionals or entirely independent) and seek to document the history of all manner of local, occupational, ethnic, faith and other diverse communities.
>
> By collecting, preserving and making accessible documents, photographs, oral histories and many other materials which document the histories of particular groups and localities, community archives and heritage initiatives make an invaluable contribution to the preservation of a more inclusive and diverse local and national heritage. (Quoted in Gilliland and Flinn 2013, 7)

Gilliland and Flinn report that the CAHG definition of *community archives* is intentionally broad in scope and uses inclusive language to account for the many forms that community archives can take. They also add that, although there is no clear definition of *community archives*, these endeavors do share common characteristics. Community archives are more likely, for example, to collect a variety of materials—for example, objects, books, and archival records—and pay little heed to traditional distinctions among museums, libraries, and archives. These organizations are also more attuned to the role of archives and the purposes of education, community building, and developing coalitions with other groups. Gilliland and Flinn suggest that community archives can also provide a social space maintained and controlled by the community, where members can exercise autonomy from mainstream society. Because many community archives develop as independent social spaces, the communities that champion these organizations often resist professional intervention and fear that their collections will be "swallowed up" and rendered inaccessible if they relinquish control. Thus, community archives tend to foreground issues of independence and autonomy even if they welcome partnerships or support from more formal heritage bodies. Gilliland's (2012) "Voice, Identity, Activism (VIA) Framework for Approaching Archives and Recordkeeping" further describes the shared characteristics among archival initiatives that evolve from grassroots, identity-based, and social justice orientations.

FRAMEWORKS FOR UNDERSTANDING COMMUNITY ARCHIVES

Researchers engaged in projects about community archives and community archiving practices have provided additional insight into the ways in which these endeavors both enhance our understanding of shared cultural heritage and challenge traditional approaches to maintaining and developing archives. These include the autonomous archives framework, participatory and Do It Yourself (DIY) archiving, and community archives as social movement organizations. These frameworks draw from interdisciplinary literatures and can help practitioners and scholars working with these organizations to better understand why they have emerged and how they develop over time. Although each framework provides a distinct approach to understanding community archives, they are not mutually exclusive, and further research may, in fact, identify parallels and complementary ideas that can further enrich the literature.

Autonomous Archives

Shauna Moore and Susan Pell first introduced the autonomous archives framework in 2010 to describe community-based collections that are constituted as social and political acts by and for emerging publics. Their work is based on case studies of three Vancouver-based archives, the Union of British Columbia Indian Chiefs Resource Centre, the Hope in Shadows Archive, and the Friends of the Woodward's Squat Archive. In each case, founders are attuned to issues of social identity, claims to place, and representation. On a very basic level, autonomous archives describe community-based collections that are collected, curated, and preserved without interference from another authority. They are constituted as conscious acts and bring together evidence to support critiques of dominant historical narratives. Moore and Pell admit, however, that this description does not waver significantly from the traditional conceptualizations of community archives as primarily regional or ethnocultural documentary projects; the boundary between their framework and more established community archives is imprecise.

What distinguishes the framework of autonomous archives is its insistence that these collections serve emerging publics whose constituent members have been traditionally excluded from or denied full participation in public discourse. Moore and Pell build on the work of a cohort of political theorists who have tarried with the definitions of public and private, many in response to the Habermasian insistence that the public sphere is an equitable site for debate and consensus making. In particular, the authors draw from Nancy Fraser's notion of counter-public and Michael Warner's more refined work on the role of publics in contemporary society. Moore and Pell argue that autonomous archives are sites of potentiality where "emergent publics" create the shared memories and heritage necessary to develop into a cohesive and recognizable public (2010, 257). They write, "Autonomous archives present a framework for understanding the archive as a creative, world-making process that contributes to shared knowledge of the past and has the power to transform modes of public engagement" (256). An autonomous archives is a site of resistance and provides the evidence for epistemological undertakings. Moore and Pell write:

> By resisting incorporation of their archives into the broad collections of national or civic institutions, these emergent publics harness the power to use the evidence of members' common pasts to develop a collective history, which provides cohesiveness to the group, and facilitates the unity of vision for the

> future and the capacity to act that is necessary for their social and political survival and success [...] The archive substantiates the community's statements about the past. (261–62)

The autonomous archives framework is most successful when it forces us to look at community archives as manifestations of the archival aspirations of local organizers. Although such artificial collections are not traditionally understood as archival in nature, the autonomous archives framework reads the activities of gathering, curating, and making accessible records as social and political acts that spring from a similar desire to memorialize and preserve evidence as would underpin the work of any archival project. Thus, under this framework, collections such as that of the Union of British Columbia Indian Chiefs Resource Centre, which collects research materials to support provincial land claims, cannot be dismissed as simply a legal service but must be recognized as an archival space. Moore and Pell do not cleave to particular definition of community archives but rather suggest a research framework for investigating the genesis and evolution of community-based collections.

Participatory and DIY Archives

A second framework for understanding community archives is informed by participatory culture and DIY movements. The concept of participatory archives is explored in more depth in Chapter 12 of this book; however, it is worth revisiting here only briefly to establish a context for community-led archiving practices. The participatory archives model was first articulated by Isto Huvila (2008) to describe the ways in which individuals can actively participate in the creation of shared heritage. Huvila draws on the concept of participatory culture, a neologism in reference of, but in opposition to, consumer culture. In a participatory culture, there are relatively low barriers to artistic expression and civic engagement, and participants are encouraged to create knowledge using extant resources and share this knowledge with others in order to achieve a common goal. According to media scholar Henry Jenkins (2006), a participatory culture is one in which every member must believe that they are "free to contribute when ready and that what they contribute will be appropriately valued" (n.p.). Within these types of cultures, individuals are not only consumers, but they also contribute to or produce the culture in which they live. Paul Willis (2003) notes that this orientation has received more attention in the wake of Web 2.0 technologies that allow Internet *users* to become *contributors* through participation in wikis and blogs or by contributing comments/feedback to news sites and other previously static Web content Web sites. Huvila's work acknowledges the potential of digitally mediated archives to create a platform for community documentation that not only encourages participation from members but also relies on their contributions to thrive. Thus, participatory archives are community-led initiatives by their very nature.

As a corollary to participatory archives, Katie Shilton and Ramesh Srinivasan (2007) have argued for a more participatory approach to the appraisal and arrangement of multicultural archival collections. Their discussion builds on an argument made by Zinn (1977) that memory institutions have ignored the experiences of marginalized peoples, creating gaps in collections that are often presented as comprehensive representations of social history. Even in cases where archives have made gestures to document marginalized communities, they have created "archives *about* rather than *of* the communities" (Shilton and Srinivasan 2007, 88). Records have been poorly described, decontextualized, or interpreted in ways that diminish the importance of local knowledge about these records. Thus, Shilton and Srinivasan suggest that a participatory approach to appraisal and arrangement could serve as antidote to some misrepresentation that multicultural communities have endured. They write:

> In this spirit, we suggest that archival principles traditionally employed in the service of both appraisal and arrangement and description can use participatory processes to facilitate the preservation of representative, empowered narratives. Re-envisioning archival principles of appraisal, arrangement, and description to actively incorporate participation from traditionally marginalized communities will not only allow these communities to preserve empowered narratives, it will allow archivists to move towards the long-debated and still unrealized goal of representative collections. (90)

Nevertheless, the archival functions that Shilton and Srinivasan reimagine, appraisal, arrangement, and description, all take place within the auspice of a traditional archives.

At the same time, Shilton and Srinivasan acknowledge that "members of marginalized groups have taken preservation into their own hands, building archives and museums devoted to community history" (92). They also recognize that, increasingly, community efforts have surfaced in a "range of settings associated with preservation, spanning indigenous museums and archives, community centres, and increasingly, grassroots digital spaces" (92). It is important, therefore, to not only move to a more participatory approach to collecting and managing multicultural collections at an institutional level but also to encourage "reconciliation" between these institutions and the myriad community-based initiatives that have surfaced as a result of institutional neglect.

Another way in which participatory culture has aligned with archives is tied up in the return to the DIY ethos that has received much attention since the mid-1990s. To be clear, DIY rarely means Do-It-Alone; our individual practices are informed by norms and values of the communities in which we participate. Moreover, projects that we consider our own have taken shape with the assistance of others, whether that be the creation of a blog using open source software or the construction of a quilt using an established design. In terms of archival initiatives, the project might begin as one person's collection of records but grow in size and scope as interest in the collection expands. The Sexual Representation Collection (SRC) at University College, for example, began as the personal collection of Max Allen, a former media producer and cofounder of the Textile Museum of Canada (University College 2014). He was passionately interested in the anticensorship debates that unfolded in the 1970s and aware that no other archives was acting to properly document this history. The SRC was thus a DIY project, until it attracted the attention of other anticensorship activists and became a central resource for their work. Similarly, the CLGA began as a DIY project championed by a collective of gay liberation activists who did not feel that their work was adequately documented by mainstream heritage institutions. Both the SRC and the CLGA were participatory endeavors in that they were created, managed, and used by the very people who they represented.

The DIY movement has been discussed in depth by English sociologist David Gauntlett (2011), who suggests that this form of passive activism has emerged in response to Western neoliberalism. In his 2011 book, *Making Is Connecting*, Gauntlett draws on Karl Marx to show that mass production technologies have parceled out tasks, thereby alienating workers from the things that they produce. In an automobile factory, for example, labor is so divided that no one person can claim to have built a car but only participated in a small part of its production. This alienation from holistic production has brought Western culture to a point in which we have become dissociated from the process of making things; we no longer knit sweaters but buy them. For the past century, things have been made for us, not by us, and we have become quite comfortable in, what Gauntlett calls, the "sit-back-and-be-told" culture (1). Moving beyond a simplistic Marxist critique of industrial labor, Gauntlett goes on to argue that, until recently, the pleasure that we once experienced through holistic creation has been satisfied through the consumption of goods. Nevertheless, shopping, as a form of psychological soma, can only keep you happy for so long or until the credit card is maxed out. This is why, in part, we are currently witnessing widespread dissatisfaction with mass produced goods and, correspondingly, a revival of DIY culture. This return to, what Gauntlett calls, a "making-and-doing" culture also signifies a rejection of cookie-cutter cultural production, as crafters, knitters, YouTube filmmakers, and self-publishers decide to tell their own stories and make for themselves the society they want to live in (1). These kinds of creative endeavors produce pleasure in ways that consumption of mass produced goods does not.

Gauntlett is clear that DIY culture is not just a social practice but also a form of political activism.

Where the DIY movement and archives have collided is in the proliferation of community-based archival initiatives since the 1970s and even more so since the introduction of the World Wide Web in the mid-1990s. Within the context of DIY culture, community archives are sites of resistance whereby custodians can build collections that challenge dominant understandings of community experiences and researchers can begin to tell stories that counter the broad cultural narratives preserved in formal heritage institutions. As Flinn and Stevens (2009) have claimed, community archives are constituted because their founders see a real or perceived failure on the part of mainstream heritage institutions to collect, preserve, and make available collections that accurately represent the experiences of community members. Community collections are, therefore, DIY projects. They take the making of heritage out of the heritage industry and back into the community context where people are doing, feeling, creating, and experiencing the world in their own ways. This resistance to dominant knowledge production is documented in Pell's (2015) ethnographic work on the 56a Infoshop, a space in which members collectivize knowledge production through DIY community archiving practices.

The implication of strong DIY foundations is that these archives likely serve few outside of their own community of creators. The point of these projects, whether implicit or made explicit, is to make something whole without, and in resistance to, state intervention (and often commercial intervention). This crafting spirit is what makes DIY archives so exciting and also what makes them vulnerable. As Moore and Pell (2010) note in their framework of autonomous archives, community-based collections are also vulnerable to the ebb and flow of archival aspirations; should members of the archives lose interest in the records or decide that housing the collection is no longer possible, the archival project may simply cease to exist. The insecurity of DIY archives also poses a challenge to traditional heritage organizations with intentions to build partnerships with the custodians of these collections. Because DIY culture is inherently counterculture, custodians may not wish to have their collections passed into the custody of a mainstream institution. Even if custody remains with the community, custodians may resist any intervention. Professional archivists must then ask, what is the value of these collections and how might we encourage community custodians to see value in partnership activities? Perhaps a more important question is, what value do these institutions have for democratic heritage? If we value the expression of culture through community-based collections, should they not remain within the community? And if the community decides the records are no longer important, can the archives be left alone for future archeologists to dig up like potsherds in the earth?

Community Archives as Social Movement Organizations

In my previous work on community archives, I have drawn heavily from the interdisciplinary scholarship on social movements to describe community archives as social movement organizations (SMOs) (Sheffield 2015). According to John D. McCarthy and Maver N. Zald (1977), an SMO is a "complex or formal organization that identifies its goals with the preferences of a social movement or countermovement and attempts to implement those goals" (20). The central task of an SMO is to aggregate otherwise dispersed resources for the purpose of engaging in action to promote social change based on the broadly held preferences and diversity of subpreferences of the social movement. At one level, resource mobilization is the task of converting adherents—individuals and other organizations that believe in the goals of the movement—to constituents who can provide resources to the SMO. On another level, resource mobilization is the task of converting non-adherents and bystander publics (neutral witnesses) to adherents. At a minimum, an SMO must possess some resources, no matter how few or what type, and claim some form of legitimacy for the work that it does. Most SMOs depend on volunteer labor, although some purchase labor, and their staff will vary tremendously in the efficacy with which they translate resources into action.

More recent studies of SMOs take into account the body of scholarship that has developed in the wake of McCarthy and Zald's foundational papers on the organizational processes of social movements. J. Craig Jenkins (1995) and John Lofland (1996) add that SMOs are those that rely on contentious action. Lofland goes on to add that tactics are less important than the types of claims made or the ideological basis of the organization. By way of illustration, this appropriately distinguishes between a corporate organization that, for example, invests in sustainability with green packaging or land management processes and a not-for-profit environmentalist organization such as Greenpeace or the Sierra Club, which engages in action for the purpose of making social change. The tactics may be similar—using green technology or mobilizing farmers to engage in more ethical and humane practices—but the ideological underpinnings are distinct. No matter how environmentally conscious, the for-profit organization exists to aggregate capital for stakeholder gain; the not-for-profit aggregates resources to achieve social movement goals.

It is also critical to understand the ways in which SMOs have been theorized within the growing body of literature on new social movements that do not always focus on political change as their central goals. As Mary Bernstein (1997) notes, movements concerned with cultural and political identities also focus on cultural, social, and economic change. This is particularly important for cultural and cognitive theories that employ an interpretive lens to understand social movements. Beth Caniglia and JoAnn Carmin (2005) suggest:

> Participants are motivated to join movements, at least in part, because they resonate with their personal values and beliefs. Analyses of new social movements advanced and crystallized this view as scholars noted that membership in the women's, environmental, and gay and lesbian movements, to name a few, often is better explained by identity affiliation than by social class. (205)

Identity is thus central to the study of SMOs that are part of new social movements, such as the feminist, gay rights, and more recently, the disability and trans movements. Collective identity has been used to refer to the shared values, beliefs, attitudes, and norms of behavior that are present within a given social movement (Johnston, Larana, and Gusfield 1994; Polletta and Jasper 2001; Taylor and Whittier 1992).

To my knowledge, social movement theory is silent on the role of community archives in collective action for social change; however, the body of literature on social movements provides useful language for talking about the ways in which community archiving practices have emerged and why they are important actors in social movements. Eichhorn (2013) has recently argued that archives are often neglected in discussions about culture and society. Although she is speaking specifically about Pierre Bourdieu's field of cultural production, her criticisms are seemingly applicable to SMO theory. She writes:

> Unlike the gallery, art museum and even academy, which more often than not endow literary or artistic work with value in the present, the archive's work is more often than not retroactive. In other words, it is uniquely located to the extent that it permits works to migrate across the fields of cultural production at different points in history ... The archives, then, is not only an institution that Bourdieu overlooks in his theorizing on the field of cultural production but also the institution that arguably holds the greatest potential to disrupt ... (25)

If, as the literature on social movements insists, the central goals of these postindustrial, postmodern movements focus not on issues of materialistic qualities such as economic well-being but on issues related to collective identities and human rights, then cultural institutions are essential to movement politics and mobilizing for collective action. In particular, community archives, which both preserve and provide the material tools necessary for the construction of collective identity, are fundamental to sustaining a movement. While they do not explicitly mobilize tangible resources for collective action (e.g., human resources or financial support), the scholarship that is produced from the evidence they preserve makes possible the social cohesion necessary for social movements to develop shared heritages that strengthen otherwise loose ties among participants.

Conceptualizing community archives as actors within social movements is useful, even if some identify as cultural institutions and not explicitly part of any contentious political action. As discussed previously, the very act of taking control of one's own documentary heritage is political. Thinking about community archives through social movement theory also suggests that these kinds of organizations not only function as SMOs but also as abeyance structures that help carry on and carry forward evidence of one generation to the next. Verta Taylor (1989) was among the first to show that movements can be understood as occurring in cycles, with periods of abeyance. During movement abeyance, she argues, organizations sustain movement continuity by providing a space to preserve networks of social movement actors and knowledge of movement histories, tactics, and goals. The concepts of movement abeyance and abeyance structures help to understand the current circumstances of community archives, namely those that emerged within the contexts of social movements that have since entered a period of decline and how practitioners, scholars, and community members can reinvigorate these organizations as vital structures for sustaining social movement continuity—what some activists might call "keeping the fire stoked."

THE COMMUNITY ARCHIVES' LIFE CYCLE

Stevens, Flinn, and Shepherd (2009) recognize that the development of community archives, particularly those with activist orientations, often aligns with social movement trajectories. Gilliland and Flinn (2013) also note that there appears to have been at least two distinct waves of community archives since the early 1970s. The first wave of community archives, which includes gay and lesbian archives, labor archives, and civil rights and women's movement collections, was established in response to 1960s protest cycles, and many of these organizations declined in the 1990s as antiestablishment social movements entered a period of abeyance. The second wave of community archives emerged in the late 1990s in response to the rise of anticapitalist, postindustrial social movements that leveraged participatory and DIY approaches to cultural production. The lull of community archiving practices in the 1990s, described by Mander (2009), likely occurred because the first wave had matured, and many of the collections created by these early community archives were integrated into mainstream heritage organizations as the social movements that inspired them went into abeyance.

The wave pattern described by Gilliland and Flinn and Mander suggests that, like social movements, community archives follow a fairly predictable life cycle. Herbert Blumer (1979) was among the first scholars to argue that social movements have life cycles. He identified four stages, which have since been refined and renamed as 1) emergence, 2) coalescence, 3) bureaucratization, and 4) decline (Della Porta and Diani 2006). In the first stage, social movements are preliminary and have little or no organization. External organizations, however, can provide the structural support for collective action, and, if this action inspires subsequent action, the movement can move to the next stage of development. Similarly, community archiving practices often emerge out of other forms of cultural production, such as the publication of a newspaper, and rely on external support from the publisher or a community service organization to survive. In the case of the CLGA, for example, the organization grew out of the working files of *The Body Politic* and was financially supported by the publishing collective for almost 20 years (Sheffield 2015). The Lesbian Herstory Archives grew first as a personal collection nurtured and cared for in its founder's own apartment (Sheffield 2015). The Hope in Shadows Archive developed out of a photography contest in Vancouver's Downtown Eastside, funded initially with support from a service organization that provides free legal service to the community (Moore and Pell 2010). In each case, the archives emerged after founders began to understand the importance of the documentation they had amassed and what a shared documentary heritage could mean for their own communities. The emergence stage is the foundational moment of constituting an archives described by Hall (2001) and Appadurai's (2003) deliberate act of intervention.

During the coalescence stage of a social movement, leadership emerges and participants begin to organize around common grievances and causes (Della Porta and Diani 2006). At this point, participants also develop informal and formal networks and establish SMOs as a way to aggregate resources needed to pursue movement goals. Community archives also moved through this stage of development, as leaders took control of the collections and introduced new energy and stability for the organizations. As noted previously, Caswell (2014b) describes how the SAADA grew out of a desire to preserve archival materials related to South Asian-American history. The digital repository now holds more than 1,600 records, documenting stories as diverse as Punjabi labor resistance in the 1910s to Muslim punk bands in the 2010s. Since its founding in 2008, SAADA has developed a network of scholars and community members who have invested in supporting the archives both financially and intellectually through further study of South Asian Americans. In some cases, leadership has remained central to the survival of the organization. Joan Nestle and Deb Edel, for example, continue to guide the Lesbian Herstory Archives as they have for more than 40 years (Sheffield 2015). In other cases, leadership has changed throughout the years, but each has added to existing support networks in their own ways. This support structure has also helped the archives move ahead, even when leaders have died or moved away from the archives due to flagging energies. Leadership has also been symbolic in some cases, in the form of a mandate or mission statement, which has provided guidance for community archivists even when archival work has been temporarily suspended.

In the third stage of the life cycle, bureaucratization, social movement actors become highly organized and start building formal infrastructures, such as incorporating as a not-for-profit, establishing a board of directors or trustees, and better organizing labor. For community archives, bureaucratization can include the development of mandates or mission statements, governance structures, and acquisition policies. Community archives may also establish formal partnerships with academic institutions and other heritage institutions as a way to raise public profile and strengthen its ties to the community, which can build capacity for fundraising and development activities. As Caswell (2014b) notes, however, many community archives have to strike a careful balance between relying on well-established institutions to provide stability and the desire to remain autonomous and community-driven. It is also true that some community archives may resist bureaucratization as a political principle, preferring to remain informal and purely grassroots; others may not ever reach the bureaucratization stage either because they become folded into the structure that initially supported them or leadership is not able or does not want to transition community archiving practices into a formal community archives.

At the final stage of their life cycle, social movements decline either because they have been successful in achieving their goals and are no longer useful or because they are subject to new forms or intensity of repression from the state or other agents of authority. As F. D. Miller (1999) points out, social movements may also be vulnerable to co-optation, if social movement organizations come to depend on central authority for funding or other resources, or if leaders take on different values than those central to the original movement. J. J. Macionis (2001) adds that some movements become established with the mainstream so that the ideology of the movement is adopted by the mainstream, and there is no longer a reason to pursue change through collective action. M. Guigni, D. McAdam, and C. Tilly (1998) also note that social movements may fall into periods of abeyance to concentrate on maintaining collective identity and shared values, which leaves open the possibility of a reemergence of more active politics at a later time and when the political opportunity structures allow participants to more easily organize.

Like social movements, community archives can also decline. Although little research has been done on community archives at this stage, Moore and Pell (2010) provide some guidance on how a community archives may decline when the emergent public that founded it achieves a certain level of acceptance in public discourse, and it ceases to be autonomous. At this point in its life cycle, the organization may be recognized and courted by traditional heritage networks and encouraged to integrate its collections into a more formal repository (e.g., a public library or a university archives). Alternatively, the archives may dissolve due to lack of resources to continue its mission, especially if the community responsible for its creation also disperses. In this sense, Moore and Pell describe autonomous archives as ebbing and flowing with the life cycle of their respective publics; they are not distinct from this emergent public but a vital aspect of the work that this public is undertaking. Mander's (2009) description of the first wave of community archives in the United Kingdom to decline in the 1990s also hints at the ways in which community archives are inherently tied to the grassroots and community building processes that create them. Diana K. Wakimoto, Christine Bruce, and Helen Partridge's (2013) work on three queer community archives in California provides additional insight into the relationships between waves of community activism and the development of community archives.

CONCLUSION

At all stages of the community archives life cycle and throughout the history of the community archives movements in the United States, Canada, and the United Kingdom, community participation is key to understanding the role that these organizations have in the creation of cultural heritage. Stevens, Flinn, and Shepherd (2009) agree that community archiving practices are part of community development and not simply the result of social activity. For this reason, community archives can be democratizing projects, whether or not the communities that create these organizations acknowledge themselves as activists or political actors. The desire to tell our own stories and to preserve our own documentary heritage without intervention are strong mobilizing factors that provide forward momentum for community archival endeavors. Independence can also propel community members to resist handing over collections to mainstream heritage institutions even when the community archives that house them are in decline. Recounting the political and social motivations that underpin community archiving practices can aid scholars and the heritage professionals to better engage with community archives and to support these organizations in a manner that is respectful, constructive, and meaningful. If the growth of community archives over the past generation is any indication of their part in cultural heritage creation, there is a broad future for these kinds of community-led archival endeavors to play a vital role in healthy communities and in shared cultural heritage that impacts more than their constituent communities.

ENDNOTE

1. This chapter is based on the author's PhD thesis (Sheffield 2015).

REFERENCES

Appadurai, Arjun. 2003. "Archive and Aspiration." In *Information Is Alive: Art and Theory on Archiving and Retrieving Data*, edited by Joke Brouwer and Arjen Mulder, 14–25. Rotterdam, Netherlands: V2.

Barriault, Marcel. 2009. "Archiving the Queer and Queering the Archives: A Case Study of the Canadian Lesbian and Gay Archives (CLGA)." In *Community Archives: The Shaping of Memory*, edited by Jeanette A. Bastian and Ben Alexander, 97–108. London: Facet Publishing.

Bastian, Jeannette A. 2003. *Owning mMemory: How a Caribbean Community Lost Its Archives and Found Its History*. Westport, CT: Libraries Unlimited.

Bastian, Jeanette A., and Ben Alexander, eds. 2009. *Community Archives: The Shaping of Memory*. London: Facet Publishing.

Bernstein, Mary. 1997. "Celebration and Suppression: The Strategic Uses of Identity by the Lesbian and Gay Movement." *American Journal of Sociology* 103 (3): 531–65.

Blumer, Herbert. 1979. *Symbolic Interactionism*. Englewood Cliffs, NJ: Prentice-Hall.

Bly, Lyz, and Kelly Wooten. 2012. *Make Your Own History: Documenting Feminist and Queer Activism in the 21st century*. Sacramento, CA: Litwin Books.

Caniglia, B. S., and J. Carmen. 2005. "Scholarship on Social Movement Organizations: Classic Views and Emerging Trends." *Mobilization: An International Journal* 10 (2): 201–12.

Caswell, Michelle. 2014a. "Inventing New Archival Imaginaries: Theoretical Foundations for Identity-Based Community Archives." In *Identity Palimpsests: Archiving Ethnicity in the US and Canada*, edited by Dominique Daniel and Amalia Levi, 35–55. Sacramento, CA: Litwin Books.

Caswell, Michelle. 2014b. "Community-Centred Collecting: Finding Out What Communities Want from Community Archives." *Proceedings of the American Society for Information Science and Technology* 51 (1): 1–9.

Chenier, Elise. 2009. "Hidden from Historians: Preserving Lesbian Oral History in Canada." *Archivaria* 68: 247–70.

Chenier, Elise. 2015. "Privacy Anxieties Ethics versus Activism in Archiving Lesbian Oral History Online." *Radical History Review* 122: 129–41.

Chenier, Elise. 2016. "Reclaiming the Lesbian Archives: How Web 2.0 Tools Can Bridge the Gap between University and Community." *Oral History Review* 43 (1): 170–82.

Cifor, Marika. 2015. "Presence, Absence, and Victoria's Hair: Examining Affect and Embodiment in Trans Archives." *TSQ: Transgender Studies Quarterly* 2 (4): 645–49.

Community Access to Archives Project. 2004. "Community Archives." nationalarchives.gov.uk. https://www.nationalarchives.gov.uk/documents/community_archives_aug2004.rtf (accessed April 17, 2016).

Community Archives and Heritage Group. 2011. "Directory." cahg.ca. http://www.communityarchives.org.uk/archives (accessed April 17, 2016).

Cvetkovich, Ann. 2003. *An Archive of Feelings: Trauma, Sexuality, and Lesbian Public Cultures*. Durham, NC: Duke University Press.

Della Porta, Donatello, and Mario Diani. 2006. *Social Movements: An Introduction*, 2nd ed. Hoboken, NJ: Blackwell.

Dicks, Bella. 2003. *Culture on Display: The Production of Contemporary Visitability*. Maidenhead, U.K.: Open University Press.

Digital Transgender Archives (DTA). 2015. "Overview." https://www.digitaltransgenderarchive.net/about/overview (accessed May 20, 2016).

Eichhorn, Kate. 2013. *The Archival Turn in Feminism: Outrage in Order*. Philadelphia, PA: Temple University Press.

English, John R. 1983. "The Tradition of Public History in Canada." *The Public Historian* 5 (1): 58–59.

Flinn, Andrew. 2007. "Community Histories, Community Archives: Some Opportunities and Challenges." *Journal of the Society of Archivists* 28 (2): 151–76.

Flinn, Andrew. 2010. "An Attack on Professionalism and Scholarship? Democratising Archives and the Production of Knowledge." *Ariadne* 62. http://www.ariadne.ac.uk/issue62/flinn/ (accessed April 26, 2016).

Flinn, Andrew. 2011. "The Impact of Independent and Community Archives on Professional Archival Thinking and Practice." In *The Future of Archives and Recordkeeping*, edited by Jenny Hill, 145–69. London: Facet Publishing.

Flinn, Andrew, and Mary Stevens. 2009. " 'It Is Noh Mistri, Wi Mekin Histri': Telling Our Own Story: Independent and Community Archives in the United Kingdom, Challenging and Subverting the Mainstream." In *Community Archives: The Shaping of Memory*, edited by Jeanette Bastian and Ben Alexander, 3–27. London: Facet Publishing.

Flinn, Andrew, Mary Stevens, and Elizabeth Shepherd. 2009. "Whose Memories, Whose Archives? Independent Community Archives, Autonomy and the Mainstream." *Archival Science* 9 (1–2): 71–86.

Gauntlett, David. 2011. *Making Is Connecting: The Social Meaning of Creativity, from DIY and Knitting to YouTube and Web 2.0*. Cambridge, U.K.: Polity.

Gilliland, Anne. 2012. "Voice, Identity, Activism (VIA) Framework for Approaching Archives and Recordkeeping." Los Angeles: Center for Information as Evidence, University of California—Los Angeles.

Gilliland, A., and A. Flinn. 2013. "Community Archives: What Are We Really Talking About?" Keynote address, *Nexus, Confluence, and Difference: Community Archives Meets Community Informatics: Prato CIRN Conference Oct 28-30 2013*, edited by Larry Stillman, Amalia Sabiescu, Nemanja Memarovic, Centre for Community Networking Research, Centre for Social Informatics, Monash University.

Guigni, M. G., D. McAdam, and C. Tilly. 1998. *From Contention to Democracy*. Lanham, MD: Rowman and Littlefield.

Hall, Stuart. 2001. "Constituting an Archive." *Third Text* 15 (54): 89–92.

Hogan, Mél. 2009. "Dykes on Mykes: Podcasting and the Activist Archive." *TOPIA: Canadian Journal of Cultural Studies* 20: 199–215.

Hurley, Grant. 2016. "Community Archives, Community Clouds: Enabling Digital Preservation for Small Archives." *Archivaria* 82: 129–50.

Huvila, Isto. 2008. "Participatory Archive: Towards Decentralised Curation, Radical User Orientation, and Broader Contextualisation of Records Management." *Archival Science* 18: 15–36.

Jenkins, J. C. 1995. "Social Movements, Political Representation, and the State: An Agenda and Comparative Framework." In *The Politics of Social Protest: Comparative Perspectives on States and Social Movements*, edited by J. C. Jenkins and B. Klandermans, 14–36. London: UCL Press.

Jenkins, Henry. 2006. "Confronting the Challenges of Participatory Culture: Media Education for the 21st Century (Part One)." henryjenkins.org. http://henryjenkins.org/2006/10/confronting_the_challenges_of.html (accessed April 26, 2016).

Jimerson, Randall. 2006. "Embracing the Power of Archives." *The American Archivist* 69 (1): 19–32.

Johnston, H., E. Larana, and J. R. Gusfield. 1997. "Identities, Grievances, and New Social Movements." In *Social Movements: Perspectives and Issues*, edited by S. M. Buechler and F. K. Cylke, 274–95. Mountain View, CA: Mayfield Publishing Co.

Ketelaar, Eric. 2005. "Sharing: Collected Memories in Communities of Records." *Archives and Manuscripts* 33: 44–61.

Kumbier, Alanna. 2014. *Ephemeral Material: Queering the Archive*. Sacremento, CA: Litwin Books.

Lee, Jamie A. 2016. "Beyond Pillars of Evidence: Exploring the Shaky Ground of Queer/ed Archives and Their Methodologies." In *Research in the Archival Multiverse*, edited by Anne Gilliland, Andrew Lau, and Sue McKemmish, 324–51. Melbourne: Monash University Press.

Lofland, J. 1996. *Social Movement Organizations: Guide to Research on Insurgent Realities*. Herndon, VA: Transaction Publishers.

Macionis, J. J. 2001. *Sociology*, 8th ed. Upper Saddle River, NJ: Prentice Hall.

Mander, David. 2009. "Special, Local and about Us: The Development of Community Archives in Britain." In *Community Archives: The Shaping of Memory*, edited by Jeanette A. Bastian and Ben Alexander, 29–46. London: Facet Publishing.

McCarthy, J. D., and M. N. Zald. 1977. "Resource Mobilization and Social Movements: A Partial Theory." *American Journal of Sociology* 82 (6): 1212–41.

Miller, F. D. 1999. "The End of SDS and the Emergence of Weatherman: Demise through Success." In *Waves of Protest: Social Movements since the Sixties*, edited by J. Freeman and V. Johnson. Lanham, MD: Rowman and Littlefield Publishers.

Moore, Shauna, and Susan Pell. 2010. "Autonomous Archives." *International Journal of Heritage Studies* 16 (4): 255–68.

Museums, Libraries and Archives Council, Archives Task Force. 2004. *Listening to the Past, Speaking to the Future*. http://webarchive.nationalarchives.gov.uk/20111013135435/http://research.mla.gov.uk/evidence/documents/atf_report_pdf_5479.pdf (accessed April 26, 2016).

Paschild, Cristine. 2012. "Community Archives and the Limitations of Identity: Considering Discursive Impact on Material Needs." *The American Archivist* 75 (1): 125–42.

Pearce-Moses, Richard. 2005. "Archives." *Glossary of Archival and Records Terminology (Online)*. http://www.archivists.org/glossary/term_details.asp?DefinitionKey=156 (accessed April 26, 2016).

Pell, Susan. 2015. "Radicalizing the Politics of the Archive: An Ethnographic Reading of an Activist Archive." *Archivaria* 80: 33–57.

Perks, Robert, and Alistair Thomson, eds. 2006. *The Oral History Reader*, 2nd ed. New York: Routledge.

Polletta, F., and J. M. Jasper. 2001. "Collective Identity and Social Movements." *Annual Review of Sociology* 27: 283–305.

Punzalan, Ricardo L. 2014. "Understanding Virtual Reunification." *The Library Quarterly* 84 (3): 294–323.

Rawson, K. J. 2009. "Accessing Transgender // Desiring Queer(er?) Archival Logics." *Archivaria* 68: 123–40.

Sheffield, Rebecka. 2015. "The Emergence, Development and Survival of Four Lesbian and Gay Archives." PhD Thesis. University of Toronto.

Shilton, Katie, and Ramesh Srinivasan. 2007. "Participatory Appraisal and Arrangement for Multicultural Archival Collections." *Archivaria* 63: 87–101.

Stevens, Mary, Andrew Flinn, and Elizabeth Shepherd. 2009. "Activists in the Archives: Making History in a Diverse Society." A summary of the report of the AHRC project, "Community Archives and Identities: Documenting and Sustaining Community Heritage."

Stevens, Mary, Andrew Flinn, and Elizabeth Shepherd. 2010. "New Frameworks for Community Engagement in the Archive Sector: From Handing over to Handing On." *International Journal of Heritage Studies* 16 (1 and 2): 59–76.

Taylor, Verta. 1989. "Social Movement Continuity: The Women's Movement in Abeyance." *American Sociological Review* 54 (5): 761–75.

Taylor, V., and N. E. Whittier. 1992. "Collective Identity in Social Movement Communities." In *Frontiers in Social Movement Theory*, edited by A. D. Morris and C. M. Mueller, 104–29. New Haven, CT: Yale University Press.

University College. 2014. "Sexual Representation Collection." http://www.uc.utoronto.ca/sexual-representation-collection (accessed April 26, 2016).

Wakimoto, Diane K., Christine Bruce, and Helen Partridge. 2013. "Archivist as Activist: Lessons from Three Queer Community Archives in California." *Archival Science* 13 (4): 293–316.

Waterton, Emma, and Laurajane Smith. 2010. "The Recognition and Misrecognition of Community Heritage." *International Journal of Heritage Studies* 16 (1–2): 4–15.

Willis, Paul. 2003. "Foot Soldiers of Modernity: The Dialectics of Cultural Consumption and the 21st Century School." *Harvard Educational Review* 73 (3): 390–415.

X, Ajamu, Topher Campbell, and Mary Stevens. 2009. "Love and Lubrication in the Archives, or rukus!: A Black Queer Archive for the United Kingdom." *Archivaria* 68: 271–94.

Zinn, Howard. 1977. "Secrecy, Archives, and the Public Interest." *Midwestern Archivist* 2 (2): 20–21.

Index

About the Editors and Contributors

Jeannette A. Bastian is a professor at the School of Library and Information Science, Simmons College, where she directs their Archives Management concentration and their satellite campus in Western Massachusetts. Formerly territorial librarian of the U.S. Virgin Islands from1987 to 1998, she completed an MPhil in Caribbean literature at the University of the West Indies (Mona, Jamaica) in 1983 and a PhD focusing on archives from the University of Pittsburgh in 1999. She has widely published in the archival literature, and her books include *West Indian Literature: A Critical Index, 1930–1975* (1982), *Owning Memory: How a Caribbean Community Lost Its Archives and Found Its History* (2003), *Archival Internships* (2008), *Community Archives: The Shaping of Memory*, edited with Ben Alexander (2009), and *Archives in Libraries: What Librarians and Archivists Need to Know to Work Together*, with Megan Sniffin-Marinoff and Donna Webber (2015).

Adrian Cunningham is the director at Digital Archives at Queensland State Archives. Previously he worked at the National Archives of Australia (NAA) from 1998 to 2011, during which time he held a variety of director-level positions and exercised oversight of the NAA's collaborations with government, industrial, professional, and international partners—particularly on matters associated with digital recordkeeping. Adrian was secretary of the International Council on Archives (ICA) Committee on Descriptive Standards (2002–2004) and treasurer of the Pacific Regional Branch of the ICA (2003–2011). Before joining the NAA, he worked as a private records archivist/librarian at the National Library of Australia, the Pacific Manuscripts Bureau, and the State Library of New South Wales. Adrian was president of the Australian Society of Archivists (1998–2000) and was inducted as a fellow of that society in 2007. He was awarded the Emmett Leahy Award for contributions to records management in September 2010.

Glenn Dingwall is a digital archivist at the City of Vancouver Archives, British Columbia, where he has been responsible for the development of the city's digital archives program since 2006. He was a member of the team that established the initial functional requirements for Archivematica and tested its early versions in its initial deployment at the city. His previous publications have addressed digital preservation, recordkeeping models, and archival ethics. Glenn is presently a researcher with the InterPARES Trust project and has been involved with the previous iterations of InterPARES. He holds a BA in history from Simon Fraser University and an MAS from the University of British Columbia.

Jennifer Douglas is an assistant professor at the School of Library, Archival and Information Studies (SLAIS) at the University of British Columbia. She earned her PhD at the University of Toronto and her dissertation, entitled "Archiving Authors: Rethinking the Analysis and Representation of Personal Archives," won the 2013 iSchools Dissertation Award. In 2014, her article "What We Talk about When We Talk about Original Order in Writers' Archives" won the 2014 W. Kaye Lamb prize from *Archivaria*, for the article that had most advanced archival thinking in Canada. Her research focuses on how and why individuals and communities make and keep archives and how archivists represent those ways and reasons. She has published articles on the principles of provenance and respect for original order, on personal recordkeeping behaviors, and on writers' archives. Her current research focuses on the role of personal recordkeeping in grieving and on online grief communities as aspirational archives. From 2016 to 2019, she is the general editor of *Archivaria*.

Wendy Duff, dean and professor at the Faculty of Information, University of Toronto, obtained her PhD (1996) from the University of Pittsburgh. At the iSchool, she teaches courses on archives and records management, with a focus on access to archival materials and community archives. She was the founding director of the University of Toronto Digital Curation Institute. She has also served as a member of the ICA Ad Hoc Commission on Descriptive Standards, the Encoded Archival Description Working Group, AX-SNet, and The Canadian Council of Archives Standards Committee.

Her current research focuses on archival users, the impact of archives on social justice archives, and archives and social media.

Terry Eastwood is professor emeritus in the School of Library, Archival and Information Studies at the University of British Columbia (UBC), where, from 1981 to 2000 he acted as chair of the Master of Archival Studies Program. He played a prominent role in the establishment of the Canadian

Rules for Archival Description. His research and writing has focused on archival theory and its application to the functions of arrangement and appraisal, including the appraisal of electronic records. He has also written about the history of archival institutions in Canada, archives and accountability, and archival education. His own research and writing was very significantly stimulated by his work supervising over 70 archival studies theses. After retiring from his position at UBC in 2007, he was called back to be interim director in 2009–2010, his third time in that role.

Alexandra Eveleigh is special collections manager at the Wellcome Library in London, where her role complements her research interests in user experiences and digital technologies in archival contexts. She trained initially at University College London and worked in both university and local government archives in the United Kingdom (University of Southampton and West Yorkshire Archive Service) before returning to University College London to complete a PhD in collaboration with The National Archives entitled "Crowding Out the Archivist? Implications of Online User Participation for Archival Theory and Practice" (2015). Alexandra is also a 2008 Winston Churchill fellow in connection to her work on born-digital archives.

Fiorella Foscarini is an associate professor in the Faculty of Information at the University of Toronto, Canada. From 2014 to 2016, she taught in the Department of Media Studies at the University of Amsterdam, the Netherlands. Fiorella holds a PhD in archival science from the School of Library, Archival and Information Studies at UBC in Vancouver. Before joining academia, she worked as a senior archivist for the European Central Bank in Frankfurt am Main, Germany; prior to that, she was head of the Records Office and Intermediate Archives at the Province of Bologna, Italy. In her teaching and research, she uses diplomatics, rhetorical genre studies, and information culture concepts to explore issues related to the creation, management, and use of records in organizational contexts.

Heather MacNeil is a professor in the Faculty of Information at the University of Toronto, where she teaches courses in the areas of archival theory and practice and the history of archives and recordkeeping. Her research and publications focus on the trustworthiness of records in analog and digital environments, archives and archival finding aids as cultural texts, and archival description as rhetorical genre. She is the author of *Without Consent* (1992) and *Trusting Records: Legal, Historical and Diplomatic Perspectives* (2000) and coeditor, along with Terry Eastwood, of the first edition of *Currents of Archival Thinking* (2010).

Sigrid McCausland was a senior lecturer in the School of Information Studies, Charles Sturt University, Australia, where she led the teaching of records and archives management in an online environment. She began her career as a reference archivist at Australian Archives (now National Archives of Australia), and her later professional positions included university archivist at the Australian National University in Canberra, where she was responsible for the Noel Butlin Archives Centre, Australia's largest collection of business and labor archives. Her PhD is in history from the University of Technology, Sydney. She has contributed to the development of the archives profession in Australia and was the secretary of the Section for Archival Education and Training at the ICA from 2012–2016, the publications focus on Australian archival history, access, and education, as well as advocacy, community cultural heritage, and how archival institutions interact with their publics.

Dr. Gillian Oliver is an associate professor in information management at Monash University, Melbourne, Australia. Her professional practice background spans information management in the United Kingdom, Germany, and New Zealand. Her research interests reflect these experiences, focusing on the information cultures of organizations. She is the coauthor (with Fiorella Foscarini) of the book *Records Management and Information Culture: Tackling the People Problem* (Facet, 2014) and is currently leading research funded by the ICA to develop an information culture toolkit for archival authorities. As recipient of an Erasmus Mundus scholarship awarded by the European Commission, she was visiting scholar at Tallinn University in 2009. She is honorary research fellow at the Humanities Advanced Technology and Information Institute, University of Glasgow, and at the Open Polytechnic of New Zealand. She is coeditor-in-chief of *Archival Science*.

Rebecka Sheffield is a senior lecturer in the School of Library and Information Science at Simmons College, Boston. She is formerly the executive director and archives manager for the Canadian Lesbian and Gay Archives (CLGA) in Toronto. She has also worked with the LGBTQ +Digital Oral History Collaboratory, which brings together a team of researchers across four community archives and five research institutions. Rebecka holds a graduate degree in archives and records management and completed a PhD at the University of Toronto's Faculty of Information, in collaboration with the Mark S. Bonham Centre for Sexual Diversity Studies.

Dr. Elizabeth Shepherd is a professor of archives and records management at University College London, Department of Information Studies (DIS). She teaches in the master's program in archives and records management and is currently director of research for DIS. She established a research center, ICARUS, to bring together researchers in records and archives management (http://www.ucl.ac.uk/dis/icarus). Elizabeth's research interests include the relationships between records management and information policy compliance (the subject of Arts and Humanities Research Council and Economic and Social Research Council-funded projects) and the development of the archive profession in England in the twentieth century. She has published numerous articles, the internationally best-selling book *Managing Records: A Handbook of Principles and Practice* (Facet Publishing, 2003), with Geoffrey Yeo, and the monograph *Archives and Archivists in 20th Century England* (Ashgate, 2009). Details at: http://www.ucl.ac.uk/dis/people/elizabethshepherd.

David A. Wallace, PhD, is a clinical associate professor at the University of Michigan School of Information. He has been a graduate archival educator since 1997. He has published and presented in a wide range of professional forums examining recordkeeping and accountability; archiving and the shaping of the present and the past; social justice impact of archives; freedom of information; government secrecy; professional ethics; electronic records management; graduate archival education; and live music archiving. He is editor of a double issue of *Archival Science* on "Archives and the Ethics of Memory Construction" (2011); coeditor of *Archives and the Public Good: Accountability and Records in Modern Society* (2002); and served as the series technical editor of 12 volumes of the National Security Archive's *The Making of U.S. Policy series* (1989–1992). Substantial consultations include the South African History Archive's Freedom of Information Program (2002–2005), Stories for Hope, an intergenerational storytelling project in Rwanda (2009–2015), and the Kresge Foundation (2014–2016).

Elizabeth Yakel, PhD, is a professor and associate dean for academic affairs at the University of Michigan School of Information where she teaches in the archives and records management and digital preservation areas. Her research interests include access to digital archives and reuse of research data. Dr. Yakel recently ended a research project entitled "Dissemination Information Packages for Information Reuse" (http://www.oclc.org/research/themes/user-studies/dipir.html) (funded by the Institute for Museum and Library Services [IMLS]), which focused on research data reuse in three academic communities: quantitative social science, archaeology, and zoology. She is now working on another IMLS-funded project: "Qualitative Data Reuse: Records of Practice in Educational Research and Teacher Development," which examines the varied uses of educational records of practice, particularly digital video of classroom activities. Dr. Yakel is active in the Society of American Archivists (SAA), where she served on the governing council and was elected a fellow in 1999.

Geoffrey Yeo is an honorary senior research fellow in the Department of Information Studies at University College London, where he was formerly director of the masters program in archives and records management. He has extensive experience as a practitioner, consultant, educator, and researcher and is the editor of the series of professional texts *Principles and Practice in Records Management and Archives*. His research interests include perceptions of the nature of records and of the origins, aims, and scope of recordmaking and recordkeeping; records' contextualization and description; and relationships between records and the actions of individuals and organizations. His published work won the SAA Fellows' Ernst Posner Award in 2009 and the Hugh A. Taylor Prize in 2013.

Made in the USA
San Bernardino, CA
22 January 2020